Costa Ⓓ BLANCA

D1458445

Chris Craggs
Alan James

A rock climbing guidebook
to the Costa Blanca area of Spain

Text and topos by Chris Craggs and Alan James
Computer artwork, design and layout by Chris Craggs and Alan James
All uncredited photos by Chris Craggs
All uncredited climbers in photos are Colin Binks
Original ROCKFAX design Ben Walker, Mick Ryan and Alan James
Printed by Clearpoint Colourprint, Nottingham
Distributed by Cordee (www.cordee.co.uk)

Published by ROCKFAX Ltd. January 2005
© ROCKFAX Ltd. 2005, 2001, 1998, 1996

ISBN 1 873341 95 4

www.rockfax.com

This page: Colin Binks on *Descoco Tensión* (6b), Marin - *page 81*
Cover: Alan James checking out *Salvea Mea* at Altea Col - *page 226*

This book belongs to:

CONTENTS

The amazing Sphynx
on the Peñón de Ifach.

3

COSTA BLANCA

The Peñón caught in the last rays of the sun as the lights come on in Calpe. The shot was taken from Olta.

The Costa Blanca has been long known as one of the best destinations anywhere in the world for winter sun rock and nowadays it attracts visitors from all over the world. Although the area is most popular as a 'sun and chips' venue, the summer's here are HOT, crowded and expensive and only mad dogs and Englishmen would try to climb in the peak holiday season. At other times of the year though the area has the almost ideal combination of a mild climate, well established infrastructure, cheap flights from most of Europe and of course masses of high quality limestone - the real white gold. The thrill of stepping on a plane on a grey English morning and emerging two and a half hours later in bright Spanish sunshine still takes some beating. More and more climbers make the regular exodus and head south for a mid-winter tonic.

The benign climate would be naught without quality climbing to go at and in that department the area really excels. Cliffs available here vary from tiny roadside offerings up through multi-pitch cragging; to extensive sea cliffs and on to some massive mountain crags. The earliest developments took place back in the 1960s and the subsequent 40 years have seen a steady growth in the climbing available right up to the present day with both locals and visitors adding new climbs on a regular basis. It will be some years yet before this area is exhausted.

Initially the climbing here was seen as practise for bigger things and routes were done on an 'anything goes' basis. Later, with the development of sport climbing, many of the shorter cliffs were bolted up and later still the locals took on the massive task of bolting some of the major lines on the biggest cliffs, giving long classics, the equal of climbs anywhere. The Costa Blanca has become a major venue, if you have never been, perhaps this guide will tempt you south to sample what the are has to offer - we will see you there.

One of the great attractions of the Costa Blanca is the multi-pitch climbing on the big mountain crags. Places like the Puig Campana, the Divino at Sella, Peñón de Ifach, the Echo Valley and the Mascarat Gorge have many superb long routes, some of which are fully-bolted and others which require carrying of a light rack to supplement the fixed gear. The photo shows the final pitch of *Las Tetas de me Novia* (6a+) an excellent 4-pitch route in the Mascarat Gorge - *page 230.*

THE BOOK

This book uses the well received full colour and highly detailed format that we have developed and used successfully in the three guides to climbing in England. Since the last Rockfax guidebook to the Costa Blanca in 2001 we have visited every crag and got a complete new set of crag photos to create the superb detailed photo-topos. On the rare occasions where the cliffs are shrouded by trees and impossible to photograph properly we have used full colour topos. The topos are closely linked to detailed route descriptions which have been significantly enhanced since the previous publications. Approaches to all the crags are detailed by many approach maps which are have all been checked and redrawn since the last book which has been essential in many cases to accurately reflect the fast pace of road development in the area.

Obviously the information is as up to date as we can make it at the time of publication but new roads will be built, new routes will be climbed and new crags will be developed. If you find anything that is incorrect, out of date or confusing then please get in touch via the Rockfax web site - **www.rockfax.com**.

THE ACTION PHOTOGRAPHS

The majority of the action shots have been taken especially for this new guide using digital cameras. The 60+ photographs without credits in the book were taken by one of the authors, Chris Craggs and many of these are of long-standing (though long-suffering might be more accurate) friend Colin (El Cap) Binks. Colin has shown a great willingness to climb photogenic routes, pause in the middle of crux sections and cope with his 'belayer' running round taking photographs. Without his tolerance the book would have be a lesser product.

Chris Craggs having a working lunch at Salem.

THE TEAM

Chris Craggs and Alan James are both from Sheffield and have collaborated on several successful projects in recent years. It was a logical progression to combine their considerable experiences of both climbing in the Costa Blanca and of producing guides to the area, to forge this new celebration of the fantastic climbing available. Chris first visited the Costa Blanca back in 1987 and has made climbing trips to Spain on over 60 occasions since then. He has written two guides to the Blanca and has several on-going projects in the pipeline covering other areas of Spain. Alan James is one of the co-founders of Rockfax; he has piloted the company from small beginnings to a major player in the production of guidebooks of the highest quality. He has climbed extensively on the Costa Blanca over the years and produced three top-selling guides to the area.

Alan James keeping in touch with his publishing empire from the Echo Valley.

EASTER EGGS

"What's that doing there?" - If you find yourself saying this when looking at one of the pictures in this book then you have found an *Easter Egg*. Not of the chocolate variety, but something hidden in a photo that shouldn't be there. There are 16 of them in all which should provide some entertainment for the long evenings. Check **www.rockfax.com** for hints and answers.

The Blanca has much to offer climbers operating in the highest grades as well as those after easy sport. Foradà North Face, Sector Deportivo at Cabezon de Oro, Wild Side at Sella, Bovedon near Gandía and the new areas of Murla and Los Pinos in the Xaló Valley are all world class crags with many routes in the highest grades. In the photo, Chris Sowden is negotiating the roof section of *Abradacabra* (7c+) on Bovedon at Gandia. This is one of the complex link-ups that make the most of the roof of this huge cave - *page 320*. Photo: Keith Sharples

WEB SITE - www.rockfax.com

The Rockfax web site is a mine of useful information about climbing all over Europe. It contains the Rockfax Route Database (see below) plus many MiniGuides and updates both complementing the printed books produced by Rockfax and also covering new areas. These downloadable guides are stored in PDF documents - a universal format which can be viewed and printed out on all modern computers using the free application Adobe Acrobat Reader. For some MiniGuides there is a small charge to download but many are free. As things develop on the crags covered in this book we will be producing updates and possibly extra MiniGuides covering any extensive new crags, so keep checking the web site.

ROCKFAX ROUTE DATABASE - www.rockfax.com/databases/

This database contains a listing of every route in this book, and most other Rockfax guide-books. Using this database you can vote on grades and star ratings and lodge general comments about the climbs. This information is essential to help us ensure complete and up-to-date coverage for all the climbs. To make this system work we need the help of everyone who climbs in the Costa Blanca. We can not reflect opinions if we have not got them so, if you think you have found a major sandbag, or discovered a hidden gem that we have only given a single star, let us know!

We also want to hear your general comments on all other aspects of this book, if you have anything to say, don't just say it to your mates down at the pub, say it to Rockfax by using the forms at **www.rockfax.com/general/feedback/**

OTHER WEB SITES

Two excellent Costa Blanca information sites
www.freewebs.com/costablancarock/
www.geocities.com/costablancaclimbing/

DOING YOUR BIT

The areas covered in this guide are very special and many are in delicate natural environments. There have already been problems at several of the cliffs created by thoughtless actions of a few. It is up to us (and that's all of us) to show due respect, help to maintain access to the areas, observe any posted restrictions and keep the places tidy so that these fine areas remain unspoiled for many years to come.

The appalling state of affairs by the parking below the Pared Negra, Orihuela.

GUIDEBOOK FOOTNOTE

The inclusion of a climbing area in this guidebook does not mean that you have a right of access or the right to climb upon it. The descriptions of routes, bolts and other forms of fixed gear within this guide are recorded for historical reasons only and no reliance should placed on the accuracy of the descriptions of the nature and position of bolts and other fixed gear. The grades set in this guide are a fair assessment of the difficulty of the climbs. Climbers who attempt a route of a particular standard should use their own judgment as to whether they are proficient enough to tackle that route. This book is not a substitute for experience and proper judgment. The authors, publisher and distributors of this book do not recognise any liability for injury or damage caused to, or by, climbers, third parties, or property arising from such persons seeking reliance on this guidebook as an assurance for their own safety.

ROCKFAX

More publications for Spanish destinations from ROCKFAX

BELLÚS MiniGUIDE (2004)
Free downloadable PDF guide to Bellús on the Costa Blanca - check **www.rockfax.com**

MALLORCA MiniGUIDE (2004 and 2001)
Updated downloadable PDF guide based on the Mallorca section of the 2001 edition of the Costa Blanca, Mallorca, El Chorro Rockfax - check **www.rockfax.com**

COSTA DAURADA (1998 and 2002)
Winter sun destination near Barcelona in northern Spain. Single-pitch sport climbing on perfect limestone. Now full colour with 172 pages, 1000+ routes and all major areas.
"It is the most comprehensive and up-to-date guide available for this area."
- John Adams, Climber, March 1999

BARCELONA and MONTGRONY MiniGUIDES (2004 and 2003)
Two downloadable PDF guides to areas near Barcelona - check **www.rockfax.com**

Other ROCKFAX print guidebooks

NORTHERN LIMESTONE (2004)
The most comprehensive guide ever published to limestone in England – weighing in at 384 pages and covering every major limestone crag between Dove Dale in the south, and Chapel Head Scar in the north.
" In terms of quality, it is what you would expect, as good as it gets."
- Adrian Berry, Planetfear.com, June 2004

WESTERN GRIT (2003) - *Outdoor Writers' Guild Guidebook of the Year 2004*
The superb climbing on the Western Gritstone edges; from Staffordshire to Kinder, Bleaklow and the Chew Valley. Also covering sections of Lancashire and Cheshire sandstone. 30 crags, 2100 routes, 304 pages, full colour throughout and over 50 action photos.
" virtually flawless climbing guide - an admirable and practical book - extraordinary clarity"
- OWG Judges, November 2004

PEAK GRITSTONE EAST (2001) - *Outdoor Writers' Guild Guidebook of the Year 2002*
The most popular UK guidebook ever covering the magnificent eastern gritstone edges of the Peak District. Full colour throughout, 288 pages, nearly 2000 routes and 50 action photos.
"..this book is as close to perfect a guidebook as we are likely to get."
- Ed Douglas, Climber, February 2002

We also have books to **Yorkshire Gritstone Bouldering (2000)**, **North Wales Limestone (1997)** and **Pembroke (1995)** for areas in the UK. With new books planned for **Dorset (2005)** and **Clwyd Limestone (2005/6)**. In the USA the current titles are **Islands In The Sky - Vegas Limestone (2001)**, **Rifle - Bite The Bullet (1997)** and the **Bishop Bouldering Survival Kit (1999)**.

In addition to this we have nearly 50 more PDF MiniGUIDES on **www.rockfax.com** covering areas from **Lofoten** in Norway to **Kalymnos** in Greece.

Leo Houlding raising the "Titanic", California, USA.
Photographer: John Dickey

Leo Houlding is a prodigy, who climbs at a level only dreamt of by most people. When he commits himself in the vertical world, the last thing Leo wants to be worrying about is his equipment or climbing partner. He works with people and gear on which he knows he can rely, allowing him to totally focus on what he is doing.

Ask Leo to explain his success and he will give you a simple answer. He puts his astounding track record down to pure self belief and an innate trust in his own ability.

INFORMATION

Before you actually touch the rock you will need to get to the area, collect a hire car (unless you are on a budget trip) and have sorted out somewhere to stay; the following section should give you some pointers. More extensive and up-to-date information is available from the ROCKFAX web site on **www.rockfax.com**. If you find any quality new information then let us know.

FLIGHTS

Alicante has an international airport with regular flights from all over Europe. The whole area is a massively popular holiday destination and the cost of flights can reflect this. The key to finding the real bargains is to be flexible, avoid school holidays and book early. If Alicante is not an option it is worth considering trying Murcia which has become increasingly popular, or Valencia. Information on charter flights is available from travel agents, newspapers and the following web sites: **www.air-travel.co.uk**, **www.flightsavers.co.uk**, **www.cheap-flights.com**, **www.charterflights.co.uk**

A more popular option, especially if you want to have flexible arriving and leaving times, is one of the many low-cost airlines now available. Alicante is served by **EasyJet** (**www.easyjet.com**) who fly from Bristol, Liverpool, Gatwick, Stansted, East Midlands, Newcastle and Luton; **BMIBaby** (**www.bmibaby.com**) who fly from Birmingham, Manchester, East Midlands, Cardiff and Teeside; **Jet2** (**www.Jet2.com**) who operate from Leeds/Bradford and Manchester. Murcia is served by **BMIBaby** from Manchester and East Midlands; **Jet2** from Leeds/Bradford and Manchester and **RyanAir** (**www.ryanair.com**) from Dublin, East Midlands, Glasgow, Liverpool, Luton and Stansted. Monarch. See.

The long and arduous drive down through France is only an option for those with a lot of time on their hands, or those on an extended climbing trip. Factor in the cost of the Channel Ferry (from £50 return - low season) the motorway tolls in France and Spain (about £90 return) and the distances involved (about 1000 miles London to Benidorm) and it is perhaps only a trip worth considering by real road warriors. A cost of £350 for the trip alone makes some of the packages available look like really good value!

CAR HIRE

Although the Costa Blanca is a good area to go if you are on a limited budget and don't want to hire a car, having your own transport is definitely preferable. Car hire is best arranged from the UK and the cost for the standard 'Group A' car starts at £80 per week. There are hire car companies at the airports and in the resorts but their prices may be higher than the pre-booked option, and there is the associated hassle of long queues at the booking office when you arrive.

Having access to a hire car opens up the hinterland of the Costa Blanca. A lunch break at Sax would have been a tough order on public transport.

Try any of the following companies:
www.europcar.com, **www.hertz.co.uk**, **www.easycar.com**, **www.carjet.com**

return charges.

TOURIST INFO - www.costablanca.org

Most decent sized towns in the area have a Tourist Office, staffed by people who are friendly, helpful and speak good English. These should be your first port of call if you need accommodation, details about local transport, market days, things worth seeing, etc.
Alicante - c/Portugal, 17 (near bus station) Alicante.
Tel: 96 592 98 02 Fax: 96 592 01 12 Email: **alicantecentro@touristinfo.net**
Benidorm - Avda. Martinez, Alejos 6, 03500 Benidorm
Tel: 90 210 05 81 Fax: 96 680 88 58 Email: **benidorm@touristinfo.net**
Finestrat - Avgda. de la Marina Baixa 14, La Cala de Finestrat, 03509 Finestrat
Tel: 96 680 12 08 Fax: 96 680 12 72 Email: **touristinfo@finestrat.org**
Calpe - Avda. Ejércitos Espanoles, 44, near the Peñón. (There is also one in the centre)
Tel: 96 583 69 20 Fax: 96 583 12 50 Email: **calpe@touristinfo.net**
Dénia - Plaza Oculista Buigues 9, 03700 Dénia.
Tel: 96 642 23 67 Fax: 96 578 09 57 Email: **denia@touristinfo.net**

MARKET DAYS

Monday - Callosa d'En Sarria, Denia, La Nucia, Parcent, Santa Pola, Ibi, Petrer.
Tuesday - Altea, Xaló, Alicante (fruit & vegetable), Elche (evening), Aspe, Jijona, Orihuela.
Wednesday - Benidorm, El Campello, Ondara, Petrel, Teulada, Guadamar, Mutxamel, Polop de la Marina, Novelda, Sax, San Miguel de Salinas, Callosa de Segura.
Thursday - Alicante, Javea, Villajoyosa, Pego, San Javier (Murcia), Rojales, Cocentaina, Villena, Aspe.
Friday - Denia (fruit & vegetable), Finestrat, Gata de Gorgos, Moraira, Torrevieja, Oliva, Elche (17.00 - 22.00), La Nucia.
Saturday - Benissa, Calpe, Alicante, Alcoy, Almoradi, Elche, Sante Pola, Pedreguer, San Miguel de Salinas.
Sunday Elche, Benidorm, Villajoyosa.

The superb Puig Campana dominates the countryside around Finestrat.

BRITISH CONSULATE

In a real emergency you may need to locate the British Consulate which is located in Alicante although best to hope you do not need to visit the place!
The address is: British Consulate, Plaza Calvo Sotelo 1, Alicante.
Tel: 5216022 and 5216190. Open Monday to Friday : 8.30 to 14.00.

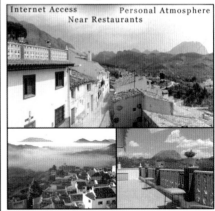

GETTING AROUND

There has been a recent expansion of the road network in the area and this continues. The maps in this guide are believed to be up-to-date, BUT don't be too surprised if there are changes. The locals appear to be especially keen on changing the road numbers on a regular basis. As a general rule it is worth avoiding towns where possible as you drive around the area since they can be horribly slow and busy. Choose routes which use the dual carriageways to avoid the towns, even over-shooting destinations on occasions in order to double back by a faster road. The final sections on some crag approaches are on dirt tracks of variable quality. These can become particularly exciting after rain!

Fiesta 1.1 versus the track from Hell, Cabezon - no contest!

WITHOUT A CAR

If you are carless the best option is Sella, where there is loads of climbing, a refuge and some basic camping. Calpe is also a possibility with the Peñon, Toix and Olta within bus/walking distance. There is a regular train service up and down the coast from Alicante to Valencia and there are local bus services. Consult the local Tourist Information to get timetables and prices - see page 14.

WHEN TO GO

The optimum time to visit is November through to April. The summer months, May to October, are very hot but and you will probably have to confine your climbing activities to the morning and evening. You may be lucky to get periods of cooler weather, but chances are it will be up in the 30s or higher and seeking shade will be the only real option.

The winter months can have periods of cold and wet weather (the *Gota Fria* is the local name for the occasional periods of very heavy rain that fill all the rivers and can even deposit snow on the high summits) but more often than not it will be wonderfully sunny and settled with cold nights and fresh days.

Rainy periods are not unheard of, especially in the autumn.

TRAVEL INSURANCE

You are strongly advised to take out travel insurance before your trip. If you are in any doubt, just ask someone who has had cause to use it!

BMC Travel Insurance (see page 9) - Tel: 0161 445 4747 or **www.thebmc.com**

SHOPS

There are major (and very cheap) supermarkets in, or on the outskirts, of all the main towns (usually shut on Sundays). Outlying villages often have a small shop or two (closed in the afternoons to 5pm) a bakery and a selection of bars.

CLIMBING SHOPS

El Refugio (opposite) - Dedicated climbing shop in the centre of Alicante with a wide range of climbing gear and all the local guidebooks.

Zero 95 (opposite) - A general sport shop with about 10% of the space given over to climbing. They sell all the basics plus a selection of guidebooks.

ACCOMMODATION

APARTMENTS, VILLAS and CASITAS

There is more accommodation available along the Costa Blanca than in most destinations anywhere in the world; cheap and cheerful self-catering apartments, all-in package deals in high-rises in Benidorm, huge villas with pools and delightful inland casitas - the choice is massive.

The Benidorm 'flight plus accommodation' packages can prove to be good value especially for small groups.

For villas, there is a premium paid for stopping down by the coast, up in the hills things are considerably less expensive. You will often have a surfeit of facilities (pool, barbecues, balconies, televisions and dishwashers) a bit of a contrast to the usual UK climbing trip! Large groups visiting out of season may find hiring a villa the cheapest option.

The inland casitas are almost certainly the best option for those who wish to get away from the hustle and bustle of the coast. Many are beautifully situated, close to the climbing, and provide a good opportunity to see another side of Spain. If you arrive with nothing prebooked, either try the local Tourist Offices (page 14) or find a tower block with a 'to rent' sign displayed (many of them have a 24 hour office) or phone one of the contacts in this book.

A villa for four to six people, with a pool, from about £150/week in the low season. The only drawback is that the pool will be too cold.

REFUGES

The only refuge in the area is at Sella which has a small shop and camping available out side. It can get noisy in the refuge at busy times but there are always others to climb with which is attractive if you are travelling alone.

Calpe and Benidorm (visible away on the horizon) have masses of accommodation which is inexpensive and often quiet out of the main tourist season.

CAMPING

There are numerous campsites to be found in along the costal strip, although these are usually closed in the winter and crowded in the summer. Also, they are surprisingly expensive and it is usually cheaper to rent an apartment. Two spots where you can camp relatively cheaply are by the refuge at Sella (page 152) and at the parking spot below Olta (page 256). Both have limited facilities.

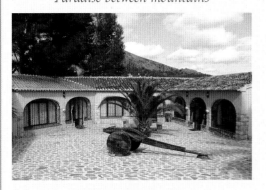

CLIMBING INFORMATION

GEAR

The vast majority of climbs in this guide are sport routes, requiring a rope and a set of quickdraws. Amongst all the sport stuff are some routes that have less fixed gear, often with fixed belays, and some form of gear near the harder moves. The symbol ⚷ is used to identify these, along with a UK grade (with a corresponding grade colour-code - see page 22). There are also many longer routes in the guide, some of which are fully-bolted and some which only have a smattering of fixed gear. Again the symbol ⚷ is used to denote these latter routes.

Here are some suggested racks of gear:

Sport routes only - 12 to 14 quickdraws and a 60m rope. 50m ropes will usually be long enough but take great care when lowering, some pitches are much longer than 25m!

Sport routes and one or two longer mixed routes - 12 to 14 quickdraws, one set of wires, a couple of medium Friends and 2 or 3 slings. Twin 50m ropes is the best option since this will allow you to abseil off. Competent climbers will be able to climb most of the mixed routes with just a rack of quickdraws and a single 60m rope although this is not advised if you are not experienced in long run-outs and descending by short abseils between insubstantial anchors!

Multi-pitch trad routes with abseil descents - 12 quickdraws, twin 50m ropes, a full normal trad rack including wires and Friends of all sizes and a helmet.

THE ENP

The ENP was a protection system, developed by Rowland Edwards, which attempted to create traditional-style routes but with removable protection on the blanker sections. It was developed for routes on Puig Campana and later used in the Echo Valley and on the Toix Sea Cliffs. Recently Rowland and his son Mark have decided to replace many of the ENPs with conventional bolts, however there are still a few routes that use them. These routes are denoted by the symbol 🔳 in the route

'Grey gold' - flutings and razors galore at Sella.

descriptions. The ENP consists of a steel tube with a plastic washer and stainless steel spring behind it. A normal wired nut (Wild Country Rock 3) is key-holed into the tube and can removed the same way. When placed properly the ENP will give a solid runner but it should not be treated as a bolt.

THE ROCK

All the cliffs described in this book are of high quality limestone, though this varies massively from grey sheets covered in razor blades to fantastic dripping tufa systems, and leaning orange walls. Climbers new to the area will find the rock hard on the fingers, much of it is both sharp and rough. It can also trash footwear at an alarming rate.

Splendid dripping tufa systems, Sector Potent, Gandia.

TOPOS AND SYMBOLS

The idea behind all the various features of a ROCKFAX guidebook is to help you find and assess the most appropriate climbing quickly and accurately. To help there are many maps, symbols, tables and descriptions, all of which are relatively simple to follow and need little explanation. If you do not like reading long-winded descriptions, or English is not your first language, then you should still be able to use the guide. Conversely, if you hate maps and your brain cannot cope with 2-dimensional representations of a 3-dimensional world, there are always the text approaches and route descriptions to fall back on.

GRADES

In general the grades are pretty friendly and consistently applied in common with most other popular Spanish areas although there will undoubtedly be some anomalies.
To help identify routes of the correct difficulty level they have been allocated colour-codes corresponding to a grade band.

GREEN SPOTS - Grade 4+ and under (*Trad routes - Sev and under*). Good for beginners and those wanting an easy life.
ORANGE SPOTS - Grade 5 to 6a+ (*Trad - HS to HVS*). General ticking routes for those with more experience.
RED SPOTS - Grade 6b to 7a (*Trad - E1 to E3*). Routes for the experienced and keen climber.
BLACK SPOTS - Grade 7a+ and above (*Trad - E4 and above*). The hard stuff! All unknown lines are also given black spots although they might not be that hard.

Routes with 2 grades

Most of the routes which require some gear to be carried have been given a normal sport grade and an overall UK trad grade in brackets. The trad grade is meant to give the correct impression of how serious the route is and the colour code has been adjusted to reflect this. For example, Route 7 on page 213 is given a grade of 6a+ (E4) and a black spot. This is because it is a relatively easy move but there is no protection and the route should be attempted by Black Spot E4 climbers and not Orange Spot 6a+ leaders!

R O U T E   G R A D E S

BRITISH TRAD GRADE (For well-protected routes)					Sport Grade	UIAA	USA
Mod *Moderate*						I	5.1
	Diff *Difficult*					II	5.2
		VDiff *Very Difficult*				III	5.3
			HVD *Hard Very Difficult*			III+	5.4
						IV	5.5
Sev *Severe*						IV+	5.6
	HS *Hard Severe*	4a VS *Very Severe* 4c			4	V	5.7
					4+	V+	5.8
			4c HVS *Hard Very Severe* 5b		5	VI-	5.9
5a E1 5c					5+	VI	5.10a
	5b E2 6a				6a	VI+	5.10b
		5c E3 6a			6a+	VII-	5.10c
			6a E4 6b		6b	VII	5.10d
				6a E5 6c	6b+	VII+	5.11a
					6c		5.11b
					6c+	VIII-	5.11c
					7a	VIII	5.11d
					7a+	VIII+	5.12a
					7b	IX-	5.12b
6b E6 6c					7b+		5.12c
	6c E7 7a				7c	IX	5.12d
		6c E8 7a			7c+	IX+	5.13a
			7a E9 7b		8a	X-	5.13b
				7a E10 7b	8a+	X	5.13c
					8b		5.13d
					8b+	X+	5.14a
					8c	XI-	5.14b
					8c+	XI	5.14c
					9a	XI+	5.14d
					9a+		5.15a

Route Symbols

 A good route

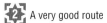 A very good route

 A brilliant route

 Technical climbing involving complex or trick moves

 Powerful moves requiring big arms

 Sustained climbing, either long and pumpy or with lots of hard moves

 Fingery climbing - sharp holds!

 A route which has ENPs in it -see page 20

 A route which requires some hand-placed gear or a full rack.

 Fluttery climbing with big fall potential

 A long reach is helpful/essential

Descent · Belay at the top · Lower-off · Abseil descent point · A · Mid-route belays · 17 · Alternatives for the same route · 16 · 18 · 19 · Photo-topos

Crag Symbols

 Approach - Approach walk time and angle

 Sunshine - Approximate time when the sun is on the crag

 Restrictions - Climbing is not allowed at some times

 Some multi-pitch routes

 A crag with mostly traditional routes

 A crag with dry climbing in the rain

 A windy and/or cold crag

 A sheltered/warm crag

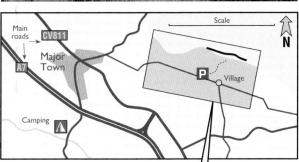

Main roads · CV811 · Major Town · A7 · Scale · N · P · Village · Camping

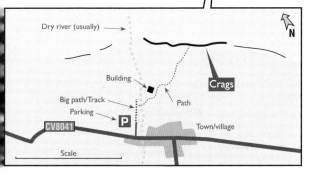

Dry river (usually) · N · Building · Crags · Big path/Track · Parking · Path · P · CV8041 · Town/village · Scale

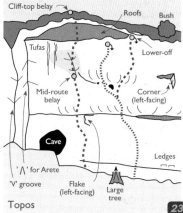

Cliff-top belay · Roofs · Bush · Tufas · Lower-off · Mid-route belay · Corner (left-facing) · Cave · Ledges · ' Λ ' for Arete · 'V' groove · Flake (left-facing) · Large tree

Topos

INTRODUCCIÓN (Español)

Bienvenido a la cuarta guía de escalada ROCKFAX que abarca la magnífica escalada en la Costa Blanca, España. Escaladores del mundo entero han considerado las tres primeras ediciones de este libro como la mejor y más fiable fuente de información sobre la escalada en esta zona, y tenemos el placer de producir ahora esta nueva versión del libro, extendida y en color.

En la Costa Blanca encontrarás una variedad increíble de escalada, con muchas paredes de vías de un sólo largo como Sella, Gandía, Foradá y la Sierra de Toix, pero también varias zonas de montaña importantes como el Puig Campana, el Peñon d'Ifach, el Valle del Eco y el Ponoch. En esta edición del libro hemos buscado aun más paredes de calidad, y aunque algunas como las de Murcia se encuentran fuera de lo que llamaríamos la Costa Blanca, proporcionan una dimensión adicional al escalador visitante. En total hay 42 paredes y más de 2300 vías que bastarán para la mayoría de los escaladores por mucho tiempo.

LA GUÍA

Toda la información sobre la escalada viene acompañada de mapas de aproximación, foto-croquis y símbolos. Aun sin hablar mucho inglés será fácil localizar las paredes y evaluar las vías. Este libro contiene información sobre las vías y paredes más importantes de la Costa Blanca, pero frecuentemente existen más escaladas de las que podemos incluir. En la página 28 reseñamos todas las guías locales actuales que contienen una mayor cobertura de vías. Todas son disponibles en las tiendas de escalada locales.

PROTECCIÓN

La mayoría de las vías en este libro pertenecen a escuelas de escalada deportiva totalmente equipadas. Existen algunas vías 'tradicionales' que requieren un juego completo de fisureros y Friends para la auto-protección. Se indica las vías que requieren protección natural con el símbolo 🪨 en el texto. Hay además varias vías en la Costa Blanca en que hay que utilizar el sistema ENP, y que se indican con el símbolo ENP. Encontrarás una explicación en la página 20.

Colores correspondientes a bandas de grados

Los números de las vías llevan un color que corresponde a diferentes bandas de grados:

❶ - 4+ o menos
❷ - 5 a 6a+
❸ - 6b a 7a
❹ - 7a+ o más

INFORMACIÓN ADICIONAL

Queremos seguir mejorando la calidad de la información contenida en nuestros libros y nos interesa saber vuestros comentarios y opiniones. Una fuente de información muy útil es la Base de Datos de Vías Rockfax en el internet. Contiene una lista de todas las vías de este libro, y permite a los escaladores votar sobre grados y símbolos cualitativos y añadir comentarios. También producimos de vez en cuando hojas actualizadas gratuitas y nuevas GUIAS Mini ('MiniGUIDES') para zonas adicionales. Éstas se pueden imprimir, en formato PDF, desde el internet: **www.rockfax.com**.

ROCKFAX

ROCKFAX consiste de Alan James, Chris Craggs y Mark Glaister en el Reino Unido, y de Mick Ryan en Estados Unidos. Llevamos 14 años produciendo guías de escalada sobre zonas situadas en todo el mundo. Podrás encontrar información detallada en el internet, **www.rockfax.com**, y en la página 10.

Símbolos de las vías

 Vía buena

 Vía muy buena

 Vía fantástica

 Escalada técnica que requiere movimientos complejos o ingeniosos

 Movimientos de fuerza que requieren brazos sólidos

 Escalada de continuidad, larga y con botellas garantizadas o con muchos movimientos duros

 Escalada de dedos – ¡Agarres cortantes!

 Vía que tiene ENP - ver página 20

 Vía que requiere algunos fisureros

 Escalada alarmante con posibilidad de caídas grandes

 Gran envergadura útil / esencial

Foto-croquis

Símbolos de las paredes

 Aproximación
Tiempo de aproximación y pendiente

 Sol
Horas aproximadas en que la pared está al sol

 Restricciones
Escalada prohibida durante ciertos períodos

 Algunas vías de varios largos

 Vías que requieren protección natural (fisureros y Friends)

 Protegido de la lluvia

 Frío / expuesto al viento

 Una pared resguardada del viento o templada

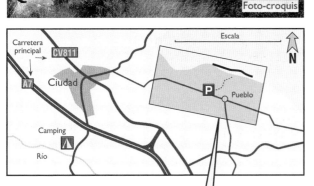

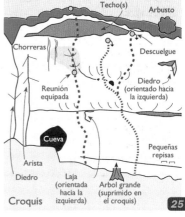

Croquis

25

EINFÜHRUNG

Willkommen zur dritten Auflage des Rockfax Kletterführers, der die hervorragenden Klettereien im Gebiet von Costa Blanca in Spanien beinhaltet.

Die ersten drei Ausgaben dieses Buchs wurden von Kletterern der ganzen Welt als die beste und präziseste Informationsquelle für die Felskletterei in diesem Gebiet anerkannt. Daher freuen wir uns nunmehr, diese erweiterte, farbige Version des Buchs herauszubringen.

An der Costa Blanca findet man eine unglaubliche Vielfalt an Kletttereien. Es gibt sowohl zahlreiche Sportrouten mit einer Seillänge wie z. B. Sella, Gandía, Foradá und Sierra de Toix, als auch einige bedeutende Gebiete mit höheren Felsen wie Puig Campana, Peñon d'Ifach, Echo Valley und Ponoch. In Vorbereitung dieser Auflage haben wir uns weiter umgeschaut, um zusätzliche bedeutende Felsen zu finden. Und obwohl sie die Grenze dessen, was man Costa Blanca nennen könnte, verschieben, werden die Gebiete um Murcia bei dem Kletterer der sie besucht, einen tiefen Eindruck hinterlassen.

Insgesamt werden 42 verschiedene Felsen mit über 2300 Routen beschrieben. Damit dürften den meisten Kletterern genügend lohnende Ziele auf Lebenszeit geboten werden.

DER KLETTERFÜHRER

Sämtliche Informationen zu den Kletttereien wurden mit Zustiegsskizzen, Fototopos sowie Symbolen ausführlich illustriert. Auch ohne umfangreiche Englischkenntnisse sollte es ein leichtes sein, die verschiedenen Gebiete aufzufinden und die Routen abzuschätzen.

Dieses Buch enthält Informationen zu den Hauptrouten und Felsen von Costa Blanca. Häufig finden sich weitere Klettermöglichkeiten, für deren Beschreibung es uns hier an Platz fehlt. Auf Seite 28 haben wir sämtliche gegenwärtig bekannten lokalen Kletterführer aufgelistet, die eine komplettere Routenaufstellung der in ihnen beschriebenen Gebiete enthalten. Diese Führer sind ausnahmslos in den örtlichen Klettergeschäften erhältlich.

AUSRÜSTUNG

Die meisten Kletterrouten dieses Buchs befinden sich an voll ausgerüsteten Sportkletterfelsen. Es existieren auch einige „traditionelle" Routen, die eine eigenhändige Absicherung erfordern. Dafür wird eine vollständige Ausrüstung an Klemmkeilen und Friends benötigt. Das Symbol kennzeichnet im Text derartige Aufstiege.

Im Gebiet Costa Blanca existieren einige Routen, die das ENP-System verwenden und durch das Symbol gekennzeichnet werden. Dieses wird auf Seite 20 beschrieben.

Farbig markierte Routennummern

Die farbigen Routennummern entsprechen den folgenden Schwierigkeitsbereichen:

- **1** - Grad V+ und darunter
- **2** - Grad VI- bis VII-
- **3** - Grad VII bis VIII
- **4** - Grad VIII+ und dar

WEITERE INFORMATIONEN

Auch weiterhin möchten wir die Qualität der in unseren Büchern enthaltenen Informationen verbessern und sind daher sehr an Kommentaren, Kritiken und Anregungen interessiert.

Für weitere Informationen bietet sich die Rockfax Routen Datenbank auf unserer Web-Seite an. Diese enthält eine Aufstellung jedes einzelnen Aufstiegs, der in diesem Buch beschrieben wird. Diese Datenbank bietet die Möglichkeit, Ihre Meinung zu Schwierigkeitsgraden und Einschätzungen („Sternchenvergabe") abzugeben, sowie auch die Kommentare anderer Kletterer einzusehen.

Ebenso werden auf unserer Web-Seite **www.rockfax.com** gelegentlich kostenfreie Updates und neue Minifführer („MiniGUIDEs") über zusätzliche Klettergebiete im PDF-Format zum Herunterladen und Ausdrucken auf Ihrem Computer zur Verfügung gestellt.

ROCKFAX

ROCKFAX sind Alan James, Chris Craggs und Mark Glaister in England sowie Mick Ryan in Amerika. Wir veröffentlichen seit 14 Jahren Führer von Klettergebieten in der ganzen Welt. Details zu all unseren Veröffentlichungen befinden sich auf unserer Web-Seite.

Symbole

 Lohnende Kletterei

 Sehr lohnende Kletterei

 Brilliante Kletterei

Technisch anspruchsvolle Tour mit trickreichen Z

Anstrengende Z kräftige Oberarme.

Durchgehend anstrengende Tour; entweder anhaltend schwer oder mit einer Reihe harter Z

Kletterei, die Sicherung durch Klemmkeile u.ä. erfordert.

ENP Eine Route, die das ENP System verwendet - Seite 20

Kleingriffige, rauhe Kletterei - nichts f

Heikle Kletterei mit hohem Sturzpotential, aber nicht allzu gefährlich.

Lange Arme sind hilfreich.

Abstieg

Abseilpunkt

Absteilstellen

Abseilpunkt

Standplatzsicherung am Aussstieg mit Klemmkeilen, Friends, etc.

Standplatz

17

Alternativen für dieselbe Route

16

18

19

Fototopos

Felsymbole

 Zugang - Zeit und Steilheit des Zugangsweges.

 Sonnenschein - Zeit, zu der der Felsen in der Sonne liegt.

 Restrictions - Climbing is not allowed at some times

 Mehrere Seillängen

 Einige oder alle der Routen erfordern ein Klemmkeilsortiment.

 Trockener Fels bei Regen

 Dem Wind ausgesetzt

 windgesch

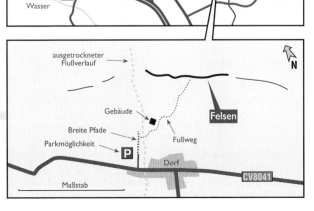

Asphaltierte Straßen CV811

Maßstab

N

Stadt

P Dorf

Camping

Wasser

ausgetrockneter Flußverlauf

N

Gebäude

Felsen

Breite Pfade

Fußweg

Parkmöglichkeit P

Dorf

Maßstab

CV8041

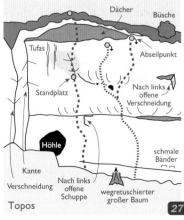

Dächer Büsche

Tufas

Abseilpunkt

Standplatz

Nach links offene Verschneidung

Höhle

schmale Bänder

Kante

Verschneidung

Nach links offene Schuppe

wegeretuschierter großer Baum

Topos

27

OTHER GUIDEBOOKS

There have been a series of guides to the area over the years, both by local climbers and outsiders. Currently there are about 10 local guides in print to the area and these are listed below. Generally the local guides are cheap and cheerful productions with simple and often very basic information. Despite this, they contain more routes and crags between them than this book and buying a copy is a way of putting a little something back into the local climbing community. The two climbing shops in the area (see page 17) usually carry a good stock of guides. Alternatively check **www.desnivel.es**.

La Panocha y la Cresta del Gallo, Guía de Escalaldas (2002) by Sergio Hernández Rodríguez and Francisco José Iniesta Gallego. A good topo-guide to this interesting cliff. 96 pages, colour photo-topos, €10.

Senderísmo y Escalada por la Vega Baja del Seguria (2003) by the Club de Montaña de Redován. A poor guide to the Orihuela area. Difficult to use and not very inspiring. 164 pages, b&w plus colour topos and line drawings, €15.

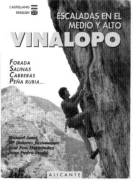

Escaladas en el Medio y Atlo Vinolopa, (1995) by Manuel Amat, Dolores Justamente, José Hernández, Juan Pedro Verdú. An extensive guide to the Alicante crags, but a little dated now. 164 pages, b&w plus colour topos and line drawings, €15.

Aitana Sur by Ignacio Sánchez Ruiz. A cheaply-produced photo-copied topo guide to Sella and the Divino. Available from the refuge. You get what you pay for. 50 pages, b&w line topos €7.

Escaladas en el Puig Campana (2003) by Manolo Pomares. A detailed guide to over 80 routes on the mountain. 240 pages, b&w hand-drawn topos (with red lines showing the routes), €18.

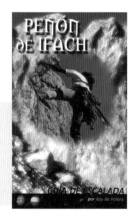

Guía de Escalada del Ponoig (1998) by Carlos Tudela. A detailed guide to over 80 routes on the Ponoch. 142 pages, b&w hand-drawn topos (with red lines showing the routes), €11.

Peñón de Ifach (2001) by Roy de Valera. Spanish and English. Uses a mixture of b&w hand-drawn topos and colour photo-topos. Very detailed though it is tricky to tease out the exact line of some routes. 120 pages, €14:50.

Gandia - Guia de Escalada, Penya Roja de Marxuquera. A free pamphlet-type guide that used to be available from the tourist office (near the station) in Gandía. 22 pages, colour photo-topos. Current availability unknown.

Guia de Escalada, Salem y Benicadel by Club Muntanyer d'Oliva. A locally-produced guide available from the bar in Salem. The topos are very crowded and the 'English' translations are hugely entertaining. 48 pages, €5.

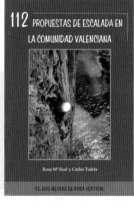

La Mola de Montesa - Escalada I Bloc (2003) by Richard Jiménez. A huge format guide with full colour photo-topos of the climbing and bouldering. Available in Montesa. 24 pages, €3.

112 Propuestas de Escalada en la Comunidad Valenciana (2001) by Rosa Real and Carlos Tudela. A 'best-of' guide covering the whole area down to Orihuela. A good guide. 128 pages, €15.

ACKNOWLEDGEMENTS

The production of this guide has been based on 17 years of climbing in the area, still my favourite foreign destination (at least in the middle of winter, Tuolomne and Lofoten still beat it in the summer!). The number of people who have helped this time round has been remarkably small; Colin Binks and Dave Gregory have made repeated visits to the area in the interests of 'checking' and have been superb, treking to out-of-the-way places, doing the routes I was interested in and keeping out of the way in the evenings when the all important 'lap-top-logging' goes on. Jim Rubery, John Addy and Dave Spencer have helped in the past 12 months and in earlier days Graham Parkes, Pete O'Donovan, Willie Jeffrey, and the late Mike Appleton have shared these great climbs.

As ever Alan James has been simply superb to work with, he has proved to be a font of knowledge and a 24 hour help-line, a shoulder to cry on and a sharp stick when needed! Of course it was Sherri's idea that we went to Spain in the first place - now I can say with true conviction, thanks for everything over the years and just look what you started!

Chris Craggs Dec 2004

The most important people who need thanking are the climbers who have equipped and climbed the routes in this book, without them we would have nothing to climb.

This is the fourth book Rockfax have published to the Costa Blanca and, as ever, we rely heavily on feedback sent in via the web site, especially this time since the routes are now all on the Rockfax Route Database. The list of all contributors is now too long to reproduce but we are very grateful to everyone who takes the time and trouble to send us their opinions and comments; keep them coming.

Once again Rowland Edwards has helped with certain sections and thanks are due to him. Others who have helped are Richard Davies, who has done a lot of proof-reading, and Adrian Bates. Both of them maintain excellent web sites with good up-to-date local information (see page 8). David Mora García has once again kept us supplied with updates on the local climbing scene and given extensive help with some sections. Other help has come from Al Evans (Segaria), Alan Leary and David Elder (who also sent a photo). Neil Foster has added his extensive knowledge of certain crags and supplied some superb photos. Keith Sharples helped with Bovedon at Gandía and allowed us to use a couple of his photos. Further photographic contributions have come from Rich Mayfield and Mark Glaister. Once again Juan Varela-Nex and Karsten Kurz have supplied excellent last-minute translations. We are very grateful to all of the above.

On the business side of things, thanks to Sally Weston, Jo Cooke, Amanda Nightingale and all at Warners for their help with advertising and promotion; to Stuart Fletcher, Peter Garley and all at Clearpoint; and to Nick Smith and Andy Hyslop for the web site work.

A few year's ago Chris Craggs and I produced rival books to the Blanca. "Great extensive text", I thought. "Good diagrams and graphics", he thought. Well the blatantly obvious partnership is now onto its fourth guidebook and may there be many more to come. Once again Chris's ability to produce the goods when required has proved to be second to none. My thanks are also due to Sherri for all the help and support she gives and, in this guide especially, for her photographic contributions.

Thanks also to Dave Gregory for his proof reading, Liz James and Mike James for thier general help and support and Mick Ryan for his input.

Finally I would like to thank the people who provide welcome noisy distractions from work: Hannah, Sam and Lydia, and to Henriette who just provides a welcome distraction whilst coping with the stresses of a print deadline once again.

Alan James Dec 2004

Photo: Chris Craggs

ADVERTISER DIRECTORY

Rockfax is are very grateful to the following companies who have supported this guidebook.

LOCAL GEAR SHOPS

El REFUGIO - Alicante (Page 17)
C/ Capitán Segarra, 29. Alicante. Tel: 965 144 922
el_refugio@eresmas.com

ZERO 95 - Calpe (Page 17)
Avda. Gabriel Miró, 14, Calpe. Tel: 965 830 589
www.zero95.com

COURSES and HOLIDAYS

DAVID MORA GARCÍA (Page 29)
Tel/Fax: +34 96 669 76 86
www.nuevoalpinismo.com

ROCK & SUN (Page 2)
Tel: +44 7880 773786
www.rockandsun.com

ACCOMMODATION and COURSES

AQUA VENTURA - Sella (Page 29)
Tel: 00 34 965 87 90 00
www.aqua-ventura.com

COMPASS WEST - Finestrat (Page 21)
Tel: 00 34 965 87 87 90
www.compasswest.co.uk

ACCOMMODATION

ASMOLADORA - Parcent (Page 19 and Inside back)
Tel: 00 34 96 640 5429
www.finca-la-asmoladora.com

ESMERO PROPERTY SERVICES (Page 19)
www.esmeropropertyservices.com

CASERÍO DEL MIRADOR - Jalón Valley (Page 29)
Tel: 00 34 607 433 349
www.villajalon.com

HOTEL LA PLANTACIÓN - Finestrat (Page 21)
Tel: 00 34 96 587 8715
www.laplantacion.com

HOTEL LOS CABALLOS - Els Poblets (Page 15)
Tel: 00 34 96 647 5177 Fax: 00 34 96 647 4988
www.ferienoase.com

ORANGE HOUSE - Finestrat (Inside front)
Tel: 00 34 965 87 82 51
www.theorangehouse.net

TERRACOTTAGES (Page 15)
www.terracottages.co.uk

VILLA PICO - Sella (Page 15)
Tel: 00 34 965 879 238 Fax: 00 34 66 000 86 93
www.villapico.com

Christmas Day on the Peñón de Ifach - enough said!

MAGAZINES

CLIMBER (Opposite)
Warners Group Publications. Tel: 01778 391117
www.climber.co.uk

OUTDOOR GEAR

BERGHAUS (Page 11)
Extreme Centre, Sunderland.
Tel: 0191 5165600 Fax: 0191 5165601
www.berghaus.com

BLACK DIAMOND (Outside Back)
Tel: 0162 958 0484
www.blackdiamondequipment.com

OUTDOOR DESIGNS (Page 15)
Tel: 01773 601 870
www.outdoordesigns.co.uk

OUTSIDE (Page 33)
Main Road, Hathersage. Tel: 01433 651 936
Baslow Road Calver. Tel: 01433 631 111
www.outside.co.uk

ROCKSPORT (Page 13)
The Edge Climbing Centre, Sheffield. Tel: 0114 275 8899 and Go Outdoors, Canley Road Coventry. Tel: 02476 671 296
www.rocksport.co.uk

CLIMBING WALLS

AWESOME WALLS (page 31)
St. Alban's Church, Athol Street, Liverpool.
Tel/Fax: 0151 298 2422
www.awesomewalls.co.uk

ENTRE-PRISE (Page 29)
Entre-Prise (UK), Kelbrook.
Tel: 01282 444800 Fax: 01282 444801
www.ep-uk.com

TRAVEL INSURANCE

BRITISH MOUNTAINEERING COUNCIL (Page 9)
Tel: 0870 010 4878 Fax: 0161 445 4500
www.thebmc.co.uk

THE AREAS

MURCIA

Well to the south of the main Costa Blanca climbing areas, and largely unknown to outsiders, Murcia offers a fine selection of cliffs with a broad range of climbs to go at. From the major long classics of Leyva, to the single-pitch sport routes of Callosa, and the fine tower of La Panocha (right) there is a week's climbing here for anyone.
Map page 42

ALICANTE

The immediate surrounds of the Alicante area do not look very promising from a climber's point of view, but venture a little way inland and the parched coast gives way to an expansive landscape dotted with orchards and some fine rocky towers. From the lower grade climbs at Marin, to the steep testpieces at Foradà, and the tall tower of Sax (left) the area has lots to offer.
Map page 76

BENIDORM

Inland from the flesh-pots of Benidorm are some impressive mountains dotted with white villages. The ever-popular Sella is the best known of the cliffs in the area and the Echo Valley also has plenty to go at. For climbers who like their sport a bit more challenging there is the big three of the Campana, Ponoch and Divino (right) to go at.
Map page 150

CALPE

Few towns have their very own mountain in the back-garden but Calpe does with the towering Peñón de Ifach (left) and its many long classics climbs. Add in the popular and extensive crags at Toix and the smaller crags of Olta, Bernia, Altea and Mascarat, and this small area has lots to offer.
Map page 218

XALÓ/JALÓN VALLEY

Just to the north of Calpe is the secluded Xaló Valley with a pleasant collection of cliffs. None of them are outstanding but together they offer an alternative to the crowded cliffs at Sella and Toix. Recent developments have increased the number of short, steep, hard routes in the area. Pena Roja (right) and L'Ocaive are the best known cliffs here.
Map page 270

GANDÍA

Running inland from the large town of Gandía is this extensive and varied region offering lots of good climbing. It is a bit of a drive from the Calpe/Benidorm area and stopping over locally is a good idea. The cliffs are extensive and very varied from Aventador (left) to Montesa, Bellús and Gandía itself.
Map page 304

Region	CRAG	Page	GRADE RANGE up to 4+	5 to 6a+	6b to 7a	7a+ and up	No. of ROUTES	Mainly sport routes	Some trad routes	Some multi-pitch
MURCIA	Leyva	44	1	3	3		83	Sport		Multi-pitch
MURCIA	La Panocha	52	4	47	3	5	79	Sport		
MURCIA	Orihuela	62	10	43		2	81	Sport	Trad	Multi-pitch
ALICANTE	Marin	78	8		15		47	Sport		Multi-pitch
ALICANTE	Salinas	84	1	0			78	Sport		
ALICANTE	Sax	92	2	33	0	4	59	Sport		Multi-pitch
ALICANTE	Magdelena	100	1	34	14	10	59	Sport		
ALICANTE	Peña del Corb	106	2	13	6		21	Sport		Multi-pitch
ALICANTE	Peña Rubia	110	1		19	19	71	Sport		
ALICANTE	Foradà North	116		1	34		71	Sport		
ALICANTE	Foradà South	124	6		1	2	35	Sport		
ALICANTE	Ibi	128	1	16	19	8	44	Sport		
ALICANTE	Reconco	132		13	0	2	35	Sport		Multi-pitch
ALICANTE	Agujas Rojas	136	1	9	11	18	40	Sport		
ALICANTE	Alcoi	142		13	9	1	32	Sport		
ALICANTE	Cabezon de Oro	146		2	4	18	24	Sport	Trad	Multi-pitch
BENIDORM	Sella	152	11	47	85	30	173	Sport	Trad	Multi-pitch
BENIDORM	Sella - Divino	172	1	3			51	Sport	Trad	Multi-pitch
BENIDORM	Sella - Hidden Valley	180			3	54	57	Sport		
BENIDORM	Puig Campana	184		4	15	8	27		Trad	Multi-pitch
BENIDORM	Ponoch	194			6	1	7	Sport	Trad	Multi-pitch
BENIDORM	Echo Valley	198	8	35	48	45	136	Sport	Trad	Multi-pitch

Approach walk	Sunshine or shade	Dry in the Rain	Sheltered	2 indy	Access	SUMMARY
40 min to 50 min	All day	Dry in the rain	Sheltered	Windy		A fine huge crag with some long multi-pitch fully-bolted classics in a magnificent setting. The 50 minute approach walk makes for long days. Also has a smaller crag with mainly harder single-pitch routes.
5 min to 10 min	Sun and shade					A popular tower of rock overlooking the city of Murcia with several associated walls dotted around it. Well-climbed on by the locals but some great routes in a fantastic setting.
5 min to 30 min	All day			Windy		A very diverse area with several big walls with some isolated multi-pitch routes plus a collection of smaller crags near Callosa. Many fine routes and well worth the long drive from the Calpe/Benidorm area.
5 min to 10 min	All day					A superb crag with loads of great easy routes on the Main Buttress offering slabby two-pitch routes on perfect rock. Western Buttress has more to offer in the mid-grades making this a very appealing crag.
10 min to 15 min	Morning				Restrictions	Beautifully-located crag with excellent mid-to-hard routes on perfect rock. The odd chipped hold and a hard approach drive. **Restriction:** No climbing from 1 March to 1 July
10 min to 20 min	Morning			Windy	Restrictions	A great set of pinnacles and walls overlooking the town of Sax. Good easy-to-mid-grade two pitch routes and a summit pinnacle. **Restriction:** No climbing on Sector Cumbre from 1 December to 1 June
5 min to 10 min	All day (1 shade wall)					A small set of cliffs in an arid setting. Not the world's greatest crag but there is certainly enough for a visit or two. The slabby routes on the Pared Negra are especially worthwhile.
20 min	Afternoon		Sheltered			A fine but neglected little cliff, set high above the Alicante to Madrid motorway. Quite a number of the climbs are two pitches and they finish at a proper summit with a big black iron cross.
5 min to 10 min	Afternoon		Sheltered			An accessible little crag with a good set of routes and shade until mid-afternoon. The harder routes are poor but the mid-grade stuff is good.
10 min	All day shade	Dry in the rain		Windy		One of the finest hard crags on the Blanca; a magnificent steep wall of perfect rock which is always in the shade. A great place to head for a work-out in the warm weather but often freezing cold in the winter.
15 min	All day			Windy		The flip side to the dark, cold and hard world - sunny and slabby with plenty of easy-to-mid grade routes. A great location for a group with mixed abilities since you can easily reach the 'hard' side.
5 min	Late afternoon	Dry in the rain	Sheltered			Short, sharp and shady, and just the job for people who are looking for short, sharp shady routes!
15 min	All day			Windy		An immaculate sheet of perfect rock covered in quality long routes. Not much very easy stuff despite the friendly angle but well worth considering for those who want a variation from Sella and Toix.
2 min	Sun and shade		Sheltered			Beautifully situated towers in a woodland setting. Small set of mainly-harder routes on good rock.
10 min	From mid morning	Dry in the rain	Sheltered			Unattractive crag in an urban setting. Mostly powerful steep climbing on pockets and the quality routes are all in the 7th grade. Good for those who need an outdoor climbing wall but don't go here for the easy stuff.
5 min to 20 min	Sun and shade	Dry in the rain		Windy		A major mountain destination, with big multi-pitch routes (some trad, some sport) and huge single-pitch sport routes. Rumours of the locals using 100m ropes might just be true!
2 min to 15 min	Sun and shade	Dry in the rain	Sheltered	Windy		The largest crag in the book has everything from short easy routes to long traditional multi-pitch offerings. Plenty of routes for everyone and enough appeal to spend your whole holiday here. It can get busy.
10 min to 1 hour	All day			Windy		This huge mountain crag dominates the Sella Valley. The routes are big and demanding traditional undertakings, with loose rock, which require commitment. The rewards are magnificent.
10 min	Mostly shade	Dry in the rain	Sheltered		Restrictions	This superb steep wall has an excellent set of hard routes which are always in the shade. **Restriction:** Access only allowed by special permission of the land owner.
1 hour	All day			Windy		Magnificent mountain crag with huge long routes. A wonderful place to spend a day providing you climb fast enough. Well worth the effort of the walk-in with good routes across the grades.
20 min	All day			Windy		One of the most awesome pieces of rock in the area which is home to many long trad routes and a few fully-bolted sport routes. Only a small selection is included in this book.
2 min to 10 min	All day	Dry in the rain		Windy		A set of buttresses offering trad and sport climbing in both single and multi-pitch variations. Easy access and plenty of routes across the grades. Slightly poor rock on some sections.

CRAG	Page	GRADE RANGE up to 4+	5 to 6a+	6b to 7a	7a+ and up	No. of ROUTES	Mainly sport routes	Some trad routes	Some multi-pitch
CALPE									
Bernia	220		5	4	11	20	Sport		
Altea	224		1	18	7	37	Sport		
Mascarat	228		9	14	10	33	Sport	Trad	Multi-pitch
Toix East and North	238	3	10	15	8	36	Sport		
Toix West, Placa, TV	242	3	51	16	6	96	Sport		Multi-pitch
Toix Sea Cliffs	252		1	10	8	19	Sport	Trad	Multi-pitch
Olta	256		9	7	6	22	Sport		
Peñón de Ifach	260		6	18	4	28	Sport	Trad	Multi-pitch
XALÓ VALLEY									
Los Pinos	272		1	8	16	25	Sport		
Peña Roja	276		5	1	11	28	Sport		
Murla/Alcalali	280	2	6	15		48	Sport		
L'Ocaive	286	2	15	10	8	35	Sport		
Covatelles	292		8	5	1	14	Sport		
Font d'Axia	294	4	5	3		12	Sport		
Pego	296	2	11	9	2	24	Sport		
Segaria	300	1	1	4		17		Trad	Multi-pitch
GANDÍA									
Gandía	306	8	43	74	48	174	Sport		
Salem	322		43	54		141	Sport		
Aventador	332	1	34	31	3	69	Sport		Multi-pitch
Montesa	340	7	43	40	7	97	Sport		
Bell s	348	5	43	71		145	Sport		
Baranc de l'Avern	358	4	36	5		117	Sport		

Approach walk	Sunshine or shade	Dry in the Rain	Sheltered	2 indy	Access	SUMMARY
5 min to 15 min	All day			Windy		A huge ridge covered with climbable rock but only with limited devlopment so far. A magnificent tufa-covered wall including the *Magic Flute*, and a mediocre area near the parking with friendly grades.
10 min and roadside	Morning and all day		Sheltered			A couple of easily accessible cliffs, one old wave and one new skool. There is stacks more rock in the hills to the west.
8 min to 15 min	Sun and shade		Sheltered	Windy		Atmospheric an very varied area. One classic easy multi-pitch route and several hard wall climbs. The experience can be tempered by traffic noise but the positions are memorable.
Roadside	Morning (1 shade wall)		Sheltered			The two developed sections on the northern side of the Sierra de Toix offer a pleasant roadside buttress with a good grade spread and a cool and shady north-facing wall with some scary hard routes.
2 min to 10 min	From mid morning		Sheltered	Windy		A favourite area which has the widest selection of easier climbs. Some of the old routes are getting a bit worn out but recent new routes, especially on Toix Placa, have added another dimension to the place.
5 min to 15 min	From mid morning		Sheltered			Two spectacular locations on the extensive sea cliffs. Raco del Corv has some great old trad routes - every one a classic! The Candelabra del Sol is has some big committing routes but on slightly crusty rock.
20 min	To mid afternoon			Windy		Beautifully-situated buttress on long ridge overlooking Calpe with magnificent views. Quality rock and routes from 4 to 6c including 2 of the area's classics. Some hold chipping on the harder routes and quite a long approach walk.
20 min	All day (1 shade area)				Restrictions	One of the main landmarks of the Costa Blanca next to Calpe. Superb long trad climbs and several stunning fully-bolted, multi-pitch routes. **Restriction:** No climbing on the North Face 1 April to 30 June.
2 min to 4 min	From mid morning	Dry in the rain	Sheltered			Short and hard routes on a sheltered and accessible crag. Good climbing but not much in the lower grades.
3 min	Morning sun		Sheltered			A great crag in convenient location. Well-sheltered and often dry in bad weather. Some good routes across the grades but starting to suffer from over-use.
2 min to 10 min	All day and afternoon	Dry in the rain	Sheltered			This long ridge has plenty of rock but only a few developed sections. Most of the climbing is hard but there are a few slabbier walls. All the routes tend to be better than they look and the rock is as good as it gets.
10 min	Late afternoon	Dry in the rain		Windy		A big crag which is finally getting the attention it deserves. The Main Wall appears vegetated but gives good easy-to-mid grade routes picking out the good rock. The new harder section has some great steep pitches.
10 min	Afternoon		Sheltered			A small crag which is easy to get to however it is probably only worth the effort if you have climbed on every other crag in the book.
5 min	Afternoon		Sheltered			Small and sheltered crag with some pleasant easy routes. A nice out-of-the-way setting for learning the ropes.
Roadside and 10 min	To mid afternoon		Sheltered			Two buttresses near the town of Pego, one good one mediocre. Sadly the good one is not the one next to the parking spot.
25 min	All day			Windy		Recently-developed mountain crag on a very extensive ridge. All trad routes at present and with scope for much development.
10 min to 20 min	All day 1 shade buttress	Dry in the rain	Sheltered		Restrictions	A popular crag with lots of steep walls and tufas. A reasonable grade spread but the best routes tend to be in the harder grades. **Access:** There are sometimes problems here at weekends
Roadside and 10 min	Sun and shade		Sheltered			Sheltered crag in a small valley. Easy access and good mid-grade routes. Over-bolted in places and the hard routes aren't very interesting.
10 min	All day			Windy		An old crag which has been well re-geared. Nicely situated above a river. Plenty of slab climbs but can get a bit repetitive and some of the lines are hard to follow because of over-bolting. Very sunny with no shelter.
5 min	All day (1 shade area)					Small well-positioned crag above an attractive town with a castle. A good grade spread and plenty in the 5 and 6 grade range. Most of the routes are only short. There is also plenty of bouldering locally.
1 min and 20 min	All day (1 shade area)		Sheltered			A beautifully situated crag in a sun-trap ravine. Loads of short wall climbs on excellent rock, plus a few steeper routes. Also a shady sector nearby with some steeper routes.
2 min to 10 min	Sun and shade		Sheltered			Some great buttresses in a gorge near Ontinyent. Fine climbing on many of the routes but the atmosphere is dominated by the busy road below.

Murcia

N

Fortuna

Orihuela - p62

A7

A30

N340

Orihuela

Mula

C415

Murcia

Alcantarille

La Panocha - p52

Leyva - p44

Alhama
de Murcia

Sierra de Espuna
National Reserve

A7

A30

20km from Murcia Airport

10km

The well-positioned, pleasant classic of *Pili* (5) on the South Face of La Panocha - *page 57*.
The climbing is typical of the cliff, a little polished but of excellent quality
and always with the striking backdrop of the city of Murcia, spread out below.

LEYVA

Although a long way south of the popular climbing areas around Benidorm and Calpe, Leyva is technically within the hinterland of the Costa Blanca and is certainly well worth a visit. It is a magnificent cliff of international significance; the main face being a 150 metre high, south-facing wall of excellent rock, not unlike the top half of the Falaise d'Escales in the French Verdon Gorge. The routes here were all done in traditional style originally but over the years there has been a substantial equipping programme and all the best climbs are now fully bolted. All that is required for these is fifteen quickdraws (some of the pitches are pretty big!) and double ropes for the abseil descent. If you prefer to travel even lighter, and just use a single rope, it is possible to walk off the right-hand side of the cliff.
To the right of the main cliff, and at a lower level, there are two smaller crags with a good selection of single pitch climbs across a range of difficulty, all of which are fully bolted. These are the Sector de la Cueva and the Sector Pecera.

Leyva is a long day's outing from the Calpe area and a good option is to consider stopping over in the area for a couple of days. There is a pleasant campsite (plus cabins) at El Berro; this is quite close to the cliff and it has the basics, including a bar and cabins. Prices are very reasonable (tent and 2 people for under €10 a night) check out **www.campingelberro.com**.

APPROACH (area map page 42)

Follow the toll-free motorway south from Alicante, round Murcia (80km) then continue southwards for another 22km to a turn off into the town of Alhama de Murcia. Turn into the centre of town and follow signs for Sierra Espuna and Baranc de Leyva. The road winds up into the hills for around 15km (the route splits at one point then rejoins a little further) to arrive at a limited parking by a barrier. The cliffs are a 30-40 minute walk up the track. This is used by locals who have properties up in the hills, its always worth sticking out a thumb as they pass - nothing ventured, nothing gained!

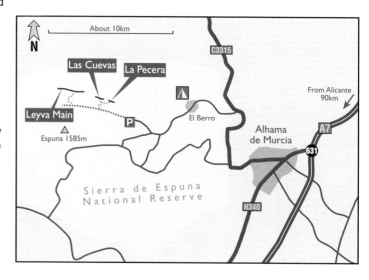

CONDITIONS

The cliff faces due south and is a great winter venue when it is possible to climb on the face in T-shirts whilst the hollows are filled with frost. If there is a wind blowing then you won't get much shelter and the climate is less reliable down here than up by Calpe. Summers are usually way too hot as all the featured cliffs face almost due south.

The striking crack-line of *Fisura Carrillo - Vera* (6b+) at Leyva - *page 47*
This fine climb forges a superb line up the Main Face, in three long pitches,
offering little chance of getting lost!   Photo: Sherri Davy
Inset: Pete O'Donovan on *Divinas Palabras* (7a+) at Las Cuevas - *page 48*

THE MAIN FACE

A magnificent wall - arguably the finest in the whole book. A wide expanse of excellent limestone, split by some fantastic lines and the place is almost always quiet. Get it pencilled in!
APPROACH - A steady 30-40 minute walk leads to a terrace wall that crosses the shallow valley, on the right. The main cliff is directly above, reached by a steep scramble up any of the scree paths.
CONDITIONS - South-facing but high enough to catch any bad weather. Warm in winter, roasting in summer.
GEAR - The routes are bolted, but these are often spaced!
DESCENT - The face to the right of *Fisura Carillo - Vera* is equipped with an abseil route. Three 45m abseils lead (the 1st goes slightly leftwards - facing in) down the smooth face. The location of the start is marked by a couple of small cairns on the cliff top. Walking round to the right is the alternative.

❶ Carillo-Cantabella . . . . . 5+

A popular classic taking a line up the disjointed grooves on the left side of the central section of the face. Start left of the toe of the buttress at a right-trending groove.
1) **4+, 40m.** Climb the ramp rightwards past a cave to a ledge.
2) **5+, 35m.** Trend left to a groove and up this to a tree.
3) **4+, 35m.** Climb the groove above then the pillar on the left.
4) **4+, 35m.** Trend left then follow cracks to a niche.
5) **5+, 40m.** Traverse right across the face then climb a groove.
6) **4+, 15m.** Finish up the groove.
FA. Juan Carrillo, Mariano Cantabella 1970s

❷ Gallego-Seiquer 6b

A big route which finishes at the hanging corner on the right side of the great block overhang near the top of the cliff.
1) **5, 40m.** A wall leads to a long groove; up this to a ledge.
2) **5+, 30m.** Up the sustained wall to a good ledge on the left.
3) **6b, 40m.** The tough wall leads to a short groove and belay.
4) **5+, 20m.** Head left up a ramp (loose blocks at the start and higher up) to the base of the groove.
5) **5+, 25m.** Finish up the chimney groove above.
FA. Miguel Angel Gallego, Jose Seiquer Carasa 1977

❸ Carrillo - del Campo . . . 6b+

A series of corners and grooves up the front of the pillar to the left of the major crack system of *Fisura Carrillo - Vera*. Start at the right-hand side of a clean 40m tower of rock.
1) **6a+, 35m.** Climb the right side of the pillar to a ledge.
2) **6a, 38m.** Move right then climb a devious series of short grooves to a small stance on a ramp.
3) **5+, 25m.** Trend left then climb direct to a stance by a flake.
4) **6a, 35m.** Up the flake, a grassy groove and a chimney to a stance on a ledge on the right.
5) **6b+, 20m.** Climb the steep wall to the final easy crack.
FA. Juan Carrillo Olmos, Carlos del Campo Fernandez 1971

❹ Riglos . . . . 🔲🔲 **6c**
A discontinuous series of cracks in the wall left of *Fisura
Carrillo - Vera* gives a good sustained climb. Start by a tree left
of the base of the groove. Also known as *Carabina Larga*.
1) 6c, 35m. Climb a crack and striated wall into a groove. Up
this to a tiny ledge and hanging stance.
2) 6a+, 40m. Climb the wall for 20m then make a short
traverse left to reach a crack. Up this to another small stance.
3) 5, 10m. A short blocky crack leads to a higher ledge.
4) 6b+, 30m. Trend right up the wall to a wide crack. Up this,
and the wall above, to the 'half-moon' crack. Up this to a ledge.
5) 5+, 25m. Traverse right to a long diedre and finish up this.
FA. Miguel Angel Gallego, Juan Carlos Gallego 1976

❺ Fisura Carrillo - Vera . . 🔲🔲 **6b+**
The prominent crack splitting the left side of the most continuous
section of the wall. Take plenty of quickdraws! *Photo page 45.*
1) 6a+, 40m. Trend left into the groove and climb it with the
occasional moves on either wall to a small stance.
2) 6b+, 38m. Climb steeply up the wall into the continuation
of the groove and follow this with sustained interest to a stance.
3) 6a, 54m. Continue up the crack (possible small stance at
25m) for ever, to a final short struggle up the final wide section.
FA. Juan Carrillo, Antonio Ruiz Vera 1972

❻ Eiger . . . . 🔲🔲 **6c**
The smooth-looking wall to the right of *Fisura Carrillo - Vera*.
1) 5+ 30m. From the base of *Fisura Carrillo - Vera*, climb rightwards then straight up a diedre to a stance in a cave.
2) 6c, 35m. Climb out of the cave and up cracks before
trending right to reach a stance on the left.
3) 5, 35m. Trend easily right for 10m then back left to enter the
steep crack. Climb this to a small stance.
4) A0 & 6a, 40m. Up the crack then move left (metal hand
hold) to enter the diedre. Up this to its top and a stance.
5) 4, 8m. Move left (loose) to a stance on the edge of the ledge.
5a) 6c, 25m. An alternative finish direct up the wall.
6) 6a, 25m. The cracks are followed with a jig left, to the top.
FA. Luis Clavel 1975

❼ Historia interminable . 🔲🔲 **6b**
Some grooves and a crack, which are split by good stances
form an interesting series of variations on *Eiger*.
1) 6a, 25m. The right-facing groove to a stance on the left.
2) 6a, 33m. Follow cracks up the wall then trend left to reach a
stance on *Eiger*.
3) 6a, 28m. Climb straight up the face into the base of the
crack on the middle pitch of *Eiger*. Up this to the small stance.
4) 6b, 40m. Follow the crack all the way to a small ledge.
5) 5, 14m. Finish up the wall and crack above.

❽ Gallego-Carillo . . . . . . 🔲🔲 **6b**
The 1st route to breach the main wall at Leyva takes a direct
line up the cliff finishing up a curving groove near the top.
1) 5+, 40m. Follow the left-trending ramp, with the odd tricky
move, to the top of the tower.
2) 6a+, 35m. Climb the double diedre (loose) then the better
wall above to a stance on a big block.
3) 4, 8m. Move left to a stance in a niche - this was the bivi-
site on the 1st ascent!!
4) 6b, 40m. Climb the hard wall to base of a developing
groove, then up this to a good stance. There may be an easier
variation to this pitch on its left.
5) 6a+, 50m. Follow the curving groove to its top then climb up
and right along a ramp and up slabs to the top.
5a) 5, 50m. Traverse left across the slab into the long groove
and follow this to the top (loose in places) past at least one
possible stance, to the top.
FA. Miguel Garcia Gallego, Juan Carrillo Olmos 1970

❾ Carnaval . . . . 🔲🔲 **6a+**
A series of grooves finishing up the left side of the great
diagonal overhang near the cliff top. Start at a left-slanting
crack under the fall-line from the great roof. There is some
loose rock near the top, care required if there are teams below
1) 6a, 40m. Climb the crack and diedre to a flake. Up this, and
the wall above, to the upper of two ledges.
2) 6a+, 30m. Climb the wall then trend right into a crusty
diedre. Climb this and the continuation crack then trend left to a
ledge - complete with loose blocks.
3) 5+, 40m. Up a short groove to a flake then move right into
the main diedre. Up this to the roof then step left to a stance.
4) 5+, 40m. An awkward chimney leads to a large ledge above
which a diagonal diedre heads for the summit.
FA. Juan Carrillo Olmos, Miguel Garcia Gallego 1971

❿ Yosemite . . . . 🔲🔲🔲 **7b**
The impressive smooth wall to the right of the great roof has a
sustained and hard series of pitches. Start in the old sheep fold
under the base of the wall.
1) 6c, 35m. Climb straight up the face to a small stance. A
right-hand start up the groove and wall is **7a**.
2) 6c, 35m. Move right to reach a left-slanting rake then follow
this as it heads to a stance between detached flakes.
3) 7a, 30m. Weave up the superb wall to a cramped stance in
the middle of nowhere.
4) 6b+, 25m. Move left then climb rightwards to an impres-
sively-situated stance under the overhangs.
5) 7b, 25m. Pull leftwards through the roof onto the hugely
exposed headwall and trend rightwards to an easier groove.
FA. Miguel Garcia Gallego, Juan Carrillo Olmos 1974

⓫ Lavaredo . . . . 🔲🔲 **7a**
A fine free version of one of the classic aid routes gives some
hard climbing up a wall and grooves. Start at the left of the
pillar below a groove leading past a prominent scar.
1) 6b, 35m. Climb a sustained groove to a small stance.
2) 6c, 15m. Straight up the wall to another tiny stance.
3) 6b+, 35m. Follow the cracks above through a recess and
onto a stance at the lower end of a diagonal ramp.
4) 7a, 25m. Climb into the smooth diedre, up this and then the
wall above to another poor stance.
5) 6a, 35m. A wall leads to easier climbing up a groove.
FA. Miguel Garcia Gallego, Miguel Sanchez Canovas 1974

⓬ Gallego - Hurtado . . . . 🔲🔲 **5+ (HVS)**
An easier offering though a lot of the gear is old - take a rack.
1) 5, 40m. Climb rightwards up a crack into the diedre on the
left-hand side of the tower. Up this to a stance on its crest.
2) 5, 40m. Trend left to a ledge then climb the steep crack that
leads rightwards to a stance in the base of a chimney.
3) 5, 35m. Climb up and right, then traverse left across the
groove then climb up and left to a red groove. Belay a short
distance up this.
4) 5+, 40m. Climb the wall on the left then traverse right to
cross the top of the groove - an exposed crux - to reach easier
ground up a ramp. The last section is also tricky.
FA. Miguel Garcia Gallego, Francisco Hurtado Martinez 1970s

⓭ Fisura Snoopy . . . . 🔲🔲🔲 **6a (E1)**
35m. The clean-cut crack-line in the left-hand side of the front
face of the buttress gives a pleasant pitch.
FA. J Matas, Javi 1984

LAS CUEVAS

Las Cuevas offers a collection of over 50 single pitch routes which vary from quite small to very large and cover the grade spectrum from 4+ to 8b, although it should be said that most of them are in the higher grades. The routes described here cover the central section of the cliff; there are a few more climbs to the left of those shown here for which few details are known. A few climbs have their names painted on the rock which helps with identification of other climbs in the area.

APPROACH - These two cliffs are reached by a steep track that starts 500 metres nearer the parking than the Main Face. It is marked by a couple of small cairns on the right-hand side of the track. The cliffs are difficult to spot from below.

CONDITIONS - Like the Main Face, this is a south-facing sun-trap. It is very sheltered and can get extremely hot at the 'wrong' time of year. The crag is steep enough to give some dry climbing in the rain although there may be some seepage.

There are around a dozen or so routes to the left of Deseo for which no details are known.

❶ Deseo **7a**
24m. The steep and heavily-cleaned groove.

❷ La proa . . . . **7c+**
22m. The wall, passing left of a prominent bush.

❸ Saltamontes cagón . . . . . **7a+**
26m. Start at some blocks on the ground.

To the right is a deep 10m high cave with two long routes starting to its left and two short ones starting inside it.

❹ La continuidad me va . . **7c**
26m. The left edge of the cave and the line directly above it.

❺ Copón de reyes . . . . . . **7b+**
26m. Start as for the last route and take the right-hand line up the wall above.

❻ Cricifixion . . . . **7a+**
10m. The short but butch line out of the back of the cave.

❼ Pelotilla colgadera **7a**
10m. A short line up the right wall of the cave.

To the right is the start of the major cave/hollow that is the main feature of the central part of the cliff. Above the left end of this are two impressive leaning grooves.

❽ El cielo puede esperar . **7a**
22m. The left-hand line has substantial glue-in ring bolts and a hard start. The lower-off is on a ramp.

❾ Divinas palabras . . . . . **7a+**
22m. The right-hand groove is approached steeply via huge pockets and leads to a lower-off out left. *Photo page 45.*

❿ Hombre wpo . . . . **7b+**
30m. Follow most of the previous route but swing right onto the arete and continue up this in a dramatic position.

The next routes are inside the steep cave.

⓫ Sube tu que de risa . . . **6b**
16m. The right-slanting traverse line under the roofs passing a couple of sawn-off tree stumps.

⓬ Soy un cagalindres . . . **7a+**
14m. A steeper, more direct start to the above via a leaning rib.

⓭ Poder de la mente **8a**
26m. Startting just to the right but crossing the traverse line of *Sube tu que de risa* and the mass of overhangs above.

⓮ Humeando y resbalosa . . . **7b+**
12m. A short, pocketed line leads directly to a lower-off below the belay at the end of the traverse line of *Sube tu que de risa.*

⓯ Quien la sigue la consigue **8a**
16m. A much harder extension to *Humeando.*

⓰ Crucifixión **7b**
14m. A right-hand start to *Humeando* is just a touch easier.

To the right are a couple of impressive routes up the steepest part of the back wall of the cave.

⓱ Señorita Calamidad . . . **8b**
28m. From a shallow cave, climb tufas into the leaning groove. Power across the left wall to a large hole and finish direct.

⓲ Café con leche Mon . . . **8b+**
28m. Climb out of the right-hand cave and follow tufas up the leaning wall to the overhang. Finish across this!

⓳ Pank Floud **7b**
14m. A shorter outing up the tufas to the right.

Murcia
Alicante
Benidorm
Calpe
Xaló Valley
Gandia

Leyva

La Panocha

Orihuela

Beyond the steepest section of the wall, the next feature is a crack rising diagonally to the right.

20 Hostia Ernesto . . . . . . 6b+
18m. Follow the crack to the lower-off hanging from the impressive bulges above.

21 Subiendo como la espuma 7a
18m. A tricky slab and thin pull gain the tufas and pockets, then easier climbing leads to the lower-off of the previous route.

22 India 7b
20m. The wall leads to the bulges. A loop to the left is only **7a+**.

23 Era un hombre 8a
30m. The extension through the bulges and up the grey wall.

To the right are red-stepped bulges in the centre of the lower wall; two routes climb through these to a shared a lower-off.

24 Los picapiedra . . . . . . 6c+
18m. The thin left-hand line.

25 Moniga atomica 6b
18m. The central, juggy and rather polished line, starting at the painted name.

26 Chúpame la minga, dominga . 6c
14m. Climb through the right side of the red bulges.

27 Yabadaba du 6b
14m. Follow easy-angled rock to a shared lower-off.

28 Pumuky 6c
10m. A short outing up the hard slab and easy groove.

29 Licantropo . . . . . . 7b+
28m. A big powerful pitch up the wall then through the capping overhangs via a large niche. Very impressive.

Away to the right the cliff becomes much more slabby and (at last) there are some amenable lines.

30 Marabunta 6a
10m. Straight up the slab to the final moves of *Pumuky*.

31 4+ que fobia . . . . 4+
10m. The flake in the centre of the slab is the easiest line here.

32 Aquí no me caigo 6a
10m. The thin crack has well-spaced bolts.

The final three routes listed go to a shared lower-off on a ledge that runs along under steeper rock.

33 Un beso o una flor . . . . 5+
10m. The left-hand line.

34 No name . . . . 5+
10m. The central one.

35 Debiste . . . . 5+
10m. ....and the right-hand one.

Beyond Debiste are a dozen or so routes and beyond these are another six based around a cave before the cliff ends. Brief details on these are on the next page.

LAS CUEVAS - DERECHA
Specific details on the routes on the right-hand side of the Sector las Cuevas have been hard to come by. That assembled here is from a series of sources. We believe the names and grades to be right, and working on the theory that some information is better than none - here it is! Any feed back re grades, descriptions and star-ratings would be much appreciated.
APPROACH - As for Las Cuevas but walk right
CONDITIONS - South facing, well-sheltered by the trees and quick drying, seepage may be a problem after rain.

❶ Pájaro loco . . . . [   ] 6a
The extension is a good looking 7a.

❷ Chicas Católicas . . . . [   ] 7b

❸ Más te vale Camarón . . . . [   ] 7b+

❹ Flaky de Maky . . . . [   ] 6c

❺ Sólo una sonrisa . . . . [   ] 6a

❻ Con pelos ne la lengua . . . . . . [   ] 6b+

❼ El bese negro . . . . [   ] 6a+

❽ La dolorosa . . . . [   ] 6b

❾ La pinochas . . . . [   ] 6c

❿ No es broma lo que desploma . [   ] 8a

⓫ Route 11. . . . . [   ] 6c

⓬ Caga superficial . . . . [   ] 7c+

⓭ Caja hondo . . . . [   ] 7a+

⓮ Tira de la cadena. . . . . [   ] 7b

⓯ Hemorroides . . . . [   ] 7a+

⓰ Cristina, venta a mi piscina . . [   ] 7a

Murcia
Alicante
Benidorm
Calpe
Xaló Valley
Gandia
Leyva
La Panocha
Orihuela

SECTOR LA PECERA

The section of rock on the far right has a collection of well-bolted routes from 5+ to 6b. The cliff here lacks the grandeur of the Main Face, or the test pieces of Las Cuevas, but if south-facing rock of a less-than-vertical nature is your cup of tea, a day here should fit the bill.
APPROACH - As for Las Cuevas but walk 100m right to locate a broad grey slab with 18 climbs on it.
CONDITIONS - South facing, well-sheltered by the trees and quick drying, a good crag for cold clear days.

① Diedro Barracuda . . . . . 🔲🔲 **6a**
20m. The right-facing groove that bounds the left side of the cliff is entered directly and exited out to the right.

② Pez globo . . . . 🔲 **6a**
20m. A direct line to the lower-off of the previous route.

③ Tiburón Martilla . . 🔲🔲🔲 **6b**
20m. A thin and crimpy slab.

④ Congerie Belga . . . . . . 🔲🔲 **6c**
18m. A direct line to, and through, the hard roof high above.

⑤ El boquerón . . . . 🔲🔲 **6b+**
18m. Climb the slab to a lower-off under the edge of the overlap that cuts across the upper part of the face.

⑥ El mero . . . . 🔲🔲 **6b+**
18m. The right-hand line leads to the same lower-off.

⑦ Nudibranquio . . . . 🔲 **6b+**
20m. The next line to the right passing through a niche.

⑧ El abadejo . . . . . 🔲🔲🔲 **7b**
20m. A fierce route up the smoothest rock around is obviously on the wrong cliff.

To the right is a bush at the base of the cliff. The next route is just left of this.

⑨ Pulpo roquero . . . . 🔲🔲 **6b**
20m. Climb to the roof at 18m and pull rightwards through it.

⑩ Lenguado Bulero . . . . 🔲 **6a+**
20m. Start to the right of the bush and climb to and through the same roof as the previous climb, by leftwards manoeuvres.

⑪ La manta ray . . . . 🔲 **6a**
18m. The second line right of the bush, with a jig right at the top.

⑫ Pastinaca . . . . 🔲 **6a**
18m. A direct to the lower-off of the previous climb starting up a shallow groove.

⑬ El metillon colaro . . . . 🔲🔲 **6b**
18m. The steep slab.

⑭ El rascacio . . . . 🔲 **6a**
18m. A slightly easier line up the slab, leading to a shared lower-off.

⑮ El sarga real . . . . 🔲 **6a+**
18m. Start up a short pillar, and press on through a hole and up to the lower-off.

⑯ La ballena azul . . . . 🔲 **6a+**
18m. A right-hand variant on the previous climb.

⑰ La tortuga carey . . . . 🔲 **6a**
18m. A pleasant rightward-trending line.

⑱ El delfín . . . . 🔲 **5**
18m. The last route, before grassier rock, is the easiest here.

LA PANOCHA

Behind the typical Spanish city of Murcia is a long range of hills. The high point is the rocky ridge of the Cresta del Gallo or the 'cock's-comb'. At one end of this is the impressive tower of La Panocha, which translates very appropriately as the 'Corncob'. This is the best climbing venue in the immediate area and a popular place at weekends with city dwellers escaping for a bit of cragging; it is the same the world over. During the week you are likely to have the place to yourself. The area has a full spread of grades with many fine face routes and a number of mini-summits to bag. Most of the routes are single pitches though the biggest of these are almost 30m long.

The local guide is *Cresta del Gallo y La Panocha* written and published by Sergio Hernandez Rodriguez and Francisco Jose Iniesta Gallego. It is a nice topo guide, only costs €10 and is available to look at from the kind lady in a Tourist Info booth by the parking, on most busy weekends.

APPROACH (area map page 42)

The crag is situated to the south east of the city of Murcia. From the north follow the A7 motorway south east then the N301 (a motorway which may be renumbered the A30 in the future) that runs round Murcia, towards Cartagena. Once past the city centre take the junction signed La Alberca and Algezares. Follow the MU302 east and drive through La Alberca then start looking for a right turn signed La Fuensanta (earlier right turns lead to the same place but by a devious road). Drive up the hill past the impressive relegious buildings to a T-junction. Turn left and follow the road past a section of one-way road to the extensive parking in front of the cliff, which is less than 5 minutes away.

CONDITIONS

The Cresta del Gallo is set at almost 500m and so can be a little cooler than the valleys surrounding it. Being a ridge there is often a breeze blowing and La Panocha has walls facing in all directions making it a viable venue at almost any time of the year.

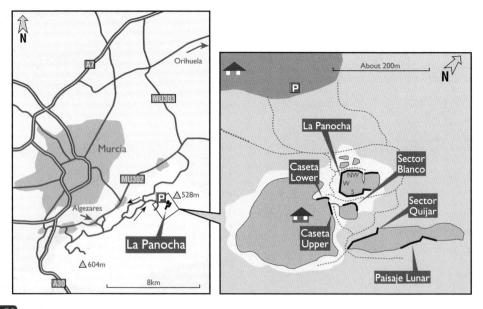

Sevi-Spiri (5+) on the South Face of La Panocha - *page 57*. An awkward start through the diagonal overlap leads to easier climbing up the face and an juggy exit through the roof of the cave.

Left margin tabs: Murcia, Alicante, Benidorm, Calpe, Xaló Valley, Gandía, Leyva, La Panocha, Orihuela

NORTH WEST FACE

The main feature here is the tall tower of La Panocha standing in front of the main edge, which has routes on all sides and a fine airy summit. The broad North West Face has a wide chimney on its left-hand side. The better climbing is on the wall to the right of the chimney with a series of fine climbs. Many of the routes originally had upper pitches but the rock on these upper sections is often poor and generally these have not been equipped.

APPROACH - The first wall reached from the parking.
CONDITIONS - The wall catches the late afternoon sun.

1 Antonio Mairal . . . . 4+
A long route up the rib, then rightwards to the top of the tower.
1) 24m. Start up the groove then climb a ramp to ledges.
2) 20m. Continue across the gap and up the slab to the top.
Descent - Abseil down the SE Face (to the left looking into the gap behind the tower) from a selection of anchors (30m).

2 Freinet 7a
18m. The steep and technical left arete of the chimney gives an excellent piece of climbing.

To the right is the deep gloomy rift of La Chimenea Panocha. Surprisingly there are half a dozen fully equipped climbs in this gloomy setting, all graded 5+ except for one.

3 Maria Angeles . . . . 5+
The first bolt-line on the right wall is as good a sample as any.
1) 5+, 22m. Climb the chimney until it is possible to transfer onto the right wall. Up this to a stance where the chimney ends.
2) 4, 14m. Climb the exposed arete to the top.

4 Directa Norte . . . . . . 6b+
20m. The prominent thin crack in the left-hand side of the North Face to a niche with lower-off just to the right.

5 Norte Baldomera 6c
24m. Weave a way up the face just left of the wide, inviting crack to pass the left-edge of the overhang then continue to a lower-off close to the Madonna.

6 Fisura Norte 6b
1) 6b, 16m. The big crack in the right-hand side leads left to a stance in a niche where it starts to lean to the left
2) 6a, 22m. Continue in the same direction, past an awkward bulge, then finish more easily.

7 Gallego - Canovas . . . . 7a+
30m. The magnificent face immediately right of the chimney. There is a lower-off at 18m for those not wanting the summit.

8 Gallego - Tirolinas . . . . . . 6c+
30m. The first 7a in the area which has typically now been down-graded. Up the crack splitting the bulges. There is a lower-off at 18m.

54

Pili

17

16

15

12 13 14

WEST FACE

These are undoubtedly the finest set of climbs here; long pitches, well-protected routes, good quality rock, all in a dramatic setting high above the city. Generally the climbs are sustained and technical on the lower wall, then ease in angle and difficulty with height.

APPROACH - From the approach path branch right under the North West Face and scramble up the blocky gully until directly under the face. It is also possible to descend the gravelly gully from the sunny classic of the South Face.

⑫ Fuensanta Maruja . . . . 🎌🖊️ [____] **7a**
26m. Start just right of the north west arete of the tower and climb the steep wall then thin cracks leftwards to a mid-route lower-off. Continue up the face until it is possible to move right to a second lower-off where the angle drops back.
FA. Jesús Martínez Fenor, Juan Ramón Bermúdez 1966

⑬ Victoria Elvira . . . . 🎌🖊️ [____] **7a**
26m. Start under the leaning wall and trend left with difficulty then climb thin cracks in the blunt rib, passing a lower-off at 20m, to one on the crest of the wall.
FA. Carlos del Campo Ferdinández, Miguel Ángel Garciá Gallego 1971

⑭ Majura Directisima 🎌🔎🖋️ [____] **6c/A0**
24m. The juggy central crack-line in the leaning face is approached up the tilted wall using a bit of aid early on. Above that it gives superb climbing bang up the middle of the face.
FA. Baldomero Brugarolas Munuera, Montesinos, Miguel Ángel Garciá Gallego 1969

⑮ Variante Majura . . . . . 🎌🖊️ [____] **6c+**
24m. A right-hand start trends left across the face and manages to avoid the aid on the regular route. Another great outing.
FA. Ginés López Peréz 1992

⑯ Gallego - Carlos . . . . . 🎌🖊️ [____] **6a**
26m. Start under the south west arete and climb up and left (crux) to a rest in a niche. Undercut awkwardly leftwards to gain the hanging groove, climb the continuation groove, then the flake left of the arete and the slab above all the way to a lower-off just below the top. Superb.
FA. Miguel Ángel Garciá Gallego, Carlos del Campo Ferdinández 1973

⑰ Pili Directa . . . . 🎌🖋️ [____] **6c.**
24m. A hard direct start to the arete up its leaning left-hand side. The main route starts around the corner to the right and is described on the next page. There is a choice of lower-offs.
FA. Antonio Gersol, Juan Ramón Bermúdez, Jesús Martínez Fenor 1966

⑨ Maneras de Sobre . . . . . . 🎌 [____] **6a+**
16m. The short overhang and wall just right of the crack.

Stood in front of the tower is a cluster of huge blocks, the largest two of these both have some short routes.

⑩ Epi. . . . . 🖋️🔎 [____] **7b**
12m. The leaning arete of the northernmost block - hard.

⑪ Buriles . . . . 🖋️🔎 [____] **7a+**
6m. The smooth west face of the smaller block - hard!

LA PANOCHA *South Face*

Murcia

Alicante

Benidorm

Calpe

Xaló Valley

Gandia

Leyva

La Panocha

Orihuela

Easiest abseil off the top

SOUTH FACE

The most popular section of the cliff is the fine South Face which has a bunch of good face routes all of which are a bit too polished to be mega-classic. Most have high lower-offs or the option of topping-out if desired. Many of the grades feel a bit tough - whether this is due to the polish or that the locals are particularly good at this style of climbing is open to debate.
APPROACH - Walk round either end of the tower, the eastern (left -looking in) route being the easier though a little longer.

To mid afternoon   6 min

CONDITIONS - It gets the sun for much of the day.
DESCENT - For the routes which top-out, abseil down to the right (looking in) which takes you down the wall by routes 12 to 16 (opposite).

① Esther . . . . 🔲🔲🔲 **6b**
24m. An eliminate taking a direct line up the face right of the arete, with a fingery start and some excellent climbing above.
FA. Miguel Ángel Garciá Gallego 1979

② Pili . . . . 🔲 **5**
22m. A classic - devious, interesting and not too hard. From a squat pedestal climb up then left to the arete. Up the balancy groove round the corner then the rib past one lower-off to a higher one. Or continue leftwards to the summit.
Photo page 42.
FA. Antonio Gersol, Juan Ramón Bermúdez, Jesús Martínez Fenor 1966

③ Niña Botina . . . . . . 🔲🔲🔲 **6a+**
22m. Another fingery eliminate. From the blocks step left and climb direct following the bolts.
FA. Mariano Ruiz Cantabella, Antonia Ruiz Vera 1980s

To the right is the 'non-line' of Climb 5+, clip the bolts to either side and ensure to wear blinkers!

④ Porki . . . . 🔲 **6a**
20m. The direct line off the big plinth is sustained and interesting to a fingery finish up the thin battered crack near the top.
FA. Mariano Miñano Lozano, Josè Mataz 1976

⑤ Pipi . . . . 🔲🔲🔲 **5+**
20m. Great climbing. Balance up the wall and pull the roof on a surprising set of holds. Very 'interesting' at the grade.
FA. Mariano Miñano Lozano 1975

⑥ Sur . . . . 🔲 **5**
20m. A worthwhile classic but very polished! Follow the slippery slanting crack to a bay then pull right from here to reach a crack (old pegs); move up and trend left to a lower-off.
FA. Antonio Gersol, Juan Ramón Bermúdez, Jesús Martínez Fenor 1964

⑦ 'M' . . . . 🔲 **6a+**
24m. An eliminate. Start up the crack of *Sur* but move out left and head up the smoother face between *Climb* and *Porki*. Finishing up *Porki* is more logical and easier!
FA. Antonio Gersol, Juan Ramón Bermúdez, Jesús Martínez Fenor 1965

⑧ Sur Directa . . . . 🔲🔲 **5+**
20m. The wall just to the right joining *Sur* at 10m.
FA. Antonio Bohórquez 1980

⑨ Murciano - Catalana . . 🔲🔲 **5+**
24m. Climb straight up the centre of the narrow wall to a cave and a little higher the lower-off. Use the bolts on *Sevi - Spiri* on the upper section
FA. Fulgencio Garijo 1980

⑩ Sevi - Spiri . . . . 🔲🔲 **5+**
24m. Climb of the wide slanting fissure and pull leftwards through the overlap (hard) then climb the face to join *Murciano - Catalana* at the cave. Climb straight through this to finish.
Photo page 53.
FA. Mariano Miñano Lozano, Antonio Bohórquez 1976

⑪ Almirante . . . . 🔲 **5**
26m. Head straight up the crack into the hanging groove above then move out left onto the face. Climb up and right into a curving layback crack and continue up the arete to a high lower-off.
FA. Miguel Ángel Garciá Gallego, Carlos del Campo Ferdinández 1972

The wall to the right faces more to the east and is slightly more sheltered. It goes into the shade earlier. It is also the section passed on the usual approach.

⑫ Mar . . . . 🔲🔲 **6c**
26m. Balance up the lower arete, or climb the short wall just left (large glue-in bolts). From the ledge continue up the thin rounded pillar above the tree.
FA. Alejandro Lozano 1982

⑬ Espolon Sureste . . . . . 🔲🔲 **5**
28m. Scramble right then back left to avoid the rounded lower part of the arete then climb the cracks just right of the upper arete. Nuts required though several of the bolts on the last route can be clipped.
FA. Miguel Ángel Garciá Gallego,1975

⑭ San Bernardo . . . . 🔲 **5**
28m. The big chimney is approached by the left-hand crack in the slab (bolt to the right) and climbed awkwardly to the top. The 1st route to climb the tower and worth doing.
FA. Luis Vidal, Juan Ramón Bermúdez 1959

⑮ Pep Camarena . . . . . . 🔲🔲 **6a+**
26m. The slabby right-hand side of the face has its moments.
FA. Antonio Bohórquez 1970s

⑯ Arista Sureste . . . . 🔲 **4**
38m. A long rambling classic with a choice of starts. A belay is possible at the top of the initial rib.
FA. Juan Ramón Bermúdez , Luis Vidal, Joaquín Asunción 1957

Murcia
Alicante
Benidorm
Calpe
Xaló Valley
Gandia
Leyva
La Panocha
Orihuela

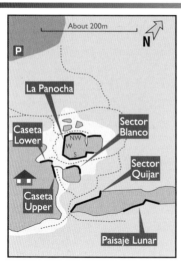

Not much sun — 6 min

SECTOR BLANCO

The steep wall opposite the slabbier South Face of La Panocha is split on its left-hand side by a thin curving crack. This is the line of *Cachondeo* - the best known climb here. All the routes are steep and fingery.

APPROACH - As for the South Face.

CONDITIONS - A very shady sector which could be useful in hot weather.

The first three routes are up the gully to the left.

① Zipe y Zape . . . . 6a+
8m. Climb the tiny and technical white wall on the left.
FA. Josè Matas 1985

② Dougal Haston 6c
16m. The centre of the white wall and the bulge to a lower-off.
FA. Miguel Ángel Garciá Gallego, Juan Carlos Garciá Gallego, 1977

③ Gato 6c
16m. The right-hand side of the wall and the bulge leftwards.

④ Cirrosis . . . . 6b+
16m. This one eases with height; no sneaking in from the left.
FA. Laureano Muñoz, Mariano Romero 1987

⑤ Flauta Mágica . . . . 6c+
16m. Start up the awkward thin crack then head up the wall.
FA. Alejandro Lozano 1992

⑥ Cachondeo . . . 6c+
16m. Follow the awkward thin crack up and out to the right by sustained and pumpy climbing until a lower-off is reached.
FA. Antonia Ruiz Vera, Carlos del Campo Ferdinández 1973

⑦ Directa Margarita . . . . 7b+
14m. Climb the centre of the wall by a thin series of moves until the break of *Cachondeo* is reached. Finish across this.
FA. Antonio Bohórquez, Mariano Miñano Lozano 1977

⑧ Matas - Ginés . . . . 7b+
14m. Fierce face climbing up the wall to the lower-off.
FA. Josè Matas, Ginés López 1991

⑨ Jaisa Tropel, no subas . . . 6a+
14m. The last line on the wall is easier. Climb diagonally left with hands on the ramp - odd!
FA. Octaviano Gálvez López, Juan Miguel Tomás Belando 2002

SECTOR QUIJAR

This sector consists of a couple of shady walls with a collection of reasonable routes. The left-hand side has a tall clean slab then at the top of the gully leading over to the Paisaje Lunar is another smaller triangular slab. The routes here drop into the quick, pleasant tick category without anything too memorable about them.

APPROACH - The wall is located on the left-hand side of the gully that runs up to the left of Sector Blanco towards the col used to access the Paisaje Lunar.

CONDITIONS - Very cool and shady.

① Pájaro **5**
18m. Climb a groove in the arete and follow it as it curves right to enter its continuation. Follow this to the lower-off.

② Variante I de la Pájaro **5**
18m. Start up the *Pájaro* groove and branch left to gain the face. Up this to a rightward exit.

③ Variante II de la Pájaro **5**
18m. A tricky start up the left-slanting crack joins the original.

④ Vistabella City **6b**
16m. A steep lower wall leads to a finish up the black streak above the ramp.
FA. Antonio Bohórquez, Pedro Pérez Gómez 1988

⑤ Sobredosis **6b**
16m. Another steep start leads to the ramp.
FA. José Matas 1982

⑥ Directa Ana, ascen, isa **6a**
16m. From the blocks climb the wall, then the face above.

⑦ Botella . . . . **3+ (Sev)**
18m. The wide crack on the right is a great line. Gear needed.
FA. Amadeo Botella, early days

The next routes are just around the corner, left of the col.

⑧ Espolón BB . . . . **4+ (VS)**
14m. The once-pegged crack and easier arete. Nuts needed.
FA. José Seiquer, José Sánchez 1973

⑨ Bonita . . . . **5+**
14m. A fingery wall to a thin break. Swing right, pull through the overlap then up the shallow groove.

⑩ Bonita Directa **6a**
14m. The direct start is just a bit harder.

⑪ Variante 2 de la bonita . . **6a**
14m. The wall left of the tree soon eases.

⑫ Variante 1 de la bonita . . **6b+**
14m. A desperate minor variation is the last route on this bit.

Change in viewing angle

Caseta - Upper

La Panocha

Approach

Not much sun — 8 min

Starts hidden by the rib

SECTOR CASETA - UPPER

Sector Caseta is the large tower opposite La Panocha, with a discreet building on its summit. It has two main faces which have a reasonable selection of routes although they are not of the same quality as many nearby routes.
APPROACH - Follow the path up left of Sector Blanco and on towards the Paisaje Lunar, but before the col turn right to locate the slab.
CONDITIONS - Shady and sheltered.

1 Placa del árbol . . . . 🔲 **5**
14m. The left side of the slab and the groove above.

2 Mariá Cristina . . . . 🔲 **6a**
16m. The thin crack that snakes up the slab to a rightward exit.
FA. Jorge Batlle, Josè Luis Patiño 1966

3 Terodáctilo . . . . 🔲 **5+**
16m. The right-hand side of the slab is thin.
FA. Josè Matas, Josè Seiquer 1981

4 Consuelo-Sevi . . . . 🔲 **5+**
16m. A right-hand variant is hardly worthy of an entry.
FA. Antonio Bohórquez, Consuelo Amoros 1984

SECTOR CASETA - LOWER

This is the lower wall that can be clearly seen from the parking, to the right of La Panocha.
APPROACH - Scramble up the steep path under the West Face of La Panocha to the base of the wall.
CONDITIONS - Facing north west, it gets the afternoon sun.

5 Voy Compadre . . . . 🔲 **6b+**
14m. The blunt left arete of the lower wall.

6 Tijuana Brass . . . . 🔲 **6a+**
14m. Climb just right of the blunt arete.

7 Lagarto Juancho . . . . 🔲 **6a**
14m. Climb the wall to finish up a crack.

8 Raquel . . . . 🔲 **6a**
14m. Another good little wall climb.

9 O.J.E. . . . . 🔲 **6a**
30m. A long route to the top of the pinnacle. The upper section may not be fully equipped. Descend by walking down the back.

10 Anfeta Local . . . . 🔲 **6a+**
18m. From the same start climb the wall then trend right.

11 Direct Anfeta Local . . . 🔲 **6a**
18m. The direct line is good and sustained.

12 Bruce Lee . . . . 🔲 **6a**
18m. The right-hand line has a choice of starts.

Afternoon — 5 min

LA PANOCHA *Paisaje Lunar*

PAISAJE LUNAR

Over the col is a different world, often sheltered from westerly winds and catching the sun until mid-afternoon. The local name of 'Lunar Landscape' is apt.
APPROACH - Follow the path round behind La Panocha and scramble up, keeping left of Sector Blanco, into a slabby bay with pine trees. Clamber over the col then turn left and down to find this attractive slab.

① Cuatro patas .... 🔲 5
20m. Take the pillar on the left edge of the wall, then pull through the overlap and make an exposed traverse right.
FA. Josè Andreu Correas 1988

② Gulliver .... 🔲 6a
20m. Start up the rounded groove with a bush then pull through the double overlap with difficulty. Trend right across the upper wall to reach the lower-off.
FA. Antonio Bohórquez, Antonio Jesús Gallardo 1970s

③ J.E.P. .... 🔲 5+
20m. A tricky start on pockets then easier climbing to the overlap. Harder moves up a crack lead to the lower-off.
FA. Josè Angel Navarro Cortés, Eduardo Pagán, Francisco Josè Carillo Vinander 1969

④ Anaconda .... 🔲 6a
20m. The left-hand side of the next slab has a hard start but the crack is easier once gained.
FA. Josè Seiguer, Julian "El Valenciano" 1974

⑤ Súperanaconda .... 🔲 5
20m. The right-hand start to the *Anaconda* crack is a bit easier.
FA. Josè Seiguer, Antonio Bohórquez 1974

⑥ Fisura de la sinfonía .. 🔲 5
24m. The awkward cracked groove leads to easier climbing then a steep finish just left of the arete.
FA. Miguel Ángel Garciá Gallego, Carlos del Campo Ferdinández 1971

⑦ Placa de la sinfonía .... 🔲 6a+
14m. Start up a crack then climb the slab parallel to the groove.
FA. Miguel Ángel Garciá Gallego, Carlos del Campo Ferdinández 1971

⑧ Sinfonía .... 🔲 4
14m. The short wall leads to the deeper central section of the groove. Up this to the lower-off on the left.
FA. Miguel Ángel Garciá Gallego, Carlos del Campo Ferdinández 1971

⑨ Espolón de la sinfonía ... 🔲 4 (HS)
30m. The cracked face on the right, then trend left. Either lower-off or head up the easy gully.
FA. Miguel Ángel Garciá Gallego, Carlos del Campo Ferdinández 1971

Across the broken gully to the right is a taller buttress, narrowing as it rises. This is reached by a short scramble.
DESCENT - *There are bolts but no real lower-off on top of the main tower. The bolts can be used to abseil but scrambling down to the right is less likely to damage the rope!*

⑩ Anda que no Andas ná . 🔲 5
20m. Climb the front face of the buttress (all a bit rattly) then a short steepening and easier rock above. Pleasant.

⑪ Comecoco. .... 🔲 6a+
20m. The right-hand side of the buttress is steeper and passing the small roof is technical.
FA. Juan Carlos Garciá Gallego, Raúl Garcia 1982

⑫ Matogrosso. .... 🔲 5
20m. The chimney groove is approached from the right. Climb it past a loose flake and exit to the right.
FA. Antonio Bohórquez, Josè Seiguer 1974

⑬ Excalibur .... 🔲 6b
20m. The left-hand side of the narrow tower has a tough finale.
FA. Juan Carlos Garciá Gallego, Josè Antonio Navarro 1981

⑭ Follando y el sol pegando. 🔲 6a+
20m. The sustained centre of the face is very well bolted.
FA. Josè Matas 1985

Murcia · Alicante · Benidorm · Calpe · Xaló Valley · Gandia · Leyva · La Panocha · Orihuela

61

ORIHUELA

The full spread of cliffs in the valley at Callosa, from the triangular tower of El Polígono, to Cueva Ahumada.

To the north of the old town of Orihuela and its smaller satellite of Callosa de Segura is a series of rugged red hills that, despite initial appearances to the contrary, contain much good climbing. From the classic multi-pitch offerings on the Pared Negra and La Pancha, to the short steep sport routes near the Cueva Ahumada, there is much here to interest the passing climber. The area is close enough to the Alicante/Benidorm area to be a reasonable objective for a day's visit, and although the cliffs have been climbed on here by the locals for over 40 years, visitors have always been few and far between. The local guide (Senderismo y Escalada por la Vega Baja del Segura) covers many more climbs in this intriguing area, and if the rumours are to be believed, there are plenty of other developed areas than even it covers.

APPROACH
(area map page 42)

The cliffs are aligned to the north of the N340 and the CV900 which are easily reached from the A7 motorway. The Orihuela junction is just over 40km south of Alicante airport. Approaches for each cliff are covered in the relevant sections of the guide; check the maps on the appropriate pages. Approach walks vary between 5 and 20 minutes.

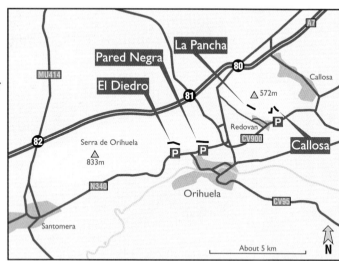

CONDITIONS

All the cliffs here get their fair share of sun and unlikely as it might seem the area around Orihuela is drier and hotter that the the country just a little further north! The crags listed here make ideal venues on clear winter days but can be a furnace at other times of the year - the cacti growing on many of the cliffs offer a good clue as to the general conditions here! The shorter routes at Callosa are very sheltered, and make a good bet on cool or windy days, whereas the longer offerings above Orihuela are exposed to the worst of the weather. All the cliffs take little seepage and dry rapidly after rain.

The pumpy single pitch route of *Ejercito Azul* (5+) on the lower walls of the Pared Negra above Orihuela - *page 66*. The main cliff has a series of fine multi-pitch outings at an amenable grade, and in as sunny-a-setting as you could wish for. The outward view is spectacular.

Murcia
Alicante
Benidorm
Calpe
Xaló Valley
Gandia
Leyva
La Panocha
Orihuela

El Diedro
El Momiot

A
Descent after abseil

To mid afternoon | 20 min | Multi-pitch | Windy

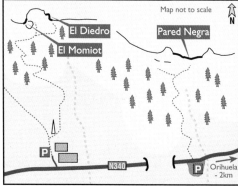

Map not to scale
N
El Diedro
El Momiot
Pared Negra

P
N340
Orihuela - 2km
P

① Momiot Ilevanti . . . 5 (HVS)

A worthwhile climb with some interesting positions. Fixed gear is adequate but rather spaced and a light rack is a good idea so the climb can be enjoyed to the full. From the col behind the tower scramble down and across ledges to the start.

1) 5, 40m. Climb grooves left of the arete until forced onto the edge. Pull over the small roof then traverse out right above the big one (exposed) and climb up to a stance with bolt belays.
2) 4, 14m. Step left and climb the short blocky arete to easy ground and a bolt belay under the final wall.
3) 5, 30m. Follow the flake crack to its end (no fixed gear) then move left to threads. Trend right across the face to a cave (threads) then step left and climb rugged cracks to the top.
DESCENT - Abseil from the final belay (30m) then follow the ledges out into the gully and scramble round to the start.
FA. M.Jaen, J.Ayats Artigas 1960s

EL MOMIOT and EL DIEDRO

A fine and complex face with massive areas of rock much of which appears to remain undeveloped.
APPROACH - Head south on the N340 past the Pared Negra and through a tunnel. A couple of hundred metres past here is a factory building on the right and immediately beyond this is a turn-off - park 50m up here on the left. Take the main track but fork right past a solitary pylon (not obvious) to reach the proper track which leads up the hill, trending slightly left, to eventually arrive by some old mine workings.
El Momiot cross rightwards under a steep tower and cut up the slope beyond then the round behind it to reach a col.
El Diedro cross the gully and scramble up the rib right then left to reach the bay below the routes.

The other routes described are based around the fine feature of El Diedro. The ledges below it are reached by a scramble right and then left up the easy-angled rib below the wall.

② El Diedro . . . . 5+

One of the classics of the area. Very popular with good climbing up a striking line and on solid rock.
1) 4, 30m. The left-hand line of bolts (red hangers) leads up short walls, cracks and grooves to a stance below a crack in the slabby right wall of the main groove.
2) 5+, 30m. Climb the sustained crack (crux) then move left to where easier rock leads up the continuation crack to a stance.
3) 4+, 14m. Trend left and climb the main groove to a stance just below the cliff top.
DESCENT - Abseil back down the line of the climb.
FA. J.Montesinos, M.Jaen 1963

CONDITIONS - The cliffs get plenty of sunshine and can be baking in the warmer months. At other times they are always worth considering unless there is a wind blowing.

3 Espero Manolo Jaen. . . 🔳🔳🔳🔳 **6a+**
A good climb although the crux is appreciably harder than the rest of the climb, especially so if the right-hand start is used.
1) 6a+, 38m. Start as for *El Diedro* but after 20m move right and climb a short hard wall (crux) to reach a good stance on the right. A start can be made up the sustained crack right of the main arete (red bolts) at **6b+**.
2) 5+, 38m. Climb up and right then follow the cracks left of the arete, tricky early on, then gradually easing with height until it is possible to escape left up grooves and ledges to reach the belay above *El Diedro*.
FA. P.Quiles, M.Pomares, A.Cayuelas 1970s

DESCENT - Abseil back down the line of *El Diedro*.

4 Maraton . . . . 🔳🔳🔳🔳 **5+ (E1)**
A fine climb up a continuous series of grooves to the right of the main arete. There is quite a bit of fixed gear but a rack (wires and Friends) will be needed by most.
1) 5, 34m. Climb the cracks and grooves steeply to a small stance on the break.
2) 5+, 42m. Step right and climb the impressive cracks (sustained) and the wall above to reach a good stance. Superb.
3) 4, 12m. Move left and climb a short groove to the top.
FA. F.Gommez, M.Angel Diaz 1984

Murcia
Alicante
Benidorm
Calpe
Xaló Valley
Gandia
Leyva
La Panocha
Orihuela

Lots of sun · 10 min

Main Face - 5 mins

PARED NEGRA
The Pared Negra is the impressive grey (!) wall rising above the road tunnel on the N340 just west of Orihuela.
APPROACH - There is extensive parking just east of the road and a good track runs up the edge of the stream bed before heading out right to the old workings at the base of the wall.
CONDITIONS - The cliffs get plenty of sunshine and can be baking in the warmer months. At other times the place is well-worth considering unless there is a wind blowing.
GEAR - Most of the routes described here are fully-bolted, however some climbers may wish to carry a small rack just in case they find the bolting a bit sparse.

⑤ Vía Nuria . . . . 6a+
A fine climb following the line of the abseil anchors. Many of the hangers were missing for a while but they are reported to have been replaced. Scramble up left to ledges under the face.
1) 5, 40m. Climb up the face, which gradually eases, to the lowest abseil bolts on a large ledge system.
2) 6a, 50m. Cross the ledges then continue up the steep face, passing one abseil point, to belay on a higher one.
3) 6a+, 30m. A fine sustained pitch to a tiny ledge and belay.
4) 5+, 30m. Finish directly up the face to the chains on the rim of the wall. Descent by abseil back down the line.

⑥ Espolón de la Pared Negra 5
A good climb, interesting and varied. Start at a scratched arrow up and right of the mine-workings.
1) 4+, 38m. Climb the slab and a short steep groove then continue up a series of short walls with the occasional awkward move before traversing left to a good stance.
2) 5, 38m. Head straight up the wall, tricky in places, to the groove that cuts past the left-hand end of the overhangs. Up this to a spacious stance.
3) 4, 22m. Trend left up the slabs more easily then climb up into the base of a groove and up this to a small stance.
4) 4+, 36m. Continue up the groove – odd and spaced fixed gear – then trend left and right up the wall to reach the big roof. Move left to a recess and climb the right wall of this to reach easy ground and a stance.
FA. J.Montesinos, Brugarolas, M.Jaén 1962

To the right is a low-relief tower, 50m high, standing at the base of the wall. There is a small collection of sport routes here, useful for a short day or getting a feel for bigger things!

⑦ Santa Faz . . . . 6b+
24m. The left-hand line is the hardest here.

⑧ Padre Bueno . . . . 6a+
24m. The right-hand line runs straight up the steep groove.

The steep groove and shrubby corner here is the original 1st pitch of Derecha del Espolón (5+) though nowadays it is usually avoided in favour of the easier groove on the opposite side.

⑨ Misa tridente 6a
30m. The first of the trio is hard if you follow the bolts.

⑩ Ejercito Azul . . . . 5+
30m. The central line gives good sustained climbing.
Photo page 63.

⑪ Padre Santo . . . . 5+
30m. The right-hand route is also very worthwhile.

ROUTES ON APPROACH
As the approach path nears the cliff, there is a buttress up and left rising above the trees. There are four sport routes here.

① El Negro . . . . 6b+
20m. The left-hand line up the broad rib and over a small roof (crux) leads to a good ledge with lower-off.

② Hoyo . . . . 6b+
20m. Powerful climbing up the tufa-groove leads to more open walls above and a shared lower-off.

③ Heaven and Hell 6a
20m. The face to the right of the depression gives a pleasant pitch; technical and fingery early on then easier, trending left.

④ Juan Iborra . . . . 5+
14m. A pleasant but short-lived face on the right.

According to the local guide there are another seven sport routes away to the left although exactly where is not clear. For the inquisitive these are, on the far left:
Sotero Guerro, 5+, 6a+, 55m - *up a wall to a stance then over a couple of overhangs.* **Rincon de Tomas, 5+, 24m** - *up a face.*
Unnamed, 5+, 30m - *up the face and through a cracked overhang. The next roues are further right and the first 3 share a lower-off:* **El Padre, 6a, 24m, El Hijo, 5+, 24m, El Espiritu Santo, 5+, 24m.** *To the right is* **Virgen Maria, 5+, 27m.**

Wire cable

DESCENT - To the south of the crest of the wall are twin abseil rings just below the ledge. Five abseils (20 – 30m with a choice of anchors on the lower section) lead down the face until an easy scramble regains the base of the wall.
Alternately head up and right (wire cable) to the top of the wall then descend the ridge (exposed) to its base. Two short abseils (20m and 30m) and some scrambling lead back to base.

⑫ Derecha del Espolón . . . . 🔲 5
A classic, the most popular climb on the cliff and with good reason. Start just right of the fall-line from the groove on the right-hand side of the pillar at a well-trodden area.
1) 4+, 60m. Wander up easy slabs to the 1st bolt then climb the groove via the odd tricky move past one stance to another on the tip of the tower - 10 bolts.
2) 5, 38m. Climb the face trending slightly leftwards until a short tricky wall (the crux - avoidable further left) leads to a groove. Up this to a good stance out on the left.
3) 4, 32m. Trend right up the wall by good sustained climbing then move up and left to a small exposed stance.
4) 4+, 28m. Up the face until a couple of tricky moves lead to easier ground. Up the gully to a stance. The abseil descent is 30m left, just beyond a bush.
FA. J.Fenor, A.Vera 1960s

⑬ Variante Pomares-Quiles . 🔲 6a+
A harder finish to the classic. Start from the stance above P2.
55m. Follow the left-hand line of red bolts up the rugged face to a niche below the top overhangs. Pull through these (aid sling in place) and finish up the short exposed wall. 22 clips.
FA. P.Quiles, M.Pomares 2003

⑭ Sombra Lunar . . . . 🔲 6a
A fine climb following a direct line up the face above the initial groove of *Derecha del Espolon*.
1) 4+, 55m. Up the groove to a stance at its top.
2) 6a, 40m. Climb up then right following the red bolts (sustained) until harder moves at 30m lead to a small stance.
3) 5, 30m. Continue in the same line to another small stance.
4) 5, 30m. Continue until the angle drops back. Escape up left.
FA. J.Vegara, P.Quiles, M.Pomares, A.Javaloyes 2001

The right-hand side of the wall has a host of routes that criss-cross the face; some are bolted and some are not - confusing!

⑮ Gallego-Carlos . . . . 🔲 5+
140m. A left-trending line with a sustained first pitch and a finish past the bush at the top left corner of the face. **5, 5+, 5, 4+**.
FA. M.Gallego, J.del Campo 1978

⑯ Somnis . . . . 🔲 6a+
150m. A direct line passing right of the olive tree. The final pitch is **7a** done free, otherwise it is AO. **4+, 6a, 6a+, 7a/AO**.
FA. J.Quesada, R.Pagán, M.Pomares 1988

The original route on this part of the wall was Directa, though it has been largly supercedded by more direct (!) lines.

⑰ Directisima . . . . 🔲 6a
140m. A fine climb, more direct than the *Directa*, on good rock. The hardest climb on the wall for years, but now a trade route. The pitches are **5, 5+, 6a, 4+, 5**
FA. M Gallego, C del Campo 1978

⑱ Teo . . . . 🔲 6a
140m. The right-hand line of bolts on the main section of the face gives a sustained climb. The pitches are **5+, 5+, 6a, 5, 6a**.
FA. C.Martínez, F.Nicolás, S.Guerrer, M.Marín

⑲ Efecto 2000 . . . . 🔲 5+
70m. A two pitch outing up the wall left of the desent abseil.

Murcia
Alicante
Benidorm
Calpe
Xalo Valley
Gandia
Leyva
La Pancha
Orihuela

LA PANCHA

"The Belly" is the best bit of rock in the area, for multi-pitch routes in the Orange/Red zone. All are fully equipped.
APPROACH - In the centre of Redovan turn onto the minor road that runs north east parallel with the hills, out towards the motorway. The cliff is visible on the right, take any of the parallel roads that run up towards it and park by gates on the right. Scramble up the side of the stream bed to the foot of the wall.
CONDITIONS - The cliff faces south east, gets plenty of sun and is rapid drying. It can be hot here even in winter.
DESCENT - Abseil back down the routes or scramble (with care) across the top to the belays above *Todos Los Santos* and abseil down this.

❶ Silvia . . . . 🔲🔲🔲 **6c**
180m. The left-hand line on the face starts with a traverse out right to gain the base of the long crack-line splitting the left-hand side of the face. It follows this and the groove above before heading left up the head-wall.
The pitches are **4, 6c, 6b, 5+, 5+.**
FA. T.Pastor, P.Hernández 1986

❷ X Capitulos . . . . 🔲 **6b**
160m. The original sport route on the face starts at the base of the crack that *Silvia* uses for its second pitch. Climb to the left of the rugged hollows in the left-hand side of the front of the buttress then continue direct. The pitches are **5+, 6a+, 6b, 5+.**
FA. T.Pastor, P.Hernández 1986

❸ Tribo . . . . 🔲🔲 **6a+**
160m. The central line on the face starts at its lowest point and is perhaps the best here. The pitches are **5, 6a+, 6a, 5, 6a**. A gradually steepening wall leads to a belay next to a big chimney alcove. The steep wall on the left leads past the crux then moves right into the dusty groove. Next is a fine airy rising traverse into the centre of the wall (good photos looking back down). An easier pitch around the big block leads to a ledge below the final pitch, which is a superb jug-infested headwall.
FA. P.Hernández, T.Pastor 1998

❹ Todos los Santos . . . . 🔲🔲 **6a+**
160m. A climb up the grey buttress that forms the right-hand side of the face. It is (marginally) the easiest way up the wall and is also the most popular descent route. The pitches are **5, 6a+, 6a, 5+.** Start with an easier pitch up to the base of a big tapering chimney. Steep cracks lead up rightwards onto the arete; up this to a belay above a steep bulge. A steep rising traverse leads left then head straight up the wall to easier ground. A final pitch is an easier version of *Tribo* top pitch.
FA. P.Hernández, T.Pastor 1998

❺ José Hernández . . . . . . 🔲🔲 **6b**
160m. The right-hand line on the face takes the clean rock up the right edge of the wall. Good climbing with long pitches and a technical crux. The pitches are **6a+, 6b, 5+.**
FA. T.Pastor, Pepe, César, Alberto 2000

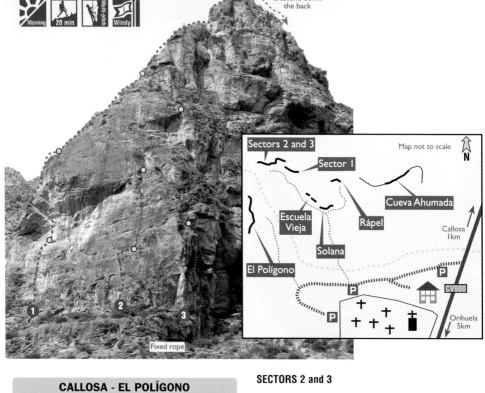

Descend down the back

Sectors 2 and 3

Sector I

Cueva Ahumada

Map not to scale

N

Escuela Vieja

Rápel

Callosa 1km

Solana

El Polígono

CV900

Orihuela 5km

Fixed rope

1 2 3

CALLOSA - EL POLÍGONO

The imposing red pyramid the blocks the upper and of the valley is home to a trio of longer outings.
APPROACH -Take the rough track that runs up the left-hand side of the stream bed (looking uphill) until it is possible to scramble up and left to a fixed rope which leads to ledges at the base of the wall.
CONDITIONS - It faces east and gets the morning sun.
DESCENT - Follow the ridge then head left, possibly following cairns, down and left past a step.

❶ Directa **7a**
140m. A line up the left side of the face and easy arete above. Pitches are **6b**, **7a**, **5**, **4**, and the route is bolted. The 1st two pitches make a good objective for the suitably competent.
FA. J.Vegara, Sergio, D.Poveda, M.Martinez, A.Monera, Alvero 1970s

❷ José Gracia . . . . **6a (E1)**
140m. The central line on the face. A fine direct climb which needs a bit of aid on the crack at the start of the last pitch. Take a rack. The pitches are **6a, 5, 6a, 6a/A1**.
FA. J.Gracia, R.Coves, M.Pomares 1975

❸ Montesinos . . . . **6a (E1)**
140m. The 1st route put up on the face follows the obvious line of weakness. It is equipped with pegs and bolts. Take a rack. The pitches are **5, 5, 6a, 4, 4**.
FA. J.Montesinos, J.Morell, M.Jaen 1967

SECTORS 2 and 3

The bulging wall on the right is home to a set of sport routes.

❹ Andrajosa **6c**
18m. Climb up the rugged grey slab above the central yellow patch (a short 4 to twin bolts) to ledges, then climb the steep rib left and then back right. Sharp and unbalanced.

❺ Jarra pellejos . . . . **6a+**
18m. Up the sharp grey rock (a short 4 to twin bolts in the break) then the steep wall above. Another unbalanced one.

❻ Zape, Zape, Zape **6a**
18m. Climb past the right-hand yellow patch then up a strenuous series of cracks. The easiest here, but not that easy!

❼ En la barra, los falsos . **6b**
14m. From the 1st painted square, climb a vague orange streak.

❽ Tomellosa **6c**
14m. Left of a black streak. Only rest in a big hole if pumped!

❾ Eugenio venta pa España . . . . **?**
14m. Start at the pile of blocks and climb through the diagonal overlap. Of unknown grade although it looks pretty hard.

❿ No metas la polla **6c**
14m. Steep climbing to enter the shallow left-facing groove (tricky 3rd clip) at which point, things ease.

Murcia | Alicante | Benidorm | Calpe | Xaló Valley | Gandia | Leyva | La Panocha | Orihuela

Murcia
Alicante
Benidorm
Calpe
Xaló Valley
Gandía
Leyva
La Panocha
Orihuela

CALLOSA - SECTORS 2 and 3

Steep sustained pitches are the order of the day here, the best destination in the area for those who like that kind of thing
APPROACH - Walk up under Sector Solana then bear left round the ridge and continue to the steep face on the far left.
CONDITIONS - South-facing getting lots of sun.

11 La pancha de blas . 8a
16m. The fiercely-steep crack was once a good peg route!

12 Al que eyacula dios 7c
16m. Climb very steeply on pockets, through the bulges, and up the pale streak, passing a shallow flared groove.

13 Ni me mires 7a
16m. Pull over the left edge of the overhang and up the good pockets that pepper the wall above.

14 Menos curas más posturas 6c
16m. A fine climb through the centre of the roof and up the white wall to a huge pocket. Take the upper roof rightwards.

15 La de Miguel Perez . . . . . 7a+
16m. A roof to start and another to finish with.

16 Con tu novia me hinchaba. 6b+
16m. The left-slanting groove is tricky to the overhang, then climb the easier rib on the right. A good long pitch.

17 Araña . . . . 6b+
18m. Start as for the previous route but fork right and climb the fine and easing rib on excellent rock.

18 Gusano. . . . . 6a+
18m. The pale wall leads past a triangular overhang, then up the fine sustained face above. *Photo page 75.*

19 Lirón Arboreo 6c
20m. Start up a grey rib and head straight up the orange face.

20 La Cueva . . . . 6b+
18m. 40m to the right, scramble up into the right-hand cave and follow the 'glue-in' staples up the left-hand wall of the big cave. A steep pitch - polished and pumpy.

Murcia
Alicante
Benidorm
Calpe
Xaló Valley
Gandia
Leyva
La Panocha
Orihuela

CALLOSA - SECTOR 1

The 1st of the newer sport venues to be developed - hence the name, with a set of short, sharp pitches

APPROACH - Walk up under Sector Solana, then bear left round the ridge, and continue to the diagonal face on the right towards the top of the slope.

CONDITIONS - South-facing and sunny.

1 La Larga................ ☐ **4+**
10m. The grey slab with tricky moves at 3m, then trend right.

2 Días de Lluvia............ ☐ **5**
12m. Start up a short wide crack then take the grey slab.

3 La libélula.........🔃📖 ☐ **5+**
12m. The steep wall has a couple of fingery moves early on and then trends right and gradually eases.

4 Ahora y en la hora....🔃📖 ☐ **6a**
14m. Fingery climbing up thin parallel cracks which get easier as you get higher.

5 Maldita sea...........📖 ☐ **6a+**
14m. The tilted grey wall is climb rightwards. Sharp!

6 Esto no es pan comido......☐ **6a**
14m. Start just left of a big bush on the ground. Climb straight up the wall passing to the left of a small bush on the rim.

7 Come bizcocho...........☐ **5+**
14m. Behind the bush, head straight up the wall.

8 Cachupín suda fuerte.......☐ **6a**
14m. Right of the bush, climb a rounded groove then pull through the bulges.

9 Nuria no Llores......🔃📖 ☐ **5+**
14m. A flow-stoned groove leads to the bulges. Power through these on (mostly) good holds.

10 Honda 1000.............☐ **6a**
14m. From a block climb the lower wall, which is tricky, and then the juggy bulges above.

11 Cojo remojo.............☐ **5+**
14m. Take the pale streak up the rib, trending slightly right.

12 Corren los cheflines........☐ **6a**
14m. Start at a white square with '5+' in it, and climb past a big hole at 4m.

13 Se aleja la almeja....🔃📖 ☐ **6a**
14m. The buttress just right of a left-slanting groove.

14 Me traicionó la piedra...📖 ☐ **5**
14m. Climb the groove on the far right then step left and head up the slab to a final fingery pull.

Sector Escuela Vieja

1 2 3

From Sector Solana

Lots of sun | 8 min | To Sectors 1, 2 and 3 | 4 5

CALLOSA - ESCUELAS

A trio of small buttresses with a pleasant selection of clip-ups which are generally in the lower-grades. Climbs on all three buttresses can easily be done in a day.

APPROACH - From the parking, the Sector Solana is obvious on the other side of the stream. Sector Escuela vieja is hidden just round the ridge to the left whilst the Sector Rappel is reached by a rather arduous scramble up and right.

CONDITIONS - South-facing and sunny and also a bit more sheltered than the buttresses up above.

SECTOR ESCUELA VIEJA

1 Vía vieja 5 . . . . [ ] **4**
14m. The left-hand slab route starting by a groove.

2 Vía vieja 4 . . . . [icon] [ ] **4**
14m. The central line is probably the best here.

3 Vía vieja 3 . . . . [ ] **4**
14m. Step out right and climb the right-hand one.

4 Vía nueva . . . . [icon] [ ] **5**
16m. The technical open groove to the juggy roof and easy ground above. Very well bolted!

5 Vía vieja 2 . . . . [icon] [ ] **5**
12m. The rickety overhang and technical slab leads to the easy groove above.

Sector Solana

Escuela Vieja

Sector Rápel

Lots of sun | 6 min

6
7
8 9
10
11

SECTOR SOLANA

6 Albertos 1 . . . . [icon] [ ] **5**
12m. The rib on sharp pockets soon eases - poor!

7 Albertos 2 . . . . [icon] [ ] **4**
12m. The open groove to a steep leftward exit is better.

8 Carmen . . . . [icon][icon] [ ] **5**
16m. The lower wall leads to a couple of tricky moves then trend right to the lower-off. Excellent. *Photo page 69.*

9 Pesahombre . . . . [icon][icon] [ ] **4+**
16m. Climb straight up the well pocketed wall to a bulge that requires a quick pull. The best here.

10 Tres Chapas Izquierda . [icon][icon] [ ] **6b**
10m. Rightwards is a cave with two short, steep offerings.

11 Tres Chapas Derecha . . [icon][icon] [ ] **6b+**
10m. The right-hand line is much the same!

Lots of sun | 8 min

Sector Rápel

12
13
14
15   16 17

Cueva Ahumada

SECTOR RÁPEL

12 Provata . . . . [ ] **4**
10m. The tiny left-hand offering - 2 bolt runners.

13 Cursillo . . . . [ ] **4**
10m. The next line is a touch longer though has no more bolts!

14 Ingenieros . . . . [ ] **4**
12m. They are getting better. Start from a hole and go direct.

15 Doctor Flemig . . . . [icon] [ ] **5**
12m. ......and better. Follow the line of half-a-dozen glue-ins.

16 La baldomera del quinto . . [icon] [ ] **4+**
24m. Now you are talking! Long pleasant and quite tricky.

17 Pedro el molisero . . . . . . [icon] [ ] **5+**
24m. Always save the best until last! A good long pitch with a tricky laybacking finale.

Cueva Ahumada

Sector Rápel

CALLOSA - CUEVA AHUMADA

In the right-hand corner of the valley is the tall entrance of the eponymous cave with a fine rounded rib to its right and long wall running away to the left with several worthwhile climbs, at least a couple of which are fully-bolted.

APPROACH - From either parking area, a series of rough tracks lead to the base of the wall. The starts of the climbs can be recognised as they are well trampled.

DESCENT - Walk left up the ridge the scramble down the steep gully the bound the face on the left. A 40m abseil leads to the base of the Sector Rápel and an easy descent. Alternately, abseil back down the route.

CONDITIONS - South-facing getting lots of sun.

❶ La Cantera **5**

110m. A fine and sustained climb up the left-hand side of the face. It is supposed to be the best of this particular selection. The pitches are **5, 5, 5+, 4+.**

FA. Germán, Olivier, Ricardo 1970s

To the right up the steepest part of the wall is the fully bolted line of La Navaja. The crux third pitch it 6a+/A0 though no other details are known other than 15 quick-draws are recommended.

❷ Sali . . . . **6a (E1)**

160m. Climb the face for one pitch then trend left to climb the face direct. The individual pitch grades are **5, 4, 4+, 4, 6a, 4.**

FA. S.Jiménez, M.Pomares 1972

❸ IX Capítulos . . . . **6a+**

140m. Start as for *Sali* but continue in a direct line. The other 'best of' climb on this wall. The individual pitch grades are **5, 5+, 6a+, 5+.**

FA. P.Hernádez, J.Vegara 1970s

❹ Trompases . . . . **5+ (E1)**

150m. The imposing rounded rib to the right of the huge cave entrance. According to the local guide (2003) this one was next in line for rebolting, so it may have been done by now. The individual pitch grades are **5+, 5+, 5+, 4+.**

FA. Germán, A. Monera i970s

The classic route of *Gusano* (6a+) on Sector 3 at Callosa - *page 71*.
The walls here have over 50 well-equipped single-pitch sport routes, and in
the background lurks El Poligon for those who fancy a little more adventure.

Alicante

Fine positions on the first pitch of *Jhonny* (3+,4) on the Main Cliff at Marin, one of the better lower-grade climbs in the book - *page 82*. Behind is the view out over Elda towards the Serra del Cid (1152m).

N

10km

Magdelena - p100

Caudete

Alcoi - p142

Agujas Rojas - p136

Reconco - p132

Ibi - p128

Yecla

Villena

Biar

Onil

Peña Rubia - p110

Castalla

Sax - p92

Cabezón de Oro - p146

Salinas

Peña del Corb - p106

Salinas - p84

Elda

Petrer

Busot

Marin - p78

Foradà - p116

Monovar

Agost

Sant Vicent

Pinoso

Novelda

Aspe

Alicante

Cocentaina

Alcoi

CV70

N344

A31

CV81

CV799

CV80

A36

N340

A36

A31

A7

CV84

MARIN

To the north west of the twin-town of Elda/Petrer is a prominent cream-coloured dome of rock where a slabby crag sits high on the crest of the hill. Developed in the 1960's then rebolted in 1992 this is not a cliff for the hard-core, on the other hand climbers who operate at HVS and below and who feel they have been hard done by when it comes to sport climbing should find a visit here very rewarding.

This Main Face of the cliff is home to 20 pleasant low-grade climbs, of a respectable length and which face south. The routes are up to 60 metres high, are very well bolted and generally are less than vertical. Many of the climbs have their names and approximate grades painted at their foot in large ugly writing. Five minutes walk further west is a newly developed crag which has a few harder offerings. Marin was originally used as a 'trad' venue and the routes were re-equipped by "Yeti" and Juan A Serrano 1992.

APPROACH
(area map page 77)

Take the A31 Madrid road north west from Alicante for 32km to Elda/Petrer, pass the castle and then continue PAST the right turn at the sign 'Centro Commercial' used on the approach to Penyal del Corb and Foradà. After a Cepsa petrol station take the slip-road off to the right signed 'Elda' and 'Hospital' then loop back over the motorway and head back towards Elda.

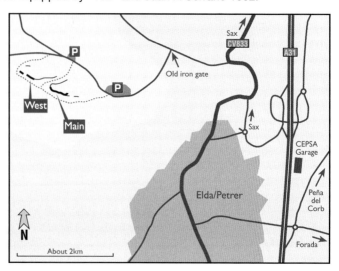

Go around a long right-hand bend (signed to Sax) and after 1km turn right at T junction (signed Sax) and drive over a col. The road descends under power-lines, on a long right-hand bend. Turn left immediately before gates set under an orange tiled roof (La Curva) and follow the track for 1.3km. Turn left through some grey concrete gate posts with old rusty iron gates and park 0.4km further on, at a bend on a broad col (1.7km from the road). A track starts on the col and ascends gradually up the slope overlooking Elda, the rocks are reached in less then ten minutes. To get to the Western Buttress continue up the road to parking on the right and follow the track up the hill, and over a col to the cliff. It is also possible to walk down the road on the left and take a track on the left that leads round the end of the cliff.

CONDITIONS
South-facing and rapid-drying though high enough to be exposed to the wind.

OTHER BUTTRESSES
To the east of the main face at Marin is a series of slabs and walls that have been developed with some short routes. No precise details are known but the routes look to be in the lower grades and worth exploring but not of the same quality as the routes on the buttresses described here.

The well-positioned left arete of the Main Cliff at Marin is tackled by *Espolon* (5+) - *page 82*. The shot illustrates the high quality (and sharpness) of some of the rock on the cliff as well as its fine setting. Inset: *Derecha de Espolón* (6a+) on Marin Western Buttress - *page 81*.

Adjoining

Main section 150m

WESTERN BUTTRESS

This fine area, to the west of the main cliff, gives a reason for climbers in the 6s and 7s to visit Marin. There are thirty or so climbs here with some steep pumpy rock and some interesting tufa features.

APPROACH - From the main cliff follow the horizontal path (yellow and white flashes) left. The crag can also be reached from the higher parking place by following a vague path over the col and down to the crag.

1 Érase una vez . . . . **5+**
12m. The short sharp rib on the left.

2 5 minutos . . . . **5+**
12m. Tackling the crack and groove is easier.

3 Tormento vertical . . . . . **6b+**
12m. The blankest part of the face has this fierce number.

4 Por aquí menos **5**
10m. The left-hand line on the right side of the buttress.

5 Por aquí cualquiera **4**
10m. .. and the right-hand line one.

6 Via Venneto **5**
16m. A steep start on good holds.

7 Hurly Burly **5**
16m. The next line has a couple of tricky moves at mid-height.

8 El sexo sentido . . . . **5+**
20m. An awkward start leads to easier ground above.

9 Out of control **4**
20m. The easiest climb here on a generous set of holds.

The best climbing on the Western Buttress is on the steep orange face 150m right of the previous routes.

10 Sobras . . . . **3+**
20m. The easy rib and mildly steeper rock above is very amenably bolted and gives an easy introduction to sport climbing.

11 Derecha corazón . . . . **5+**
20m. Take the slab then steeper rock to a pull left into the base of the 'heart'. The groove on the right is tricky to enter (try laybacking) but soon eases.

Murcia
Alicante
Benidorm
Calpe
Xaló Valley
Gandía
Marin
Salinas
Sax
Magdalena
Peña del Corb
Peña Rubia
Forada
Ibi
Reconeo
Agujas Rojas
Alcoi
Cabezon

⑫ Espolón gris . . . . . 🔲🔲🔲 **6a+**
20m. The grey rib on the left-hand side of the biggest cave leads, to a steeper final section on chipped holds. A hard crux!

⑬ Derecha de espolón 🔲🔲🔲 **6a+**
20m. Climb the right-hand side of the rib throughout. Again the crux is the chipped upper section leading to a short final slab.
Photo page 79.

⑭ Descoco Tensión . . . . . 🔲🔲 **6b**
20m. The left-hand wall of the cave leads right then steeply back left to reach the capping roofs. Finish powerfully through these. Excellent - all the right holds just where you need them!
Photo page 1.

⑮ El Mono mecánica . . . . 🔲🔲 **6c**
18m. The orange wall on the right side of the large recess and the rib above leads to easy ground. Trend left more steeply to the final overhang which is crossed on the left by a brief grovel.

⑯ El Vuelo del Murciélago . . 🔲🔲 **6c+**
18m. The crack in the right-hand rib of the cave. Lowering off above the first roof gives a pleasant **6a**.

⑰ Techitos Frie . . . . 🔲🔲 **6b+**
18m. The orange rib is hard if done direct, then easier ground leads to the capping overhang which is soon over.

⑱ Un lugar liberado . . 🔲🔲🔲 **7b+**
20m. The big tufa-encrusted roof is the toughest here. The lower wall is easy enough but the roof isn't.

⑲ Alegrar final . . . . 🔲🔲🔲 **7b+**
18m. The right-hand side of the big roof is approached up the lower-wall via bolt line that splits at 8m.

⑳ El vuela del bellaco . . . 🔲🔲 **6b**
18m. At the junction take the right-hand line then haul through the juggy roof by powerful moves.

Next is a 15m gap that is undeveloped - at the moment!

㉑ El machazo . . . . 🔲🔲 **6b**
16m. The wall just to the left of the left-hand grey streak.

㉒ Mi ultima palabra . . . . 🔲🔲 **6b+**
16m. ... and directly up the right-hand one.

㉓ Pillete que . . . . 🔲🔲 **6a+**
14m. The steep wall is climbed slightly rightwards passing a useful tree in a hole - just grab it.

㉔ Paranoia . . . . 🔲🔲 **6a**
14m. Start by a spiky bush in a hole and climb the rib trending rightwards to a pumpy final section up the leaning tufa wall.

To the right are three shorter routes starting from a dusty hollow reached by a short scramble.

㉕ Desportillada . . . . . . 🔲🔲 **6b**
14m. The steep wall from the left-hand side of the bay has a hard start on drilled holds. The upper section is better.

㉖ Hueco Roja . . . . 🔲🔲 **6b**
14m. The central line from the bay is precarious then strenuous to enter and leave the red niche.

㉗ Un diá balan . . . . 🔲🔲 **6a+**
14m. The right-hand line out of the bay is pleasant enough with sustained climbing on sharp rock.

㉘ D.2 Mágicos . . . . 🔲🔲 **6b**
14m. The brown crack is harder and steeper than it looks. The crux is where the crack ends!

㉙ Miedo me Da . . . . 🔲🔲🔲 **6b**
14m. The short wall on the right of the brown crack.

Lots of sun | 10 min | Multi-pitch

Descent - scramble down the gully behind

MAIN FACE

The Main Face at Marin consists of a fine 50m high slabby face with the best selection of lower grade climbs anywhere on the Costa Blanca. Add in the short approach, the superb outward views and the sunny aspect and it is obvious why the place is so popular.
APPROACH - The Main Face is best approached from the lower parking spot direct by a well-marked path.

❶ Aniversario . . . . . . 　　　　 **5+**
20m. Climb the groove in steep rock on the far left. An awkward start and blocky middle lead to fine finale on rugged rock.
FA. F.Rico, V.Freire 1979

❷ Jhonny . . . . 　　 **4**
1) 3+, 28m. A low grade classic. From the green writing, move right and climb the lower rib past a tree to a stance in a niche.
2) 4, 16m. Step left and continue up the steeper upper arete to finish. Scramble across the hillside and descend the gully.
Photo page 76.
FA. Pepe Navarro 1962

❸ Espolon . . . . 　　　 **5+**
18m. The rounded arete has a brutal start then eases.
Photo page 79.

❹ Anibal . . . . 　　 **6a**
1) 18m, 6a. Climb the bulge on good holds to a cave belay.
2) 30m, 4+. Climb the right rib then step back left into the groove above the cave, climb this to the final rib of *Jhonny*.
FA. Rovira, Maestre 1971

❺ Fuerza bruta . . . . 　 **6c**
1) 6c, 10m. A short hard pitch leads to a stance in the groove.
2) 4+, 40m. Continue more easily (spaced gear) up the groove.
FA. Cosme 1990s

❻ El Nombre de satan . . . . . 　 **6b+**
12m. The bulges give a short struggle. 3 bolts only.
FA. Cosme, Luis 1993

❼ Petreles . . . . 　 **5**
The deep, twisting chimney is worthwhile and interesting.
1) 5, 32m. Enter the fissure steeply then continue up the groove and narrowing slab above to a choice of stances.
2) 4+, 14m. From the upper belay traverse out left onto the rib - exciting; or continue up the slab above - more logical.
FA. Avelino, Pallisa 1970s

❽ Mermelada del futuro . . . . 　 **6a**
10m. The steep wall gives a short steep struggle.
FA. Cosme 1990s

❾ Placa gris . . . . 　　　　 **5+**
1) 5, 28m. An excellent route. Start at a triangular hole and climb up steeply then follow the slab, keeping left of the brown streak, to a stance in the left-hand edge of the cave.
2) 5+, 20m. Climb the steep rib then step right and traverse into the slanting groove above the cave. Exposed.
FA. Manolo Amat, Biberon 1979

❿ Prats . . . . 　　 **4+**
1) 4+, 28m. Devious but excellent. Start by the old green name and trend left above the overhangs to the second bolt-line. Climb the face, steep and tricky to start, then step right to a belay on the edge of the cave. Twin bolts hidden in the shadows.
2) 3+, 24m. Climb the red groove then step out left - exposed - and finish up the upper slab of the chimney of *Petreles*.
FA. Pepe Navarro 1963

Decent over the back and down the gully

DESCENT - It is possible to scramble down the gully behind, heading leftwards. It is also possible to make 2 abseils down *Agust*. Check no-one is climbing up first.

Right side tabs: Murcia · Alicante · Benidorm · Calpe · Xaló Valley · Gandía · Marin · Salinas · Sax · Magdelena · Peña del Corb · Peña Rubia · Forada · Ibi · Reconco · Aguas Rojas · Alcoi · Cabezon

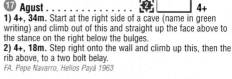

---

⑪ Susetec a la cuchara . . 🔒🗝 [ ] **6b**
1) 4+, 28m. From the name, trend left past a bush then climb the right side of the brown streak to the large cave. Pleasant.
2) 6b, 18m. Climb the back wall of the cave by powerful moves.
FA. Cosme 1992

⑫ Kiki . . . . 🗝 [ ] **5+**
1) 4+, 34m. Start between bushes and climb a brown scoop, then bear right up the edge of the cave to a stance in a hollow.
2) 5+, 12m. Climb steeply rightwards then finish more easily. There is also a left-hand finish which is much easier, **3+**.
FA. Antonio Drogero 1963

⑬ Carmela . . . . 🛠 [ ] **4**
34m. A varition start to *Kiki* without the luxury of fixed gear.

⑭ Maika . . . . 🗝 [ ] **4+**
1) 4+, 34m. Start just left of the cave and head straight up the slab - slippery - then trend right to a bulge. Over this to a belay.
2) 4, 12m. Finish up the straightforward slab above.
FA. Pepe Navarro, Maestre 1967

⑮ Paquita trueno . . . . 🔒🗝 [ ] **5+**
1) 5+, 32m. Climb out of the left side of the cave by one tough move, then continue up the slab to a good stance.
2) 4+, 18m. Finish more easily in the same line.
FA. Manolo Amat 1981

⑯ Dalia . . . . 🗝 [ ] **5**
1) 5, 30m. Climb out of the cave steeply (**5+** if you don't sneak right) then take the left-hand bolt line to a superb stance in a large solution hollow with a choice of belays
2) 4+, 18m. Pull left onto the wall and finish direct.
FA. Manolo Amat 1981

⑰ Agust . . . . 🗝 [ ] **4+**
1) 4+, 34m. Start at the right side of a cave (name in green writing) and climb out of this and straight up the face above to the stance on the right below the bulges.
2) 4+, 18m. Step right onto the wall and climb up this, then the rib above, to a two bolt belay.
FA. Pepe Navarro, Helios Payá 1963

⑱ Jake mate . . . . 🗝 [ ] **5+**
1) 5+, 30m. Start at the name and climb the smart, sustained rib to a choice of a stances on the routes to either side.
2) 4+, 18m. Choose a finish or abseil off.
FA. Jesus Ruiz 1979

⑲ Puente aereo . . . . 🗝 [ ] **5**
1) 5, 34m. Climb into a hollow and then follow good holds to a stance and belay below the right side of the roof.
2) 4+, 20m. Pull left on to the steep wall then finish up the rib.
FA. Manolo Amat 1979

⑳ Manolito . . . . 🔒 [ ] **5**
48m. From the high 1st bolt climb the face in one huge pitch or if required take belay in a niche below the final overhang.

㉑ Capicua . . . . 🗝 [ ] **4+**
Start on the far right side of the main face at a scratched cross.
1) 4+, 30m. Climb easy white slabs, then an imposing brown streak, up the right side of the open bay to a stance on the ridge.
2) 4, 30m. Trend leftwards back up the left side of the rib to eventually join the ramp that runs across the upper part of the main face.

SALINAS

Salinas is a pleasant crag in a peaceful situation, well-geared and has a good grade spread of high quality routes. You couldn't ask for much more perhaps though almost inevitably there are couple of minor problems; firstly, many of the harder routes are a bit hacked about and secondly there is the seasonal bird-ban which can interfere with your plans if you are here in the spring, especially annoying if you have made the long haul from the coast! Despite this the routes are mostly superb and sustained, following steep pockets and thin vertical walls. It shouldn't just be considered a crag for the hard-core as there is a decent selection of fine easier climbs on Sector Picara Viborita and on the edges of the higher sectors. The locals know the cliff as Alto Don Pedro after the hill behind it.

ACCESS

There have been restrictions in the past with no climbing from 1 March to 1 July because of nesting birds. Check for signs on the approach to the cliff which are only posted if the birds are nesting. This restriction has been known to vary from year to year sometimes starting in February.

CONDITIONS

The crag is basically a ridge with faces on both sides. The upper section faces east and the lower section faces west. With most of the best routes being on the upper section the crag is really a morning venue in the winter and a useful shady afternoon retreat in the summer. It is not too exposed and can be considered an all year round crag except perhaps on the coldest of days, or when it is windy. Most of the upper sectors are over-hanging and may give some dry climbing in light rain, although only in the upper grades.

APPROACH (area map page 77)

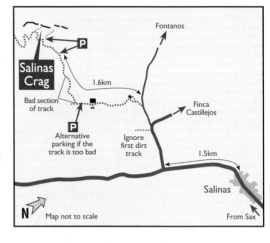

The crag is situated near the town of the same name which is 8km west of Sax and is best approached from there. Drive from Alicante towards Madrid on the A31 (a free dual carriageway). Turn off at Sax and drive into the town. At the first roundabout turn left, signed 'Salinas'. Follow this for about 8km to the small village of Salinas and drive straight past it. (Note: water is available in the centre of the village). After you leave the town, continue for 1.5km and turn right (signed 'Finca Castillejos'). At this point the ridge of the crag can be seen ahead on the left. Ignore the first dirt track on the left and on the next right-hand bend continue straight onto a wide dirt track (signed 'Fontanos'). Turn left off this onto another dirt track and follow it towards the crag past two sets of buildings. Keep left at the first branch and right at the second. The road after the second bend is particularly bad, care is needed! Park at a clearing on the right or press on to a higher parking area - steep! Continue walking up the track to find a path on a bend. This leads straight to Sector Picara Viborita. It is also possible to park just past the second building and be faced with a slightly longer walk.

Chris Craggs climbing *Cefalinpadus* (6b), one of the better lower grade routes on Sector Picara Viborita at Salinas - *page 90*. In the distance is the town of Salinas and the salt pan that gave the place its name; a sign of how hot the summers are here. Photo: Sherri Davy Inset: Olive groves below Salinas. Photo: Alan James

Sector La Higuera

SECTOR FINAL

The highest sector up the ridge is also one of the best here. The routes are on superb rock, up some dramatic orange streaks, and are especially suited for those who like blank 7c's, with no holds! However there is also something for people who like swinging between juggy pockets at a slightly more amenable grade.

APPROACH - Walk left, under the main face, from where the approach path arrives at the crag. You will immediately pass over a lower wall of broken rock. A little further up the hill is a gap in the ridge, keep left here and continue uphill past Sector Ratoli and La Higuera.

⊖ **ACCESS** - NO CLIMBING FROM 1 MARCH TO 1 JUNE BECAUSE OF NESTING BIRDS.

The first route is on the left-hand side, almost starting from a bush, and below a grey rib.

❶ Manzanita verde . . . . . 🔲🔲 ⎯⎯ 6b+
14m. The nice-looking rib is a bit precarious and the finish has a hard move. Avoid the bush at the start.
FA. Jose Hernandez, L.Justamante 1994

❷ Terranova . . . . 🔲🔲 ⎯⎯ 6c
16m. The second line leads to a bulging finish.
FA. Jose Hernandez, J.Vicente 1993

❸ Serrano - Magui I . . . . . . 🔲 ⎯⎯ 6b+
18m. The bolts go over a steep bulge but you are forced rightwards onto a flake.
FA. Juan Serrano, Magui 1993

The next two routes are up an extremely blank wall.

❹ Crucifixión . . . 🔲🔲🔲🔲 ⎯⎯ 7c
20m. The left-hand side of the grey wall. You'll just have to use your imagination and a little levitation since there aren't any actual holds.
FA. Jose Hernandez, L.Justamante 1993

❺ Ahí va la liebre . . . 🔲🔲🔲 ⎯⎯ 7c
20m. The right-hand side of the grey wall is about as blank as its near neighbours.
FA. Chiri Ros, Isabel Pagan 1992

❻ Danza interrumpida 🔲🔲🔲 ⎯⎯ 7c
20m. The grey rock between the two orange streaks. It is chipped but still sharp, and manages to be brilliant.
FA. Juan Serrano 1992

❼ Mata-Hari . . . . 🔲🔲 ⎯⎯ 7a+
20m. A stunning route up the pockets in the large orange streak. Finish left or right over the top roof via chipped pockets.
FA. Chiri Ros, Yeti 1992

❽ Metamorfosis . 🔲🔲🔲🔲 ⎯⎯ 7c
22m. Yet another hold-less horror!
FA. Jose Hernandez, J.Vicente 1993

❾ Línea maestra . . . . 🔲🔲🔲 ⎯⎯ 7b+
22m. The line of resin bolts has an outrageously hard start past the big (useless) holes. Above that it gives a superb 7a+.
FA. Chiri Ros, Isabel Pagan 1993

To the right is an obvious gap based around the orange streak, and beyond this is an attractive curving arete.

❿ Donde dices que vas . . 🔲🔲 ⎯⎯ 6a+
22m. The curving rib has good moves on good rock. The route is a lot less 'fingery' than those to the left!
FA. Juan Serrano 1992

⓫ La silla de la Reina . . . 🔲🔲 ⎯⎯ 6b
14m. Climb to a deep pockets then use rounded holds on the crux bulge. It is easier above.
FA. Juan Serrano 1992

Murcia | Alicante | Benidorm | Calpe | Xaló Valley | Gandia | Marin | Salinas | Sax | Magdalena | Peña del Corb | Peña Rubia | Forada | Ibi | Reconco | Agujas Rojas | Alcoi | Cabezon

SECTOR LA HIGUERA

The sectors at this end of the crag are all very similar; superb routes on orange streaks and interesting pockets. Mainly harder grades, easy routes at the edges, and all better than most of the bolted routes in Britain.

APPROACH - Walk left, up under the main face, from where the approach path arrives at the crag. You will immediately pass over a lower wall of broken rock. A little further up is a gap in the ridge, keep left here. Continue uphill past Espolón Mágico to the buttress on the left.

⊖ ACCESS - NO CLIMBING FROM 1 MARCH TO 1 JUNE BECAUSE OF NESTING BIRDS.

The first route is left of the steep middle section, just right of a curving groove.

① Serrano - Magui II . . . . ☐ **6a**
22m. The steep wall and bulge leads to easier rock above.
FA. Juan Serrano, Magui 1993

② Lloviendo sale corriendo . 🖼☐ **6a**
18m. Climb the ramp and pull through the roof of the cave (or skirt round it) and finish direct.
FA. Martinez, Serrano 1993

③ Pequeña y juguetona . . 🖼🖼☐ **6c+**
14m. A short route with a delicate traverse and a drilled mono on the crux.
FA. Yeti, Magui, Jose 1992

④ Babieca . . . . 🖼🖼🖼☐ **7b**
18m. A brilliant route which follows the pocketed wall to a finish just left of a thin roof.
FA. Jose Hernandez, L.Justamante 1994

⑤ El gran cañón . 🖼🖼🖼🖼☐ **7b+**
20m. Start in the same place as *Babieca* but move right and finish over the thin roof. Hard!
FA. Jose Hernandez, L.Justamante 1995

⑥ Reina de corazones 🖼🖼🖼☐ **8a**
20m. *The Queen of Hearts* - face climbing at its hardest.
FA. Jose Hernandez, L.Justamante 1994

⑦ Africa . . . . 🖼🖼🖼☐ **7c**
18m. The steep face has a couple of useful elongated pockets - and not much else!
FA. Jose Hernandez, L.Justamante 1994

⑧ Puerco espín . . . . . 🖼🖼🖼☐ **7b+**
18m. A good route just right of a right-facing groove.
FA. Jose Hernandez, L.Justamante 1994

⑨ Papa ven en tren . . 🖼🖼🖼☐ **7a+**
16m. Straight up the orange streak looks unlikely at the grade!
FA. Juan Veliz, Raul, Jose 1992

⑩ Hay canto . . . . 🖼🖼🖼🖼☐ **7b+**
18m. The next line rightwards should have been called *Directisima*, it shares the same lower-off.
FA. Jose Hernandez, L.Justamante 1994

⑪ Directisima . . . . 🖼🖼☐ **6b+**
18m. Start left of some bushes and climb the tough lower wall passing a scar then trend left under a bush to reach the lower-off. No, its not really very direct is it?
FA. Juan Serrano 1992

⑫ Roca loca . . . . 🖼🖼☐ **6a**
18m. A sustained pitch straight up the wall.
FA. Jose Hernandez, L.Justamante 1992

⑬ Saltimbanqui . . . . 🖼☐ **6a**
16m. Start left of the trees at a vertical slot and climb slabby rock eventually into a left-facing corner.
FA. Jose Hernandez, L.Justamante 1992

⑭ Pepito conejo . . . . 🖼☐ **5**
15m. Start just left of the gully and right of some pine trees and climb straight up the rib.
FA. Jose, Lola, Magui 1992

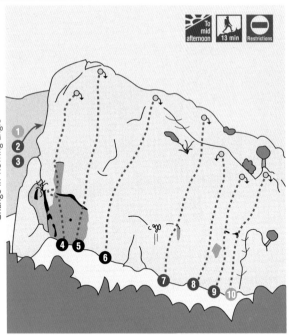

Change in viewing angle

Sector La Higuera

SECTOR ESPOLON MAGICO
The 'Magic Pillar' is slightly over sold by its name, but the smooth wall to its right is quite good.
APPROACH - Sector Ratoli is the first decent wall you come to as you walk leftwards up the hill from the approach path. Take care to drop down slightly left at the col by the top routes on Sector Picara Viborita.

ACCESS - NO CLIMBING FROM 1 MARCH TO 1 JUNE BECAUSE OF NESTING BIRDS.

The pillar faces south and is just down the slope from the last routes on the Sector La Higuera.

❶ Fisura mágico . . . . ☐ **6a+**
22m. The initial crack is followed almost to its end then the thinner continuation on the left leads to the summit
FA. Jose Hernandez, L.Justamante 1993

❷ Placa mágico . . . . ☐ **6b+**
22m. The initial crack and wall left of the arete is 'squeezed in'.
FA. Jose Hernandez, L.Justamante 1993

❸ Espolón mágico . . . . . ☐ **6b**
22m. The initial crack and well-positioned arete on the right is the best of the trio here.
FA. Jose Hernandez, L.Justamante 1993

❹ Los dedos del mono . . . ☐ **7a+**
18m. Head up the orange streak, right of the corner. At this grade, most people will accept the beckoning rest on the tree just to the left (7b without).
FA. Jose Hernandez, L.Justamante 1992

❺ Marca pasos . . ☐ **7a+**
20m. Brilliant climbing and probably the best here. The upper section is very blank.
FA. Jose Hernandez, L.Justamante 1992

❻ Agárrate donde puedas. ☐ **7b**
16m. Hard climbing up the gently leaning wall, initially to the left of a flake crack.
FA. Jose, Lola, Juan 1992

❼ 7b el plumero . . . . . . ☐ **7a**
18m. Straight up the wall passing to the right some flowstone lumps at 5m and pulling through a mid-height bulge.
FA. Jose Hernandez, L.Justamante 1992

❽ Cangrena . . . . ☐ **6c+**
14m. A fingery pitch trending rightwards up the wall.
FA. Jose, Lola, Juan 1992

❾ Paprika . . . . ☐ **6b**
14m. Just right of a scar on the wall, another fingery pitch passing through a small overlap.
FA. Jose Hernandez, L.Justamante 1992

❿ Avoriaz en pelotas me verás . . ☐ **5+**
14m. The easiest on the wall - by a mile.
FA. Jose Hernandez, L.Justamante 1992

Murcia
Alicante
Benidorm
Calpe
Xaló Valley
Gandia
Marin
Salinas
Sax
Magdelena
Peña del Corb
Peña Rubia
Foradà
Ibi
Reconco
Agulas Rojas
Alcoi
Cabezon

SECTOR PICARA VIBORITA

This is the most popular buttress at Salinas; not surprisingly it has the best spread of grades and is closest to the car. The routes vary from nice and slabby on the left-hand side to steep, orange and generally harder away on the right. Fingery climbing is the order of the day whatever the grade.

ACCESS - NO CLIMBING FROM 1 MARCH TO 1 JUNE BECAUSE OF NESTING BIRDS.

The first routes are reached by a short scramble up the slope, and are located at the left-hand end of the wall.

① Dartacán. 6c
12m. The overhanging red wall almost on the back of the fin.
FA. Jose Hernandez, Yeti 1991

Back on the main face, just before the end of the buttress, is a small grey slab with three routes and one lower-off.

② Aramis 5
12m. The left-hand line.
FA. Jose Hernandez, Jose Serrano 1991

③ Portos 5
12m. The central line, direct to the lower-off.
FA. Jose Hernandez, Jose Serrano 1991

④ Atos 5
12m. The right-hand line gives more of the same.
FA. Jose Hernandez, Jose Serrano 1991

⑤ No te lo pongas . . . . 4+
18m. There is an awkward move after the first bolt though it is still the easiest route on the cliff!
FA. Juan Serrano 1991

⑥ Pónselo 6a
18m. Good climbing up the blank looking scoop. Left of the scoop is a bit easier (**5+**) but also feels less worthwhile.
FA. Jose Hernandez, Yeti 1991

⑦ Póntelo . . . . 5+
18m. Pleasant, though with a hard bulge just below the belay.
FA. Pedro Lopez 1991

⑧ Jarpichuela. . . . . 5+
18m. The clean face just beyond an area of broken rock.
FA. Yeti 1991

⑨ Pero yeyo 5
16m. Head to and through the large diamond-shaped scoop.
FA. Yeti 1991

⑩ Amonite . . . . 5+
18m. 3m down the slope this passes a couple of 'eye holes' early on and is pleasantly sustained above.
FA. Jose Hernandez, L.Justamante 1991

⑪ Sancho Panza 6a
18m. Just right again a fingery bulge early on leads to easier climbing above. From now on the routes get harder!
FA. Yeti, Jose Luis 1991

Murcia · Alicante · Benidorm · Calpe · Xaló Valley · Gandía · Marín · Salinas · Sax · Magdalena · Peña del Corb · Peña Rubia · Forada · Ibi · Reconco · Aguas Rojas · Alcoi · Cabeceon

SECTOR PICARA VIBORITA - RIGHT
These routes are up the fine domed wall directly above where the approach path meets the crag.

ACCESS - NO CLIMBING FROM 1 MARCH TO 1 JUNE.

❶ Ali Baba y los 40 .. 🎫 6b
14m. The wall has a hard start past the beckoning pocket. The rib above is fingery and sustained.
FA. Jose Hernandez, L.Justamante 1991

❷ El canto de la abubilla . 🎫 6b+
14m. A fingery start leads to a pleasant, delicate groove.
FA. Juan Serrano 1991

❸ Lolitus .... 🎫 7a
18m. The blunt rib on the right-hand part of the face is technical. There is a **6c+** detour around the hard section near the top.
FA. Jose Hernandez, L.Justamante 1991

❹ Me estoy multiplicando 🎫 6b
20m. A good route up the shallow, fingery groove and upper rib.
FA. Juan Veliz, Yeti 1991

❺ Así habelo Pepetrusta . 🎫 5+
18m. A pleasant pitch up the left-bounding rib of the wall.
FA. Juan Serrano 1991

❻ Andrea .... 🎫 6b+
20m. A direct line to and through the widest part of the roof.
FA. Jose Hernandez, L.Justamante 1991

❼ Flash Bea .... 🎫 6b+
20m. A squeezed in eliminate line.
FA. Juan Serrano 1991

❽ Bocadillos de micros .. 🎫 6b
20m. Tasty moves leading to the right edge of the roof.
FA. Juan Veliz 1991

❾ Lenin .... 🎫 6c
18m. The orange streak and line of big pockets gives a good pitch, thin early on then strenuous above and high in the grade.
FA. Jose Luis Pienado 1991

❿ Cernicalus .... 🎫 7a
12m. A short pitch that runs into a blind alley finishing in the middle of the blank wall.
FA. Jose Hernandez, Yeti 1991

⓫ Cefalinpadus .... 🎫 6b
18m. A brilliant route up the pocketed wall with hard moves on sharp holds where the big jugs run out. *Photo page 85.*
FA. Yeti, Jose Hernandez 1991

⓬ El abominable .... 🎫 6b
16m. Better than the name suggests. Pull over a thin overlap early on, then go!
FA. Yeti, Paqui Barcelo 1991

⓭ Machu que pichu ..... 🎫 6b+
16m. The left-hand side of the scoop, trending left to finish up the hanging groove at the side of the roof.
FA. Jose Hernandez, L.Justamante 1991

⓮ Le puerta de Anubis ... 🎫 6a+
18m. Climb up a shallow scoop and make a steep rightwards pull through the diagonal bulges to a finish up the short wall.
FA. Pedro Lopez 1991

⓯ Sube golondrina ...... 🎫 6c+
18m. This one is probably **7a** if you climb direct but it is very escapable on the left of the first bulge.
FA. Jose, Lola, Juan 1991

⓰ Chiri Rosmoya. 🎫 7c
18m. The superb curving line of steep pockets with a hard crux.
FA. Chiri Ros, Isabel Pagan 1991

⓱ Alicantorroca . 🎫 8a
18m. The steep bulges and hanging rib above give one of the hardest offerings here.
FA. Chiri Ros, Yeti 1993

⓲ Destroyer .... 🎫 6c+
12m. A short steep route up the right edge of the wall.
FA. Jose Hernandez, Yeti 1991

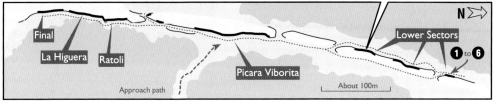

LOWER SECTORS

There are a couple of short steep walls hidden over on the other side of the fin of rock which forms the ridge. The routes here are not popular being mostly hard, or short, or both. They get the afternoon and evening sun.
APPROACH - From the open area below the crag (the highest parking) continue horizontally along the track to a col. Scramble down the other side of the col and the first routes can be seen on your right-hand side.

ACCESS - NO CLIMBING FROM 1 MARCH TO 1 JUNE BECAUSE OF NESTING BIRDS.

The routes are described from left to right up the hill. The first route encountered on the approach is Impone El desplome.

SECTOR DESPLOME

This steep cave is situated some distance down the hill and is awkward to reach, requiring a scramble under a large roof to get there. The routes are short and several seem to be forgotten projects.

1 Ajo Power. . . . . ☐ Project

2 Cho-oyu '93 . . . . ☐ 6b+
5m. A poor route. Don't come down here to do this one.

3 Wonder Bra. . . . . ☐ Project

4 Por Pelos . . . . ☐ 8a
8m. This one can be identified by its conspicuous sika hold.

5 Totem. . . . . . . ☐ 7c+
8m. Up a steep rib.

6 La era del tiempo . . . . ☐ Project
8m. Manufactured holds.

Back up the hill the routes are more interesting.

7 La primera y la ultima . . . ☐ 6b+
12m. At the bottom of the slope is this short steep buttress.
FA. Jose Hernandez 1993

8 Selva vertical . . . . ☐ 6a+
16m. The rib and scoop above are pleasant enough.
FA. J.Martinez, R.Martinez 1994

9 Atácale. . . . . ☐ 6b
16m. Climb the attractive scoop by interesting moves.
FA. Jose Hernandez, L.Justamante 1993

10 Licor armago . . . . ☐ 7a+
16m. The steep rib on the right is tough.
FA. Jose Hernandez, L.Justamante 1993

11 Tortura Contínua . . ☐ 8a
16m. A good looking hard route on the tiniest of holds.
FA. Jose Hernandez, L.Justamante 1992

12 Project . . . . ☐
16m. A steep and technical line.

13 Roca de Pandora . . . . . ☐ 7b+
16m. Steep climbing just up the knobbly crack then through the steep bulges above.
FA. Jose Hernandez, Mati 1992

14 Impone el desplome . . ☐ 7b
16m. More steep work right of the hole, via some mini tufas. The best looking route here, and probably worth the 5 min approach if you are up to it - the route that is, not the walk!
FA. Jose Hernandez, Mati 1992

SAX

Above the historic town of Sax is an impressive series of towers, perched high on the hill, overlooking the wide valley of the Vinalopo. There are two main climbing areas; the towers of the Peñas del Rey, which is the most popular area; and the open wall of the Sector Cumbre, higher up the hillside. Most of the climbing is slabby with the occasional bulging bit and the grades range from quality 4s to technical 6bs. Many of the pitches are long and there are some excellent two pitch climbs on the main Peñas del Rey.

Sax has been used by the Spanish for years and consequently some of the routes are a little polished but most of the good lines have been rebolted. Many of the routes reach the top of the crag and walking down is the least stressful way off. An exposed ridge and short slippery scramble leads down to the col behind the tower.

These towers have been called Cabreras in previous guides but we are now referring to them by their more commonly used name.

APPROACH
(area map page 77)

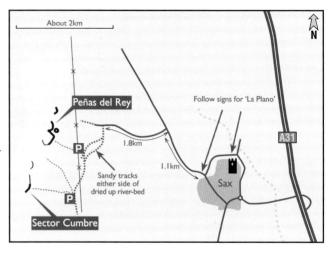

Drive from Alicante towards Madrid on the A31 and turn off at Sax. Drive towards the town, cross the river then turn right and follow the road as it loops round the town passing below the castle walls. Follow signs for La Plano as they head out of town for 1.1km then fork left - still on tarmac. 1.8km down here turn left down a dirt track. Follow this towards the Peñas del Rey, which is now clearly visible on the hillside.

For Peñas del Rey - Keep right at the first fork, and right at the second (sandy) to reach a parking spot directly below the crag.

For the Sector Cumbre - Keep right at the first fork, left at the second and continue up the hill to a level area some distance below Sector Cumbre high on the hillside. Walk round the end of the cultivated land to where a yellow/white flashed track heads diagonally to the right. From the start of this an ill-defined and sparingly-cairned track runs straight up the hill to the cliff.

ACCESS

No climbing is allowed on the upper sectors of the crag from 1 December to 1 June because of nesting birds. Please respect this arrangement. It sometimes starts earlier and stays on longer depending on the actual activities of the birds. Signs are usually posted.

CONDITIONS

The main areas face east which making it a good morning crag in winter and a good after-noon crag in summer. The exposed position on the hillside means that it catches the wind although it is usually possible to still find some shelter on the Peñas del Rey.

Chris Craggs on the pleasant two-pitch route *Blanes* (4+) on Peñas del Rey at Sax - *page 97*. The routes here tend to exhibit the characteristics of climbing on a mountain crag - a proper summit, walk-down descents and well-positioned mid-route belays, with fine views out over some spectacular scenery.

Murcia
Alicante
Benidorm
Calpe
Xaló Valley
Gandía
Marín
Salinas
Sax
Magdalena Peña del Cerí Peña Rubia
Forada
Ibi
Reconco Aguas Rojas Alcoi Cabezon

Descent

Sector Cumbre

Zona del Buho (not described)

SECTOR CUMBRE

Sector Cumbre is perched high on the hillside south (left looking in) of Peñas del Rey. The wall described here contains some great routes on immaculate rock the only drawback being the slightly tortuous ankle-scratching approach slog up the slope to get to the buttress. Since the routes on the Peñas del Rey equally good as those here, Sector Cumbre is probably best reserved for those making their second visit to Sax or those after a bit of peace and quiet.

Many of the routes have well-spaced bolts so carry a few wires if you have them.

ACCESS - NO CLIMBING FROM 1 FEBRUARY TO 1 JUNE BECAUSE OF NESTING BIRDS. This restriction is put in force when the birds nest; it has been known to have been in place as early as December. Check the sign at the start of the path.

APPROACH - From the upper parking spot, walk round the end of the cultivated land to where a yellow/white flashed track heads diagonally to the right. From the start of this an ill-defined and sparingly-cairned track runs straight up the hill to the cliff.

DESCENT - Some of the routes have lower-offs and some top-out. For the ones which top-out, a selection of gear is probably required for the belay, if not on the route itself. From the top, walk down the left-hand side (looking in) of the crag.

The first routes are on the short wall just left of the main buttress.

❶ Moreno machacón . 　　　　7b+
14m. Disproportionately hard for this crag.
FA. Chiri Ros 1989

❷ Rompe bragas. . . . . 　　6a+
14m. Up the right-facing corner.
FA. Chiri Ros, Moreno 1989

❸ Polla asesina . . . . 　　6c
14m. The right-hand of the trio past some holes and a bulge.
FA. Chiri Ros 1988

To the right is an attractive open groove/crack line.

❹ Homicidio frustrado 　　　　6c+
18m. The wall left of the main groove is thin.
FA. Chiri Ros, Isabel Pagan 1989

⑫ Fiesta salvaje . . . . 🪨⚡▢ **6b+**
The central line of the face is well worth doing.
1) 6a+, 18m. Up the thin pocketed seam to small stance.
2) 6b+, 14m. Move left and power past the bulge.
FA. Chiri Ros, Manolo 1988

⑬ Busque y compare . . . . . . 🪨▢ **6a+**
Another route with spaced bolts and its name at the base.
1) 6a+, 18m. The face right of the central groove, sustained.
2) 6a+, 14m. Sneak to the right of the capping bulge.
FA. Manolo, Chiri Ros 1989

⑭ De película . . . . 🪨🪨▢ **6b+**
1) 6a+, 16m. Start by a detached flake and head straight up the wall, marked by newish bolts.
2) 6b+, 18m. Continue directly to the top - probably the best protected pitch on the cliff.
FA. Chiri Ros, Isabel Pagan 1989

⑮ Toreros muertos . . . . . 🪨🪨▢ **6b+**
1) 6a+, 14m. Start at the name and climb straight up the wall.
2) 6b+, 18m. Head up the shallow groove line directly above.
FA. Chiri Ros, Isabel Pagan, Manolo 1989

⑯ Demonio con faldas 🪨🪨✊▢ **7a**
1) 6a+, 18m. Spaced bolts lead up the wall to a small stance.
2) 7a, 16m. Thin moves lead quickly to easier ground.
FA. Chiri Ros, Isabel Pagan 1990

⑰ Lucecitas de colores . . . . 🪨▢ **6a+**
1) 6a+, 16m. Start right of a shallow scoop, then traverse above it to gain a groove line and a small stance.
2) 6a+, 22m. Climb the groove to the top.
FA. Paco, Pedro 1990

⑱ Jabato con pie de gato . . . 🪨▢ **6a+**
1) 6a, 24m. From the name, a long pitch with sustained moves.
2) 6a+, 14m. On to the top in the same line. Short and sharp.
FA. Chiri Ros, Clavel, Manolo 1988

⑲ Gringo . . . . 🪨▢ **6a+**
1) 6a+, 20m. Up the face to a belay in a shallow scoop.
2) 6a+, 16m. Direct to the top from the stance.
FA. Chiri Ros, Clavel, Manolo 1988

⑳ Civera . . . . 🪨▢ **5+**
1) 5, 20m. The prominent groove is followed to the cave.
2) 5+, 14m. Finish out left from the stance in the cave.
FA. Cosme 1989

㉑ Sensaciones azuladas . 🪨🪨▢ **6a+**
1) 5+, 20m. The wall to the right of *Civerea*. Share its belay.
2) 6a+, 14m. Finish out rightwards from the cave.
FA. Cosme 1990

ZONA DEL BUHO
About 200m to the right of Sector Cumbre are a few more routes dotted around a more broken section of rock. The routes here are not particularly good and the path to them is awkward. The most obvious feature here is a large triangular pinnacle at the base of the wall. Left of a pinnacle is a clean wall with two **6c**s and a **7b** on it. The pinnacle itself has two **5+** routes on it. Further right are another seven routes in the **6b** to **7a** range.

⑤ Asesinato premeditado . 🪨🪨▢ **6b+**
18m. The crack line in the groove is not very helpful. The wall to the left is of material assistance.
FA. Chiri Ros, Manolo 1989

⑥ Ingreso cadáver . . . . . . 🪨🪨▢ **6b+**
22m. A tricky wall climb. Poor belay on the top.
FA. Pedro Luis 1989

⑦ Pincha pansida . . . . . . 🪨⚡▢ **6a**
18m. The pleasantly sustained slab.
FA. Chiri Ros, Isabel Pagan 1988

⑧ Gorilero . . . . 🪨▢ **6a**
18m. The left-trending line requires some delicate slab work.
FA. Chiri Ros, Isabel Pagan 1988

⑨ Tauro . . . . 🪨❤▢ **6a**
18m. The name is painted on the bottom. To get rid of the flutter symbol, carry a few wires.
FA. Manolo 1988

⑩ Tubular Bells . . . . . 🪨🪨❤▢ **6b+**
The name is painted at the bottom.
1) 6b+, 18m. A technical wall with spaced bolts.
2) 6b+, 14m. Move out right and then skirt past the bulge on its left-hand side.
FA. Chiri Ros, Manolo 1988

⑪ Zombis . . . . 🪨🪨▢ **6b**
20m. A good pitch up the wall.
FA. Paco, Pedro 1990

Murcia · Alicante · Benidorm · Calpe · Xaló Valley · Gandia · Marin · Salinas · Sax · Magdalena · Peña del Corb · Peña Rubia · Forada · Ibi · Reconco · Agulas Rojas · Alcoi · Cabezon

PEÑAS DEL REY

The main crag at Cabreras is centred on a fine tall tower known as the Peñas del Rey. The routes here are mostly well-bolted but have a mountain crag feel about them with belays and walk-down descents. Many of the routes converge at the top of the main pinnacle and following an independent line on the upper sections is often a bit tricky but this is usually above all the difficulties, on the slabbier upper walls.

CONDITIONS - The tower gets the sun until around noon. It is exposed to the wind although some shelter can be found in the central recess. In hot weather it makes a good afternoon crag.

DESCENT - For most of the routes scramble off the back and down leftwards - exposed. It is also possible to abseil off after some of the first pitches from rings set at the change in angle.

The main pinnacle has a clean slabby wall as its left-hand face which is covered with some superb pitches. The corner left of the face has a two pitch trad route in it.

1 G.E.F.C. . . . . 5+

1) 5+, 24m. The left-hand bolted line on the face past holes and through a steep bulge to reach a stance out on the ridge.
2) 4, 34m. Continue up the ridge more easily.

2 Innominado . . . . **6a+**
1) 5, 34m. The rugged slab gives a good pitch to bolts below the upper wall. Lower-off or throw yourself at.....
2) 6a+, 22m. The left-hand line on the steep wall.

3 Blanes . . . . **4+**
1) 4+, 34m. A pleasant classic. Climb the rounded rib to the overlap, cross this then trend right to a small stance.
2) 4+, 30m. Step right and climb a short wall, then take the enjoyable grooves all the way to the top.
Photo page 93.
FA. Pepe Navarro, Helios, Blanes 1960s

4 Caballo Loco . . . . **6a+**
1) 6a+, 30m. The scoopy groove is tricky to start and again at the steepening. The steep slab to the right of the upper part of the pitch offers a more sustained alternative.
2) 6a+, 30m. The right-hand line in the headwall is steeper!
FA. Chiri Ros, Manolo, Caballo 1982

5 Anduriña **6a**
1) 6a, 30m. Follow the steep technical slab (prominent old bolt marks) to a belay left of the cave. Another excellent pitch.
2) 4+, 34m. The easy groove after a steeper start.
FA. J.M.Rico, Julio Guerrero 1981

6 Kabronkon **6b**
18m. A fine pitch up the crinkly wall plugging one of the more obvious gaps here. Start at the plaque and balance up the wall to crucial moves at half-height using a thin undercut.

7 Liga Humana . . . . . . **6a+**
1) 6a+, 30m. Follow the fine slab via a small roof to a cave.
2) 6a, 36m. Pull steeply onto the pillar on the right and finish up this in a superb position.
FA. Manolo, Chiri Ros, Paco 1982

8 Tupungato . . . . **5+**
1) 5, 30m. Climb into the reddish groove at 16m then follow the delightful slab to a comfortable belay in the cave.
2) 5+, 34m. Pull out leftwards into a smaller cave above (a wire may be needed by some) then step right and finish more easily.
FA. Bravo, Pepe Navarro 1970

9 Muerte Sabrosa **6b**
30m. Make a hard start to reach the orange patch beneath the cave. Abseil off or finish up one of the other routes.
FA. Chiri Ros, Tekila 1988

10 Innominado dos . . . . . **6a+**
1) 6a+, 30m. Take the right-hand side of the orange patch steeply to a stance in the cave. A good long pitch.
2) 6a, 34m. Pull though the high point of the cave then follow the narrowing slab to the top which gets easier higher up.

11 Super Directa **6a**
1) 6a, 34m. Climb a 6m high detached block, and the wall, into a hanging groove (threads). Move out right and take the long juggy rib before escaping left to the stay.
2) 5+, 30m. Step back out right and continue up the exposed and sustained rib above, gradually easing.
FA. Pepe Navarro, F.Mola 1970

12 Directísima **6a**
1) 6a, 34m. Start by a smaller pillar and pull through the left side of a small shattered overhang. Climb past a big hole and up the scoopy wall, move out left to belay in a shallow bay.
2) 6a, 34m. The second pitch climbs straight up the steep arete and wall above the stance with continuous interest.
FA. Manolo, Biberon, Chiri Ros 1981

13 La Mulxaranga **6b**
1) 5+, 34m. The direct line from the start of *Central* via a niche and then the sustained rib to a small stance.
2) 6b, 34m. The slab above leads to a junction with *Central*.

14 Central . . . . **5+**
1) 6a, 40m. Climb to the centre of the overlap and then round its right side. Up the rib to a small niche, exit steeply left from this to locate a small stance on a ramp.
2) 5+, 30m. Step left and climb the slab to a short awkward wall, up this then follow the obvious left-trending line to the final bulges and pull through the left edge of these.
FA. Pepe Navarro, Helios 1970s

15 Límites Realidad . . . . . **6a+**
Protected by good bolts but a little run-out.
1) 6a, 40m. From the left-hand of a pair of blocks climb up leftwards to join *Central* and continue to its stance.
2) 6a, 30m. Climb straight up the steep wall above to the top.
FA. Moreno, Diego, Fede 1984

16 Diedro Dinamita . . . . **6b (E3)**
38m. The left-facing corner groove needs a collection of wires. Finish up any of the other routes or abseil off.
FA. Manolo, Tekil 1982

17 Polvos Mágicos **6a**
1) 6a, 40m. A bit run-out at the bottom. Start at a 'ban-the-bomb' sign, climb through an alcove and up the wall then trend left into a corner. Up this then keep right up the rib to a stance up the ramp from *Central*.
2) 6a, 24m. Continue up the left side of the final rib via a sustained shallow groove.
FA. Manolo, Biberon 1980

18 Hollywood . . . . **6a+ (E2)**
34m. A single pitch marked by a thread and a peg. Take some wires. Abseil off or continue up one of the upper pitches.
FA. Pedro Luis 1991

The next three routes are located in the back left-hand side of the gully, between the two pinnacles.

19 Navarro 1 . . . . **6a**
An expedition up the front of the leaning block and wall above.
1) 5+, 10m. Scramble up onto the top of the pinnacle (possible belay) then climb the steep wall above to the break.
2) 6a, 34m. Make a hard move up and left into a scoop and climb direct up the wall to finally merge with the other routes.
FA. Pepe Navarro, P.Navarro 1970s

20 Navarro 1 Variante **6b**
A variation to the last pitch, up the blunt rib on the right.

Murcia
Alicante
Benidorm
Calpe
Xaló Valley
Gandía
Marin
Salinas
Sax
Magdalena
Peña del Corb
Peña Rubia
Foradà
Ibi
Reconco
Agulles Rojas
Alcoi
Cabezon

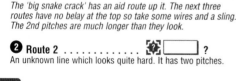

PEÑAS DEL REY - RIGHT

At the back of the gully between the two main pinnacles is an impressive steep wall which contains the best steep routes at Sax. To the right is a prominent tall narrow pinnacle standing in front of the main crag.

CONDITIONS - The enclosed nature of this section means that it only sees the sun in the early morning. It is better-sheltered than the rest of the crag and great in hot weather. The two pinnacles are more exposed to the elements.

DESCENT - For the back wall routes, scramble off the back left-hand side (looking in) of the Peñas del Rey - exposed.
For routes which reach the top of the free-standing pinnacle, make one 30m abseil from a cable, down into the central gully.

14 15 on the wall up the slope

12 13 on the back of the pinnacle

---

① Chimenea Groen 70 . . . 5 (HVS)
1) 5, 20m. Squirm up the chimney at the back left-hand corner of the gully. Fun if you like that sort of thing.
2) 5, 34m. Pull back right into the corner and continue the fight all the way to the top. Interesting!
FA. A.Botella, Aranda 1969

The 'big snake crack' has an aid route up it. The next three routes have no belay at the top so take some wires and a sling. The 2nd pitches are much longer than they look.

② Route 2 . . . . ?
An unknown line which looks quite hard. It has two pitches.

③ Elena de Pablo . . . 7a
The magnificent route with a brace of 3-star pitches.
1) 6a+, 24m. Steep, juggy and exhilarating though also shiny and fairly hard work for the grade.
2) 7a, 34m. More technical than the lower section although the real difficulties are only short.
FA. Pepe Navarro, Bravo 1970

④ Chinche 6b
1) 5+, 24m. A superb first pitch at an amenable grade.
2) 6b, 34m. There is one hard move just above the stance then spaced gear and good holds lead all the way to the top.
FA. F.Rico, P.Amat 1984

⑤ Espolón Luis Rico . . . . . . 🔲 6a
1) 6a, 20m. Climb the chimney by the block on the right-hand side of the recess to a belay on the col.
2) 6a, 34m. Finish up the long arete above.

The next routes are on the bulging wall on the right-hand side of the central gully.

⑥ Retri . . . . 🔲 6a+ (E2)
25m. A big single pitch to the top of the tower. There are bolts but they are pretty well spaced.
FA. Domingo, Rovera 1974

⑦ QE2 . . . . 🔲 6a
25m. Start as for *Retri* but break right and follow spaced gear up the steep face. It can be split at half-height if needed.
FA. Paco Amat, F.Rico 1982

⑧ Techo . . . . 🔲 7a+
15m. The direct start to the next route is very technical. Finish up *Carrasco* or lower off from the mid-height belay.
FA. Chiri Ros 1989

⑨ Con cuarto basta . . . . 🔲 6a+
25m. An odd eliminate which makes a rising traverse above the scoop. Join and finish up *Carrasco*. Not shown on topo.
FA. Pedro Luis 1989

⑩ Churrasco . . . . 🔲 5 (HVS)
25m. A good route up the front left-hand side of the pillar, the best equipped and easiest way up the tower. It can be split at the mid-height belay if needed.
FA. Pepe Navarro, Helios 1965

⑪ Rafael Vercher . . . . 🔲 5 (HVS)
30m. The line is marked by two pegs so take some wires. It can be split at a belay on a ledge.
FA. Chiri Ros, Caballo, Manolo 1981

At the back of the pinnacle is a narrow gully. The next two routes are on the left of this gully.

⑫ Sombra del pájaro . . . . 🔲 6a+
15m. Straight up the face - easing with height.
FA. Chiri Ros, Manolo, Isabel Pagan 1985

⑬ Carrozas Climb . . . 🔲 7b
15m. A wicked test-piece up the side wall overlooking the gully.
FA. Chiri Ros, Isabel Pagan 1990

There are two more routes are on the wall beyond the pinnacle.

⑭ Aspirante carroza . . . . . . 🔲 6a
An interesting route up the long rib.
1) 6a, 20m. Climb the rib past a small overlap.
2) 5+, 30m. Continue in the same line to the top.
FA. Biberon, Juan Ma 1991

⑮ Marco Antonio . . . . 🔲 5 (HVS)
55m. A long and wandering line which requires gear. It can be done in two or even three pitches. All pitches are grade 5.
FA. Domingo, Rovera 1980s

THE ELISA-BELTRÁN PINNACLE
To the right of the main sectors is another shorter pinnacle with a bulging side wall and a fine front arete.

⑯ Moreno . . . . 🔲 6a+
18m. The left-hand line on the side-wall.
FA. Pedro Luis 1989

⑰ Super miembro . . . . 🔲 6c+
18m. The line up the centre of the side wall.
FA. Pedro Luis, Paco 1988

⑱ Elisa-Beltrán . . . . 🔲 4
40m. A good route up the front arete which can be split at a mid-height belay.
FA. Pepe Navarro 1992

MAGDELENA

This is not a major venue and it is a long way from the coast, hence it doesn't see much in the way of visitors. It has a varied selection of 60 or so routes all in a rather scruffy and very arid setting. Although probably not worth a visit from afar, if you are in the area it is worth considering calling in for a couple of hour's sport. The best piece of rock here it the Pared Negra which has a pleasant collection of lower-grade slab climbs in a very sunny setting, worth a day if you climb at 5/5+ and want to tick plenty of routes without too much effort. The Pared Roja has some short and fierce routes, whereas the secluded Pared del Salto is home to the really steep stuff. Generally speaking the grades here are all rather tough. The fixed gear is excellent on all the decent routes.

Technically speaking the crag is actually in the Murcia region, though it fits more logically in the Alicante section because the usual approach is from that direction, hence its inclusion here.

APPROACH (area map page 77)

From Villena on the A31 Madrid road drive past the town, through a tunnel then turn right off the dual carriage way to pass back under it and pick up signs for Yecla. Follow the ring road round Villena until the main CV81 road is joined then head cross country (where it changes to the C3314!) to Yecla for 20km. Just before Yecla, bear left onto the new ring road (N334) and follow this for 8km until the road from the centre of town comes in from the right. Just under 1km from here, and opposite a wired enclosure on the left, is a nondescript dirt track branching off to the right. Follow this to a right fork by a sunken water tank. Continue along this bearing left at a ruined house then right at a T-junction just beyond a new house. Continue along the road through a low point in the ridge as it swings up and right to an open parking area; the last section is steep and rough. This is 4km from the road.

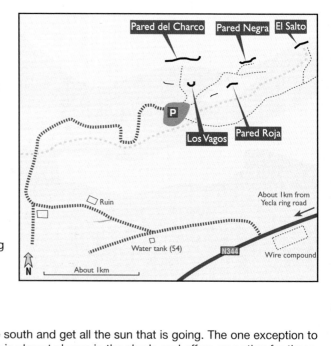

CONDITIONS

Three of the main cliffs face south and get all the sun that is going. The one exception to this is the Pared Roja which is almost always in the shade and offers an option for those in search of steep, shady sport on hot days. All of the faces dry rapidly after rain and the whole valley is well sheltered from the wind.

Murcia
Alicante
Benidorm
Calpe
Xalo Valley
Gandia
Marin
Salinas
Sax
Magdelena
Peña del Caro
Peña Rubia
Forada
Ibi
Reconco
Agulas Rojas
Alcoi
Cabezon

Chris Craggs on *Ultimatun* (5+) on the Pared Negra, Magdelena. Although not typical of the off-vertical face routes here, it is worth doing for some interesting jug pulling. - *page 104*. Photo: Sherri Davy

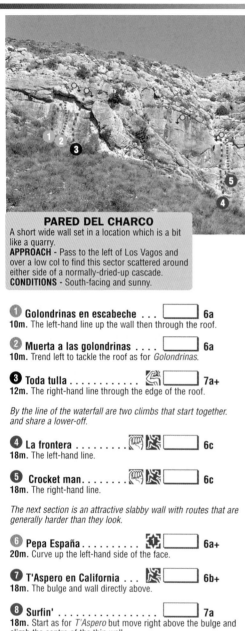

PARED DEL CHARCO

A short wide wall set in a location which is a bit like a quarry.
APPROACH - Pass to the left of Los Vagos and over a low col to find this sector scattered around either side of a normally-dried-up cascade.
CONDITIONS - South-facing and sunny.

1 Golondrinas en escabeche . . . ☐ 6a
10m. The left-hand line up the wall then through the roof.

2 Muerta a las golondrinas . . . . ☐ 6a
10m. Trend left to tackle the roof as for *Golondrinas*.

3 Toda tulla . . . . 🎽☐ 7a+
12m. The right-hand line through the edge of the roof.

By the line of the waterfall are two climbs that start together. and share a lower-off.

4 La frontera . . . . 🧤🎽☐ 6c
18m. The left-hand line.

5 Crocket man. . . . . 🧤🎽☐ 6c
18m. The right-hand line.

The next section is an attractive slabby wall with routes that are generally harder than they look.

6 Pepa España . . . . 🔧☐ 6a+
20m. Curve up the left-hand side of the face.

7 T'Aspero en California . . . 🎽☐ 6b+
18m. The bulge and wall directly above.

8 Surfin' . . . . ☐ 7a
18m. Start as for *T'Aspero* but move right above the bulge and climb the centre of the thin wall.

9 Mas se perdido en Cuba . . 🔧☐ 6a+
18m. From *T'Aspero*, keep heading right along the seam to climb easier-angled rock to a lower-off just below the crest.

10 Puta navidad. . . . . ☐ 6a+
18m. A direct start to *Mas se perdido en Cuba*.

11 Notecorras en mi Polla . . . . . . ☐ 6b
14m. Steep climbing through the inverted A-shaped notch.

12 Cruisin' . . . . ☐ 6b+
14m. The left-hand side of the rib and smooth face.

13 El vipolador de chotas . . . . . . ☐ 7b
14m. The last offering here has a tough finish.

LOS VAGOS

14 Metehe goles . . . . ☐ 6a
8m. Out left then back right via the flake.

15 Samba pa ti . . . . 🎽☐ 6b+
8m. Direct up the centre of the rounded rib on sharp holds.

16 Gozas negro . . . . ☐ 6a
8m. Trend right up a groove then back left to the lower-off.

LOS VAGOS

Three tiny offerings on the small tower near the car park.
APPROACH - A one minute dash from the car.

Not much sun | 8 min

Pared Negra

Approach

PARED ROJA

Looking up the gully to the east of the parking is this short wall with a solitary tree stood in front of it. This crag is home to a small collection of fierce fingery routes and is always in the shade. Some of the rock is a little dubious but the big beefy bolts make up for this.

APPROACH - Walk up the sandy gully east of the parking and this is the second crag on the right.

CONDITIONS - The only shady climbing around here.

1 Puec .... ⬜ **6a**
10m. The left-hand line starting through a diagonal overlap.

2 Mollunga gongorino ..... ⬜ **6c**
10m. Start up a flake then head for the same lower-off.

3 Masturbaciones sensaciones ⬜ **7c**
12m. The fierce fingery wall passing an overlap high up.

4 Reine matadora ...... ⬜ **6c+**
14m. The pocketed centre of the wall.

5 Corleone .... ⬜ **7b**
14m. Arduous moves up the diagonal seam.

6 Volver a empezar ..... ⬜ **6a+**
14m. Start as for *Corleone* but avoid the issue by trending right up the pocketed wall to a finish over the overlap.

7 Seta negra ...... ⬜ **6c**
14m. Climb through the big hole then trend rightwards up the face to a short leftward traverse to the belay. More direct is **7a**.

8 Es doz .... ⬜ **6a**
14m. Follow the flake rightwards strenuously to a hole with lower-off. Press on to the next one just up and right.

9 Soy un borracho .... ⬜ **6b+**
8m. Straight up the wall to the lower-off in the hole.

10 China blue .... ⬜ **6c+**
10m. Direct to the lower-off of *Es doz*.

11 Blue bayou .... ⬜ **6a+**
10m. The right edge of the wall trending left.

104

Lots of sun
10 min
Approach
Main Face 50m
1
2
3

PARED NEGRA

Arguably the best bit of rock in the area, the 'Black Wall' is especially worth a visit if you are looking for a collection of low-grade and (relatively) low-angled climbs.
APPROACH - Walk up the gully that contains the Pared Roja and continue over the col, the Pared Negra is on the left. Watch for snakes!
CONDITIONS - South-facing and sunny.

1 A pan y agua . . . . 1 star 5+
20m. Climb through the overhangs to a finish up a rugged rib.

2 Ulimatun . . . . 1 star 5+
20m. Direct via the big hole in the cave roof. *Photo page 101.*

3 Primera . . . . 1 star 5+
22m. Take the slab on the right then the upper face direct.

The main section is 50m further right.

4 Calienta motores . . . . 1 star 5
14m. Climb out of an orange niche and up the slab past a flake.

5 Al loro con el cazarlo . . . . 5+
14m. Barely independent at the start and not at all above!

6 Treinta cinco . . . . 5+
16m. Up the centre of the slab (red bolts) then trend right.

7 36 . . . . 5+
16m. The right-hand line on the slab past silvery bolts.

8 Ciento veinte dos . . . . 4+
16m. Start up a pocketed crack on the next slab and trend left.

9 Jubito poco . . . . 2 star 5
20m. Start up the pocketed crack (or to the right) to a curving ledge, then up and left via the left side of the fine tower. Good!

10 Etiopyn boys . . . . 1 star 5
20m. Climb just left of the black streak past a large flake.

11 Papa mateo . . . . 1 star 5+
18m. Just right of the black streak, climb the blunt rib via a broken flake to a ledge (crux) then the easier face above.

12 Capfrutica roja . . . . 2 star 5
18m. Approach the flake-crack from the right then climb it, and the rib, up and right by pleasant moves.

13 Rambla matxaka 5
18m. The narrow face is climbed past a chevron-shaped niche, then the right side of the rib above.

14 Cornered . . . . 5+
18m. A scruffy slab leads to better climbing up the rib above.

Lots of sun
10 min
Approach
4
5
6
7
8
9
10
11
12
13
14
15
16
17
18
19
20
21

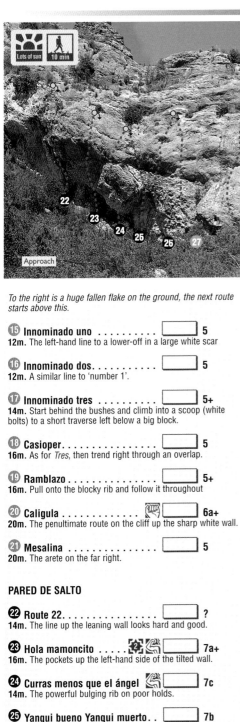

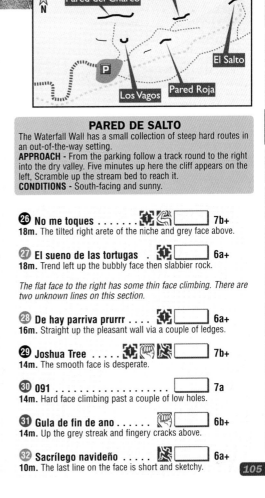

To the right is a huge fallen flake on the ground, the next route starts above this.

⑮ Innominado uno . . . . [⬜] 5
12m. The left-hand line to a lower-off in a large white scar

⑯ Innominado dos. . . . . [⬜] 5
12m. A similar line to 'number 1'.

⑰ Innominado tres . . . . [⬜] 5+
14m. Start behind the bushes and climb into a scoop (white bolts) to a short traverse left below a big block.

⑱ Casioper. . . . . [⬜] 5
16m. As for *Tres*, then trend right through an overlap.

⑲ Ramblazo . . . . [⬜] 5+
16m. Pull onto the blocky rib and follow it throughout

⑳ Caligula . . . . [🖐][⬜] 6a+
20m. The penultimate route on the cliff up the sharp white wall.

㉑ Mesalina . . . . [⬜] 5
20m. The arete on the far right.

PARED DE SALTO

㉒ Route 22. . . . . [⬜] ?
14m. The line up the leaning wall looks hard and good.

㉓ Hola mamoncito . . . . . [📷2][🖐][⬜] 7a+
16m. The pockets up the left-hand side of the tilted wall.

㉔ Curras menos que el ángel [🖐][⬜] 7c
14m. The powerful bulging rib on poor holds.

㉕ Yanqui bueno Yanqui muerto. . [⬜] 7b
14m. More pockets up the inverted niche to easier ground.

PARED DE SALTO
The Waterfall Wall has a small collection of steep hard routes in an out-of-the-way setting.
APPROACH - From the parking follow a track round to the right into the dry valley. Five minutes up here the cliff appears on the left, Scramble up the stream bed to reach it.
CONDITIONS - South-facing and sunny.

㉖ No me toques . . . . . . [📷][🖐][⬜] 7b+
18m. The tilted right arete of the niche and grey face above.

㉗ El sueno de las tortugas . [📷][⬜] 6a+
18m. Trend left up the bubbly face then slabbier rock.

The flat face to the right has some thin face climbing. There are two unknown lines on this section.

㉘ De hay parriva prurrr . . . . [📷][⬜] 6a+
16m. Straight up the pleasant wall via a couple of ledges.

㉙ Joshua Tree . . . . . [📷][🖐][🖐][⬜] 7b+
14m. The smooth face is desperate.

㉚ 091 . . . . [⬜] 7a
14m. Hard face climbing past a couple of low holes.

㉛ Gula de fin de ano . . . . . . [🖐][⬜] 6b+
14m. Up the grey streak and fingery cracks above.

㉜ Sacrílego navideño . . . . . [🖐][⬜] 6a+
10m. The last line on the face is short and sketchy.

Murcia · Alicante · Benidorm · Calpe · Xaló Valley · Gandia · Marin · Salinas · Sax · Magdelena · Peña del Corb · Peña Rubia · Forada · Ibi · Reconco · Aguilas Rojas · Alcoi · Cabezon

Murcia
Alicante
Benidorm
Calpe
Xaló Valley
Gandia
Marin
Salinas
Sax
Magdalena
Peña del Corb
Peña Rubia
Forada
Ibi
Reconco
Aguas Rojas
Alcoi
Cabezon

PEÑA DEL CORB

A short distance north of the centre of Petrer/Elda is 'the tower of the raven', set high above the valley, with a black metal cross on its summit. This west-facing cliff is home to twenty worthwhile climbs, several of which are in the lower grades. The routes are up to 30m in length, often of two pitches, and are well bolted. The rock is generally less than vertical and many of the routes finish on a true summit. The place well worth a day if you are in the area and climb at the appropriate grade. The cliff is also known as Espolón de la Sierra del Caballo.

The climbing here was first developed in the early 1960s. In the mid 1990s many of the routes were rebolted by J.P. and V. Verdú.

APPROACH (area map page 77)

Take the A31 Madrid road (toll-free motorway) north west from Alicante for 32km to Elda/Petrer, pass the castle and turn right at the sign 'Centro Commercial'. At the junction head straight across onto a smaller road. Continue straight up this passing a tiny cross-roads and after 0.4km the road forks. Bear right gradually rising for another 0.5km until the Tarmac ends, 0.2km further on is parking on the right by a solitary tree. The path starts here and zig-zags up the grassy rib (two to the right of the prominent cliff) until it contours away to the left to arrive at the right edge of the cliff.

CONDITIONS

The cliff faces west and so get the afternoon and evening sun. It is quite exposed but dries rapidly after rain due to it being a free-standing summit.

The short-lived but well-positioned route of on *Pipona* (6b) on Peña del Corb - *page 109.*

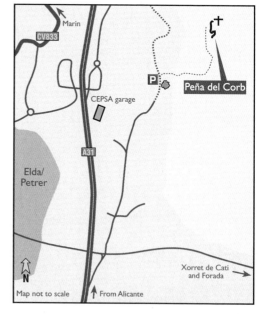

Chris Craggs and John Addy on *Pascual Navarra* (6a+,5) on Peña del Corb. An excellent two pitch offering on this fine but neglected crag - *page 109*. Photo: Sherri Davy

Descend by abseil off the back

SOUTH WEST FACE

A good set of slab and face climbs often two pitches long and leading to a mini-summit. The routes on the right tend to be steeper and harder than the offerings futher left.
DESCENT - From the cross, either abseil back down the front face (two ropes required) or make a 12m abseil down the back of the tower into the notch. From here you can scramble right (facing the summit) down the steep scratchy gully, passing under several good climbs, or trend down and across the rocky slope to the left until easy scrambling leads back to the foot of the cliff. Avoid the direct descent of the south side gully as it contains some steep steps.

1 Larga 4
1) 3, 14m. The left arete of the cliff is the easiest route here.
2) 4, 16m. Keep to the right of the crest (or 4+ to the left). Abseil off or scramble to the summit cross.
FA. Jose Navarro, Jose Poveda 1963

To the right a ramp runs leftwards under the wall with three new bolt lines (and a line of rusty old ones) starting off it.

2 Espolón oeste norte oeste . . . 5
28m. The line just to the right of the left-bounding rib of the cliff gives a long pleasant pitch, easing with height.
FA. Jose Peréz, Antonio Martínez 1977

3 No se sabe 6a
28m. The central line off the ramp passes a large scar, then head between bushes and continue direct. Pleasantly sustained
FA. J.P.Verdu, V.Verdu 1994

4 Pedro ayuste . . . . . 6a+
28m. Start 8m up the ramp and climb the awkward steep wall then much easier rock above. One of the best here.
FA. Moneo, Antonio Martínez 1977

5 Penélope 6a
1) 6a, 20m. Start right of the lowest point of the cliff and climb into the groove via a curved flake. Continue using continuously surprising holds to reach a good stance.
2) 4, 10m. Step left and pull through the edge of the bulge.
FA. Mataix, Berbegal, M.Juan 1975

6 Marina . . . . 6a+
1) 6a+, 20m. Start at a 2m high cave. Climb the sharp pocketed crack up the right side of a scoop to a comfortable stance.
2) 5, 10m. Climb above the stance and pull through the bulges.
FA. Jose Navarro, Elios Paya 1965

7 Daniel Esteve . . . . 6c+
1) 6c+, 16m. The hardest climb on the cliff, with two contrasting pitches. Climb thin pocketed seam in the wall with difficulty and when thing ease traverse 3m right to a stance in a hollow.
2) 6c+, 18m. Follow the ramp up to the left then power through the double overhangs finishing up a red streak.
Variante Rovira, ? - Direct above the stance is an unknown.
FA. M.Maestre, R. Vicedo 1969

8 9 d'Octubre 6b
14m. Starting at a head-high flake is this direct line with good climbing. Pass a large hole then make a couple of tough moves just before the angle eases. Lower off.
FA. V.Freire, R.Villena 1980s

⑨ Isabel . . . . 🔲 6a

1) 6a, 14m. The easiest climb up the central section of the cliff with only a couple of harder moves on the first pitch. Start at a left-trending rib and climb this to some large pockets. Make steep move back right then climb easily to a good stance.
2) 3, 20m. Follow the left-trending ramp to outflank the impressive double overhangs and finish easily.
FA. Riqueime, Domingo, Marti 1971

⑩ Directa Franciso Moya . . . 🔲 6c

1) 6c, 14m. An unbalanced climb. Start in a 'sentry-box' just left of the arete and follow the steep pocketed seam up and slightly leftwards to a stance in a bay on *Isabel*.
2) 4+, 20m. Step back right and follow the wide easy corner-groove to a two bolt belay just below the cliff top.
FA. M.Maestre, Riqueime, Botella 1971

⑪ Pascual Navarra . . . . . 🔲 6a+

1) 6a+, 14m. The right arete of the cliff is excellent. Start in the gully to the right and climb a bulge to a ledge. Step left and head up the face left on good holds to a stance.
2) 5, 14m. Easier climbing up the arete above until it is possible to step into the gully on the left. Up this to a two bolt belay.
Photo page 107.
FA. Jose Navarro, Elios Paya 1968

⑫ Pascual Soler . . . . 🔲 A2+

24m. The steep wall above the gully on aid, with an hanging stance if required. I don't think it gets done much these days!
FA. F.Rico, V.Freire 1980

NORTH FACE

⑬ Triento y uno . . . . 🔲 3 (Diff)

18m. Down the slope from the col behind the tower is the easiest way to the summit. Mild but sparingly-bolted. Trend left across the undercut slab to reach the base of an open groove then continue leftwards around the arete to reach easy ground.
FA. M.Maestre, M.Bravo 1970

⑭ Diedro del mechero . . . . . 🔲 5 (HVS)

14m. The groove passed by the last route has no fixed gear.
FA. M.Maestre, Rovira 1977

⑮ Corta . . . . 🔲 4+ (VS)

12m. The shortest way to the summit. Start at the top of the slope behind the tower and climb up to the top of a large fallen block and then up the short flake crack above.
FA. Jose Navarro, Jose Poveda 1963

⑯ Fuerza futura . . . . 🔲 6b+

12m. The right side of the arete at the top of the gully has a couple of fierce moves early on (chipped pockets) and then eases dramatically.
FA. Cosme 1989

⑰ Pipona . . . . 🔲 6b

12m. The right arete of the short side of the tower gives a pleasant and photogenic pitch with a couple of long reaches between good holds. *Photo page 106.*
FA. Jose Navarro 1964

⑱ Ma-ma . . . . 🔲 6c

14m. The steep line passing to the left of the prominent black streak near the top of the wall is hard, especially if you don't use the chipped holds when passing the bulge.
FA. M.Maestre, Simón Diego Macia 1972

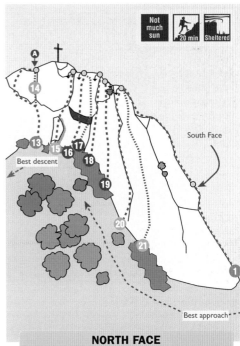

South Face

Best descent

Best approach

NORTH FACE

The other routes here are found behind the main face in a steep gully filled with scratchy vegetation. The routes here face north (cool in the middle of the day) and are described from left to right as the are passed when descending from the col. The first couple of routes are on the eastern side of the col behind the tower.

⑲ Estilo libre . . . . 🔲 6b

14m. The line of bolts running up the slab to the left of the obvious crack is harder than it looks, particularly the bulge at three quarters height.
FA. Cosme 1989

⑳ Greta 472 . . . . 🔲 6a

16m. The once-pegged thin crack with 'EJOR' scratched near its foot is good and is harder than it looks. Exit right and lower-off the large ring bolt on the ledge.
FA. M.Maestre, A.Higueruela 1972

The last route climbs the attractive grey slab near the base of the gully.

㉑ Senda paras tus dedos . 🔲 6a+

16m. The slab gives a nicely technical pitch with several sketchy moves until the angle eases. Lower-off the large ring bolt on the next ledge up, as for the last climb.
FA. Cosme 1989

PEÑA RUBIA

Peña Rubia has been quite popular in the past and it does have some good climbing though a rogue reputation for harsh grades and polished routes hasn't done the place any favours. Probably its main claim to

fame is the proximity of the 'Boreal' factory and the fact that many famous climbers have tested their sponsored boots on these humble walls. There is a full grade range from 4s to 8s. Most of the harder routes only have short technical sections on steep bulges using chipped pockets. The easier routes are more interesting, especially some of the longer ones in the Centre Sector.

The whole crag is fully equipped with good lower-offs. Some of the routes have two pitches but in most cases you can run them together with a 60m rope.

APPROACH
(area map page 77)

From Alicante, take the A36, pass Castella and follow signs for Villena and Biar (CV799), then take the Villena road and turn left onto the A31 and immediately left again to Peña Rubia. You can see the crag on the hillside to the left of the mast. See the map on the right for the few turnings. Drive through the impressive

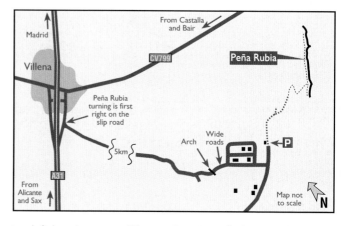

archway and tack up to the top left-hand corner of the road system. A short sandy track leads up to the crag. Don't leave any valuables in your car.

CONDITIONS

The crag faces north west which means that it only gets the afternoon sun. It is relatively sheltered from the wind and makes a good morning venue in hot weather. Like most of the cliffs hereabouts it is far too hot in the summer months. Its accessibility means this is a reasonable 'airport day' crag providing you can leave a sunbathing team to look after the car and the luggage!

Mike Appleton on *Los 4 chinetes* (6c+) on Peña Rubia - *page 114*. The crag has had a bit of a rogue reputation and it has to be admitted some of the harder routes are chipped and polished. Despite this there are many worthwhile routes here, spread across the grades.

Adjoining

Approach

Routes 1 to 9

SECTOR GANDALF
The furthest section consists of a couple of thin slabs and the steep side wall of a tower.
APPROACH - The routes start at various points above a broken and vegetated lower wall. Walk left to the far end of the crag and either stay low for the far end, or scramble up the ramp (scratchy) to reach the tower.

❶ No sabe no contesta. . . . . [ ] **5**
22m. The first route is at the extreme left-hand end, up an open corner and then the face above.
FA. Pascual Canto 1989

❷ El espejo de Galadriel . . [ ] **7b+**
14m. Thin climbing up the slabby wall right of the corner.
FA. Chimo, José Miguel 1988

❸ Sauron . . . . . . [ ] **7a+**
14m. More bald slab climbing passing a bulge early on.
FA. Chimo, José Miguel 1988

The next three routes are on a rounded pillar towards the right-hand side of the wall. Scramble up to them from below.

❹ Condón Simón. . . . . [ ] **6a+**
18m. The left-hand line. Needs rebolting.
FA. José Miguel 1988

❺ Hells Bells . . . . [ ] **6c**
18m. The central line. Could do with rebolting.
FA. José Miguel, José Antonio 1988

❻ Samsagaz. . . . . [ ] **6b+**
18m. The crack and streak above - the best here.
FA. Chimo, José Miguel 1988

To the right is a gully which is overlooked by the north-facing side wall of a tall orange pillar. There is a wire cable below it.

❼ Me de la mismo . . . . . [ ] **5**
18m. The twisting crack-line. Good climbing.
FA. José Miguel, José Antonio 1991

❽ Smaug el dorado . . . . . [ ] **6b+**
16m. The centre of the face is sharp.
FA. Chimo, José Miguel 1988

❾ Gandalf el gris . . . . . [ ] **6a+**
14m. The well-positioned arete of the tower.
FA. Chimo, José Miguel 1988

SECTOR CHIMET
To the right of the tower is a short undercut wall with half a dozen short offerings which are best reached by scrambling up from the right-hand side.

❿ Voltage . . . . [ ] **6a+**
14m. The left edge of the wall finishing rightwards.
FA. José Antonio, José Miguel 1992

⓫ Seamos peligrosos . . . . [ ] **6a+**
14m. The left-trending scoop with a tufa-feature.
FA. José Antonio, José Miguel 1992

⓬ Por si el Sidra. . . . . [ ] **6b+**
12m. The grey slab is short and sharp. Four bolts.
FA. José Antonio, Andres 1990

⓭ Póntelo Pónselo . . . . [ ] **6a**
12m. Pull through the roof just left of a large hole.
FA. Chimo, José Miguel 1989

⓮ Cinco contra el calvo . . . . [ ] **6a**
12m. The right-hand side of the roof has a butch start.
FA. José Antonio, Fulgen 1992

⓯ El chico del loro . . . . [ ] **5+**
12m. Skirt the edge of the steep rock then head left.
FA. Chimo, José Antonio 1993

Below the undercut face are three short offerings.

⓰ Piñerus . . . . [ ] **7a+**
10m. A contender for the most pointless route in this book.
FA. Who cares?

Murcia | Alicante | Benidorm | Calpe | Xaló Valley | Gandia | Maria | Salinas | Sax | Magdelena | Peña del Cot | Peña Rubia | Forada | Ibi | Reconco | Aguas Rojas | Alcoi | Cabezon

Murcia
Alicante
Benidorm
Calpe
Xaló Valley
Gandia
Marin
Salinas
Sax
Magdeluna
Peña del Corb
Peña Rubia
Forada
Ibi
Reconco
Águiles Rojas
Alcoi
Cabezon

SECTOR CHIMET

A tall slabby wall with a vegetated mid-height ledge. Here are some longer routes at a lower grade then the rest of the cliff - although not fantastic, they are worth doing for climbers operating at that grade.

17 ¿Paraqué? 6b
10m. A short bulging wall.
FA. Piñero, Paraguayo 1988

18 Pilarín . . . . 5+
16m. The rib is more worthwhile although that's not hard!
FA. Chimo, Carujo 1988

19 El vuelo del Mono 5
1) 5, 16m. Climb the left side of the open groove then step right across its closure to reach a broad grassy ledge.
2) 5, 16m. The second pitch passes a variety of fixed gear to finish just left of a block at the top of the cliff.
FA. Chimo, Carujo 1988

20 Tampones lejanos . . . . . . 6a+
12m. A short route which starts up a broken groove then bales out before the ledges.
FA. Chimo, José Antonio 1993

21 Chimet . . . . 4+
1) 4+, 14m. Start at the green name, climb the rib and slab pulling over, or around, a couple of bulges, to a large ledge.
2) 4+, 18m. Trend leftwards, passing the edge of an orange niche, then climb the pleasant slab. Reaching the initial bolt on this pitch is probably the crux of the climb and the gear is rather spaced above this!
FA. Chimo, Carujo 1987

22 El ultimo Yeclano 5
22m. A long and pleasant slab climb. Follow new bolts up the slab and through a band of steeper rock to a lower-off below the overhangs at the top of the cliff.
FA. Chimo, José M.Bufan 1989

23 Moco de pavo . . . . 6b+
22m. Climb slabby rock (most of the next route) to a short sharp climax over the bulge above the wall. An oddity.
FA. Chimo, José Antonio 1993

24 Caru 5
28m. Start at the name on the rock. Climb straight up ambling slabby rock to steeper stuff then cross the slabs rightwards to the lower-off of *Medio metro*.
FA. Chimo, Carujo 1987

25 Sharon Pistones 7a
10m. Start just left at a head-height hole and a strange 'space-man/bishop' drawn on the rock. Short and sharp.
FA. José Antonio 1992

There may be a short unnamed 6a between these routes.

26 Medio Metro 6a
24m. Interesting scoopy climbing. Start at the name. Climb the initial pockety groove then escape out right before trending generally left up slabs to a lower-off just to the right of a series of orange roofs.
FA. Pascual Canto 1988

SECTOR CLAVELES

For the best climbing at Peña Rubia look no further! The routes here tackle steep bulges or slabby grey faces and often make strenuous use of large pockets. Sadly many of the better climbs have become polished through over-use.

❶ Pari-Dakar . . . 🔳🔳🔳 ▱ **7b+**
12m. The pink scoop and short wall above.
FA. José Miguel, José Antonio 1989

❷ Txavo tu vales mucho . . 🔳🔳 ▱ **8a**
10m. Intense but short-lived climbing up the blank face.
FA. Txavo Vales 1988

❸ Kortatu . . . . 🔳🔳🔳 ▱ **6c+**
22m. The long sustained face on sharp holds. The angle and difficulties ease with height.
FA. José Miguel 1987

❹ Los 4 chinetes . . . 🔳🔳🔳 ▱ **6c+**
22m. A long bulging slab with a low crux. *Photo page 111.*
FA. José Miguel 1988

❺ Vacilando con lobos . . . . . 🔳 ▱ **6a+**
22m. Climb the juggy left wall of the red groove keeping left where the line splits to outflank the capping overhang.
FA. Chimo, José Antonio 1992

❻ Te cuelgan . . . . 🔳🔳 ▱ **6b+**
22m. Start as for the previous route but where the line splits take the harder road and tackle the tough overhang.
FA. Chimo 1991

❼ Verás que fuerte . . . . . 🔳🔳 ▱ **5+**
20m. Climb the long red groove to an awkward rightward exit.
FA. José Miguel 1987

❽ Inomminata . . . . 🔳 ▱ **5+**
20m. The blunt arete just right of the red corner.

❾ La muerte de la higuera . . 🔳 ▱ **6b+**
20m. Climb left of the spidery tree and finish left of the prow.
FA. José Miguel 1989

❿ Claveles . . . . 🔳🔳 ▱ **6b**
24m. A great route up the pocketed wall and short slab above.
FA. José Miguel, Pedro Lillo 1987

⓫ Te tiemblan . . . . . 🔳 ▱🔳🔳 **7a+**
14m. Steep moves past a hole to a lower-off on the rim.
FA. José Miguel 1990

⓬ Viviendo en una súplica . . 🔳 ▱ **6a**
24m. Follow the long groove leftwards then lower off or (better and harder) traverse right. The wide crack of the **Direct Finish** is best avoided! A right-hand exit through the bulges is **6b+**.
FA. Chimo 1989

⓭ Anda tié huevos . . . . . . 🔳🔳 ▱ **7b**
24m. The hard bulge via a ragged crack.
FA. José Miguel 1990

⓮ Cocodrilo Din Don . . . . 🔳🔳 ▱ **7b+**
20m. Climb into the scoop and finish up a steep diagonal crack.
FA. José Miguel 1989

⓯ La Ira del Tiempo . . . . 🔳 ▱ **7a**
20m. Up the rounded arete and bulge above.
FA. José Miguel 1987

⓰ El Amperio contra Paca 🔳🔳 ▱ **7a+**
24m. A steep start past a hole and a slab to a bulging finish.
FA. José Miguel 1988

㉓ Vamos Joaquín 6c
12m. The flake and blunt rib on the left is a soft-touch.
FA. Chimo, José Miguel 1988

㉔ Placa Solar . . . . 5+
12m. The polished central line is entertaining for the grade.
FA. Chimo, José Miguel 1988

㉕ Huesitos Krac 6b
12m. Tricky friction climbing on glassy holds.
FA. Chimo, José Miguel 1988

SECTOR POCKER DE BASI

㉖ Aquaforce 7c
8m. The bulging wall right of the tree is terrible.
FA. Chimo, José Miguel 1988

㉗ ? . . . .
10m. A new route following the bolts rightwards.

㉘ A Bassi le faltó . . . . ?
8m. Has it ever been done? Terrible and chipped.
FA. Roberto Bassi 1988

㉙ Lluvia de Arañas . . . . ?
10m. The diagonal crack-line is also probably incomplete.
FA. José Miguel 1988

㉚ Pocker de Bassi 8a
12m. The left-trending scoop and pockets.
FA. Roberto Bassi 1986

㉛ Hombres de Paja . . 7b
10m. Straight past the hole.
FA. John Bachar 1986. Whilst on a visit to the local Boreal factory.

㉜ Men of Still 6c
10m. Follow the pockets leftwards through the yellow scoop.
FA. John Bachar 1986

㉝ Estalactus Topus 7a
8m. A steep tufa and fierce undercut move.
FA. Chimo, José Miguel 1989

㉞ Mantequila de Nápoles . . . 6c+
8m. Just left of the wall follow the crack leftwards.
FA. Chimo, José Miguel 1990

⑰ Hambre de gamba . 8a
12m. Short and fierce.
FA. Machaca, Iván 1992

The next four routes have no topo but take lines up the right-hand side of the wall.

⑱ Txavito clavó 7c
12m. A short hard number.
FA. Txavo Vales 1988

⑲ Rompe Pelotas . . . . 7a+
24m. Start up the bubbly crack. There is a mid-height lower-off.
FA. Chimo, José Miguel 1988

⑳ Wary Wary Yeah . . . . . 7a+
10m. Direct to the lower-off of *Rompe* is short and technical.
FA. Chimo, José Miguel 1988

㉑ En la espera te esquino . . . . . 6a+
10m. Start at the 'beehive' and loop out right.
FA. Chimo, José Miguel 1988

㉒ María A . . . . 5+
12m. A short but not unpleasant slab.
FA. Chimo, José Miguel 1988

SECTOR POCKER DE BASI
The first sector encountered when you arrive at the crag is an extremely steep and bulging wall with some poor steep routes. Walk on by for better quality stuff.

Evening | 8 min | Sheltered

Change in viewing angle

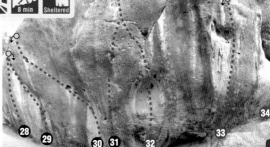

Murcia
Alicante
Benidorm
Calpe
Xaló Valley
Gandia
Marin
Salinas
Sax
Magdelena
Peña del Corb
Peña Rubia
Foradà
Ibi
Reconco
Agujas Rojas
Alcoi
Cabezon

115

FORADÀ

A fine varied cock's comb of a cliff which has a mega north-facing wall which gives some of the best steep climbing around. Pride of place has to be Sector Super Heroes; a steep wall of soaring, overhanging pocket-lines, a must for people into steep grade 7s and 8s. The other sectors on the north side are much the same as Super Heroes except on a lesser scale. Foradà also has some attractive easier routes on the slabby southern side; this a totally different proposition with routes at a much friendlier angle and in a beautiful sunny setting, with magnificent views. A couple of sectors have the odd trad route, but most climbs are well bolted with good lower-offs. A 60m route is useful for Sectors Super Heroes and Elecciones.

CONDITIONS

Apart from the 'soaring overhanging pocket-lines' the other major attraction of this crag is its useful-ness in extreme weather. The Foradà North Face is a great place to head for if it is really hot and it also has plenty to go at in wet weather, but it can be very cold compared to other crags in the area because of the altitude, at almost 1000m. In cold weather clever climbers will head straight for the South Face so that while the 'hard' team are freezing in search of a 'big tick' on the North Face, the less ambitious members of the team can sun themselves just round the corner.

APPROACH (area map page 77)

From junction 69 (University) on the A7, take the A36 as far as the first turn off for Castalla. Take this and follow the road into Castella and picking up brown signs Xorret de Cati - a rather fine hotel up in the mountains. Follow these steeply uphill and over the col to Xorret de Cati. Keep left and then turn left onto a track by a small pond just after the red-roofed hotel. Follow this to a sharp turn left where a chapel, partially hidden in the trees, can be seen up ahead. Continue to car parking on the left from where the crag is clearly visible. There are two easy routes on the wall behind the parking, both around grade 5. The left-hand track is the fastest way to the South Face and the business end of the North Face. Alternately approach the hotel of Xorret de Cati from Alicante via the A31 Madrid motorway. After about 30km take the exit signed 'Petrer, Elda, Centro Commercial'. Double back right off the exit road and follow signs (and the narrow bendy road) to Xorret de Cati, for 11km, to join the approach described above.

There is now a Refugio de Montana up the hill from Xorret de Cati.

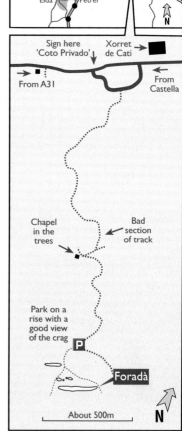

Mike Appleton on the mega-classic of *Elios* (7a+) on Sector Super Heroes at Foradà - *page 120*. Originally aided in the early 1970s, it was converted in to a great free climb in the 1990s. At an altitude of 1000m this north-facing wall is not an ideal winter venue - remember that woolly hat!

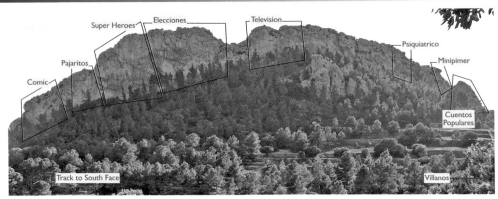

SECTOR VILLANOS

This small sector has several short routes which are quite tough for their grades. There are better routes on the main crag.

APPROACH - This is the short low wall passed on the right as you follow the right-hand approach track to the crag.

CONDITIONS - It faces north and gets little sun but is slightly more sheltered than the main North Face.

❶ Cabrales . . . . ☐ 6a+
10m. Slabby rock and a rightwards traverse.

❷ Valapenos . . . . ☐ 7a
10m. Direct to the same lower-off as *Cabrales*.

❸ Joker . . . . ☐ 7a
10m. The crimpy wall, trending left.
FA. Chiri Ros, Isabel Pagan 1990

❹ Pancho Villa . . . . ☐ 7a+
10m. The bulge and wall.
FA. Chiri Ros, Isabel Pagan 1991

❺ Doctor No . . . . ☐ 7a
10m. The thin crack is the best route here.
FA. Pedro Luis, Paco, Pedro 1989

❻ Lutor . . . . ☐ 6c+
10m. The overlaps right of the crack.
FA. Pedro Luis, Paco, Pedro 1989

❼ Esquelotor . . . . ☐ 6c+
10m. Past the half-height overlap.
FA. Pedro Luis, Paco, Pedro 1989

❽ Phantomas . . . . ☐ 7a+
10m. The penultimate route crosses the edge of the bulges.
FA. Pedro Luis, Paco, Pedro 1989

❾ Barrabas . . . . ☐ 6c
10m. Start where the overlaps disappear into the ground.
FA. Chiri Ros, Isabel Pagan, 'M' 1991

Murcia | Alicante | Benidorm | Calpe | Xaló Valley | Gandia | Maria | Salinas | Sax | Magdelena | Peña del Corb | Peña Rubia | Foradà | Ibi | Reconco | Agujas Rojas | Alcoi | Cabezon

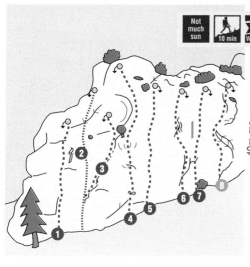

SECTOR COMIC/PAJARITOS

The first section of the North Face of Foradà is at the left-hand end where a series of short walls and slabs offer some interesting routes that are always in the shade.
APPROACH - The left-hand path to cliff leads straight here.
CONDITIONS - Shady and north-facing, this is a wall for warmer weather only.

❶ El pequeño Franenstein .. 🔲 **6c**
12m. The leftmost line on the wall starts just to the right of a huge fir tree and is a little horror.
FA. Chiri Ros 1990

❷ Mundo mutante ...... 🔲 **6c+**
14m. The wall directly above the rightward-leaning crack.
FA. Pedro, Paco 1989

❸ Pedrusco .... 🔲 **6b+**
14m. The slanting crack is very good.
FA. Chiri Ros, M.Amat 1990

❹ Sara .... 🔲 **6c**
18m. A great little climb over two bulges.
FA. Chiri Ros, Isabel Pagan, Paco 1989

❺ Torpedo .... 🔲 **6b+**
16m. Start up the slope to the right, climb past a hole with a small bush and then the right side of the bulges.
FA. Pedro Luis 1989

❻ El mercenario ...... 🔲 **6c+**
16m. The bulging wall is quite tough.
FA. Pedro Luis, Paco, Pedro 1989

❼ Legionario .... 🔲 **6c**
16m. The wall and then the overlaps immediately to the left of a left-facing flake system.
FA. Pedro, Paco 1990

❽ Comic .... 🔲 **5+**
16m. The left-facing flake and rather totty wall above are no laughing matter.
FA. Pedro, Paco 1989

There is then a short gap before a few more slabby offerings.

❾ Nuevo .... 🔲 **5**
14m. Just off the topo to the left.

❿ Chorlito .... 🔲 **5+**
12m. Share a lower-off with the next route.

⓫ Route 11 .... 🔲 **6a+**
14m. The slab with glued-on hold.

⓬ Gorrión .... 🔲 **6a+**
18m. The left-hand line leads through an overlap past the old belay to a recently moved lower-off. It is quite good fun.
FA. Pedro, Paco 1991

The next three routes share the same lower-off.

⓭ Golondrinas .... 🔲 **6a**
14m. Climb up to and through a bulge then step right.
FA. L.Montesinos, M.Amat 1989

⓮ Cucú .... 🔲 **6a+**
12m. The centre of the slab. This route can be continued, on natural gear, to the top of the crag if you really want to!
FA. L.Montesinos, M.Amat 1989

⓯ Periquito .... 🔲 **5**
14m. The right side of the slab trending left.
FA. L.Montesinos, M.Amat 1989

The start of the Sector Super Heroes is immediately to the right.

SECTOR SUPER HEROES

For those who are up to it this is the best sector at Foradà, in fact one of the best in the whole Costa Blanca. The climbing is unrelentingly steep but mostly on good holds and virtually all the routes are superb challenges.
APPROACH - From the main track that passes to the left of the ridge, pick up a track leading to the tallest wall just left of centre of the magnificent North Face.
CONDITIONS - It can be very cold in winter but once you start wrestling with these routes you will soon warm up. Finding someone to hold your ropes can be tricky though, especially if you are in for a long session. The wall gets no sun except on summer evenings but it can be lovely and cool here in the warmer months.

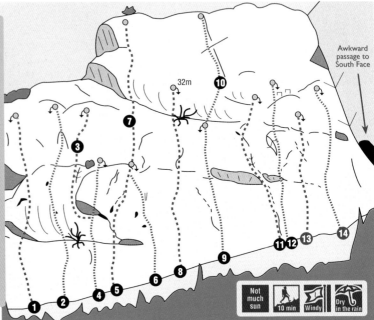

Awkward passage to South Face

32m

Not much sun | 10 min | Windy | Dry in the rain

❶ Escalibur ...... 🔲 **8a+**
30m. A huge pitch forging a line up the rock on the left-hand side of the biggest bulges. The left-hand finish is also **8a+**.

❷ Tundra ..... 🔲 **8a+**
32m. Pass the dead tree in the break and push on up the massively steep wall above. There are several good rests and the route is thought to be 'only 8a' by some.
FA. Jose Serrano, Jose Herdenández 1995

❸ Batman izquierda. 🔲 **8a**
32m. The left-hand finish to *Batman*. A long-time project which the locals now do laps on!

❹ Batman .... 🔲 **7b+**
24m. A powerful route through the bulges and substantial roof with an especially-tough clip near the lip though easier above.
FA. Pedro Luis, Paco, Pedro 1989

❺ Muscleman ...... 🔲 **7b**
24m. The overhanging groove and juggy pockets with a tough sequence just below easy ground is superb, especially if you get someone else to put the clips in! Low in the grade.
FA. Chiri Ros, Isabel Pagan 1991

❻ Rock'n Roll Exprés .... 🔲 **8a**
24m. A left-trending line to the *Muscleman* lower-off. Less good than its neighbours with some unpleasant moves.
FA. Chiri Ros 1992

❼ Satori .... 🔲 **8b**
30m. A soaring pitch from the *Muscleman* lower-off that goes on for ever up to the crest of the wall.

❽ Radicales libres .. 🔲 **8a+**
32m. A long sustained route which leads onto the head-wall.
FA. Jose Herdenández, Jose Serrano 1995

❾ Thor .... 🔲 **7b+**
26m. Intricate and sustained climbing which waits until you are pumped before turning really hard. Lower off or attempt ....
FA. Pedro, Paco 1989

❿ Plasticman .... 🔲 **8a+**
26m. The line of glued-on blobs above is **8a+** to the last bolt!
FA. Jose Herdenández, Jose Serrano 1994

⓫ Elios .... 🔲 **7a+**
28m. The majestic diagonal pocket-line gives a superb pitch. Lots of hard moves broken up with reasonable rests and a distinct crux on the bulge. *Photo page 117.*
FA. V.Freire, Santiago (aid) 1974. FFA. M.Amat, Tekila 1991

⓬ Guerrero del antifaz 🔲 **7b+**
28m. The continuously-leaning wall to the right of the thin crack is mostly 7a apart from a fierce crux pulling through the roof. Hard to on-sight.
FA. J.L.Clavel, M.Amat, L.Mont 1995

⓭ Spiderman ...... 🔲 **7a**
24m. The broad rib on the right is climbed on good but slick pockets until you thought it in the bag, and then there is a horrible precarious move to easy ground. **6c+** in the local topo!
FA. Pedro, Paco 1989

⓮ Starman .... 🔲 **7a**
24m. The broad rib before the major diagonal break gives an excellent pitch of pocket-pulling, easing after half-height. Easier than *Spiderman* - but only just.
FA. M.Amat, Juanvi 1994

32m

10m gap of poor rock

Sector Television 50m

Not much sun | **10 min** | **Windy** | **Dry in the rain**

Passage to South Face

THE PASSAGE - The passage between the two sectors can be used to access the South Face. It is awkward with a sack on but okay for between red-point sun breaks. A much safer approach is walk round the bottom of the fin.

SECTOR ELECCIONES

The wall right of the diagonal slit is almost as impressive as Sector Super Heroes. It is made up of a series of bulges and open grooves leading to a break below the bulging upper wall. Not surprisingly all the routes bale out at this point.
APPROACH and CONDITIONS - As for Sector Superheroes.

❶ Baby boom ... 🔲 **8b**
30m. The super-steep side wall of the gully complete with plenty of glued-on holds and upside down climbing.

❷ Bombe bombero .. 🔲 **8a+**
24m. A shorter rightward finish to *Baby Boom*.

❸ Los patos de la Moncloa. . 🔲 **7b+**
22m. Start just right of the huge slanting break and climb the lower wall to fingery moves on small holds where the rock turns white. Climb the slab above to finish.
FA. Chiri Ros, Isabel Pagan 1992

❹ Cámara Alta . . . . 🔲 **6c+**
22m. A steep start leads to the finish of the previous climb. An excellent long pitch and mild at the grade.
FA. Chiri Ros, M.Amat 1992

❺ Disturbio vertical . . . . . 🔲 **6c**
24m. Just to the right of the tree, tackle the wall and bulges. A fine route with a bit of everything including an obligatory jam!
FA. M.Amat, Tekila 1994

❻ El golfo de la guerra . . . . 🔲 **6b+**
20m. A bulge-laden line. Easy at the grade.
FA. Chiri Ros, M.Amat 1992

❼ La guerra del golfo . . . 🔲 **6b+**
20m. Climb through a red groove and continue over the bulges above. Given **6c** in the local topo.
FA. Lina, Manolo, Antoñin 1991

❽ Abstención . . . . 🔲 **6c**
18m. Attack the steep lower wall and a crinkly slab above then another tough wall section.
FA. L.Montesinos, M.Amat 1991

❾ La fuerza del parábola . 🔲 **6a**
16m. Start directly below a small red hole at 12m. Passing this hole is the crux.
FA. Lina, Manolo, Antoñin 1991

❿ Galimatías . . . . 🔲 **6c+**
32m. A slippery, slabby lower section leads to a series of bulges climbed on sharp holds and leading to a spectacular finish high on the arete. Highly entertaining.
FA. M.Amat, Tekila 1995

The next section of rock has no routes. 10m further right is a much shorter wall.

⓫ Pictolin . . . . 🔲 **6a**
14m. Pull onto a ledge and through a rickety bulge to reach a flake, exit to the right over another bulge. The bolts are good though it is a pity about the rock!
FA. Pedro Luis 1989

⓬ Sugus. . . . . 🔲 **6a+**
14m. The right-hand line is precarious low down and eases with height. Once again, the rock is not of the best quality.
FA. Pedro Luis, M.Amat 1989

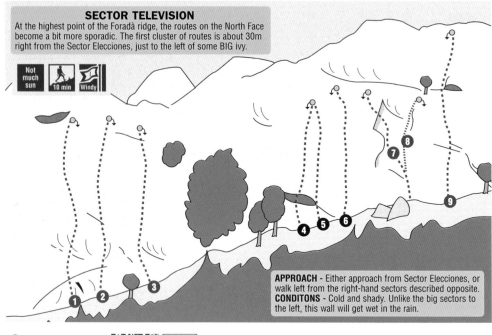

SECTOR TELEVISION
At the highest point of the Foradà ridge, the routes on the North Face become a bit more sporadic. The first cluster of routes is about 30m right from the Sector Elecciones, just to the left of some BIG ivy.

Not much sun | **10 min** | **Windy**

APPROACH - Either approach from Sector Elecciones, or walk left from the right-hand sectors described opposite.
CONDITONS - Cold and shady. Unlike the big sectors to the left, this wall will get wet in the rain.

❶ La calle de ritmo 6c+
20m. Climb two bulges to a lower-off below a small roof.
FA. Chiri Ros, Manolo, Tekila 199

❷ Waku-Waku 6c
20m. The central line leads through the large bulge.
FA. Chiri Ros, M.Amat 1990

❸ Sesión de tarde 6c
20m. The line just right of a small tree.
FA. Chiri Ros, Isabel Pagan 1990

The next routes are past the ivy to the right, by a small roof.

❹ El último mohicano 7c
20m. Pull over the roof on the left - protected by big ring bolts.
FA. John Bachar 1990

❺ Quieres que el tigre 7b+
20m. Steep wall climbing on small holds, easing with height.
FA. Chiri Ros, Isabel Pagan 1991

❻ Bum-Bum 7a+
20m. A fine climb. A bouldery start leads to slopers.
FA. Chiri Ros, Isabel Pagan 1990

❼ Recién venido 6b+
18m. The large flake/corner is protected with white bolts.

❽ El precio justo 7a
16m. Start in the same place as the previous route but move right over a bulge, via a crack. The second clip is tricky and the end is a bit sudden.
FA. Pedro Luís, Paco, Pedro 1989

❾ Carta de adujiste 7a
24m. The right-hand climb in this sector has a technical central bulge and a delicate finish past a dodgy-feeling flake.
FA. Pedro, Paco 1991

SECTOR PSIQUIATRICO
About 80m down the hill, from the highest point on the ridge, is a short wall with two steep routes on it.

❿ Carne de psiquatrico 7a
12m. Climb into a horizontal slot and over the bulge above.
FA. Pedro Luis, Biberón, 'M' 1989

⓫ Bloqueo mental 7b
12m. The wall past a useful tufa.
FA. Pedro, Paco 1989

SECTOR MINIPIMER
At the very bottom of the ridge is a short wall that gets the evening sun.

⓬ Termomix 7b
14m. The left-hand line is very technical.
FA. Chiri Ros, Paco 1989

⓭ Picadora Mulinex 7a+
14m. Start as for *Termomix* but trend right across the wall.
FA. Chiri Ros, M.Amat 1989

⓮ Minipimer 7a+
14m. Steeper but less sustained than its neighbours.
FA. Txavo Vales 1988

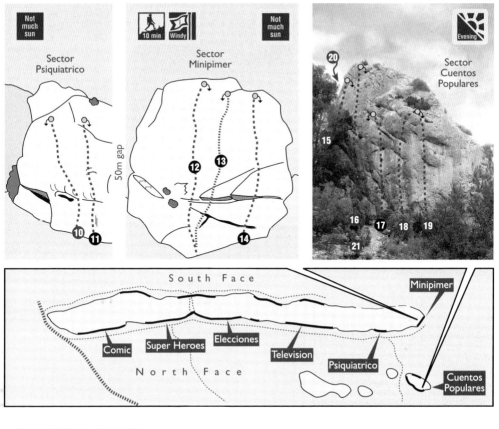

SECTOR CUENTOS POPULARES
This is the left-hand (looking at the North Face) of the two pinnacles in front of its right-hand side. It has several routes on its shady side. The other pinnacle has little of interest.

⑮ Tres cerditos . . . . 🔳🖼 ▭ **6c**
20m. The steep face just right of the arete.
FA. Pedro Luis, Paco, Pedro 1989

⑯ Cuentos populares . . . . 🔳🖼 ▭ **7a**
22m. The centre of the highest part of the face.
FA. Pedro Luis, Paco, Pedro 1989

⑰ Dumbo . . . . 🖼 ▭ **7a+**
14m. The short wall and small bulges just to the right.
FA. Pedro, Paco 1990

⑱ Pinocho . . . . ▭ **6b+**
14m. The warm up for the face.
FA. Pedro, Paco 1990

⑲ Juan Sin Miedo . . . . 🖼 ▭ **7a**
14m. A direct line to the lower-off of the previous route, passing the left edge of an overlap at half-height.
FA. Chiri Ros, Paco 1989

NORTH FACE - RIGHT
The right-hand (west) end of the massive north face of Foradà, is less appealing to climbers and only offers a few worthy sections of rock.
APPROACH - Follow the right-hand branch of the main approach track towards the pinnacle of Cuentos Populares and further on, to the wall with the other two sectors.

On the south side of the pinnacle is a short tufa line.

⑳ Las botas de 7 leguas . 🔳🎗 ▭ **6c+**
14m. Plough up the enticing tufas.
FA. Txavo Vales 1988

The smaller pinnacle to the right (looking at the North Face) of the main pinnacle, has a solitary route.

㉑ Chiquitín. . . . . ▭ **6b+**
10m. The bolted slab with a steep start.
FA. M.Amat, Chiri Ros 1989

SECTOR PETORRI/DESCOTE

The sunny south face has some pleasant slab climbing and superb views. The routes on offer tend to be at a lot friendlier grades than the steeper North Face.

The highest sectors on the ridge consists of a couple of clean walls with a good set of routes.

APPROACH - Follow the main track which passes under the lowest point of the ridge. Then turn the corner and head up the hill, arriving at Sector Goteta first. You can also approach from the other end of the fin or through the middle of the cliff via an awkward scramble (not advised).

CONDITIONS - This superbly-situated wall catches every ray of sunlight going until late in the day. It can be extremely warm and pleasant, or hot and oppressive. However, it is exposed to any wind that there is and the whole crag is quite high so it will be a LOT colder up here than down at the coast at all times.

① Fácil . . . . **3+**
10m. An easy and tiny climb on the far left. A connection across to the next route is better, but a bit harder.

② Bon día **5**
14m. Climb a left-sloping ramp and a bulging rib then traverse right below the roof to a lower-off on the next climb.

③ Cursilería **4**
14m. An excellent beginner's climb. Start just right of a large bush and pull over an overlap then pass left of a tufa streak to reach the lower-off.
FA. V.Freire, J.Pedro Verdú 1991

④ Lo corto . . . . **5+**
10m. The short line of four bolts to a big lower-off.

⑤ Fama de gos . . . . . **5+**
16m. Start left of the blunt rib, left of the 'X' shaped crack. Make sustained moves up the slab with a crux move over the centre of the final bulge.
FA. J.Pedro Verdú, V.Escolano 1990

The next section of the slab has a lot of bolts and it is rather easy to get confused. All the routes are worth doing.

⑥ Pilar **5**
16m. One of the best in this sector is the direct line, starting at the left edge of the X, and pressing up superb rock above.
FA. V.Freire, Pilar Perseguer 1990

⑦ Noche golfa . . . . **5+**
16m. Climb through the right side of the X then directly up the slab (blinkers!) before moving left to join the last climb. It is also possible to trend right to join the next route.
FA. J.Pedro Verdú, V.Escolano 1991

⑧ Paula . . . . **5+**
16m. Start up a right-slanting crack to reach holes and a flake then head on up the pleasantly-sustained slab slightly rightwards to chains set above a bulge.
FA. V.Mialles, V.Freire 1975

⑨ Tiburón . . . . **5+**
16m. Start at a wide crack, leading to a break containing a small shrub, and climb via a mid-height bulge. Then follow the slab and a final groove to the shared lower-off.

⑩ Otra ruta . . . . 🔆🔲 5+
18m. Start up broken yellow rock and climb to a short crack to a taxing exit. Move right to a lower-off below a bulge.

⑪ Nuevo ruta . . . . 🔆🔲 6a+
18m. Climb broken rock (1st bolt in a bulge) then up cracks to steeper territory. Step right and climb the shield (steep) to easier ground above.

10m to the right is an easier slab with two pleasant lines. This section is referred to as Sector Descote in the local guide.

⑫ Left . . . . 🔆🔲 4
14m. The left-hand line has a steep but juggy upper section.

⑬ Right . . . . 🔲 3
10m. The tiny right-hand offering.

The next climbs are 20m to the right where a slabby groove forms the left-hand edge of a narrow slab.

⑭ Caballería . . . . 🔆🔲 4+
A two pitch route, on natural gear. It isn't popular.
1) 4, 14m. Start up a right-facing corner (peg) to reach a stance and two peg belay on the left.
2) 4+, 16m. Continue up the slab then a right-trending groove before moving right to a belay/lower-off just short of the ridge. Abseil off.

⑮ Marisol . . . . 🔆🔲 6a
16m. The left-hand side of the slab right of the groove, is climbed direct and is well equipped. There is a thin bulge early on and then it is much easier.

⑯ Freire sin aceite . . . . 🔆🔲 6a
16m. The centre of the slab gives a good pitch with a 'bloc' move passing the small slab at two-thirds height. A line of black bolts marks the way.

⑮ Espolón derecha . . . . 🔆🔲 6a+
16m. The right-hand side of the blunt rib is the hardest here.

⑱ Mujer furtivo . . . . 🔆🔲 6a+
16m. The line up the bubbly rock is pleasant and not too hard for the grade.

⑲ Route 19 . . . . 🔲 5+
12m. A shorter line on the right, passing a couple of old pegs.

⑳ Cosme . . . . 🔲 5+
16m. Beyond a long broken corner is a rib that starts at the foot of a blocky ramp, on the other side of the gully. Follow this throughout with two crux sections; a delicate one early on, and a strenuous one higher up.

SECTOR DEL FORAT/GOTETA

The lower section of the South face has two developed areas; the left-hand one has some routes around the exit-hole from the through-cave, and the right-hand area is the good clean slab down to the right, below a large curving roof. All the routes here are worthwhile.

APPROACH and CONDITIONS - As on previous page.

① La golondrina . . . . 6a+
14m. The left-hand line up a fine flake gives sustained climbing. Gold-coloured bolts and a thin move at two-third's height.

② Mama Ukri 6b
16m. Sustained face climbing passing a crucial bulge near the top on poor pockets. Silver bolts protect.

③ Chorro sin agua 6a
16m. The central line to the shared lower-off starts just to the right of a flake with a small bush. Avoid the use of the flake for the full effect

④ Sube que es gratis . . . . 6a+
14m. Climb the steep face using good pockets with one move on crimps. Good climbing.

⑤ Ana A2
A curious route which sees little attention.
1) A2, 14m. Aid up the bolt ladder on the leaning wall to the left of the ramp to a small stance.
2) A1 and 5+, 10m. Pull over the bulge on aid and free climb to the top.

⑥ Route 6 . . . . ?
18m. The leaning wall and roofs above the through-tunnel looks like it is going to be quite taxing.

⑦ Del Forat . . . . 5+
22m. Climb the ramp to the right of the through cave. Good climbing but with a hard crux bulge.

⑧ Javier Muñoz . . . . 6a+
12m. Start at the white arrow and climb the short bulging rib past some awkward moves.

⑨ Plutga . . . . 5+
24m. Follow the bulging ramp to its end then climb steeply and trend back left to the lower-off. An excellent route and very atmospheric considering its size.

⑩ Route 10 . . . .
18m. The leaning wall and roofs above look very hard!

On the left is an old line leading up the flakes below the crack in the big overhang. It is not equipped and no details are known.

⑪ Mayaya . . . . 5+
20m. Pull over an overlap early on (old first couple of bolts) then pass round the left edge of another overlap by steep moves and continue on sharp holds. Quite tough at the grade.

⑫ Llei dels Maleans 6a
20m. A steep start up a crack (stand on the loose block) and a crucial bulge (wire thread) at half-height are the main difficulties on this one. The finish is rather prickly. *Photo opposite.*

The next three routes share the same initial bolt reached from a ledge behind the bushes.

⑬ McFlay . . . . 5+
20m. From the ledge, climb left of the bolt, up a crack. Then pass the overlap and gain the slab before trending slightly left to tricky and sharp moves up to the large lower-off.

⑭ Panchuflas . . . . 5+
20m. From the ledge, follow the central bolt line with sustained (and sharp) interest until it is possible to pull rightwards across an overlap to reach the lower-off.

⑮ Cristina . . . . 5+
20m. The final equipped route off the ledge proves to be the best route here, initially passing right of the first bolt and with thin moves into and out off the scoop at half-height.

Chris Craggs on *Llei dels Maleans* (6a) on Sector Goteta at Foradà - *opposite*. Photo: Sherri Davy

IBI

A closely packed set of routes running steeply up the side of a 'barranco' or rocky ravine. The ravine is called the Barranco de los Molinos and at least one the mills (a water-powered affair) is still there. The routes are well protected and tend to be steep, strenuous and fingery; some of the rock is rather suspect though most of it is fine. As is so often the case with 'out-of-the-way' locations, the grades here veer towards being on the harsh side; be prepared to either drop your sights a little or have a tussle. Climbers who operate in the 6s and low 7s and who enjoy technical faces should find enough climbing for a good day's sport here. Many of the climbs have their names painted on the rock or stamped on the first bolt bracket. Much more in the way of descriptions would be superfluous, just pick a line and go for it.

Almost all climbs here were originally equipped single-handedly by Miguel Muñoz back in 1989/90 - a fair effort!

APPROACH (area map page 77)

Leave the A7 at junction 70 which is initially signed to 'San Vicente' and then 'Alcoi' and take the A36 road past Castalla to Ibi. Turn into the town and use the map to the right to navigate your way to the Baneres (CV801) road on the northern edge of town. About 1km after leaving the town there is a right turn, just before the second bridge, and just beyond a 'no overtaking' sign. Drive down the track past a red 'probihut fer foc' sign and park on the right after 100m. Leave nothing in the car. Walk to the mill (water, water - everywhere!) and climb steps just in front of it to reach the base of the crag. Scramble up the slope to find the object of your desire - and some flat ground!

CONDITIONS

The cliff faces north west and thus only gets the sun quite late on in the day, because of this it can be a rather cool venue in the winter. Early in the day it provides a shady retreat in hotter weather. There is often a breeze blowing down the Barranco which helps keep things cool when the heat is on and makes conditions bitter when the weather is cold!

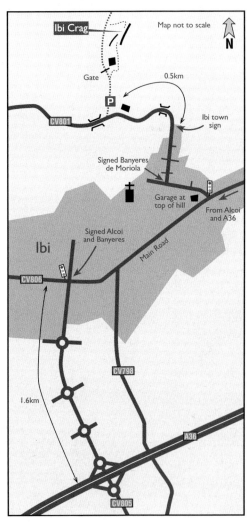

Dave Spencer enjoying a bit of morning shade on *Chorizo Bailarin* (6a+) on the rocky tower of the Peña Almarra, at Ibi - *page 131*.

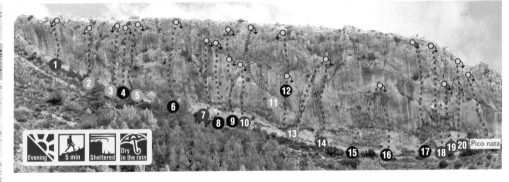

BARRANCO DE LOS MOLINOS
At the top of the slope is a long leaning wall of variable quality rock. The crag gets the sun late in the day and is a good venue on hot days. The descriptions are like the routes - short and sharp!

1 Woldan .... `7a`
12m. The tufa on the far left currently needs rebolting.

2 Búho .... `5`
12m. The steep (and hopefully owl-less) crack.

3 Chinto fano .... `6a+`
12m. The leaning wall is well supplied with jugs.

4 Carlo y bruña .... `7b`
12m. The tough pillar to the left of the crack systems.

5 Stalak .... `5`
14m. The bulging crack leads to ledges. More of the same above. Gear needed.

6 Rompe dedos .... `7b`
20m. The leaning wall leads to ledges and an easier finish.

7 Mediterráneo Free ...... `6c+`
18m. The pocketed grey rib on good-but-spaced holds.

8 Bacalao de Bilbao .... `7a+`
18m. Climb the steep wall to a good flake and a leaning finish.

9 El vira .... `7b`
22m. Start up the wide awkward crack but leap left into a thinner crack. Up this to the bulges (6c to here) and the crux.

10 Route 10. .... `7a`
12m. The short steep wall right of the crack.

11 La traverse de les figúrese ... `6a+`
22m. Climb the pocketed wall to a vague diagonal line and follow this to a steep finishing crack on the left.

12 La chica yeye .... `7b+`
18m. Start as for *La traverse..* but climb the wall to the bulges (7a+ to here). Finish with great difficulty.

13 Variante Pontect .... `4`
14m. The steep juggy diagonal needs gear - pity really!

14 Pontect. .... `6c`
14m. The leaning crack to a juggy hole, then more of the same.

15 No name dos. .... `7a+`
14m. The pumpy diagonal splitting the rust-coloured rock.

16 La cegaste Burlan Castor . `8a`
14m. Directly up the leaning wall to a hard exit.

17 Bon perfil .... `7b`
24m. Climb the steep wall to the right of a dead tree with difficulty, then on up still steep rock to a ledge. Finish direct.

18 Intron 'A' .... `7a`
24m. Climb through the overhangs and up a short smooth wall then take the juggier arete above.

19 Paranoia. .... `6c`
14m. A shorter pitch through the widest part of the overhang.

20 Viril os .... `6c`
22m. Climb the steep wall to the right of the overhangs to reach a ledge then the easier ground above.

Barranco de
Los Molinos

PEÑA ALMARRA

A fine wall of compact grey limestone running up the side of the steep slope directly above the mill. The routes tend to be steep, fingery and quite hard for the grade and really they are too closely packed.

① Pico nata . . . . 6a+
20m. Climb through the inverted scoop (steep!) to jugs then trend left across the wall (still steep) to a lower-off on the edge.

② Que potiti . . . . 6c+
12m. A short route up the right edge of the orange streak and the leaning wall above.

③ Figurita 6a
16m. The scoopy slab an leaning wall to jugs.

④ Valla marrón 6c
14m. The right arete of the slab and leaning pillar above.

⑤ Tela con la Paula 6c
16m. A leaning wall leads to a slab and an easy groove.

⑥ Artero no seas duro . . . 7a
16m. A very thin wall climb.

⑦ Licencia para matar . . . . . 6c+
16m. A steep start and technical finish.

⑧ Maldita hepatitis . . . . 6b+
16m. The scoops offer a relatively easy way up the wall.

⑨ Linda bonita 6b
16m. Pull into the shallow groove and bridge up this.

⑩ No te inquietes un 7 . . . . 6b+
16m. The leaning wall leads to an easier rib above.

⑪ Uhele a bacalao 6b
16m. From a grassy niche climb the steep wall leftwards.

⑫ Show de yemas . . . . 6b+
20m. The sustained wall from the right-hand side of the niche.

⑬ Chorizo Bailaran . . . . 6a+
20m. The right-hand side of the tall tower is good.
Photo page 129.

⑭ Capullos en flor 6a
14m. Fingery moves right if the orange scoop.

⑮ H.M.T. 6b
14m. Hard climbing left of the water-streak.

⑯ Hola mi Belén . . . . 5+
14m. The rib right of the water-streak is hard!

⑰ Taifons S2. . . . . 6a+
16m. Technical climbing past a couple of clumps of grass.

⑱ Hipermania 6a
14m. An hour-glass shaped pillar leads to good climbing above.

⑲ Mama ya lo sabe 5
14m. A steep start then easier beyond.

⑳ Ali Baba . . . . 5+
14m. Pleasant enough.

㉑ Leiva show 5
14m. The blunt rib that is the last real feature of the wall.

㉒ Las pelotas rosas 5
10m. Short and with a steep start.

㉓ Luz solar . . . . 5+
10m. A 'quickie' that gets the sun first.

Murcia · Alicante · Benidorm · Calpe · Xaló Valley · Gandia · Marin · Salinas · Sax · Magdelena · Peña del Corb · Peña Rubia · Forada · Ibi · Reconco · Agujas Rojas · Alcoi · Cabezon

RECONCO

Reconco is a superb crag with a good range of middle grade routes on perfect, slabby rock; it is a great pity the place is not a couple of kilometres wide! It is beautifully situated on a hillside above a pleasant rural valley and is easy to find. The only slight drawback is its distance from the main accommodation spots but stick to the motorway and you'll get there surprisingly quickly. As a venue it makes a superb alternative to the popular and polished areas at Toix and Sella with a similar grade range and significantly more routes that have not been battered to death yet!

Most of the routes are long single pitches, although there are some two pitch routes on the right-hand side, and most of these prove to be particularly good. All the routes are clean and well-equipped but the rock has many small pockets and is a bit sharp and taxing on the skin. Route finding shouldn't be a problem as the names and grades are stamped on tags on many of the first bolts and there is the occasional painted name on the rock.

All the routes here were equipped and climbed by Juan Mario Marcos and José Aurelio with a few additions by Miguel Muñoz between 1989 and 1993.

CONDITIONS

The crag faces south east and is exposed so it also catches plenty of sun and any wind that is going. There is little shelter at the base of the wall apart from a single almond tree. Access isn't a problem at the moment but try to park with consideration to avoid antagonising the locals and don't block the access track.

APPROACH (area map page 77)

Recent road improvements have made getting to Reconco a bit easier although exactly where all the new roads are going remains a bit unclear. Development continues so please inform us of any new developments. From the coast leave the A7 at junction 70 which is initially signed to 'San Vicente' and then 'Alcoi' and take the new A36 road to Castalla. After passing Castalla head west on the CV80 towards Sax and Villena and get off at the next junction (signed to Biar and Onil). Turn towards Onil and 0.7km after the roundabout is a white house on the right with black and gold railings. Opposite this are several tracks, take the right-hand one (rough!) nearest to Onil, and park a little way up this on the left. The cliff is clearly visible on the hillside directly above. Follow the sandy track up through the trees and the steep, open hillside above.

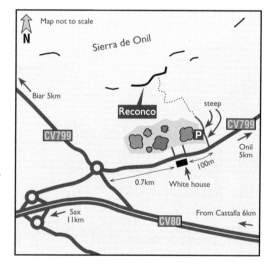

John Addy shadow dancing on *Dit-Laser* (6a+) Reconco -*page 134*. This route is typical of many on the cliff, offering sustained climbing up superb sheets of compact grey limestone. A stiff pair of boots and strong fingers are great assets here.

RECONCO

Murcia
Alicante
Benidorm
Calpe
Xaló Valley
Gandia
Maria
Salinas
Sax
Magdalena
Peña del Cerro
Peña Rubia
Forada
Ibi
Reconco
Agujas Rojas
Alcoi
Cabezon

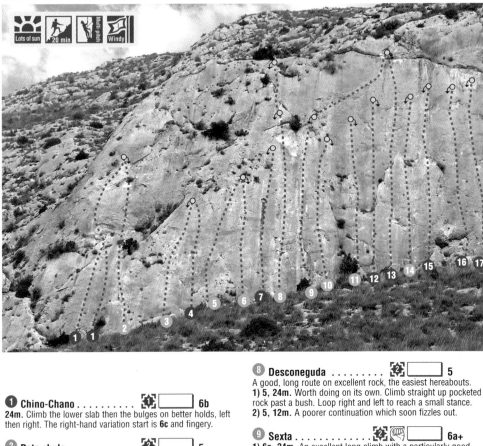

❶ Chino-Chano . . . . 🔲 6b
24m. Climb the lower slab then the bulges on better holds, left then right. The right-hand variation start is **6c** and fingery.

❷ Pata chula . . . . 🔲 5+
24m. Excellent. Climb a grey tufa streak and thin layback crack then move left. Steeper rock and a thin slab lead to the belay.

❸ El Rey del seis A . . . . 🔲 6a+
14m. Climb the rounded rib (hard) then go rightwards.

❹ Corbella . . . . 🔲 6b
14m. Start in an orange scoop and climb up this on pockets and past shrubbery onto a steep bubbly wall.

❺ Pa en cubitos . . . . 🔲 6a+
16m. Climb out of the right side of the scoop and trend slightly rightwards to a lower-off at the level of some ledges.

❻ Gorbachov . . . . 🔲 6a
16m. Follow small sharp holds and then jugs as thing steepen to a lower-off at the change in angle.

❼ Tachar . . . . 🔲 6b+
18m. Climb to and straight up the brown streak to the hole at its apex. Sharp, sustained and hard for the grade.

❽ Desconeguda . . . . 🔲 5
A good, long route on excellent rock, the easiest hereabouts.
1) 5, 24m. Worth doing on its own. Climb straight up pocketed rock past a bush. Loop right and left to reach a small stance.
2) 5, 12m. A poorer continuation which soon fizzles out.

❾ Sexta . . . . 🔲 6a+
1) 6a, 24m. An excellent long climb with a particularly good second pitch. Climb flakes and cracks up a grey streak then past a white scar to a belay in a niche.
2) 6a+, 20m. Traverse a long way up and right to the roof. Pull over to finish. Take care if you lower off.

❿ Paris-Texas . . . . 🔲 6a+
28m. Start at the blue painted name and climb the white rib passing a thread, and then some ledges to a lower-off in a bay.

⓫ Canal . . . . 🔲 6a
26m. The left side of the scoop with a tricky start and finish.

⓬ Servina . . . . 🔲 6b+
28m. Excellent climbing up the rounded scoop. The bulge at the start is tricky, as is the finish.

⓭ Directa . . . . 🔲 6b
1) 6b, 28m. Start at the scratched name and climb the right rib of the scoops to a small ledge.
2) 6a+, 12m. A short pitch to the lower-off of *Sexta*.

⓮ Dit-Laser . . . . 🔲 6a+
28m. Start at a crack that rises diagonally to the right. Climb the broad front of the buttress to chains below the overlap.
Photo page 133.

㉒ Chica de moda . . . . . . 🔲🔲🔲 6b+
1) 6a+, 26m. Climb right of the flake crack then pull through the centre of the over-lap to reach a tiny stance.
2) 6b+, 26m. A long and surprising pitch up the steeper wall and a delectable blank slab to easy ground.

㉓ Ruda . . . . 🔲🔲🔲🔲 6b+
1) 6b, 22m. The centre of the slab is sustained and crimpy with crucial moves at half height to a poor stance just below a bulge.
2) 6b+, 28m. Pass the bulge by moving out left (crux) then continue on finger holds through another bulge to easy ground.

㉔ La lágrima . . . . 🔲🔲 6b
1) 6a, 30m. A good easier pitch. Steep moves lead to a hole, and leaving this is tricky and sustained to a cramped stance.
2) 6b, 24m. Pull left through the bulge and into the large hole of 'the teardrop'. Exit from this (crux) and head for the top.

㉕ La lágrima derecha 🔲🔲🔲 7a
1) 6a, 30m. As for *La lagrima*.
2) 7a, 26m. A superb right-hand finish along the undercut flakes with some well-positioned moves into the scoop.

㉖ La Pelma . . . . 🔲 5+
18m. Tackle the left-hand line keeping left of the vegetated rock then move slightly right to the belay.

㉗ Sense por . . . . 🔲 5
18m. From the bay follow a pleasant flake up leftwards.

㉘ Fama de fuga . . . . . . 🔲🔲 7a
1) 4, 20m. The easy slab to a stance.
2) 7a, 24m. A sustained wall leads to the bulge before the pleasant finishing scoop.

㉙ Super Ali . . . . 🔲🔲 6c
1) 4, 20m. The unremarkable grassy slab.
2) 6c, 24m. A hard finish up the centre of the wall.

㉚ Tedy Man . . . . 🔲🔲🔲 7a
1) 4, 20m. As for *Super Ali*.
2) 7a, 24m. A reach-dependent alternative finish to *Super Ali*.

Right of here is a large roof with no climbs.

RECONCO - FAR RIGHT
There is another small buttress down and right of the main wall which is worth seeking out if it is windy. The six routes are all good but no details are known apart from the grades.

㉛ Route 31 . . . . 🔲 7a

㉜ Route 32 . . . . 🔲 6b+

㉝ Route 33 . . . . 🔲 6c

㉞ Route 34 . . . . 🔲 6a+

㉟ Route 35 . . . . 🔲 6b

⑮ Lengua Free . . . . 🔲 6b+
24m. A good lower section climbs through the diagonal over-lap. Sustained face climbing leads to a final hard moves to the lower-off. Sadly it is easier to step left to join the last route.

⑯ La perla del Caribe . . . 🔲🔲 6c
28m. Two squares left of the tree. Climb to an overlap then pull through this and on up the sustained grey face to a hard finish.

⑰ Chunay-Free . . . . 🔲🔲 6c+
28m. Start left of the tree and climb steepening rock into a scoop. The leftward exit from this proves to be the crux.

⑱ En busca del Postes 🔲🔲🔲 7b
28m. Behind the right edge of the tree, an easy start leads to sustained climbing trending leftwards up the tan-coloured wall.

⑲ No es tan guay . . . 🔲🔲🔲 7a+
26m. Climb past the left edge of the prominent overlap then head up the steep sharp wall to a lower-off by a tree in a bay.

⑳ Gemma Boom . . . . 🔲🔲🔲 7a
30m. Start behind the tree and climb the left-hand side of the pale grey streak by a fiercely sharp and sustained pitch.

㉑ Central . . . . 🔲 5+
18m. This delightful route follows the big flake and right-slant-ing overlap to a mid-height lower-off. The groove is mostly juggy but there is one tricky section.

Murcia · Alicante · Benidorm · Calpe · Xaló Valley · Gandia · Marin · Salinas · Sax · Magdalena · Peña del Corb · Peña Rubia · Forada · Ibi · Reconco · Aguila Rojas · Alcoi · Cabezon

AGUJAS ROJAS

Agujas Rojas is a small collection of pinnacles, in a picturesque woodland setting, on a secluded hillside just north of the town of Onil. The orange and yellow coloured walls offer about 40 routes for face-climbing enthusiasts; all well-bolted climbs and generally on good quality rock. Most of the routes are in the high 6s and 7s with only a small selection routes below 6a and unfortunately the very best of the climbs here also look like the hardest! The approach is very easy, being only minutes from the parking, and the crag could be a good one to combine with a visit to Reconco or just a place to enjoy a bit of peace and quiet away from the crowds at Sella and Toix. Quite a few of the harder (and even some of the easier) routes are chipped and glued, which is sad really.

The ever productive Miguel Muñoz discovered, bolted and climbed virtually every single route at this crag between 1991 and 1994.

APPROACH
(area map page 77)

From the coast leave the A7 at junction 70 to access the A36, which is initially signed to 'San Vicente' and then 'Alcoi'. Follow the A36 north to Castalla. As you pass Castalla follow signs off the motorway to Onil. Continue towards Onil until just short of the town you arrive at a roundabout and turn right. This turns into the Baneras Road; follow it for less than a kilometre to a left fork that heads uphill. Go up this for about 1.3km, past a pink house ('El Pan Sucre') on the left. The crags are visible as a series of tawny-coloured faces just uphill from the

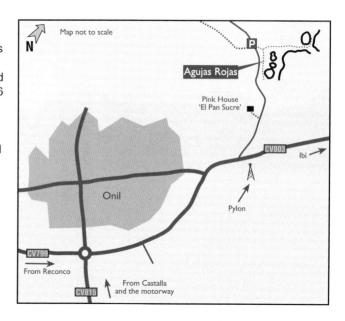

road. Park just beyond the cliff at a small gravelled shoulder just off the road and within sight of the crag. There are several paths leading from the road up through the woods to the crags. Leave nothing in the car.

CONDITIONS

Although there are some south and some north-facing routes, most of the main faces are tipped towards the west sky. The sparse tree cover offers some shelter from the sun and the wind (and makes photography a pain) however there is not much climbing on offer here in the rain. The position of the cliff, on the edge of the valley, means it is often breezier than you might be expecting. The crag is quick-drying, as the towers take little in the way of drainage.

The right-hand exit to *Escupe cubatas* (6b) on Sector Las Esfinge at Agujas Rojas - *page 141*. The photograph illustrates both the climbing and the setting here; steep orange walls in a sparse Mediterranean pine forest and only seconds from the road.

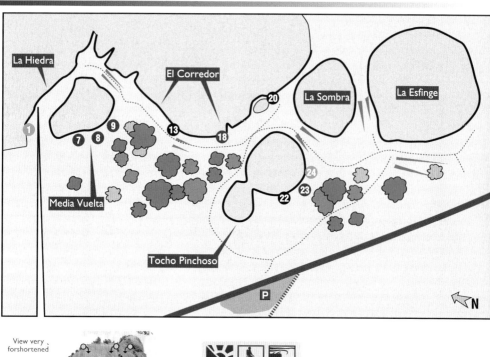

Murcia
Alicante
Benidorm
Calpe
Xaló Valley
Gandia
Maria
Salinas
Sax
Magdalena
Peña del Conó 'Peña Rubia
Foradà
Ibi
Reconco
Agujas Rojas
Alcoi
Cabezon

View very forshortened

Afternoon | 3 min | Sheltered

❸ Jumpin' Jask Flash . . . 🔧🪨 [____] **7a**
24m. Hard work up the slightly overhanging arete.

❹ Niu de arrayanes . . . . . 🔧🪨 [____] **7c+**
24m. The same start then tackle the superb scoop to the right.

❺ Jack el destrepador . . . 🔧🪨 [____] **7c+**
28m. An overhanging face climb with small shallow pockets up the streak to the pocket then wall above.

❻ Lagramusa . . . 🔧🪨🪨 [____] **8a**
28m. The fantastic scooped wall on the right side of the face.

SECTOR MEDIA VUELTA
The pinnacle in front of Sector La Hiedra has three unremarkable lines on it. See the map for their locations.

❼ Route 7 . . . . [____] **?**
14m. The back of the pinnacle.

❽ Route 8 . . . . 🪨 [____] **6c**
14m. The central line.

❾ Route 9 . . . . [____] **?**
14m. The right-hand line.

SECTORS LA HIEDRA/MEDIA VUELTA
The furthest sector up the hill is a tall vertical wall behind the pinnacle of the Sector Media Vuelta. It is reached by a short scramble under the rest of the cliff. The routes are mostly hard and very smooth; steel fingers are a must. In the main, they look excellent - well worth the effort.

❶ El Raco . . . . 🔧 [____] **6b**
14m. A short pitch just right of the dry-stone walling.

❷ Stalak . . . . [____] **(8a?)**
20m. The smooth leaning wall right again.

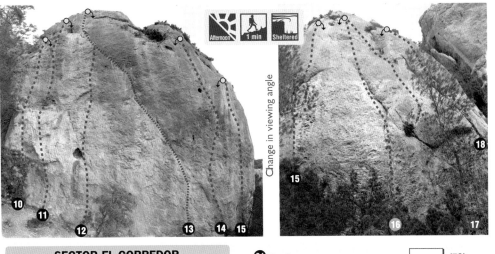

Change in viewing angle

SECTOR EL CORREDOR

The most important sector here with a bunch of routes in the Black Zone. Steep, sharp and sustained is the name of the game. The routes get the sun late on in the day and provide welcome shade at other times.

⑩ Edu el travieso 7b
14m. The left-most route on the wall.

⑪ Nit de bruixes .... 7b+
16m. Sustained climbing up the blunt rib.

⑫ My Gym .... 7b+
18m. The direct start to *L'Babao* via the huge pocket. Hard!

⑬ L'Babao 7b
22m. The thin and intermittent crack is quite superb.

⑭ Chip-Chop .... 7b+
18m. The thin wall past the big pocket to a high crux.

⑮ Mama Chicho . 7c
14m. The last route before the arete.

⑯ Mentireta .... 6a+
24m. The shallow slanting groove on the left side of the face is a corker giving sustained climbing to a final blank section.

⑰ Los tarugos 6b
22m. Pull through the centre of the overlap and then climb the flake and the face above to the lower-off of *Mentireta*.

⑱ Un 6b I si no tambe .. 7a+
22m. The right side of the face starting by a flake and leading to some very sketchy face climbing on the grey slab above.

⑲ Turbo deisel 7a
26m. The crack and hanging prow above is another cracker, though lovers of elegant face climbing won't enjoy the start!

⑳ Hay bruneta .... 7c+
28m. Superb climbing up the leaning wall.

㉑ Route .... (7?)
26m. The right-hand side of the face looks tough.

SECTOR TOCHO PINCHOSO
A short, red tower has three lines on it.

㉒ Marabu .... 7a+
12m. The left-hand line.

㉓ Cipriano toca el piano 6c
12m. The middle line has a bulge at mid-height.

㉔ Hay Madonna .... 6a+
12m. The right-hand line.

Murcia · Alicante · Benidorm · Calpe · Xaló Valley · Gandia · Marín · Salinas · Sax · Magdalena · Peña del Corb · Peña Rubia · Forada · Ibi · Reconco · Agujas Rojas · Alcoi · Cabezon

SECTOR A LA SOMBRE
This smaller pinnacle sits in the shade of the larger La Esfinge. There are two short, slick, slabby offerings here.

1 Fumador no .... 🧗📋 **6a**
12m. The flake and slab on the left is quite tricky, the polished holds at the start don't help, though it is usual to smoke up it!

2 Cruz .... 🧗📋 **6a+**
12m. The sharp arete has a tricky start and midway bulge.

To the right is a short slab of good quality rock that hasn't been developed as yet.

SECTOR LA ESFINGE
The big tower closest to the road has a steep sunny side and a slabbier shady one round the back.

3 ? .... 📋 **6a**
8m. Up the slab with just one hard move.

4 ? .... 🔲🧗🗿🕯️📋 **7b**
8m. A move of UK 6c - and on a slab!

5 ? .... 🗿🧗📋 **7a+**
8m. The right-hand side of the slab on sika crimps - shoddy!

6 A la sombría .... 🔲📋 **6a**
12m. Climb delicately to the flake and swing right to finish.

7 Clip-clap .... 🔲🪄🗿📋 **7c**
16m. The tough line up the left side of the arete.

8 Rompe techos .... 🔲🪄🗿📋 **7b+**
16m. The very steep blunt arete is tackled via a tough bulge, then press on up the grey rib above.

Not much sun | 1 min | Sheltered

SECTOR LA ESFINGE

This is the tower nearest the road, it has routes on all sides. On the northern side the is a short slab with technical offerings whereas those facing the road and the car park are steep sustained and hard. There are a couple of easier routes on the far right. The first routes are around the back.

9 Escupe cubatas ... 🔲 **6b+**
20m. Start where the crag swings round and climb the lower wall on good holds trending right, step left and make a thin pull to easier angled rock. Finish up the steepening slab and shallow groove; or alternatively finish out right at **6b**. *Photo page 137.*

10 La tufona ...... 🔲 **7b**
20m. The line to the right of the large red cross, featuring hard climbing and at least one very long reach.

11 Besuga .... 🔲 **7c+**
20m. This impressive line is spoilt by the bolt-on holds, though without them it would be impossible! Low in the grade.

12 Innominado. .. 🔲 **6c+**
22m. The next line has a sharp undercut start, tricky moves up and right, and then trends left by good climbing.

13 El cap. .... 🔲 **6a+**
10m. The short, steep rib to join the next route.

14 Gonso .... 🔲 **4+**
10m. The rib on the left of the grey slab has an awkward start on strange 'stuck on' holds' and is much easier above.

15 Rufo. .... 🔲 **6a**
10m. The centre of the slab has been bolted so there is no need to solo it now! The crux is quite tricky if you are puritanical!

16 Pequeños .... 🔲 **5**
8m. The thoroughly bolted slab on the far right gives a pleasant if short introduction to sport climbing with an awkward start and much easier climbing above.

141

ALCOI

This is not the most popular crag in this guide. It not that the climbing is bad - though it is hard - it more that the place is poorly situated above a busy town and is really awkward to get to from the coast. In spite of these drawbacks, a worthwhile day's climbing can be had here since the actual routes are quite good, especially in the harder grades. It also has the added attraction that the bars and restaurants are only a short stumble down the hill, if you get bored or too hot. The crag consists of a steep diagonal buttress of compact limestone just above the town. It is highly-featured, covered in edges, tufas, pockets and big holes but sadly, even with all these natural holds, many of the routes have chipped holds as well.

The routes are well equipped with new bolts and lower-offs. The grades tend to be a notch harder than elsewhere and it is probably only of real interest to people who lead 7a and above, although the slab at the top of the crag has some easier offerings and the classic of *Mosca* (opposite) is worth calling in for.

Desnivel's Escuelas database (**www.escuelasdeescalada.com**) lists two more crags in the Alcoi area; the Barranc del Sinc and the Barranquet de Ferry. If you are in the area for a few days it might be worth exploring the canyons behind the town.

CONDITIONS

The crag faces south and is sheltered making it a real sun-trap. Due to its angle, it will stay dry in light rain but will get wet pretty quickly in heavier stuff.

APPROACH
(area map page 77)

Alcoi is approximately 50km north of Alicante, in the middle of the mountains.

From the Coast - Drive south on the A7 to junction 70. From here, take the A36 north towards Alcoi.

From Benidorm - Follow the CV70 past Polop and the Echo crags and on to Guadalest (a fast 18km) and its continuation (a slow 36km to Alcoi). Rather than head straight into the city, nip across the CV7880 to join the coastal approach.

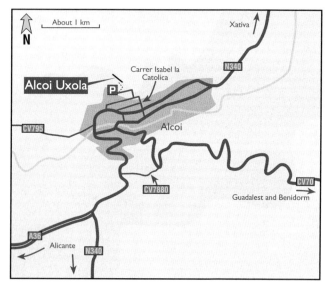

On entering the built-up area you will cross a large bridge, continue on the same road towards the city centre (and Cocentaina) looking for the *Carrer Isabel la Católica* which cuts across your direction of travel. Turn left onto this and follow it up hill. At its top, bear left then right onto the *Carrer Font de la Vixola* and at its top bear left again to the parking by the road end - easy! From the parking by the turning-circle follow any of the short paths to the base of the cliff.

Dave Spencer tackles the striking diagonal line of *Mosca* (6a+) probably the best of the 'easier' routes at Alcoi - *page 144*.

ALCOI *Uxola*

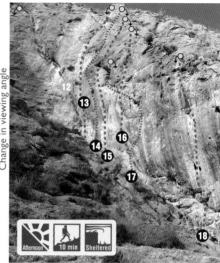

The first routes described are located on the slab at the top left corner of the crag, reached by scrambling up under the face.

1 Gusano loco . . . . 5+
14m. The unremarkable first (or last) line on the cliff.

2 Nen butrut 6a
20m. Start left of the shrubbery and go direct.

3 Susi 6a
22m. Start at the name *Acido* and trend left up the slab to join the last bit of the previous climb.

4 Acido . . . . 6a+
22m. Start as for *Susi* but go direct, keeping right of the grass.

5 Mírate . . . . 6a+
22m. Start at the name and trend right up the sustained slab.

6 Mírate variación . . . . 5+
22m. An easier variation starting from just down the slope.

7 Migueleño Schwarzeneger . . . 5+
22m. The shallow groove in the centre of the slab.

8 Vampiro . . . . 6a+
22m. The bubbly grey rib from a small left-slanting ramp.

9 Beso negro . . . 6c
22m. Climb direct to the bush on *Mosca*, then up the steep rib.

10 Flipo 8a
22m. Over the smooth bulge and up the red streak! Thin!

11 Orinal con pedales. 6c+
24m. The bulge to the right has larger holds. Start left of the ramp and climb the wall on pockets (threads) and holes.

12 Mosca . . . . 6a+
30m. Excellent climbing up the obvious diagonal corner/ramp. The crux is a tricky bulge low-down and the lower-off is out left on the slab. Well worth the effort.
Photo page 143.

13 Jetro 7b
24m. Up the bulging yellow wall above the tip of the ramp of *Mosca*. Long reaches between big pockets.

14 Vómitos leprosos. . 7b+
30m. A fine sustained offering up the pocketed leaning wall 3m right of the base of the ramp of *Mosca*.

15 Pestañas postizas . 7b
30m. The wall and rib left of the cave with chains. Pumpy!

16 Super flan. 7c
22m. A technical and pumpy one up the shallow scoop - nasty!

17 Guapo del sapo 7b
18m. Short and pumpy with a low crux, but it is still desperate!

18 Mejillas tiernas 8a
18m. A steep line past the pair of large 'eyes' early on.

19 Moldura 8a
22m. From the orange streak, battle it out with the tufas.

20 Mescalito 8a
20m. The tilted wall (name) is the best of the trio of 8a routes.

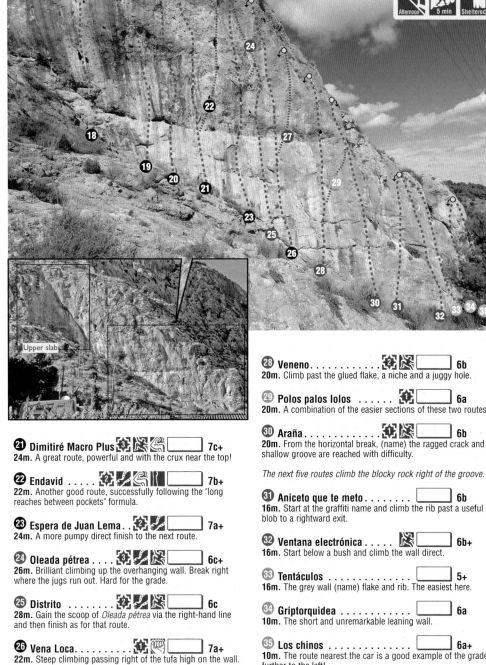

Murcia
Alicante
Benidorm
Calpe
Xaló Valley
Gandía
Marín
Salinas
Sax
Magdalena
Peña del Corb
Peña Rubia
Forada
Ibi
Recanco
Agujas Rojas
Alcoi
Cabezon

28 Veneno. . . . . 🔲 **6b**
20m. Climb past the glued flake, a niche and a juggy hole.

29 Polos palos lolos . . . . . . 🔲 **6a**
20m. A combination of the easier sections of these two routes.

30 Araña. . . . . 🔲 **6b**
20m. From the horizontal break, (name) the ragged crack and shallow groove are reached with difficulty.

The next five routes climb the blocky rock right of the groove.

31 Aniceto que te meto . . . . 🔲 **6b**
16m. Start at the graffiti name and climb the rib past a useful blob to a rightward exit.

32 Ventana electrónica . . . . . 🔲 **6b+**
16m. Start below a bush and climb the wall direct.

33 Tentáculos . . . . 🔲 **5+**
16m. The grey wall (name) flake and rib. The easiest here.

34 Griptorquidea . . . . 🔲 **6a**
10m. The short and unremarkable leaning wall.

35 Los chinos . . . . 🔲 **6a+**
10m. The route nearest the car is a good example of the grades further to the left!

21 Dimitiré Macro Plus 🔲 **7c+**
24m. A great route, powerful and with the crux near the top!

22 Endavid . . . . . 🔲 **7b+**
22m. Another good route, successfully following the "long reaches between pockets" formula.

23 Espera de Juan Lema . . 🔲 **7a+**
24m. A more pumpy direct finish to the next route.

24 Oleada pétrea . . . . 🔲 **6c+**
26m. Brilliant climbing up the overhanging wall. Break right where the jugs run out. Hard for the grade.

25 Distrito . . . . 🔲 **6c**
28m. Gain the scoop of *Oleada pétrea* via the right-hand line and then finish as for that route.

26 Vena Loca. . . . . 🔲 **7a+**
22m. Steep climbing passing right of the tufa high on the wall.

27 Que se mueran los feos . . 🔲 **7a**
20m. An easier right-hand finish to *Vena Loca.*

CABEZON DE ORO

Travelling north from Alicante, the first mountain of any significance is the broad hump of the Cabezon de Oro (1209m) away on the left-hand side. The mountain is most famous for the show caves of the *Cuevas de Canalobre* and, although the seaward side of the hill looks tame, the western face features extensive sheets of rock with many fine trad climbs. Accurate information has been difficult to come by although the locals have been exploring these hills for years. The ridge has three main areas of interest to climbers; on the left is the rocky ridge of the *Pared de los Alcoyanos* with its huge south west face, whilst the right is the twin-peaked top of the *Peña de Alicante*. This has an imposing west-facing wall with a collection of very impressive sport routes, and beyond this, the fine buttress of *Espolón Paiju* rising to the right-hand summit.

Looking back down at Andy Gledhill following the 6th pitch of *Espolòn Paiju* (5+/A1) on the Peña de Alicante - *page 149.* Photo: David Elder

APPROACH
(area map page 77)

From the A7 at Alicante, follow signs to Busot and the Cuevas de Canalobre (N340 then CV773). A kilometre of so before the parking for the caves there is a right-hand bend with a signboard and a track branch off to the left. To reach the Peña de Alicante take this and follow it about 1km to parking just beyond where the first section of tarmac ends. A track passes to the right of the wall (cairn) on the right-hand side of the road and runs up the stream bed to reach the climbing.

To reach the Alcoyanos, continue along the track (past one especially rough section) to parking (2 cars) by a small house on the left. The path to the cliff starts opposite and zig-zags up to arrive just to the right of where 'VIA GENE' is scratched on the rock.

CONDITIONS

The cliffs face south west and are exposed to the weather. They provide morning shade in hot weather and afternoon sun when its cooler. The Sector Deportivo is in the shade until mid-afternoon.

Pared de los Alcoyanos

Sector Deportivo

Pena de Alicante

Rough section of track

For Cuevas de Canalobre

CV776

N

About 1km

From Busot and Alicante

Murcia
Alicante
Benidorm
Calpe
Xaló Valley
Gandia
Marín
Salinas
Sax
Magdelena
Peña del Corb
Peña Rubia
Forada
Ibi
Reconco
Agulas Rojas
Alcoi
Cabezon

Descend down the back

❶ Zarabanda . . . . . . 🏔️📷🔧 ⬜ **6c+ (E4)**
A direct line up the left-hand side of the buttress, starting 20m left of where *Gene* is scratched on the rock. It follows the face in five long pitches. The rock is good and although there is quite a lot of fixed gear (and bolts on the stances) it is not a sport route so take a rack. To descend, abseil down the route or head over the back as for *Gene*.
The pitch grades are **5, 6b+, 6c+, 6b, 6b**.
FA. J.Ruiz, M.Pomares 1983

❷ Vía Gene . . . . 🏔️🔧🪨 ⬜ **5 (VS)**
A good route following a strong natural line and with a grand finish. The whole thing can be managed on a single rope. Start at the groove where the name is scratched. We have done this one so you get a full description!
1) 4+, 45m. The vegetated groove, and its cleaner continuation lead to a tree belay. The groove 12m to the left is a better and cleaner alternative, with no change in the grade.
2) 4, 45m. Traverse diagonally right to a tree and continue past a pair of bolts to a belay on a pair of pegs.
3) 4+, 30m. Move right into a groove with a bush and climb this. At the its top move right up slabs to belay on a huge ledge.
4) 4+, 55m. Scramble up right to a left slanting break (possible belay), and climb this to a long ridge. Follow this to the top of a pillar and a two bolt belay in a corner.
5) 5, 50m. Move up and left into a groove and left again into another. Up this to an exit on the left to ledge and peg belay.
6) 5, 45m. Continue up the ridge (pegs) to reach a ledge just below the crest, single peg belay.
7) 3, 45m. Move up right onto the ridge and traverse right to first deep notch in the ridge, and a 3 bolt belay with wire cable.
FA. P.Notario, G.llobet 1974

PARED DE LOS ALCOYANOS
Over 25 routes weave their way up this fine 250m high face, and, although they all contain some fixed gear, a rack and double ropes are needed on most of them. The four climbs listed here are believed to be the best of the bunch.
APPROACH - A short path leads from the parking straight up to the foot of the face in less than 10 minutes.
DESCENT - Either abseil back down the line of ascent, or abseil off the back of the face - single rope can be used to reach the ground in four abseils, with double ropes the ground can be reached in two abseils. Then descend scree leftwards to the foot of the face and contour to the south around the end of the cliff and follow an improving path back round to the start of the routes.

❸ El Don de Volar . . . 🏔️📷🔧 ⬜ **6c+ (E4)**
This route follows the buttress below the upper section of *Vía Gene* and contains much fixed gear though a lot of it is rather old. Start 20m right of where *Gene* is scratched on the rock. The grades are **6a, 6c+, 6b, 5+** and **5**. Descend as for *Gene*.
FA. J.Ruiz, C.Ramirez, M.Pomares 1982

❹ Delicatesen . . . . . 📷🏕️🏔️ ⬜ **6b+**
A fully-equipped sport route up the right-hand side of the face and the wall above the huge ledge. It can be done up and down on a 70m rope. The pitches are **6b, 6b+, 6b, 6b+**.
FA. D.Mora, J.Quesada 1992

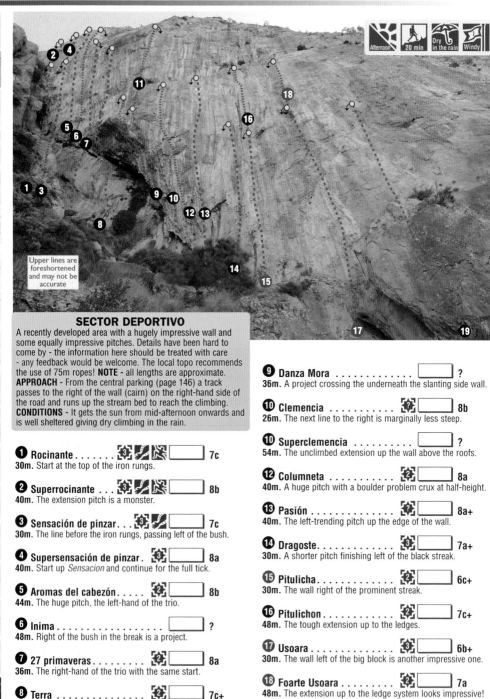

Upper lines are foreshortened and may not be accurate

SECTOR DEPORTIVO

A recently developed area with a hugely impressive wall and some equally impressive pitches. Details have been hard to come by - the information here should be treated with care - any feedback would be welcome. The local topo recommends the use of 75m ropes! **NOTE** - all lengths are approximate.
APPROACH - From the central parking (page 146) a track passes to the right of the wall (cairn) on the right-hand side of the road and runs up the stream bed to reach the climbing.
CONDITIONS - It gets the sun from mid-afternoon onwards and is well sheltered giving dry climbing in the rain.

❶ **Rocinante** 7c
30m. Start at the top of the iron rungs.

❷ **Superrocinante** 8b
40m. The extension pitch is a monster.

❸ **Sensación de pinzar** 7c
30m. The line before the iron rungs, passing left of the bush.

❹ **Supersensación de pinzar** 8a
40m. Start up *Sensacion* and continue for the full tick.

❺ **Aromas del cabezón** 8b
44m. The huge pitch, the left-hand of the trio.

❻ **Inima** . . . . ?
48m. Right of the bush in the break is a project.

❼ **27 primaveras** 8a
36m. The right-hand of the trio with the same start.

❽ **Terra** . . . . 7c+
34m. The right side of the lower wall and off the roof above.

❾ **Danza Mora** . . . . ?
36m. A project crossing the underneath the slanting side wall.

❿ **Clemencia** 8b
26m. The next line to the right is marginally less steep.

❿ **Superclemencia** . . . . ?
54m. The unclimbed extension up the wall above the roofs.

⓬ **Columneta** 8a
40m. A huge pitch with a boulder problem crux at half-height.

⓭ **Pasión** . . . . 8a+
40m. The left-trending pitch up the edge of the wall.

⓮ **Dragoste** . . . . 7a+
30m. A shorter pitch finishing left of the black streak.

⓯ **Pitulicha** . . . . 6c+
30m. The wall right of the prominent streak.

⓰ **Pitulichon** . . . . 7c+
48m. The tough extension up to the ledges.

⓱ **Usoara** . . . . 6b+
30m. The wall left of the big block is another impressive one.

⓲ **Foarte Usoara** 7a
48m. The extension up to the ledge system looks impressive!

⓳ **Fiager** . . . . 7a+
30m. The front face of the big 'boulder' then the wall above.

Cabezon del Oro 1209m

Pared de Los Alcoyanos

Sector Deportivo

Peña de Alicante

Descent

PEÑA DE ALICANTE

The fine summit that forms the right-hand bulwark of the cliffs here is home to several routes, including the one classic described here.

APPROACH - From the central parking follow the path towards the Sector Deportivo but where this start to bear away left scramble right out of the stream bed up to the base of the buttress. Alternately start from the lower parking, follow the track past the houses and vague paths up towards the buttress.

DESCENT - At the top, walk right to tick the summit, then drop down the south east (right - looking in) side of the hill and skirt back to the base of the buttress as indicated on the top photo - a gentle 20 minutes back to the base of the buttress.

CONDITIONS - This gets the afternoon sun but is exposed to any bad weather.

---

1 Espolón Paiju . . . . . . 🔲🔲🔲 5+ (HVS)

The compelling arete is a regional 'classic' following the huge rib towards the right-hand side of the cliff right under the summit of the Peña de Alicante. It has a short crux section that is normally aided to keep the grade at a consistent 5/5+. Take a rack, with a some big stuff. The penultimate pitch is a finely exposed, although rather retro, aided traverse along the diagonal crack that can be seen clearly from the approach track below. The aid section is equipped and will be straight forward for any competent team with a sense of adventure and a couple of foot slings. A little ingenuity with medium wires and cams is required to pass the odd blank gap and one awkward section. The crux aid pitch can be climbed free at 6b.
Start at a cleared patch in the undergrowth just up and right from the lowest part of the rib.
Photo page 146.

Espolón Paiju continued...
1) **4+, 35m.** Climb straight up cracks in the slab and then traverse left to move up a steep corner and belay on the rib.
2) **5, 30m.** Climb to a steep crack on the left and then continue up and right to a belay.
3) **5, 45m.** Continue up and leftwards moving over a terrace to belay in a corner below a steepening in the rib.
4) **4+, 25m.** Follow the line up the corner to a belay ledge
5) **4+, 30m.** Continue up the groove to below the headwall and a semi-hanging stance on a wooden wedge and in-situ thread.
6) **5+/A1, 35m.** Launch out left along the crack following a variety of fixed gear. Halfway along awkward moves lead down to a niche and back up to rejoin the crack. Belay with wires in a block at the far end of the terrace. Can be free climbed at 6b.
7) **2, 10m.** Up the easy gully to the top
FA. J.Agulló, F.Durá 1973

Alan James enjoying the perfect blend Sella manages to do do so well; beautiful weather, a stunning setting and the immaculate quality of the rock. The route is *Desperate Dan* (6c), Sector Final - *page 167*.

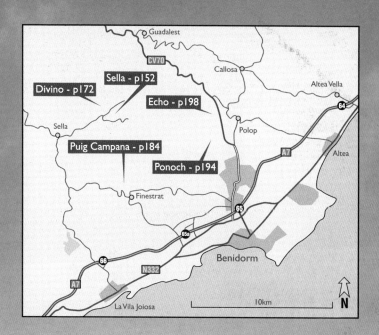

Guadalest

CV70

Sella - p152

Divino - p172

Echo - p198

Callosa

Altea Vella

84

Sella

Polop

Puig Campana - p184

A7

Altea

Ponoch - p194

Finestrat

65

65a

66

Benidorm

A7

N332

10km

N

La Vila Joiosa

Benidorm

SELLA

Sella is the most important, extensive and popular area in the whole Costa Blanca. There is enough climbing so that you could easily spend a whole week's holiday here and only leave the valley to top up on your supplies at the super-market. The most popular section is the long ridge in the centre of the valley which has a superb south-facing series of walls and buttresses. However if you stray from the crowds, you may be rewarded with some peace and solitude. In hot weather the north-facing Pared de Rosalía is well-worth considering with its fine long routes in the mid and harder grades. Further along the road from the main area is the Mecca for hard climbers called the Hidden Valley and you can't

The Techo del Rino and Sector Marión, with the Divino beyond.

really miss the final jewel in the crown - The Divino sits majestically above everything and is worthy attention from all those who demand a little bit more from their climbing.

The routes in the main area tend to be fingery and technical on single pitch slabs and low-angled walls. All the routes are well bolted with solid lower-offs. On the Pared de Rosalía it is worth getting your rack out, especially if you intend to tackle one of the longer routes. In the Hidden Valley you will find yourself grappling with tufas and pockets on wildly steep walls but it is only really worth considering if you lead 7a or above. The Divino has mainly long traditional routes, but the lower sections do contain some sport routes albeit mostly in the harder grades.

Graham Parkes getting technical on the final moves of the leaning wall of *Acróbata porcino* (7a) on the Techo del Rino at Sella - *page 161*. Most of the climbing at Sella is on less-than-vertical sheets of rock so this area is a little unusual.

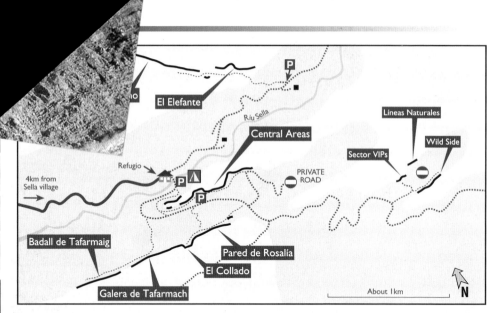

Map labels:

El Elefante

Líneas Naturales

Riu Sella

Central Areas

Wild Side

Sector VIPs

Refugio

4km from Sella village

PRIVATE ROAD

Badall de Tafarmaig

Pared de Rosalía

El Collado

Galera de Tafarmach

About 1km

N

APPROACH (area map page 151)

Sella is situated about 20km inland from Villajoyosa on the A7 motorway.

To reach it from the north - Leave the A7 at junction 65a (Terra Mitica) or 65 (Benidorm) and follow signs for Terra Mitica and then Finestrat. Drive around Finestrat, always following signs to Sella, and continue to a T-junction. Turn right and 5km of twisty roads lead to the outskirts of Sella. Just before entering the village, turn right down a short straight road and turn right again at the end of this and drive past the cemetery. Follow this track for 4km to the refuge and crags.

From the south - Turn off the A7 at junction 66 (Villajoyosa) and head inland following signs to Sella to join the above description at the T-junction 5km before Sella village. This approach is the fastest from either direction as it involves the least driving on minor roads.

CONDITIONS

It is usually possible to find sun or shade when required, although it is rather less of a winter-sun venue than you might think since the tall surrounding walls tend to keep the low sun

Springtime in Sella - almond blossom.

off except in the middle of the day. Most of the crags are well sheltered except for the Pared de Rosalía and the Divino. These two should be treated as mountain crags. The main area will dry quickly after rain. If it is raining then most of the Hidden Valley crags will stay dry, however they will seep after prolonged spells of bad weather.

The three pitch classic of *Marión* (5) has become one of the post popular climbs in the whole valley. It offers a great introduction to multi-pitch face climbing - *page 163*.

Murcia
Alicante
Benidorm
Calpe
Xaló Valley
Gandia

Sella

Puig Campana

Ponoch

Echo Valley

Evening | Roadside | Dry in the rain | Sheltered

CABEZA DE RINO

The 'Rhino's head' is the crag directly opposite the refuge. It is shorter than most of the other sectors at Sella but the main section leans steeply giving some powerful routes. The right-hand side was a very popular easy area with some technical slab climbs which inevitably and unfortunately have become very polished.

CONDITIONS - This is a useful shady retreat in hot weather and it also has some routes that stay dry in the rain. The buttress can be cool and damp in the depths of winter.

❶ Bajo las ruedas **6a**
10m. A short offering away on the left. The bolts may be old.
FA. N.Sánchez 1990s

❷ La sombra de Caín.   **6c**
30m. A long route which is worth seeking out. Scramble up the ramp then climb the wall on the left to a final devious section.
FA. N.Sánchez 1990s

❸ Compuesta y sin novio . . . . . .   **6b+**
26m. Further up the gully and reached by a tricky scramble.
FA. N.Sánchez 1990s

❹ L'eura **6b**
14m. The 1st route on the main face. A strenuous pull leads to the pleasant slab above, keeping just right of the floribunda.
FA. N.Sánchez 1990s

❺ Chapo el secundo **6a**
14m. Climb the pillar and the leaning wall above on good holds.

❻ Route 6 . . . .
14m. A hard new line up the steep, blank pillar.

❼ Encadena - 2 . . . . .   **7c+**
14m. Climb up and then left with difficulty (it used to be easier but a hold fell off). A nasty move using a chipped one finger pocket reaches the buckets.
FA. S.Sánchez, M.Sánchez 1990s

❽ Menestral Pescanova . .   **7b+**
18m. Climb the steep wall using pockets and finger jams until a difficult traverse left can be made on more pockets.
FA. Llopis

❾ Síndrome del Betún   **7a+**
16m. Follow *Menestral Pescanova* for a couple of moves along the hand-rail then finish direct. Easier than the hand-traverse.

❿ Próximo Bautizo . . . . .   **7a+**
16m. Gain and climb the short steep crack that shoots straight up the wall to a blind flake with a tricky exit. Short but sustained.
FA. J.M.Ramírez, N.Sánchez 1990s

⓫ Comtitapel **7a**
16m. A steep line starting up *Diagonal* then tackling the short right-hand crack of the three.
FA. J.M.Ramírez, Q.Barberá 1990s

⓬ Diagonal. . . . .   **7a+**
24m. The best route on the wall. Follow the rightward-slanting crack throughout. Mostly good holds but a tricky exit.
FA. J.M.Garciá 1990s

13 Hombres de poca fe 🔧🪣🪥⬜ **8a**
14m. The direct start to *Comptitapel* is extremely fingery, very steep and devious to boot. The hardest here.
FA. Iván Hernández 1990s

14 Multigrado ...... 🔧🪨🪥⬜ **7c**
14m. A hideously rounded layback and the odd chipped hold - though the moves are good!
FA. J.M.Garciá 1990s

15 Región Pagana ... 🔧🪨🪥⬜ **7c**
14m. The hard crack features some chipped holds.
FA. N.Sánchez 1990s

16 Julio César .... 🪨⬜ **6c+**
14m. From the overhung ledge climb the leaning wall on surprising holds to tricky final moves.
FA. Llopis 1990s

17 Chulearías .... ⬜ **6c**
14m. The right-most line weaves up the leaning arete on poor rock. There are (much) better routes not too far away.
FA. N.Sánchez 1990s

The slabby right-hand sector is based around The Horn. It is easy to reach from the lower parking. The routes were equipped by N.Sánchez and J.M.Garciá early in the 1990s.

18 Pequeñeces .... ⬜ **3+**
14m. The left-most line starts by stepping off a block and gives well-bolted but slippery climbing.

19 La Tina de Turner .... ⬜ **6a**
12m. Start at a white patch and climb direct on good rock and with some surprising holds. Very polished now.

20 Taís tos tolais .... 🪨⬜ **6b**
14m. Start just left of a bush and climb to a stiff couple of moves past the second bolt. The upper rib is easier.

21 Frustración agrícola ..... 🔧⬜ **5**
14m. Start just right of a bush and climb into a groove which you follow to an exit left to the belay of the previous climb. The first bolt is rather high.

22 Quisiera ser un octavo ... 🔧⬜ **5**
16m. From the left side of a niche climb a thin crack (keep to its right) and shallow groove (keep to its left). Well-spaced bolts can be supplemented with wires. High in the grade.

23 Verglas que sí .... ⬜ **5+**
14m. From the right side of the niche climb direct on flaky rock with sustained difficulty.

24 Registro sanitario . 🔧🪨🪣⬜ **6b+**
14m. Start at the narrowest point of the path and climb the smooth slab to easier but sustained climbing above. Passing the second bolt is thin but is avoidable on the left at **6a**.

Murcia
Alicante
Benidorm
Calpe
Xaló Valley
Gandia
Sella
Puig Campana
Ponoch
Echo Valley

CULO DE RINO

The first section on the popular sunny side of the ridge is around the corner and up the hill from the Cabeza de Rino. The climbing here is excellent with a good selection of slabby or vertical routes, on good rock, within 5 mins of the car. It is getting polished.
APPROACH - See map on page 154.
From the refuge - walk up the road until you are almost level with the end of the Cabeza de Rino, then take a path up through the bushes and around leftwards to the wall.
From the middle car park - Walk leftwards (looking in) from the parking area below the Techo del Rino.
CONDITIONS - The wall gets plenty of winter sun and is well sheltered. The right-hand side goes into the shade earlier than the left.

CULO DE RINO - LOWER

Before you get to the quality climbing there are three hidden routes on the other side of the Rhino's horn. The bushes have grown around these routes and they are hard to find but they aren't really worth the effort anyway.

1 Todo por la punta patria . . 7c
10m. A short and very blank three-bolt-wonder.

2 Aqui no pinta nadie nada . . . . 5+
10m. Another three bolt offering.

3 Más fácil todavia . . . . 4+
12m. The right-hand line is marginally the best of this bunch.

CULO DE RINO - MAIN

Further up the slope the climbing starts to improve.

4 Timatiriticón 6a
14m. The left-hand line is polished and the bolts are old.

5 Pies de minino . . . . 5+
16m. Trend right up the buttress.
FA. J.M.García 1990s

6 Chusmaniática . . . . . . 6a+
16m. A fingery bulge provides the crux.

Take care when lowering off the next set of routes, they are all long and there have been accidents.

7 Otigofrénicia 7c
20m. A desperate fingery boulder problem up the blank wall just right of the corner.

8 Denominacíon de origen . . 6a+
26m. A good wall climb. Trend left up the sustained white wall with thin moves off a small tufa at half-height.
FA. J.M.García 1990s

9 Camilo el rey 6b
28m. A classical pitch on great rock up the centre of the wall to the right of the corner. Passing the central bulges is tricky.

10 Valor y Coraje . . . . 6a+
30m. The third of this excellent trio and another long pitch. Trend right up the wall to reach parallel flakes and continue to a lower-off high on the right.
FA. J.M.García 1990s

11 Martillazos de maricona . . 6b+
30m. The next line has a poor start but improves higher up and is another very long pitch.

To the right is one of the most popular walls at Sella which has some great long pitches on the customary perfect rock.

12 Sense Novetat . . . . 6a+
20m. 2 bolts lead up into a corner, from on here you will need runners, shock horror!
FA. J.M.García 1990s

13 Los refugiados . . . . . . 5+
18m. A good little route with a steep and sustained upper wall.
FA. J.M.García 1990s

14 A diestro y siniestro 6a
20m. A fine climb that weaves up the wall and has the crux where it should be - right at the top.
FA. J.M.García 1990s

15 A golpe y porrazo 5
24m. A worthwhile longer pitch.
FA. J.M.García 1990s

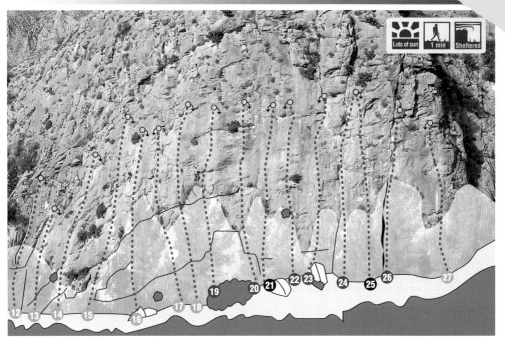

Alicante

Benidorm

Calpe

Xaló Valley

Gandia

Sella

Puig Campana

Ponoch

Echo Valley

16 Vía del Indio . . . . 5+
20m. Climb the wall passing between the bushes, taking care with the occasional loose block. Good climbing but polished.
FA. J.M.García 1990s

17 Divinas Chapuzas 6a
22m. Start behind a pine tree, left of a cream rock scar (name). A two-move-wonder with spaced bolts up the lay-back crack.
FA. J.M.García 1990s

18 Tú dirás . . . . 6a+
22m. From a big flat block, trend left then back right. The final section is taken on the left and is steeper than it looks. The hard start can be avoided by using *Divinas Chapuzas*.
FA. Llopis 1990s

19 Vino d'Oporto 6c
22m. The next line in gives fine varied climbing passing round the left side of a small overhang, with the crux at the top.

In the past there has been a project up the wall in between these two routes but currently it doesn't have any bolts.

20 Guija loca . . . . 6c+
22m. Begin below and right of a flake. A desperate starting sequence to pass the first bolt (avoidable on the right) gives access to the fine, sustained upper wall.

21 Kina borregada 7b+
22m. Starting behind a white block climb sporadic tufas to reach a thin seam high on the wall. Follow this with escalating interest. Bolted for a national climbing competition and, unlike most competition routes, it is vertical and fingery.
FA. M.Muñoz 1990s

22 No frenes mis instintos. 7a
22m. Starting behind a white block climb sporadic tufas to reach a thin seam high on the wall. Follow this with escalating interest. The crux is very fingery. There is a lower-off over to the left at the top.
FA. Originally led on gear (E7 6b) by Mark Edwards as Edwards' Wall.

23 Suspiros de dolor 7a
22m. From a 2m high fallen flake, climb rightwards then awkwardly up the wall to a hidden jug. The crux section is taken left then right and locating the drilled holds is not that easy!

24 La cosa 7a
22m. The shallow groove is climbed on prickly rock, initially via the right rib and finishing by trending right through the bulges.
FA. J.M.García 1990s

25 A golpe de pecho. . 7a+
22m. The steepening wall to the right of the groove is climbed trending left. The lower part is pleasant but the bulging section has a 'bloc' move on small drilled holds and a tricky clip. Jugs above lead to the lower-off. Low in the grade.

26 Con las manos en la Cosa. 6c
22m. A spiky groove gives a fine pitch, with hard moves at its closure, swinging up and over to the right. It is no pushover at the grade and is supposedly harder then *Kashba*.
FA. N.Sánchez 1990s

27 Días de lluvia . . . . . . 6a+
20m. The right side of the rib, just before the cliff swings and round trending right to finish Steep and technical climbing on side-pulls and sprags. Rainy days indeed - just imagine!

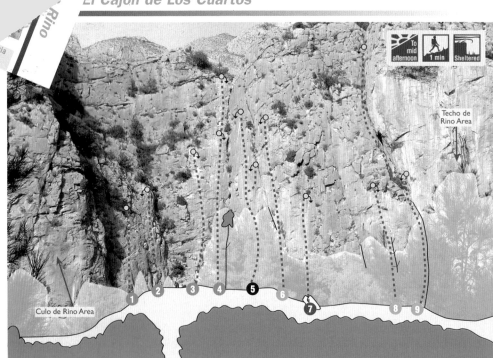

Rino

García

Alicante

Benidorm

Calpe

Xaló Valley

Gandía

Sella

Puig Campana

Ponoch

Echo Valley

Techo de
Rino Area

Culo de Rino Area

EL CAJÓN DE LOS CUARTOS

A short section of bolted slabs with some popular easier routes. It is a good area for beginners though the routes are getting pretty badly trashed through over-use.
APPROACH - This is the bay above and left of the main parking area. Now you know why it is so popular!
CONDITIONS - Sunny and sheltered although it gets the shade earlier in the day than some of the other walls.

① Dime dime . . . . **3+**
12m. The left-hand line in the bay is pronounced 'dee-may dee-may'. It is popular and has become extremely polished so take care not to slip off before you get to the second bolt.

② Con mallas y a lo loco . . . **3+**
14m. PPP - pleasant, popular, polished!

③ Pequeñecos II **4**
18m. The left-hand line in the centre of the bay.

④ Pequeñecos III . . . . **4+**
1) **20m, 4+** Entertaining climbing up the right-hand line, pleasant but polished, and quite hard at the grade.
2) **12m, 4+** Not as good as the 1st pitch but the view from the top is worth the effort. Abseil descent.

⑤ Porko niente lire . . . . . **7a+**
22m. A technical little number up the smooth scoop, keep left for the full tick. The right-hand line at the 'fork' has its own lower-off and is a bit of a cop-out at **6c+**.

⑥ Cuidado con mi sombrero . **6a+**
20m. The worthwhile steep groove even has some jams. The tricky top crack can be by-passed on the left.

⑦ Fulanita y sus menganos . **6b**
14m. Short but quite absorbing.

⑧ Zig-zag atómico **6a**
14m. Up the wall behind the trees to a lower-off below the overhang. Now polished and a bit of an unpleasant sand-bag!

⑨ Two Nights of Love . . . . . . **5+**
1) **5+, 18m.** Climb right into the corner then follow this to a belay in the gully. Either lower off here or:
2) **4+, 22m.** Cross the gully leftwards then climb up the slab and groove above. One 50m abseil reaches the ground.

TECHO DEL RINO

⑩ Blanco nato **6b**
22m. Follow the edge of the wall starting up an awkward crack, with sustained interest. The initial moves are polished.

⑪ Martín Galas . . . . . **6b+**
20m. Start at the name. A fine sustained wall climb but a bit of an eliminate. Climb direct passing a big flake to a crimpy crux.

The next three routes start from above Blanco nato.

⑫ Pesos pluma . . . . . **6b+**
16m. From the belay, climb out left then up to the edge of the big roof. Exposed and improbable on sticky rock.

Murcia · Alicante · **Benidorm** · Calpe · Xaló Valley · Gandía · **Sella** · Puig Campana · Ponoch · Echo Valley

TECHO DEL RINO

This is the steepest sector on the main area at Sella, which is dominated by a huge square roof on its upper left, with the magnificent bulging wall of *Kashba* below and right. There are several fine, steep pitches in this area.
APPROACH - It overlooks the central parking area.
CONDITIONS - Very well sheltered and a real sun-trap.

13 La Explanada . . . . **8b+**
16m. This tricky 'created' roof climb is one of the hardest in the area. Originally done with a bolt-on hold.
FA. Iván Hernández 1990s

14 Vía Pecuaria **6b**
14m. A gripping and exciting trip up the groove then out under the right-hand side of the roof to a lower-off right on the lip!

15 Vaya tipo el de Oti . . . . **6c+**
18m. An easy lower section on sharp rock leads to steeper climbing above, the crux being the last couple of moves.

16 Cardo Borriquero . . . . . **6c+**
A fine climb that can be done in one pitch with a suitable rope!
1) 6a, 18m. A lower pitch which can be done in its own right.
2) 6c+, 20m. The superb leaning arete. Climb the left side of the arete until forced round the exposed corner.
FA. J.M.García 1990s

17 Acróbata porcino **7a**
22m. Start left of the block and climb to the base of the steep wall. Good flowstone layaways and undercuts allow for rapid progress to the last crucial moves. *Photo page 153.*
FA. M.Muñoz 1990s

18 Sorbe verge . . . **7b+**
26m. A very bouldery middle section provides the difficulties.
FA. M.Muñoz 1990s

19 Kashba . . . . **6c+**
26m. Classic climbing and one of the best routes at Sella. Sustained, superb and only a little over-graded.
FA. M.Muñoz 1990s

20 No me bajes tan **7a**
22m. A bit of a one-move-wonder. Grab the side-pull and jump!
FA. J.M.García 1990s

21 El torronet . . . . **5+**
26m. A worthwhile easier climb on good rock and with the crux right at the top. If in difficulty, try stepping left then back right.
FA. J.M.García 1990s

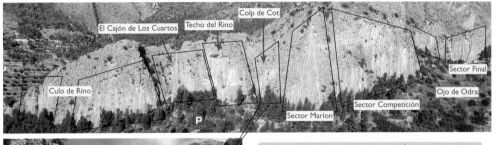

SECTOR MARIÓN
One of the best known features of Sella is the broad arete of *Marión* and its three pitch classic. There is almost always a team in-situ. The wall to the left of this has also been developed with a fine set of climbs.
APPROACH - It overlooks the central parking area.
CONDITIONS - The huge arete of Marión catches the sun until late in the day.

⑥ Bolt Tax . . . . 🔲🔲 6a
16m. The first line on the wall gives good technical climbing.
FA. J.M.Garciá, N.Sánchez 1990s

⑦ Deja vu . . . . 🔲🔲 5
20m. A worthwhile line, though with some loose rock.
FA. J.M.Garciá, N.Sánchez 1990s

⑧ Cartujal . . . . 🔲🔲 5+
22m. More fine climbing, quality rock and a good long pitch. With some of the other climbs having been over-used, this is currently one of the best hereabouts.
FA. J.M.Garciá, 1990s

⑨ Cul de sac . . . . 🔲🔲 5+
1) **5, 18m.** The first line of (spaced) bolts to the right of a bush.
2) **5+, 18m.** Continue in the same line up smoother rock.
FA. J.M.Garciá, N.Sánchez 1990s

⑩ Prusik . . . . 🔲 6a+
1) **5+, 20m.** A popular and pleasant first pitch.
2) **6a+, 30m.** Good sustained climbing trending to the right but be wary of the huge loose-looking flake below the lower-off.

⑪ Anglopithecus Britaniensis 🔲 6a+
24m. The fingery bulge is the crux - the rest is much easier.
FA. J.M.Garciá, N.Sánchez 1990s

⑫ Mister Pi . . . . 🔲🔲 5+
24m. Start by bridging up the groove. Hard 6a if you stick to the most direct line but you can escape right into the crack.

⑬ Marión . . . . 🔲🔲 5
The prominent arete offers one of Sella's best known climbs. The grades suggested for the pitches seem to vary a lot, though they are all somewhere in 4+ and 5 zone. *Photo page 155.*
1) **5, 24m.** Hard moves over a bulge then trend left to ledges.
2) **4+, 22m.** Continue to another stance (50m to ground).
3) **5 (VS 4b) 22m.** Follow a small groove to a tricky bulge (2 bolts). Pull over this then use the lower-off on the left or continue to the top on wires.
DECENT - Make two abseils down the line. Alternatively, walk right along the ridge to reach the Ojo de Odra cave from behind.

SECTOR COLP DE COT
To the right of the main wall is a short wall with some short and frequently-climbed routes. Sadly they have all become horribly polished over the years and can no longer be recommended except to Avon devotees.
APPROACH - It overlooks the central parking area.
CONDITIONS - Very well sheltered and a real sun-trap.

① Colp de Cot . . . . 🔲 6b+
16m. A short and desperate mid-height section.

② Hola Patricio . . . . 🔲 6b
16m. More polished pocket pulling past well-spaced bolts.

③ Puntea que no tienes . . 🔲🔲 6a+
18m. The right-hand line is the best but also rather tired. The hard move is at about 1/3 height, above that it is a steady 5+.

The next two routes are much better, and considerably longer. In fact they are 38m and have a very high first bolt. They can be done back to the ground on a 70m rope - otherwise use the one-third-height chain. Take care.

④ Culo Ipanema . . . . . . 🔲🔲 6b
38m. A huge pitch with a good technical wall climbed left then right with an easier finish up the wall above the big flake.
FA. J.M.Garciá, N.Sánchez 1990s

⑤ Rosalind Sutton . . . 🔲🔲🔲 6b
38m. An excellent route of escalating interest with thin moves at mid-height and a nice left-trending crack at the top.
Culo Sutton Combination - Combine the first half of *Culo Ipanema* with the top section of *Rosalind Sutton* for the most sustained climbing. A bit harder though at **6b+**.
FA. J.M.Garciá, N.Sánchez 1990s

Murcia · Alicante · Benidorm · Calpe · Xaló Valley · Gandia · Sella · Puig Campana · Ponoch · Echo Valley

SECTOR COMPETICIÓN

This is one of the show-piece areas of Sella with many long climbs on perfect rock, set at an angle from steeply-slabby to just off vertical. The climbing tends to be very technical with fingery and sustained moves. Some of the routes are quite long so take care when lowering.

APPROACH - Walk rightwards (looking in) from the parking below Techo del Rino. There are several paths through the bushes.

CONDITIONS - as with most of the sectors on this crag, it is a south-facing sun-trap. It is also rarely windy and dries very quickly after rain.

The first routes are down and left of the main wall. These are generally easier than those further right and are a bit polished. Despite this they still give good climbing.

❶ El gran coscorrón. . . . . . 🔲🔲 🔲 **6a+**
22m. Great and sustained climbing on 'goutes d'eau'.

❷ Nido de Piratas . . . . 🔲🔲 🔲 **6b**
22m. Straightforward climbing to the bulges which provide the crux. Above these, things ease again.

❸ Y tú ¿Quién eres? . . . . . . 🔲 🔲 **6a+**
22m. A once fine and popular pitch has suffered from over-use.

❹ Desbloquea que No . . . . . 🔲 🔲 **5**
20m. This is the easiest route on this wall but it still has its moments towards the top.

❺ Perlita . . . . 🔲🔲 🔲 **5+**
18m. A short route. Harder (**6a**) for the short but tricky for the tall as well! If it proves too easy have a go at.....

❻ Perlita Extensión . . . . 🔲 🔲 **7a+**
30m. A hard extension up the brittle upper wall. The line on the topo is only approximate.

The next two routes start from the big vegetated ramp and finish high on the wall above.

❼ The Wasp Factory . . . . 🔲🔲 🔲 **6c+**
1) **6a, 24m.** A good pitch, worth doing on its own.
2) **6c+, 26m.** Pumpy and sustained in its upper section though passing the 'wasp factory' is probably the psychological crux!
FA. J.M.Garciá, H.Romero 1990s

❽ Ratito de gloria . . . . . . 🔲🔲 🔲 **7a**
1) **6a+, 28m.** A good pitch, again worth doing on its own.
2) **7a, 24m.** This one has very distinct crux move past a roof.
FA. J.M.Garciá, H.Romero 1990s

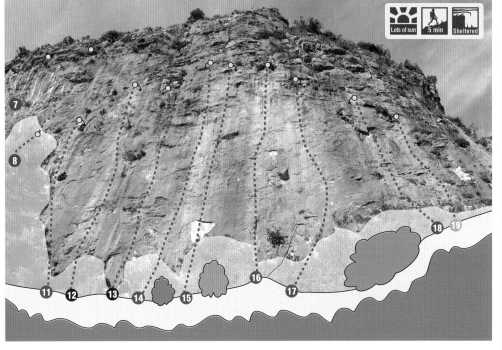

9 Martxa d'aci . . . . 🔳⬛ 6a
22m. The left-hand line is a classic though it is getting polished. Climb on good holds until forced right into a groove. Bridge this to chains just above.

10 Relleno de crema . . . . . . 🔳⬛ 6b
20m. Good climbing up the wall just right but it is barely independent and is hard above the third bolt.
FA. N.Sánchez 1990s

11 Dingo boingo . . . . 🔳👐❤⬛ 6c
24m. Excellent and a little 'run-out'. Entering the scoop above the third clip is the crux, though the interest is well maintained.

12 Pedro, estás inspirado . 📐👐⬛ 7c
28m. Starting at the name follow the desperate line passing to the left of the tree, up the smoothest part of the wall.

13 The Second Coming . . 🔳📐⬛ 7c
26m. Another technical horror. The crux may be V7 or V8 and clipping the bolt is desperate. There are variations around the hard moves on the right.
FA. Pat King 2000

14 Sopa de marsopa . . 🔳💧📐⬛ 6b+
30m. Start below and left of the prominent scar and follow a line slightly rightwards. The crux is at half height, gaining and leaving a small pillar, and the pitch is quite hard for the grade.

15 Odio los domingos . 🔳👐📐⬛ 6c+
28m. Step off the fallen flake and make very thin moves up to a small scar (crux). Continue in the same line with sustained and sharp climbing. Another cracking pitch and a tip-shredder.
FA. J.M.García 1990s

16 Tecnócratas . . . . 🔳📐👐⬛ 6c
28m. Climb the steep wall, sustained and sharp with the crux being the shallow groove.
FA. F.Durá 1990s

17 El vuelo de la máquina . . . 🔳⬛ 6b+
28m. Great climbing on good holds, generally to the right of the bolt line and with a tricky finale up a steep wall. It has become a bit polished hence it is no longer worth 3 stars.

Past some bushes are 2 more recent routes.

18 García uno . . . . . . 🔳📐👐⬛ 6b
22m. You can finish by stepping right onto the slab which is a bit easier than direct (which is **6b+**).
FA. J.M.García 2000

19 García dos . . . . 📐👐⬛ 6a+
22m. The last line before the cliff swings round is worthwhile.
FA. J.M.García 2000

The first routes in the Ojo de Odra sector are just to the right.

Murcia · Alicante · Benidorm · Calpe · Xaló Va ley · Gandia · Sella · Puig Campana · Ponoch · Echo Valley

Ojo de Odra
(hidden)

Sector Final

OJO DE ODRA

Around the corner and up the hill from Sector Competición is a steep wall leading to a shorter section of cliff with an amazing water-worn hole through it. Further right is another short wall which has seen some recent development with a handful of unspectacular routes.
APPROACH - Parking on the bend is frowned upon, though that doesn't stop the locals. The easy 10 minute walk from the main parking is probably the best idea.
CONDITIONS - The routes to the left of the hole of Ojo de Odra face south east getting morning sun and going into the shade from mid-afternoon.

The first two routes are just around the corner from Sector Competición. They are excellent lower-grade offerings.

❶ Almorranas Salvajes . . . . 🔲 **4+**
24m. The left-hand line eases as height is gained. Enjoy.

❷ Alí Babá y 40 Komandos. . 🔲 **4**
26m. The right-hand line gives more of the same.

The upper section of the wall has some steep, orange rock.

❸ Kamikaze . . . . 🔲 **7b**
25m. Start behind a bush and climb slabby rock left of a detached flake at 4m then on up steeper terrain to a couple of taxing moves to better holds. Trend right then back left (hard clip) to easier ground. A superb route with great climbing.

❹ Seventh Samurai . . . . . 🔲 **6c**
25m. Start at a head-height cave/hole and climb straight up the wall passing some suspect rock to the lower-off used by *Kamikaze*. More run-out than its neighbour but better bolted!

❺ Fisura con finura . . . . . 🔲 **6a**
22m. The long flaky crack-line gives a very pleasant pitch with a stiff little layback as the crux about halfway to the chains.

❻ Roberto Alcázar . . . . 🔲 **6a+**
22m. A technical start followed by a long reach then some juggy moves to the top.

❼ Espíritu de Satur . . . . . 🔲 **6c**
22m. The crinkly and technical wall just left of the cave.

The next feature is the famous hole known as Ojo de Odra. If you scramble up the back of this hole you can get an amazing view of the Divino framed by the tunnel. The wall to the right has been developed but non of the routes is especially worthwhile. A place to avoid the crowd perhaps.

❽ Ojo de Odra . . . . . 🔲 **6c**
14m. Start in the hole and swing out of the left-hand side (looking in) on sharp, polished holes, then haul to the chains.

❾ Los coreanos . . . . 🔲 **6c+**
14m. The line of pockets right of the hole, past a sling.
FA. H.Romero 1990s

❿ Els nuciers . . . . 🔲 **7a**
14m. A bit of a non-line up the wall and across the groove.
FA. 'Pitu', 'Coco', N.Sánchez 1990s

⓫ Mel de roma . . . . 🔲 **6b**
16m. A nasty fall is possible from the last move on this one.
FA. J.M.Garciá, N.Sánchez 1990s

⓬ Skid mark . . . . 🔲 **6b**
20m. Steep and strenuous on good holds up the pale wall.
FA. J.M.Garciá 1990s

⓭ Los remeras . . . . 🔲 **6c**
14m. A short and sharp up the slab and rib.
FA. J.M.Garciá 1990s

⓮ Baladas para un sordo . . . . . . 🔲 **6a+**
16m. The steep wall leads into the hanging groove.
FA. 'Pitu', 'Coco' 1990s

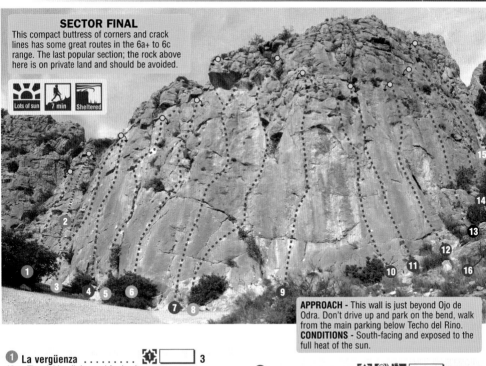

SECTOR FINAL

This compact buttress of corners and crack lines has some great routes in the 6a+ to 6c range. The last popular section; the rock above here is on private land and should be avoided.

Lots of sun | 7 min | Sheltered

APPROACH - This wall is just beyond Ojo de Odra. Don't drive up and park on the bend, walk from the main parking below Techo del Rino.
CONDITIONS - South-facing and exposed to the full heat of the sun.

1 La vergüenza **3**
16m. The slabby rib is good for beginners.

2 La vergüenza II .... **3+**
18m. The right-hand side of the rib is even better for beginners.

3 Speedy González ..... **5+**
16m. Start up the slab but trend right to enter the groove (crux) then climb the pleasant wall above, direct.

4 El Pixoncet **6b**
18m. A once great pitch, now with shiny crux moves! Start from the dirt heap, climb onto a flake then take a line up the centre of the buttress - delightful, apart from the crux!

5 Con mallas y a lo loco . **5+**
18m. The groove separating the two buttresses has a bushy start and pleasant (if you like jamming) climbing above.

6 Aquí no nos dejan aparcar **6a+**
20m. Start left of the lowest point of the buttress. A thin and slippy lower section (easier on the left but a harder clip) leads to a steep rib and a much easier groove above.

7 Aquí tampoco . **6c**
22m. Great climbing up the technical wall and over the tough roof which is tackled on the right. The short (and anyone struggling) can sneak up the left-hand edge of the roof at **6b**.

8 Wagageegee .... **6a+**
22m. The big corner is good and low in the grade. Originally climbed without bolts at E3 5c.
FA. J.M.Garciá, N.Sánchez 1990s

9 Desperate Dan ... **6c**
20m. The awkward, pocketed crack has good but spaced holds. *Photo page 150.*

10 Kilroy was 'ere ... **6c+**
20m. Climb a 'crinkly' wall in to the base of the shallow groove then trend left to the lower-off of the previous climb.

11 El Agüí .... **6c+**
20m. The shallow groove running the full height of the cliff, is entered with difficulty, followed with interest and exited with more difficulty.

12 Grillos Navajeros **6c**
20m. Just left of the bank, climb a 'spiky' slab leftwards to its apex then swing onto the steep wall and sprint up this.
FA. J.Ruiz, C.Maracu 1990s

13 Mandolin Wind ...... **7a+**
16m. The wall above the bank has a very hard start.

14 Año Dracula **6c**
16m. Another with a hard start.

15 El pellizco .... **6a+**
18m. The retiring crack line is worth seeking out.
FA. J.Romero 1990s

16 IQ - 18/30 .... **6b+**
20m. The final route here starts up the pillar behind the tree. Sustained and worthwhile but with a single bolt lower-off.

PARED DE ROSALÍA

This vast face is frequently stared at by climbers basking in the sun on the popular areas at Sella. Most climbers don't bother to make the effort of actually walking up which is a shame since it is one of the best crags in the area for people leading in the upper 6s and 7s. There are some superb, fully-bolted routes, with great lines, on good rock. Most of the pitches are at least 30m which can make lowering-off awkward. The best advice is to climb on two 50m ropes.

APPROACH - Park in the main area, below Techo del Rino. Go back down the road for about 100m until you find a path on the left. This leads steeply up through the trees to the bottom of the cliff. This path also seems to be a very popular toilet - users please go somewhere else!

CONDITIONS - The wall faces north making it an attractive venue in hot weather. During the winter months it never sees any sun but at other times it is possible sometimes to climb here in beautiful evening light. It is much more exposed to the wind than the main areas.

DESCENT - You can abseil straight back down most of the routes using double 50m ropes. Failing that, locate the anchor at the top of *Sonrisa Vertical*. One long abseil leads to the belay at the top of pitch 2 which is 50m from the ground.

❶ Luna 7a
A good long route which starts up a left-trending flake on a small clean slab. The last pitch is to the right of a large recess high on the face and provides a hard finale. Fully bolted.
1) 6b+, 28m. 2) 6b, 26m. 3) 6b+, 20m. 4) 7a 24m.
FA. Ruiz, Barber, Sánchez 1990s

❷ Esto escampa . . . . 7a+
A majestic, fully-bolted route with two technical pitches in the middle and on quality rock throughout.
1) 6b, 28m. 2) 7a+, 30m. 3) 7a, 24m. 4) 6c 24m.

❸ Lejos de la multitud 7a
Two good hard pitches after an poor start.
1) 4, 26m. Scramble up the approach slopes to a belay.
2) 6c+, 30m. 3) 7a+, 28m. Directly up the wall to the left of the long curving corner.
FA. J.M.García 1990s

❹ Venus erycina . 7b
A brilliant line up the long sustained corner. It is seldom climbed, probably because the top pitch is E6.
1) 4, 26m. As for *Lejos de la multitud*.
2) 6c, 34m. 3) 7b, 28m. Two desperate trad pitches up the long curving groove.
FA. J.M.García, N.Sanchez. FFA. M.Edwards 1990s

❺ El Ojo de Yavé 7a
33m. A scrappy start but fine climbing near the top.
FA. N.Sánchez 1990s

❻ Anillos de Saturno . 7b
30m. Another slow starter but it improves a lot above.
FA. N.Sánchez 1990s

❼ Molly Highins 6c
35m. A long single pitch which is excellent.

Murcia · Alicante · Benidorm · Calpe · Xaló Valley · Gandia · Sella · Puig Campana · Ponoch · Echo Valley

El Collado

⑭ Calfamusculus 6b
28m. The line above directly where the approach path arrives. Excellent grey limestone but a bit of an eliminate.

⑮ Caleidoscopio 6a
20m. A superb route just to the right of of *Calfamusculus*.

⑯ Barco pachero 6c
20m. More quality rock and a bit run-out to add a bit of spice. Fortunately where the bolts are spaced the moves are easier!
FA. J.M.García, N.Sanchez.

⑰ Línea caliente . 7b
Three great hard pitches plus one short connector pitch.
1) 6c, 20m. 2) 7b, 30m. 3) 4, 15m. 4) 6b+, 35m.
FA. N.Sánchez

⑱ Pretoriana . . . . 6b+
28m. The sustained pumpy line of holes is a bit loose and scary
FA. Juan C. and Jesús Romero

⑲ As de copas 7a
25m. This one has thin climbing with spaced bolts.
FA. N.Sánchez

⑳ As de bastos 7a
28m. A long line with an airy feel about it.
FA. N.Sánchez

㉑ Sin comentarios 7b
1) 7b, 35m. A desperately thin and fingery pitch.
2) 6b+, 30m. A long but rather anti-climatic continuation.

㉒ Arte del olvido . . . . . . 6c+
38m. An enormous single pitch.
FA. N.Sánchez 1990s

㉓ Project . . . . (6c+)
38m. Another huge pitch.

㉔ Unnamed . . . . . . 7a+
A long and majestic trad route. Take a full rack.
1) 7a+, 30m. 2) 6b, 28m. 3) 6a, 30m. The odd bit of tat marks the way though the route sees little attention.
FA. M.Edwards, R.Edwards 1990

㉕ Rosa de piedra . . . 7a+
Two hard pitches but on friable rock. **1) 7a, 30m. 2) 7a, 30m.**
FA. N.Sánchez 1990s

㉖ Route 26. . . . . 7b
18m. A shorter offering aiming for the base of the big groove.

㉗ La pistola 6b
18m. A crack and groove.
FA. Juan C. and Jesús Romero 1990s

㉘ La Vergonya 4
20m. A scrappy pitch on the edge of the wall which is not really worth walking up here for.

⑧ El martillo de Thor 6c
30m. A right-hand finish to *Molly* is of less sparkling quality.
FA. N.Sánchez 1990s

⑨ Tanit . . . . 6b+
A superb long route and the easiest way up the whole wall. The first 3 pitches are well bolted but there is little fixed gear on the last pitch so take a small rack. The first pitch is 3 star and well worth doing even if you don't want to go any higher.
1) 6b+, 30m. 2) 5+, 26m. 3) 6a+, 24m. 4) 6a+, 20m.

⑩ El endemoniado 7a
30m. A fine single pitch which is well worth the walk up.
FA. J.M.Ruescas, N.Sánchez 1990s

⑪ La estación de la bruia . 6c
Another fully-bolted mega route.
1) 6c, 30m. 2) 6b+, 28m. 3) 6b+, 28m.
FA. N.Sánchez 1990s

⑫ Armagedón . . . . 6c+
30m. A left-hand start to *Sonrisa Vertical*.
FA. J.M.Ruescas, N.Sánchez 1990s

⑬ Sonrisa Vertical . . 7a
One of the best routes around with superb climbing on the first two pitches. Fully bolted and best done on two 50m ropes.
1) 6c, 30m. Worth doing in its own right.
2) 7a, 20m. An immaculate sustained pitch.
3) 6a+, 40m. Straight on all the way to the top.
FA. Salva, Higinio, Jesús 1990s

Not much sun | **15 min**

❹ Metal guru . . . . 🔲🔲 [____] **6c**
25m. A left-hand start to *Quita* is a little run-out.
FA. Javi Metal

❺ Quita la música . . . . . . 🔲🔲 [____] **7a+**
25m. Superb steep climbing with too many holds on the crux.

❻ Final d'estiu . . . . 🔲🔲 [____] **7b**
25m. Good climbing up the steep wall.

❼ Felanicula . . . . [____] **8a+**
25m. A former competition route so expect chipped holds.
FA. M.Edwards 1989

❽ Los Avutardos . 🔲🔲🔲🔲 [____] **7c**
25m. The overhanging crack and corner.

GALERA DE TAFARMACH

❾ Route 9 . . . . [____] **6c**
28m. A solitary pitch away on the left.

❿ Sporty Spice . . 🔲🔲🔲🔲 [____] **7a+ (E5)**
A wild outing with a remote feel. It is partly bolted but take a
small rack including Friends. Start about 100m right of where
the path meets the face. The first bolt can be seen 20m up.
1) 6b+, 40m. Easily up a recess then left to the bolt. Head up to
some good holds then gain a line of undercuts leading left to a
bolt below the belay ledge. Bolt belay.
2) 6b, 20m. Climb cracks (bolt) to the next belay, bolt and peg.
3) 7a+, 40m. A long pitch, take 12 quickdraws and a Rock 5.
Up the beautiful pocketed shield to nut belay in a deep cave.
4) 6b+, 30m. Leave the cave rightwards then move back left,
past a peg, to the foot of a crack-line in an exposed position.
Climb the crack to the top.
DESCENT - Walk down the ridge to the top of El Collado then
off the back to a track which leads around to the main track.
FA. Andy Hyslop, Tim Lofthouse 2000

EL COLLADO
Up and right of the main face of Pared de Rosalía is a short
wall in a bay with a recessed cave up and left.

❶ Manhatten Blues . . 🔲🔲🔲 [____] **7a**
26m. Start at the top of the slope, inside the cave. Climb the
steep wall on pockets and tufas. Gets very steep very quickly.

❷ Parado de la duración . 🔲🔲 [____] **6c+**
30m. Another fine long pitch up the right wall of the cave.
FA. J.M.García 1990s

❸ La indecisa . . . . . . 🔲🔲🔲 [____] **7b**
30m. A good route up the grey slab and into the open scoop
right of the cave but with a perplexing move. Low in the grade.

GALERA DE TAFARMACH
Right of El Collado is a massive wall which is in
reality a continuation of Pared de Rosalía.
APPROACH - Walk up the clear area directly
from the first bend in the track, after the refuge.
This brings you out at the foot of *Mujer Lampréa*.
There is also a path from below El Collado.
CONDITIONS - Mostly shady and cool/cold
except on the longer evenings when the wall is lit
up by the evening sun.

Not much sun | **20 min** | **Windy**

Murcia | Alicante | Benidorm | Calpe | Xaló Valley | Gandia | Sella | Puig Campana | Ponoch | Echo Valley

BADALL DE TAFARMAIG
The continuation wall. The first routes are centred on a steep recess with well-featured rock.

Not much sun | 25 min | Multi-pitch | Windy

⑯ Route 16 . . . . 6b+
15m. The bolted right-hand finish to the previous route.
FA. J.M.García, S.Barber, J.C.Romero 1990s

⑰ Vía de Bea 6c
15m. Direct to the lower-off on *Route 15*.
FA. J.C.Romero 1990s

The next line is a project.

⑱ La red del diablo . . 7b
22m. The centre of the orange wall on the right.
FA. J.C.Romero, N.Sánchez 1990s

⑲ Algol 7a
FA. J.C.Romero, N.Sánchez 1990s

⑳ Zafiro 6b (E3)
The right-hand wall of the cave and the grooves above.
1) 6a, 2) 6b, 3) 6a.
FA. R.Edwards, S.Perez 1990s

㉑ Badall de Tafarmaig . . . 6c (E4)
1) 6b, 2) 6c, 3) 6a.
FA. Albert Lloret, Sebastía Pérez 1990s

㉒ Scenic Express 6c (E4)
A brilliant top pitch but it requires some effort to get there.
1) 6c, 2) 6b+.
FA. R.Edwards, M.Edwards 1990s

㉓ Figures in the Mind . . . 8a/7b
An impressive long route which is fully bolted.
1) 7a, 2) 7b, 3a) 8a. The right-hand branch.
3b) 7b. The left-hand branch.

㉔ Mighty Whitey . 7c
The slab to the first belay of *Figures in the Mind*.
FA. A.Hocking 2001

㉔ Gran diedro rojo 6c (E4)
The long red corner on the next section of the wall. 1) 6c, 2) 6a.
FA. R.Edwards 1990s

⑪ Gato negro, gato blanco . . 7b
1) 6c, 2) 7b, 3) 7b.
Three very long pitches. Long ropes needed to abseil off.
FA. François Clair, Benjamin Stach 1990s

⑫ Mujer Lampréa 6c
1) 6c, 2) 6b, 3) 6c, 4) 6c+.
The only details known abou this one are that it is fully bolted, brilliant and a little run-out.
FA. N.Sánchez 1990s

BADALL DE TAFARMACH

⑬ Route 14 . . . . 7b
25m. The left-hand side of the wall directly above where the approach path meets the wall. It is about 12m left of *Phoenix*.

⑭ Route 13 . . . . 7c
25m. The left-hand wall of the recess. Given 7c but it may actually be harder than that.

⑮ Phoenix Zone . . . . . . 7a+ (E5)
32m. A single pitch trad route.
FA. M.Edwards, R.Edwards 1990s

Murcia | Alicante | Benidorm | Calpe | Xaló Valley | Gandía | Sella | Puig Campana | Ponoch | Echo Valley

THE DIVINO

The most impressive bit of rock in Sella is also one of the least popular of the developed areas. The climbing is divided into two main categories. The lower walls which have some shorter (one or two pitch) sport routes; and the upper walls, which have some multi-pitch traditionally protected routes.

APPROACH FROM ABOVE (Pared de la Cima and Upper Pared de la Taula) - The recommended approach for the upper sectors is by driving around the back to get within easy walking distance of the summit of the mountain. Drive through Sella village away from the coast. 4.1 km from the village is a right turn on a left-hand bend signed 'Benifato 16.2km'. Follow this tarmaced road up the hill keeping to the main road, passing Remonte Alemana at 3.2 km, until it turns to dirt, at a parking area by a water tank, 6.3 km from the main road. Continue on foot spiralling round behind the peak to a large chimney construction (a pigeon roost - drivable to here in a 4-wheel-drive vehicle) and continue up to the summit. From here you can walk down the edge of the cliff to the grassy ramp between the 2 upper walls (see photo above). This ramp leads down, past one awkward section, to the terrace below both Pared de la Cima and Pared de la Taula.

APPROACH FROM BELOW (El Elefante, CP10M, Techo Placa, Espolón Pertemba, Lower Pared de la Taula) - From the refuge, take the left-hand fork of the road up the valley. 100m past a house on the right, a track doubles back on the left, park here (space for 2 cars but don't block the road). Walk leftwards along a rough path up the hillside. The first buttress is El Elefante, to the left is Sector CP10M. Continue up the hillside to the cave of Techo Placa. Just beyond this is the rounded rib of *Espolón Pertemba*.

For Pared de la Taula - Continue walking up left to the foot of the long broken ramp dropping down from the upper walls. Scramble (3) up here and gain the diagonal ramp which runs up beneath the face. Walk up here to reach both upper sectors.

DESCENTS - These are listed with each section. The main terrace descent is indicated above. If you have approached the upper two sectors from below then the scramble down towards Sector Pertemba involves an awkward section which is equipped with a belay for abseil.

The route below is worth a brief mention because it provides a relatively easy way up the Divino, with continually interesting climbing. The line is marked on the photo above.

❶ Amor de Odio . . . . 🔲🔲🔲🔲 ☐ 6a
A great long expedition (12 pitches) which follows the lower ramp-line below Pared de la Taula, then continues up the slabs right of the diamond of Pared de la Cima. There are a couple of 6a pitches on it, and a diagonal abseil at the start of pitch 3 - take a full rack of gear. Pitch grades are 1) 5, 2) 5+, 3) 6a, 4) 5+, 5) 4, 6) 3, 7) 5, 8) 3, 9) 5, 10) 6a, 11) 5+, 12) 5+.

PARED DE LA CIMA
The diamond-shaped buttress which rises to the summit of the mountain is home to some impressive routes with striking lines. They require a competent approach since inevitably there is some loose rock and route-finding can be intricate. Those looking for big-mountain adventures will find little better in this book. Allow plenty of time, carry water and make sure someone back on the ground knows your plans.
APPROACH - The best approach for the wall is from above (see opposite).
DESCENTS - If you have parked at the top then you won't need to descend. If you approached from below then see the terrace descent from Pared de la Taula.

Approach from rake between Cima and Taula

❶ **Mamtastic** ...... 6c+
A superbly positioned sport route on the upper left edge of the wall. Reach the start by locating some abseil bolts near the summit and abseiling down the line.
1) 6b, 25m. Trend left onto the front of the pillar.
2) 6b+, 15m. Superb climbing up the crest.
3) 6c+, 25m. The climax, follow the bolts - excellent sport.
FA. Andy Hyslop 1990s

❷ **Diedro Edwards** ... 6b (E3)
A striking line though the option of escape left spoils it somewhat. Start at the base of the ramp below the wall.
1) 5+, 25m. Climb a pillar and slab then move left to a ledge.
2) 6a+, 35m. Continue up the slab and over the overlap.
3) 6a, 20m. Move back onto the slab and follow it to a niche.
4) 6a+, 30m. The slab leads to a roof. Move left to a bolt belay.
5) 6a+, 15m. Step left then go up right (bolt) to a bolt belay.
6) 5, 25m. Climb over a roof onto a slab. Move up left then climb a crack on the right to a ledge. (It is possible to continue in the same line and escape at grade 5).
7) 5, 25m. Climb the crack on the right, past some bolts (shared with *Mamtastic*) to a belay.
8) 6b, 25m. Follow the crack past 2 overhangs (2 bolts) to a finish over loose blocks.
9) 5+, 45m. Climb the groove, moving left to the top - poor.
FA. R.Edwards, S.Perez 1993

❸ **Notario** 7a (E5)
The original climb on this wall follows the striking diagonal crack line, mostly on trad gear, with some bolted belays. There are some variations possible though only the modern and most popular line is described here.
1) 6a+, 25m. Get onto the slab (loose), up this and cross onto the wall then traverse the ledge (thread - *E.o. t.W.* belay). Continue right to the edge of a pillar and up this to a belay.
2) 6b, 27m. Climb the broken cracks direct. At the top, move left to a sloping ledge and bolt belay.
3) 6a, 30m. Climb the slab on the left to a spike, left to a groove and climb this until it is possible to move left and follow a fault to a bolt belay (same as *Eye of the Wind*).
4) 6b, 28m. Climb broken cracks on the left then follow the right-hand branch to a stance. The left one is *Eye of the Wind*).
5) 6c, 32m. Climb left to a steep corner and pull around the arete leftwards into a diagonal crack. Traverse this to a corner then move left and up to a hand traverse left across to a stance.
6) 6c, 50m. Follow the shallow depression to bolts above the roof. Pull over and traverse right into cracks. Follow these to the large ledge and traverse left to a bolt belay.
7) 7a, 50m. Climb the short crack left to a shallow depression (bolt). Ascend leftwards (bolt) to the arete and follow the crack (3 pegs) to ledges which lead to the top.
FA. (Aid) P.Notario, Maldonado 1983
FFA. R.Edwards, M.Edwards 1993

❹ **Eye of the Wind** 7c (E6)
Takes an uncompromising line up the centre of the wall.
1) 6a+, 25m. Climb a shattered pillar to the slab, up this and cross onto the wall then traverse the ledge to a thread belay.
2) 6c+, 35m. Climb to a bolt then right (2 bolts) to a groove. Up this to a another groove to its top. Move right to belay.
3) 6a, 30m. Climb the slab on the left to a spike, move right to a groove and climb this then move left along a fault to a stance.
4) 6b, 35m. Follow the shallow groove below the broken cracks until it is possible to climb along a faint crack which leads to a groove. Climb the groove and cross right to a bolt belay.
5) 7c, 30m. Up the fault (threads) then a groove to a slab. Pull over a roof then up the groove and cracks to a bolt belay.
6) 6b, 25m 6b. Follow the cracks past a small tree, and pull over a small overlap to a good ledge.
7) 4, 15m. Traverse the ledge left to a bolt belay.
8) 6c, 48m. Up the right-slanting crack then move left onto the wall. Up then right to another crack and follow this to a ledge on the right. Move left to undercuts, pull over and climb the slab and cross the roof on the left.
9) 4, 15m. Climb up ledges to the top of the wall.
FA. R.Edwards, M.Edwards 1993

Descent down terrace

Lots of sun | 1 hour | Multi-pitch | Windy

10

7

2
1
3
4
5 6

8

9

11 12

A

Approach scramble

13

The ledge beneath the first two routes is reached by a grade 4 scramble. Climb them with double ropes and abseil off.

PARED DE LA TAULA

The central section of the Divino is more developed than the upper walls. Most of the routes on this wall are long, hard and of unquestionable quality but the easiest one has pitches of 6c and the rest are much harder. Most are traditionally protected, although there is some fixed gear, and there is also loose rock, as expected on a big mountain. Take plenty of water and make sure you let someone on the ground know your plans.

APPROACH - From above or below. See page 172.

CONDITIONS - This huge wall catches most of the sun that is going, making it an oven in hot weather but a better bet in the colder months. It is high up so it will be exposed to wind and rain if the weather turns.

TERRACE DESCENT - Descend down the grassy ramp between Cima and Taula, past one awkward section, to the terrace below the upper walls. Drop down this until you are past a large cave on the left. Find the fixed belay and make 1 abseil to the ground (or down climb at grade 3 or 4).

❶ **Class for Today . . .** 6a (E1)
40m. The cracks in the left side of the wall. Take a full rack.
FA. R.Edwards, S.Perez 1993

❷ **Toda. . . . .** 7a (E5)
40m. The right-hand crack is a lot harder. Take a full rack.
FA. F.Durá, J.F.Carbonell

The next line is under the centre of the large triangular wall.

❸ **La Taula/Regalo de díaz** 7a+
One of the best-situated sport routes on the Blanca which has great climbing. Check on the state of the gear at the refuge.
1) 6c, 45m. Climb the slab right to a crack and up it to a niche.
2) 7a, 40m. The crack leads to a stance below an overhang.
3) 7a+, 50m. Climb the roof on its left, then follow cracks to a peg. Traverse right into the wider crack and belay.
4) 6a, 30m. Climb the crack to the top.
FA. (Aid) Q.Soler, J.M.Orts. FFA. R.Edwards, M.Edwards 1992

❹ Wish You Were Here 🎀🖼️🔩 [____] **8a (E8)**
An arduous outing with four hard pitches. The belays are bolted but a full rack is needed including lots of micro-wires. Start below a faint crack-line to the right of *La Taula.*
1) 3, 15m. Climb up easily to a ledge below the crack.
2) 6a+, 25m. Gain the crack and climb it to a bolt belay.
3) 7b, 25m. Continue in the same line.
4) 8a, 25m. The big pitch! Follow the very faint cracks above to another bolt belay. Small wires essential.
5) 7b, 25m. Continue up the cracks to a belay below a roof.
6) 7a, 25m. Climb the steep groove to the right of the roof, then the crack above. Move right into another crack. Up this to belay and junction with *La Taula.*
7) 6a, 30m. Finish up the crack as for *La Taula.*
FA. M.Edwards, R.Edwards 1995

❺ Fisura de Edwards . 🎀🔩🖊️ [____] **7a (E5)**
The natural crack system in the middle of the wall. Take a full rack and plenty of quickdraws. Start in the centre of the wall.
1) 7a, 50m. Climb the cracks then traverse right past a bolt to a ledge. Climb the bulge on the right, then left out of the hollow above to reach a flake. Climb to a crack which leads to a belay.
2) 7a, 25m. Descend right to a groove, up this then move left onto a wall. Cross left to where cracks lead back right to a hole. Climb the flakes and corner above to a ledge.
3) 7a, 40m. Traverse left, then move up into cracks. Follow these past threads, some difficult moves and 2 bolts, to a ledge.
4) 5+, 50m. Climb the groove above to an overhang. Step left to another groove and follow this to the top.
FA. R.Edwards, S.Perez 1993

The next two climbs are started from ledges reached by descending right from the centre of the face to the base of a long sloping crack.

❻ Excitación/Waiting for the Sun
. . . . 🎀🔩🖊️ [____] **6c+ (E4)**
A route up the right-hand side of the wall based on an old route called *Excitation*. Take a full rack.
1) 5, 25m. Climb cracks to a niche.
2) 6b, 25m. Climb the steep wall then move right and up another wall. Traverse left to a small cave and thread belays.
3) 6c+, 35m. Climb up then right to cracks, up these to a belay.
4) 6c, 25m. Climb cracks on the right past a peg and over a small roof to a stance in a niche.
5) 6b+, 25m. Follow the obvious traverse leftwards, past 2 bolts, to a crack. Climb up, then left and up to a ledge.
6) 6a+, 30m. Climb over the bulge on the left and continue leftwards past a peg until you can climb direct to the top.
FA. (Excitación) ? and J.Garcés. FA. (WFS) R.Edwards, S.Perez 1994

❼ Lloret/Pérez/Edwards . 🎀🔩🖊️ [____] **6c (E4)**
The easiest line on this wall. Take a full rack with a lot of quickdraws. From the broken ledges scramble down right to a rib.
1) 4, 40m. Climb the rib and wall then move up to a small tree.
2) 5, 25m. Climb rightwards to a recess and bolt belay.
3) 6b, 50m. The crack on the right leads to a scoop.
4) 6c, 25m. Move left to a crack. Climb this then move left and back right then continue up the crack to a hanging stance.
5) 6a, 30m. Climb the crack then a shallow groove on the left, over an overhang to a ledge.
6) 5, 30m. Traverse left, then up to a small ledge and belay.
7) 5, 30m. Move left then climb up and left near the top.
FA. A.Lloret, S.Pérez, R.Edwards 1993

The large cave below the huge triangular wall is home to a lone sport route. It is best reached from below.

❽ Ópera Orni . . . . . 🎀🖊️🖼️ [____] **7b**
25m. A lone sport route through the roof of the cave.
FA. I.Sánchez

The right-hand side of this wall is bounded by a huge chimney/ corner in its upper section - La Canal. The next route starts below this and is best reached from below.

❾ La Canal . . . . 🔩🖊️ [____] **6a (E2)**
The striking line has drawn many climbers to it but most come back with horrific tales of loose rock, thorns and gorse bushes. 8 pitches with a hardest grade of **6a**.
FA. J.C.Chorro, M.Pomares

❿ La Chino . . . . 🔩🖊️ [____] **5+ (HVS)**
This is the easiest way up the Taula wall although it shouldn't be underestimated. The climbing is straightforward but the situation and rock quality are not. 8 pitches at around **5/5+**.
FA. Coves, Jiménez

The next three routes need different scrambles to gain their starts. Most of the climbing is easy but take care with loose rock.

⓫ Blood on the Rocks . . . 🎀🖊️ [____] **7a+ (E5)**
A big route taking the impressive red-streak in the big wall right of the main bulk of Pared de la Taula. A full rack is needed with a few thin threads. Start by scrambling up a ramp onto the grassy terrace. Continue left until almost under the red streak.
1 to 3) 5, 90m. Take three relatively easy pitches up the lower wall to reach a belay below the smooth wall.
4) 7a, 45m. Climb direct to a thread, then left up a pocketed slab, past some bolts, to a belay.
5) 7a+, 40m. Follow the fully bolted line above.
6) 6c, 40m. Climb a groove on the right then move left into a groove. Follow this past bolts to a ledge on the left.
7) 6b, 35m. Climb the wall above then swing left and follow grooves to a large ledge.
DESCENT - Make 5 abseils starting from threads and blocks down and left. Alternatively, walk across the ledge and follow *La Chino* (4) to the top.
FA. M.Edwards, R.Edwards 1993

⓬ Milongas sangrantes . . 🎀🔩🖊️ [____] **7b**
Running parallel to *Blood on the Rocks* is a fully-bolted route. No exact details are known but it is likely to be very good. Start right of *Blood on the Rocks* on the terrace.
1) 6b, 2) 7a/A0. This might be an aid point or just a short, hard section which is by-passable with a quick pull on a bolt.
3) 7b (6c+ with aid) 4) 6a+, 5) 6a+, 6) 6a
FA. Domenec Rus, E.Pereres

⓭ Alcudia . . . . 🔩🖊️ [____] **5+ (E1)**
A diagonal line starting from just left of the pillar of *Espolón Pertemba*. Rumoured to be loose and full of prickly bushes.
1) 4+, 2) 5+, 3) 4, 4) 4+, 5) 4+, 6) 4+, 7) 3
FA. R.Moltó, M.Pomares

ESPOLÓN PERTEMBA and TECHO PLACA

On the lower section of the wall is a long rounded rib up which *Espolón Pertemba* finds a way. Right of the rib is a vertical wall known as Techo Placa.

APPROACH - Walk up from the valley under the El Elefante and Sector CP10M.

CONDITIONS - It catches most of the sun that is going making it an oven in hot weather but a better bet in the colder months. This lower section is quite well sheltered.

Descend by the terrace

Alcudia

① Espolón Pertemba

.... 5 (HVS)

A good line up the long rounded pillar which is the most popular long route on the Divino, however it is a serious undertaking; the route finding is awkward and there is a fair amount of loose rock about. Take a full rack. Start below the rounded rib left of the arching roof of Techo Placa.

1) 4+, 40m. The centre of the rib, past two ledges, to a third ledge.
2) 5, 45m. Climb direct then trend left and back right to pegs. Move up and left again to a ledge.
3) 4, 40m. Climb right then left over a bulge. Continue upwards, keeping right of the gully, to a ledge on the arete.
4) 4+, 30m. Head up the vegetated groove, then press on up the slabs heading slightly left.
5) 4, 20m. Climb a slab then trend left to a belay.
6) 4, 40m. Move up rightwards to easier ground and the top.

Variation Finish
6a) 5, 25m. Climb the slab on the left to blocks and a belay.
7a) 5+, 50m. Follow the slab above past a hard move to the right.

DESCENT - Walk up the mountain until the Pared de Cima comes into view. Then descend as described on the previous page.
FA. J.García, M.Pomares, J.M.Ramírez.
FA. Variation Finish - El Edwards

② Enlaces ... 6c (E4)
The left-hand line. It might have some fixed gear.

③ Tesores ... 8a
The right-hand bolted line is steep.
FA. N.Sánchez

④ Voyages 6c (E4)
The left-hand side of the wall has a testing pitch.
1) 6c+, 34m. There is some fixed gear in the pitch, but take a full rack of wires to supplement this.
2) 4, 16m. Traverse right to an abseil point.
FA. R.Edwards, S.Perez

⑤ Hidden Glory..... 5+ (E1)
Good climbing along the dog-leg cracks. Take a full rack.
1) 5, 20m. Follow the cracks as they lead up and right to a stance in the middle of the wall.
2) 5+, 20m. The leftwards crack leads to a belay on *Voyages*. Finish as for *Voyages*.
2a) 4, 20m. A variation finish can be made up the continuation line of the first pitch to the other abseil point.
FA. R.Edwards, S.Perez

⑥ Techo Placa 7a (E4)
A worthwhile route on the right-hand side of the wall. Consider taking a rack to supplement the spaced fixed gear
1) 6c, 30m. Climb direct up the wall past some fixed gear (but not enough) to a small stance in the middle of nowhere.
2) 7a, 25m. Break right out from the stance up the bolt line and follow this to the crest of the wall. Abseil off.
FA. R.Edwards, M.Edwards

⑦ Duel in the Sun ... 6a (E1)
A amenable route following a line of weakness across the bolts of *Techo Placa*.
1) 6a, 30m. Follow the line of weakness to the belay.
2) 6a, 30m. Head up leftwards to the main abseil point.
It has been extended upwards to the top of the crag in four more pitches (hardest grade 5).
FA. R.Edwards, M.Edwards

Neil Cummins the major tufas of *Ya Somos Olimpicos* (7b+) on Wild Side at Sella - *page 182*. The disturbance caused by climbers at this crag has resulted in the landowner banning free access and you must now get special permission in order to climb here. Yet another example of how thoughtless behaviour by some can spoil it for everyone. Photo: Keith Sharples

EL ELEFANTE

The lower section of the Divino has some very impressive dome-shaped walls. El Elefante is the larger of the two on the right and CP10M is the one on the left. Unlike the upper Divino walls, these buttresses have been developed mostly with sport routes and feel more like the main sectors of Sella than the bigger mountain crag higher up the hillside. The climbing here is very technical with lots of sustained moves on small holds. Many of the routes are sparingly bolted which gives them an exciting feel.

APPROACH - From the refuge, take the left-hand fork of the road up the valley. 100m past a house on the right, a track doubles back on the left, park here (space for 2 cars but don't block the road). Walk left-wards along a rough path up the hillside.

CONDITIONS - Sunny and open but slightly more sheltered than the higher walls.

TOXTO EL FALO

Toxto El Falo is a tiny tower down and left of Sector CP10M. It has some short hard routes with dubious bolts and lower-offs.

1 Pene-tra-2 . . . . 6c
10m. Short, sharp and old bolts.

2 Morfigrey . . . . 6b+
10m. This one has a poor lower-off, so use the tree as well.

3 Escalera De Color 7c
10m. A boulder problem start with hard clips above. Keep left of the bolts over the roof.
FA. I.Hernández

SECTOR CP10M

The fine wall left of the main Elefante.

4 Jesusunu el Africano . . . . 6c+
10m. Old bolts up the nice-looking red groove. No lower-off.

5 Rigoleto 6b
14m. Old bolts protect the right-trending line.

6 CP10M 6b (E3)
30m. Abseil or continue to the top at 5+. Needs a small rack.

7 Tramontana tremens 7c
32m. A stunning long climb. Take care when descending.
FA. N.Sánchez 1990s

8 Lyon's Den . . . 8a
30m. Known locally as *Plasmagoratron*.
FA. M.Edwards 1992

9 Hostia succidanea . 7c
20m. Technical climbing up some thin cracks.
FA. N.Sánchez

10 Pontifex maximus . 7a+
22m. A superb wall climb, finishing over a little roof.
FA. N.Sánchez

11 Cortes en los labios . . . 6a (E1)
1) 6a, **30m.** The wall left of the pillar. A full rack is needed.
2) 5+, **20m.** Two abseils lead back to the ground.

12 Mediodía . . . . 4+
30m. Pleasant climbing up the pillar. Fully bolted.

13 JJ Motos . . . . 5 (HVS)
60m. The long groove on the right is climbed in two pitches. Take a full rack, secateurs and gardening gloves!

Walk down descent

Lots of sun | 10 min | Multi-pitch

14 15 17 18
16
19
20
21 22 23 24 25
26

EL ELEFANTE

⑭ San Alejo . . . . 🔾🔾 **6c**
30m. The left-hand line on the face is excellent.
FA. N.Sanchez 1990s

⑮ Candyman . . . . 🔾 **6b**
The left-hand edge of the wall has this sparsely bolted route.
1) 6b, 25m. Up the slabby face to a stance, recenty rebolted.
2) 6a+, 25m. Continue directly to the top. Abseil off.
FA. R.Edwards, M.Edwards 1987

⑯ Faraód de la chica . . . . . . 🔾 **6c+**
30m. The bolt line paralleling *Candyman* p1.
FA. N. Sanchez 1990s

⑰ Scorpion . . . . 🔾🔾 **7a**
A big route which follows the line of grooves and tufas.
1) 6c, 20m. Rebolted. Use the mini-lower-off to belay.
2) 7a, 40m. A fine long pitch.
FA. R.Edwards, M.Edwards 1980s

⑱ Lupu . . . . 🔾🔾 **6c**
20m. A short curving line past a hole.
FA. N.Sánchez

⑲ Top rope a cinco . . . . 🔾 **7b**
20m. The direct line to the same lower-off.
FA. N.Sánchez 1990s

⑳ The Tongue of the Snake . . 🔾 **7c**
1) 7c, 45m. A long sustained pitch.
2) 7c, 20m. The left-hand variation middle pitch is 7b+.
3) 7a, 20m. The wall above.
FA. M.Edwards, R.Edwards 1987

㉑ Edward's Wall . 🔾🔾🔾🔾 **8a**
50m. A big pitch! It is usually climbed to the mid-height lower-off at a lesser 7b. Descend on a single 60m rope in 2 abseils.
FA. M.Edwards 1991

㉒ Divine Inspiration . 🔾🔾🔾 **7c**
1) 7b, 25m. Past some tufas to a ramp.
2) 7c, 30m. Sustained wall climbing.
3) 7b, 20m. ..and on to the top. Abseil back down.
FA. M.Edwards, R.Edwards 1986

㉓ El Arúspice . . . . . . 🔾🔾🔾 **7b+**
25m. A good single pitch to the lower-off on *Divine Inspiration*.
FA. N.Sánchez 1990s

㉔ Wallmarks . . . . . . 🔾🔾🔾 **8b**
An old project with a good first pitch and a stunning second.
1) 6c+ 20m. Sustained moves up the vertical, red wall.
2) 8b, 30m. The superb continuation. Given 6c+ locally.
FA. M.Edwards 1997

㉕ Gran fisura . . . . . . 🔾🔾🔾 **6b+**
The big corner gives a classic trad route.
1) 6b+, 30m. Struggle up the groove and belay in the back.
3) 6b+, 30m. More of the same to a fixed belay on top.
DESCENT - Abseil via the fixed belay.
FA. R.Edwards, S.Perez, A.Lloret 1989

㉖ The Naked Edge 🔾🔾🔾🔾 **6c**
A superb and sustained arete but with an awkward descent.
1) 5+, 30m. Climb the crack to a bolt belay on the pinnacle.
2) 6c, 30m. Crank to the top - brilliant!
DESCENT - The mid-route belay is poor so it is best done in one huge 60m pitch. Abseil off down *Gran fisura*.
FA. R.Edwards, M.Edwards 1987

Murcia
Alicante
Benidorm
Calpe
Xaló Valley
Gandia
Sella
Puig Campana
Ponoch
Echo Valley

SECTOR VIPs

This short overhanging buttress, of compact smooth limestone, is the home of some very difficult routes. There are some natural routes but most are heavily chipped and glued. This may create some good athletic exercises - but is it cricket? It is up to you to make your mind up.

CONDITIONS - The wall is very steep and sheltered and will stay dry in all but the heaviest of rain although it may seep if it has been very wet. It is south-facing and gets very hot in sunny weather.

APPROACH and ACCESS - See opposite.

① **Akuna Patata.** . . . . 6c+
10m. Just right of the terracing on the far left.

② **La invasión de las morcas** 7b+
12m. A short, sharp route up the wall just right!
FA. Carlos Porcell 1990s

③ **Hazlo ahora** . . 8b
14m. The leaning and smooth wall via a weedy tufa.
FA. Iván Hernández

④ **Jumping mecha flash** . . 8a
16m. Pass the break and head for the hanging flake.
FA. Agustín Gómez, Mecha, I.Hernández 1990s

⑤ **Desert Storm.** 8a
16m. A fingery boulder problem start followed by strenuous jugs and a powerful move to finish.
FA. M.Edwards 1989

⑥ **El valle de los locos.** . . 8b
16m. The direct on *Desert Storm* misses out all the jugs.
FA. Iván Hernández 1990s

⑦ **Ejecutión radical** . . 8c+
16m. Sella's hardest route runs up the centre of the wall.
FA. Iván Hernández 1990s

⑧ **Mark of the Beast** . 8a
18m. More sustained but less cruxy than *Desert Storm*.
FA. M.Edwards 1990

⑨ **Torrente** . . . . . 8b+
16m. Another outrageous line trending right up the wall.
FA. Iván Hernández 1990s

⑩ **Bullarenque** . . 8c
14m. Starting from the top of the block and head left.
FA. Iván Hernández 1990s

The next line is a spectacular project.

⑪ **La generación yogur** . . 7a+
16m. Superb climbing with an E2 jamming crack to finish. The start is harder than it looks. Requests to up-grade it to 7b have been ignored!
FA. J.García, I.Hernández 1990s

⑫ **La fuerza de la costumbre** 7c
18m. Start up a couple of pockets then climb the rib above.
FA. J.García, I.Hernández 1990s

⑬ **Conecta cuarto** . . . 7c
18m. The left-hand branch above the diagonal crack.
FA. Iván Hernández 1990s

⑭ **Estratego** 7c
18m. The diagonal pocket line has some reachy clips.
FA. Iván Hernández 1990s

⑮ **Copacabana** . . . . 7b+
14m. The last two routes start above the terracing on the far right. This is the left-hand line.
FA. Agustín Gómez 1990s

⑯ **El mejor matarife.** 7a
20m. The right-hand line from the same start.

Murcia · Alicante · **Benidorm** · Calpe · Xaló Valley · Gandia

HIDDEN VALLEY

This is an area of steep crags in a short deep valley to the east of the main areas. Most of the climbing is steep and overhanging with some superb routes in the grade 7 and 8 category. Please read the access information carefully.

APPROACH - From the refuge, drive up the track past the main climbing areas and continue on the right fork of the road over the top of the ridge and down into another valley. Approximately 3km from the refuge you reach a sharp bend at

LÍNEAS NATURALES

The tall crack-seamed buttresss up and right of the Sector VIPS sees little attention. All the routes require a rack and the fixed gear is 15+ years old on 3 of the routes. If they were re-geared then they would be high quality challenges.

CONDITIONS - A tall south-facing wall which gets plenty of sun. Less sheltered than the other crags in the Hidden Valley

APPROACH and ACCESS - See opposite.

the bottom of a valley. From here you can glimpse Sector Wild Side on the right-hand side of the valley ahead, through the trees. Park here and walk up the track. Wild Side is reached from the first bend and VIPs is further up the track.

IMPORTANT ACCESS INFORMATION - Currently the landowner is unhappy about allowing climbers on this crag. This is because of noise, litter and bad parking by climbers in the past and this is unlikely to change. However, he is a reasonable man and sometimes allows small groups onto the crag providing that they seek his permission first.

Park sensibly off the road at the bottom of the track. Walk up under Sector VIPs and continue to a small house. The owner lives here and speaks English. Every climber who doesn't go and ask permission makes it more likely that there will be a total ban on climbing here.

① Final Exam 7c
As its name suggests, this is the hardest route of the trio, up the smooth left-hand side of the wall.
1) 6a+, 20m. Scrappy climbing up and right to a ledge.
2) 7c, 35m. A big pitch but the bolts are not trustworthy.
3) 6c, 20m. Continue to the top. Abseil off.
FA. R.Edwards, M.Edwards 1990

② Midterm Exam . . . . ⊖🔲🗲✎🔲 7a+
The central crack line could also do with some new bolts.
1) 5+, 20m. easy climbing to the ledge.
2) 6c, 35m. The right-hand corner-line. Left-hand variation is an easier way to the same stance - 6a+.
3) 7a+, 20m. A hard final pitch.
FA. R.Edwards 1990

③ Entrance Exam . . . . ⊖✎🔲 6c
The first route of the degree course follows an elegant line up the right-hand side of the wall.
1) 6b+, 15m. Climb direct to the base of the slim groove.
2) 6c, 35m. Straight up the groove.
FA. R.Edwards, M.Edwards 1990

④ Teorema Chino de los Restos . 7b+
The local topo lists a fully-bolted route somewhere nearby, probably up the hill to the right.
FA. Iván Hernández 1990s

Sella · Puig Campana · Ponoch · Echo Valley

HIDDEN VALLEY - WILD SIDE

This large and impressive overhanging wall is one of the steepest crags in the area with some classic climbs up improbable tufas.

IMPORTANT ACCESS INFORMATION - Currently the landowner is unhappy about allowing climbers on this crag. This is because of noise, litter and bad parking by climbers in the past and this is unlikely to change. However, he is a reasonable man and sometimes allows small groups onto the crag providing that they seek his permission first.

Park sensibly off the road at the bottom of the track. Walk up under Sector VIPs and continue to a small house. The owner lives here and speaks English. Every climber who doesn't go and ask permission makes it more likely that there will be a total ban on climbing here.

CONDITIONS - The wall is very steep and sheltered and will stay dry in all but the heaviest of rain although it may seep if it has been very wet. It is north facing and gets very little sunshine so consequently can be cold.

APPROACH - From the parking area on the main road walk up the track to a bend. From here find a track through the woods which leads easily to a ledge below the wall.

ACCESS - Please do not park by the bend in the track; leave your car down on the main track.

❶ Black is Black 7b
25m. The tufa on the far left of the cliff to the first lower-off.
FA. Iván Hernández 1990s

❷ Watermark . . . 8a+
38m. The vague crack and tufas up the big black wall is done in one big pitch. To the first lower-off is an excellent **8a**.
FA. M.Edwards 1991

❸ Ya Somos Olímpicos . . 7b+
A brilliant route up overhanging tufas which can be led in one mega 40m pitch from the ground.
1) 7b+, 22m. Follow the leaning tufas. The direct start is harder.
2) 7a+, 22m. Continue up the corner in a spectacular situation.
Photo page 177.
FA. J.M.García 1990s

❹ Propiedad privada . 7b+
14m. A short hard pitch up the tufa right of *Somos Olímpicos*.
FA. S.M.Sánchez 1990s

❺ Nameless 7b
20m. A left-hand start to *Keep the Faith* is very good. Use the mini lower-off or press on.
FA. Mechas, Sulcina 1990s

6 Keep the Faith. . . . 🔲🔲🔲 **7c**
20m. The overhanging ramp line to a crux on smooth rounded tufas and pockets. Can be split at a mid-height lower-off or continue in one long pitch to the top. The upper section is 7b.
FA D.Lyon, C.Greatwich

7 Cuestión de estilo . 🔲🔲🔲 **7c**
24m. The right-trending crack-line has a hard crux move. Finish on the belay of *Dosis* or continue to another lower-off (easy).
FA. J.M.García 1990s

8 Dosis . . . . 🔲🔲🔲🔲 **8b+**
24m. A very difficult line up the smooth overhanging wall. Chipped but still manages to be brilliant.
FA. I.Hernández 1990s

9 Project . . . . 🔲
24m. Makes *Dosis* look like a path. Outrageous.

10 Ergometría . . . . . . 🔲🔲🔲 **8a**
26m. A mini *Lourdes* with a hard start followed by pumpy moves up rounded tufas. There is one hands-off rest and several knee-bars if you can find them.
FA. J.M.García 1990s

11 Project . . . . 🔲
20m. Another improbable-looking line.

12 Océano. . . . . 🔲🔲🔲 **7b**
20m. A 7b route to first belay chain. A project (8b+) to the top.
FA. A.Gómez 1990s

13 El último mono 🔲🔲🔲🔲 **8b**
32m. A stunning line up some vague tufas, all the way to the top. It is 'only' 8a+ to the first lower-off.
FA. I.Hernández 1990s

14 Project . . . . 🔲
24m. The pocketed wall. The bottom half looks okay!

Approach

15 Nido amoroso . . . . 🔲🔲🔲 **7b+**
28m. The left-hand finish provides a 7c+ option. Chipped.
FA. I.Hernández 1990s

16 La criatura . . . 🔲🔲🔲🔲 **8b**
30m. An interesting (and big) pitch, despite 3 glued-on stones. The second bolt is very high.
FA. A.Gómez 1990s

17 Septiembre. . . 🔲🔲🔲 **8b+**
28m. Climb tufas to a roof then pull over this to finish.
FA. A.Gómez 1990s

18 Sweet Lady. . . 🔲🔲🔲🔲 **8a**
28m. Start just right of a corner/ramp and climb up to the blank headwall. A strange start and a boulder problem finish.
FA. A.Gómez 1990s

19 Dimensión diamante . . 🔲🔲 **8a+**
28m. Another excellent route. Climb past a long sling to a slot then continue, finishing up a left-facing groove.
FA. A.Gómez 1990s

20 El gremio . . . . . . 🔲🔲🔲 **7c+**
28m. A superb climb up the blue streak. The start and finish are easy. The hard move is only short and can be by-passed by a loop out to the right lowering the grade to 7b+.
FA. L.Birch, J.M.García 1990s

21 El pito del sereno . 🔲🔲🔲 **7c+**
28m. A bouldery start leads to a virtual no-hands rest. Use it because the next 15m are steep and sustained on pumpy holds to a shake-out. The finish is hard, fingery and tricky to read.
FA. Iván Hernández 1990s

22 La hora de Millau . 🔲🔲🔲 **7c**
26m. Start up the 'inverted-V' tufa. Hardest at the start but sustained with a tricky upper section which is a bit run-out. Close to *El pito* in its middle section but still a brilliant route.
FA. Franceses 1990s

23 La forqueta del diablo o Romocop
. . . . 🔲🔲 **8a+**
26m. The line is marked by some double bolts with tat.
FA. Pep Ginestar 1990s

24 Celia . . . . 🔲🔲🔲 **7c+**
26m. 7b up to the top tufa system (good rest). Then steep and powerful moves up the tufa to finish. Hard 7c+ but easy to read on sight and never 8a.
FA. Pep Ginestar 1990s

A 50m gap of blocky but climbable-looking rock.

25 Llanuras bélicas . . . . . 🔲🔲 **7b**
25m. The blue streak and tufas on the left edge of the wall.
FA. Goicoetxea, N.Sánchez 1990s

26 Todos los caminos . . . . 🔲🔲 **7b**
25m. A good route up the vague tufa/crack system.
FA. J.M.García 1990s

27 Si te dicen que caí. . . . 🔲🔲 **7a**
25m. The prominent corner gives intricate climbing. Finish up the right arete at the top.
FA. J.M.García 1990s

PUIG CAMPANA

As you drive up and down the coastline, there is one impressive bit of rock which stands high above all the other impressive bits of rock, the 1406m high Puig Campana behind the small town of Finestrat. Along with the Peñón de Ifach, this mountain has been a focus of climbing in the Costa Blanca since the 1960s. However owing to the long approach walks, and the existence of other significantly more accessible crags, Puig Campana hasn't been developed nearly as much as it deserves. Despite this it is still home to some superb and important routes, which will provide many memorable days of climbing for those into long, traditionally protected climbs. The actual climbing is seldom hard, except on the newer routes. The three main classics on the south face, *Espolón Central*, *Diedro Gallego* and *Diedro Magicos,* along with *El Diamante* and *Espolón Finestrat* on the Aguja Encantada, are the only routes on which you are likely to have company. If you enjoy exploring the mountain, the local guide (Escaladas en el Puig Campana by Manolo Pomares) list over 80 routes on the various face, enough to keep most people busy for several years.

APPROACH (area map page 151)

Puig Campana is approached from the village of Finestrat.

From the North or South - Leave the A7 at junction 65 or 65a and follow signs for Terra Mitica and then for Finestrat. Once there follow the road round the village to a T-junction. Turn right here (left leads to Sella) then left and drive towards the mountain on the road to the popular water source of the 'Font de Moli'. Continue along the metalled road, up the hill, around a series of bends and over a bridge. There are usually cars parked here as this is the most popular point to start your walk up to the summit. For climbing, it is quicker to continue for about 1km to a short track on the right-hand side of the road. Park here and follow a path up the hill for 200m. Just after some pine trees on the right, and by a cairn, is a small track leading off to the right.

For Sector Central - Follow the small path until it is possible to scramble up onto a big plateau. A well-marked path leads from here up under the face.

For Sector Aguja Encantada - Continue along the lower path until the first track on the right at a junction marked by a cairn. Continue to another cairn which marks a track that zig-zags up the screes directly below the face. This sector stays in the shade longer than the main south face routes.

CONDITIONS

This is a big mountain with a climate more familiar to alpine peaks than Spanish crags - snow is not unknown up here in winter. The length of the routes means that it will take you most of the day to get up and down your chosen climb and, as there are no professional rescue teams in the region, it is best to chose the right objective according to your skills, gear and the available hours of daylight. It is obviously essential to carry water but also take some spare clothing for the upper sections, which are frequently colder than you might expect. Indeed the top is often shrouded in mist which makes descents difficult and potentially hazardous. Having said this, you are probably more likely to suffer from sunburn than anything else, so light long-sleeve tops and neck scarves are also a sensible addition to your gear along with the 'factor 15' sun cream.

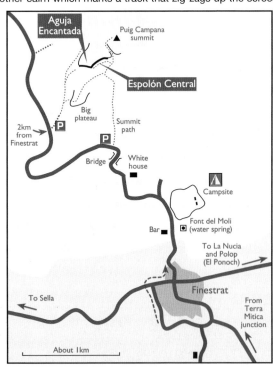

The magnificent Puig Campana towering above Finestrat, with the line of *Sur Central* clearly visible centre-stage.

Murcia
Alicante
Benidorm
Calpe
Xaló Valley
Gandia
Sella
Puig Campana
Ponoch
Echo Valley

AGUJA ENCANTADA

The West Face of Puig Campana is complex area with many pinnacles and walls. By far the most impressive section is the Aguja Encantada which has a number of fine trad climbs. The routes are not as long as on the south face but they are still big undertakings and should not be underestimated.

GEAR - Most of the routes require a full rack although there is some fixed gear. Two of the routes are equipped with the ENP protection device (see the notes on page 20).

CONDITIONS - This huge wall is exposed to the mountain climate and is not a place to go if the weather forecast is poor. However in good weather it catches plenty of afternoon and evening sun, perhaps a bit too much for some people's liking; remember to take plenty of water with you.

DESCENTS - For some of the routes you can just abseil down the line which is sometimes easier since you know where the belays are. There are two general abseil lines which are also worth considering.

Routes 1 to 3 - From the top, abseil back down to the mid-height ledge. Then abseil down the line of *La Flecher*.

Routes 4 to 9 - Abseil down the line of *El Diamante* (see topo).

① La Flecher .... 🔲🖊️⬜ 6a (E2)
Start below a pinnacle on the slab. Take a full rack.
1) 5, 25m. Climb cracks to the base of the pinnacle.
2) 5+, 20m. Climb the pinnacle, step left and up cracks.
3) 5+, 25m. The steep crack on the left leads to a ledge.
4) 6a, 30m. Climb up right up the shallow groove (bolt) and at its top traverse left to the arete. Up this to a ledge.
5) 5+, 20m. Follow cracks to ledges and a tree.
FA. R.Edwards and students 1994

② Aorangi .... 🔲🖊️⬜ 6c+ (E5)
Maori for 'cloud piercer'. Take a full rack.
1) 5+, 25m. Climb the slab to the pinnacle.
2) 5+, 25m. Up the pinnacle then the groove and crack above.
3) 6c+, 45m. The groove (bolts) then on past a flake to a ledge, cross the slabs to the wall behind.
4) 5, 20m. Climb the wall past a sloping ledge. Up left to belay.
5) 6a, 30m. Climb left over a small roof. Cracks and corners lead to a large ledge.
6) 3, 25m. Scramble across broken rock to below a long crack.
7) 5, 20m. A broken wall leads to a ledge.
8) 6b, 45m. Climb the crack then the wall on the left. Move back to the crack and up to a cave.
9) 6a+, 45m. Exit the cave up a chimney; cracks lead to the top.
FA. R.Edwards, S.Pérez 1994

③ Dancing on Crystals 🔲🖊️⬜ 6c (E4)
A fine climb with contrasting climbing. It has 6 ENPs (see page 20). Start below and right of the large pinnacle.
1a) 45m. Climb the slab right to belay below the red wall.
2) 6c, 30m. The groove leads up the steep red wall, 6 ENPs.
3) 6b, 20m. Climb the groove on the right to a ledge. Continue up to another ledge with bolt belays. 2 ENPs.
4) 5, 45m. Go across to a broken corner, and up to a cave.
5) 6a, 30m. Climb the steep wall, move leftwards to a slab and up this to a ledge. 3 ENPs.
6) and 7) As for *Aorangi*.
8) 6b+, 40m. Up *Aorangi* but pull right to a crack, up to a cave.
9) 6b+, 50m. The roof on the right, trend left to join *Aorangi*.
FA. R.Edwards, C.Edwards 1996

④ Diedro Edwards-Pérez 🔲🖊️⬜ 7a (E5)
Climbs the right-hand side of the red wall. Take a full rack.
1) 5, 25m. Climb the wall to a good ledge.
2) 5+, 20m. The black slab leads to the base of a steep crack.
3) 6a, 25m. Follow the crack to a ledge and bolt belays.
4) 7a, 35m. Climb to the corner, past a tufa then make a hard traverse leftwards to a good ledge.
5) 6b+, 30m. Follow the long corner above.
6) 6b+, 35m. Climb the wall left of the belay to a ledge then up past pockets. Move left to a ramp, over a roof and up a groove.
7) 5, 35m. Climb rightwards to an abseil station.
DESCENT - Abseil down *El Diamante*.
FA. R.Edwards, S.Perez 1994

⑤ Pilar de Finestrat ..... 🔲🖊️⬜ 6b+ (E4)
A good climb up the 'Enchanted Pillar'. Take a full rack.
1) 5, 25m. Climb the wall rightwards then move left to a cave.
2) 6b, 30m. Climb up a groove and slab to a roof. Pull over this to a crack on the left then up to a ledge, bolt belay.
3) 6b+, 30m. Climb right then up to a crack, up this then right.
4) 6a, 45m. Climb right then up, past blocks, to a small roof. Over this to the arete on the left, then up to a cave.
5) 5+, 40m. The groove above leads to the abseil station.
DESCENT - Abseil down *El Diamante*.
FA. R.Edwards, A.Lloret 1994

⑥ El Diamante .... 🔲🖊️⬜ 6a+ (E2)
A popular route up the right-hand side of the pillar. Take a rack.
1) 5+, 44m. Start as for *Pilar de Finestrat* and climb the ramp and grooves to the top of a pinnacle. Move right to belay.
1a) 7a+, 30m. A direct start, though the bolts are well-spaced.
2) 6a, 25m. Climb out right, over a bulge, then up a slab to a groove. Follow the groove to a ledge and bolt belay.
3) 6a+, 45m. Up to a slab then the arete. At the last bolt move right to a ledge (belay?). The slab and wall above lead to a cave.
4) 5+, 18m. The pocketed wall leads up a slab to a ledge.
5) 5+, 32m. A groove in the arete leads to the abseil station.
Photo page 193.
FA. R.Edwards, S.Perez 1994. Direct Start R.Edwards 1994

⑦ New Generations .... 🔲⬜ 6b+ (E3)
An ENP route up the wall between the two older classics. Start below a slab, down and left of *Espolón Finestrat*.
1) 6b, 35m. Up the slab to a roof, and right to a ledge, 4 ENPs.
2) 6b+, 50m. Climb the slab above leftwards, then move up to a crack. Follow this to a ledge. 6 ENPs.
3) 6a, 40m. The broken groove and wall leads to another ledge.
4) 6a+, 45m. Climb the slab on the right then up a steep groove. Swing right and cross a roof. Up to the abseil station.
FA. R.Edwards, C.Edwards 1995

⑧ Espolón de Finestrat .. 🔲🖊️⬜ 5 (HVS)
An older route, easier than most hereabouts. Scramble up the ramp below and right of the main pillar. Belay at a tree.
1) 5, 25m. Climb the slab leftwards to a ledge and bolt belay.
2) 4, 20m. Follow ledges out right then back onto a pillar.
3) 3, 25m. Follow the ramp left to a bay. Belay bolt on the left.
4) 4, 20m. Out left into a groove, up to a pinnacle on the left.
5) 5, 20m. Climb the groove on the right. At its top either climb up left or go direct (harder) to a cave.
6) 5, 15m. Follow the arete on the right and move left to belay.
7) 5+, 30m. Climb up right then move leftwards across a ledge. climb a crack to an arete and follow this to the abseil station.
FA. M.Pamares, F.Garcia 1984

⑨ Talisman .... 🖊️⬜ 6a+ (E2)
Start on top of a boulder 4m up from *Espolón Finestrat*.
1) 6a, 20m. Traverse into the middle wall, climb direct, then right, and direct again to a block. Move left to a ledge.
2) 5, 35m. Move left to a groove, over a roof then follow a slab over another roof to easy ground. Belay on the right.
3) 6a, 25m. Climb the right side of the pillar, loop left then right then gain a shallow scoop. Continue up a blocky chimney.
3a) 6a+, 25m. Get into a cave and then out right onto the face. From the next cave, move left into a groove. Up this to a ledge.
4) 6a+, 50m. Move left up the wall, over two overhangs to a slab. Up this and the roof to the slabs above. Continue slightly right to a crack on the headwall. Finish up this.
FA. R.Edwards, R.Birch, B.Birch 2000

⑩ Flamingo Dancer ..... 🔲🖊️⬜ 6a+ (E2)
An extension route. You should already have a full rack!
1) 5, 25m. Cross the pillar into the gap, climb to the right arete.
2) 5+, 25m. Climb the broken groove on the left, then move left to belay below a corner. (The corner is a 6a pitch to the top).
3) 6a, 40m. Move left across the wall, past bolts, to a cave.
4) 6a+, 30m. Move back right to a groove, up this to the top.

⑪ Corazón en la Roca ... 🔲🖊️⬜ 7b+
A sport route reached by climbing one of the lower routes.
1) 6b, 40m. Follow the bolts up the pillar then out right onto the wall. This pitch can be split at a stance at 25m.
2) 7b+, 15m. A hard pitch but it can be aided at 6c/A0.
3) 6a+, 30m. One more pitch leads to the top.
FA. R.Edwards, S.Pérez 1994

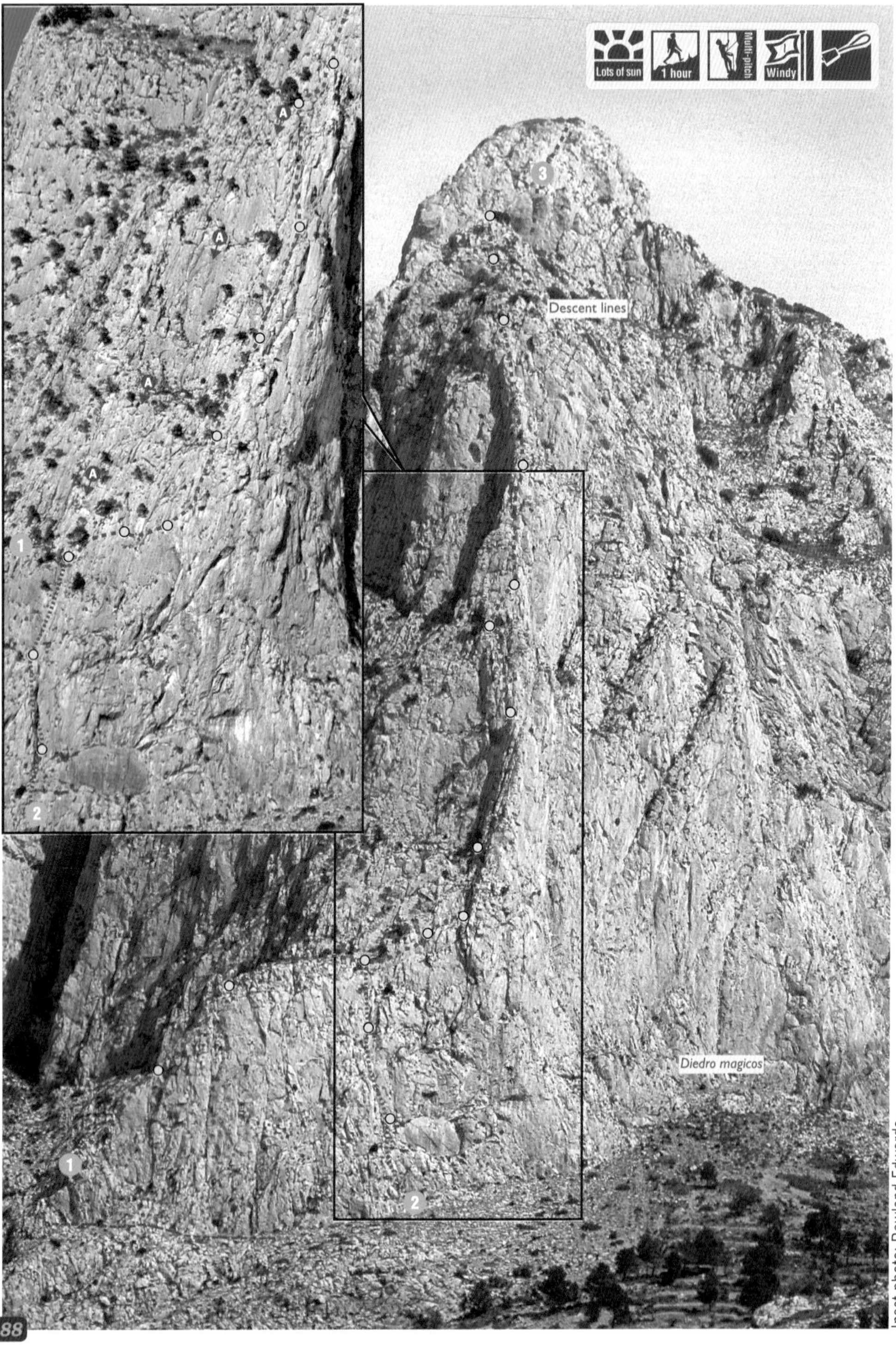
Lots of sun
1 hour
Multi-pitch
Windy
Descent lines
Diedro magicos
1
2
3
A

ESPOLÓN CENTRAL

The huge south face is a massive and complex bit of rock dominated in its centre by the long slender ridge known as the Espolón Central which is home to the classic trad route of the same name.

WHERE ARE YOU? - The local rescue services are often called out to Puig Campana to rescue people who aren't real in difficulty, and quite understandably, they are getting a bit annoyed about this. To avoid this please please make sure that you plan your ascent, that your plans are made known to others and that you stick to them. If you intend to spend a night on the mountain then leave a note in your car to this effect. If you get delayed, but are not in difficulty, then let someone know by mobile phone if necessary.

① Espolón Central . . . 🔲🔲🔲 □ 4+ (HS)

One of the longest routes in the book is a great mountaineering experience. It follows the huge pillar on the left-hand side of the face at a relatively easy grade (British 'Severe' at most) if don't you stray off route. Despite this, the route shouldn't be underestimate since route-finding can be tricky, and the length of the climbing makes for a very tiring day with descents in darkness not uncommon. This route has a bad reputation amongst the local rescue service for accidents many of which happen on the descent. If in any doubt about your ability to climb and descend the route quickly, make sure you start as early as possible. A fast ascent will take around 6 hours but allow yourself at least 10 hours of daylight. Also ensure that you inform someone where you are going and when you expect to be back, or leave a note in your car to that effect.

APPROACH - Walk up the scree slope going up to the centre of the lower half of the South Face. You arrive on a wide ledge below the face itself, the area of the *Direct Start*. Continue leftwards to a cairn below a short steep wall. Scramble up this - the timid may need a rope. Continue up rightwards to reach the rib forming the edge of the buttress.

1) 2) and 3) grade 3, 120m. Follow the right edge of the ridge selecting belays where convenient to reach the large ledge which splits this part of the mountain.

1) to 3) Quick Alternative. Continue up the broken ground behind the ridge, in a gully, until you reach a groove with a large pine at its top. Climb right to the same ledge as above. Walk along the ledge to its end, above is a slab with trees.

4) 3, 45m. Climb the slab to the tree and continue up broken grooves and aretes, trending right, to reach another large ledge.

5) 25m. Scramble horizontally right to the arete proper, threads. Avoid the broken grooves on the left or slabs above the ledge.

6) 4, 25m. Climb up the arete to the next good ledge.

7) 4, 50m. Up the arete moving left at the top to a ledge and peg belay. Retreat is possible from here using a bolt on the left.

8) 4, 35m. Climb the groove on the left of the pillar and continue up easily to a large tree.

9) 10m. Scramble right over ledges to the base of a steeper wall.

Alternative to pitches 8 and 9 -

8a) 4, 35m. Climb the right side of the pillar then hand traverse left onto the arete, up this and the short wall above to a ledge.

9a) 4, 25m. Follow the arete to the base of the wall.

10) 4, 30m. Trend left and follow the groove to the crest, or climb the groove to the left, or the centre of the wall (slightly harder). Beware loose blocks near the top of this pitch.

11) 4, 50m. Climb the arete by the groove on the left. Continue up ledges to a good thread belay.

12) 4, 30m. Climb the ridge by cracks and grooves to the large ledge. Climb the zig-zag crack to a good belay but poor pegs.

13) 4, 30m. The groove on the right leads to easy ground. A further 20m of scrambling reaches a boulder with a faded red paint mark on it. From here a long traverse right (cairns) can be made to reach the far gully - see photo opposite.

FA. J.Roig, C.Torregrosa, M.Gascon 1965

② Espolón Central Directa 🔲

A touch harder than the original wa[...] a groove containing a small bush. [...] route, if that is indeed possible!

1) 3+, 30m. Climb the wall to a sh[...] and continue up the broken groov[...]

2) 4+, 30m. Climb left across the groove and up [...] (pegs) to a ledge. Take care with loose rock on this pitch.

3) 4, 30m. Climb directly up the grooves above to reach the large ledge mention on the normal start.

③ The Edward's Finish 🔲🔲🔲 □ 5 (VS)

A continuation to the top is long and devious - stick to the description! Start above the end of the main route. Whether it is worth the extra effort depends on how tired you are!

1) 175m. Scramble up the broken ridge to a stance below the below the pinnacles that block the way.

2) 2, 50m. Scramble along the ridge then follow ledges that lead across the face on the left to a stance in a col.

2a) 3, 50m. The col can also be reached by following the ridge till it steepens, step right and climb to the top of the pinnacle. (4). Abseiling from a spike into the gully.

3) 4, 26m. From the col climb the wall behind the huge chockstone for 5m then aim left to the blunt arete to find a stance and thread belays.

4) 4, 30m. Choose any line (all much the same grade) to the top of the climbing. From here a final 175 m of scrambling gains the notch at the top of the mountain.

DESCENT - See below.

FA. R.Edwards 1984

GEAR - A full rack of wires and Friends is required for all these trad routes. Take double 50m ropes and some tat for abseiling - just in case. Take plenty of water and spare clothing.

DESCENTS - There are frequently problems when people try and descend the mountain, especially if darkness is falling. As a precaution you should always carry one head torch per person in case you get caught out and please try and familiarise yourself with the descent paths as you approach the mountain. Allow at least a couple of hours to get off the mountain.

DESCENT FROM THE TOP - As you get to the top of the climbing and the terrain flattens out. Follow the path and it takes you into the big notch on the summit. From the notch, drop down about 30m on the seaward side, then traverse until you reach a three bolt belay with a wire 'via ferrata'. Abseil 25m then a good path leads to the main gully descent.

DESCENT FROM THE TOP OF ESPOLÓN CENTRAL - Scramble carefully rightwards, descending slightly into a easier angled area (marked by red dots and with fixed cables on most of the steep sections). Continue traversing around the bottom of a spur then over a ridge to start dropping down a steep gully. The main summit path lies below. Don't try and drop down the slope too early since this is where a lot of the accidents and problems have been caused in the past. The photo above shows the correct line. Note that the whole mountain is covered with goat tracks and goats don't always know where they are going.

DESCENT BY ABSEIL DOWN THE ESPOLÓN CENTRAL LINE The abseil descent, down the left-hand side of the pillar, can be joined at various points from the routes to the right. Remember that abseiling often takes significantly longer than walking down so it may be quicker to head upwards fro a couple of pitches and join the descent above. From the large tree on the ledge at the top of pitch 8a) of *Espolón Central*, abseil from the bolt and thread belay to a ledge (50m). Walk left (facing in) to a cable thread and abseil to another ledge (50m). Walk left and down to another cable. Abseil 25m to a wide bay. Walk down around the base of a rib on the left (facing out) and descend easy rocks to the bottom.

PUIG C

Murcia   Alicante

Beni

Calpe

Xaló Valley

Gandia

Sella

Puig Campana

Ponoch

Echo Valley

VÍA JULIA PILLAR

te *Espolón Central* avoids much of the lower section of the pillar. This is tackled by a nber of significantly harder routes that take intricate lines up it, mostly arriving at the top of pitch 8 on *Espolón Central*. These routes are all worthwhile and have straightforward abseil descents.

GEAR - Most of the routes require a full rack of gear and 2 50m ropes. The route *Nueva Edicion* has several ENP devices on it (see page 20).

DESCENTS - The route *Edge of Time* has well bolted belays and can be used for a quick direct abseil descent from some routes. For the routes which get to the top of the pillar see the abseil descent from *Espolón Central* described on the previous page.

Climbers

Route on previous page

Route on previous page

Photo: Rowland Edwards

❹ Directisima . . . . . 🔣🔣🔣🔣 ⬜ **6a (E2)**
A three pitch route which can lead on to bigger things. Start below a left-sloping ramp, below a large overhang high up.
1) 4, 20m. Climb the ramp to a good ledge.
2) 6a, 40m. Climb the steep wall to a shallow groove (pegs). Enter the groove on the right and climb the excellent crack to its top. Climb rightwards across slabs making for a cave high up. Thread and peg belay.
3) 6a, 45m. Climb the red groove. Near its top move right and climb the steep wall (threads) to reach less steep rock. Follow the cracks on the right to reach the belays of *Vía Julia*.
DESCENT - Abseil off or continue up one of the routes above.
FA. Juan Marti, Pep Camarena 1976

❺ Nueva Edición . 🔣🔣🔣🔣 ⬜ **7a (E5)**
Exposed climbing with several ENPs. It has a UK grade of E5 6a. Start to the left of a ramp and directly below a faint crack coming down from the right side of an overhang high up.
1) 6b, 50m. Follow thin cracks to a shallow groove right of the roof. Climb this to a belay on blocks.
2) 6b, 25m. Climb up to a pocket and continue to a bay on the right. Follow the thin crack above to belay in another bay.
3) 6c, 35m. Climb the steep wall above and left of the cave. Join *Vía Julia* at the end of the layback.
4) 6a, 45m. Climb the groove on the left, move right and up to a tree. Make a rising traverse across the wall to a small niche.
5) 6a, 25m. Climb to a thread and continue up a scoop. Move up and right, then direct to a large flake crack. Belay.
6) 7a, 35m. Climb the middle of the wall (thread) then continue straight up. Take the crack on the right to reach a stance.
7) 4, 25m. Climb the steep slabs to the ledges on the left and a belay shared with *Vía Julia*.
DESCENT - Either continue to join the descent for *Vía Julia*, or, abseil back down *Edge of Time* via the bolt belays.
FA. R Edwards, C.Edwards 1995

❻ Edge of Time . . 🔣🔣🔣🔣 ⬜ **6c (E4)**
A good hard climb. Take a full rack. Start at the top of a ramp, just right of *Nueva Edición*.
1) 5+, 45m. Climb up to a faint groove. Follow the grooves rightwards to another wider one which leads to the belay ledge of *Vía Julia*.
2) 6c, 50m. Climb the thin flake above the belay to a thread. Ascend to a small ledge and then to a small groove. When it becomes steep, move right (thread) and climb slabs and a small roof. Traverse right to belay.
2a) Sin Salida - 5+, 45m. Ascend right to the first shallow groove. Climb this then pull left into another groove. Follow cracks to a ledge. Climb the wall above (peg) then shallow grooves to a good stance.
3) 6a, 20m. Climb to a wall then move right to a ledge. Follow the groove on the left until a crucial hold allows moves onto the left wall. Move up past a peg to belay in a niche.
4) 6b, 40m. Follow the rightwards-slanting cracks to a groove. This leads past a flake to a ramp and groove above (peg). Climb the steep crack to a ledge. Bolt belay.
4a) Sin Salida - 4, 25m. Climb left across the wall to a crack. Climb this to join and finish up *Vía Julia*.
DESCENT - Either continue to join the descent for *Julia*, or, abseil back down the route via the bolt belays.
FA. R.Edwards, C.Edwards

❼ Vía Julia . . . . . 🔣🔣🔣🔣 ⬜ **6a (E1)**
A classic with some great climbing. Take a full rack and large gear for pitches 3 and 5. Start at the foot of the pillar where the name is painted on the rock.
1) 4, 30m. Climb shallow grooves and cracks to a ledge (can be reached by walking around to the right).
2) 6a, 45m. Climb the steep wall and cracks above to a ledge. Continue up more cracks to the top of a pillar. The pitch can be split at a spectacular stance on the half-way flake.
3) 5, 25m. Move left, climb a groove and slab to an overhang (peg). Pull over into a groove (possible belay) then move left to a steep, wide crack. Climb this to a belay.
4) 4, 25m. This can easily run together with pitch 3. Climb cracks in the slab then a corner above.
5) 5, 30m. Follow the widening crack to join *Espolón Central*.
FA. Chema Ramirez, Manolo Pomares 1982

❽ Diedro Gallego . . . 🔣🔣🔣🔣 ⬜ **6a (E1)**
An old classic which follows the huge groove/corner in the centre of the South Face. Start below the long crack.
1) 3, 20m. A wall leads past a tree to a chimney/crack. .
2) 6a, 35m. Follow the crack to a cave.
3) 5+, 25m. Climb up to the roof then onto the face on the left and up a small corner. Move right into a corner and spike belay.
4) 5, 20m. The corner above leads to the final chimneys.
5) 4+, 40m. Follow the chimney past 3 caves to a larger cave.
6) 4, 30m. Bridge the final chimney then climb the right wall to the ridge of *Espolón Central*.
FA. M.Angel, J.Luis, J.Carlos García Gallego 1977

❾ Espolón Edwards . . . . . 🔣🔣 ⬜ **6c+ (E5)**
A route up the narrow pillar of rock immediately to the right of *Deidro Gallego*. Mostly fixed protection but you should carry a good selection of nuts and one or two Friends.
Start right and up from the big crack of *Deidro Gallego*, below a narrow rib of rock going up to an crack at 20m.
1) 5, 25m. No fixed protection. Climb the slabs to the crack and belay on a small ledge just beyond this.
2) 6c+, 25m. Climb the slab and then move left to the overlap and surmount this onto the slab above. Climb to a thread on the left and then move right and then up to a good belay.
3) 6c, 35m. Climb up into the caves above then move left into a groove. Up this and swing left onto the steep slab. Climb up then follow a faint depression left to the roofs. Traverse these right until you can climb up to a peg. Continue direct to reach a good ledge and belay.
4) 6c+, 45m. Climb to the foot of the red wall above and move left to climb some small overlaps. Move right then direct and swing left into the bottom of a groove. Climb this to its top where you can swing right again onto the steep wall. Climb this direct onto a sloping ledge. Climb the leaning wall to its top.
5) 6a+, 40m. Climb the centre of the pillar finishing up a shallow groove on the right
FA. R.Edwards, M.Edwards 2001

❿ Viaje en el tiempo . 🔣🔣🔣🔣 ⬜ **6b+ (E3)**
Pitch 4 can be aided to make the whole route around 6a (E1).
1) 5, 40m. Climb the slab then a blunt arete to a groove. Follow this to a palm tree.
2) 6a, 25m. The steep wall on the right leads to a corner and cracks. Up these to a ledge belay.
3) 4+, 25m. Broken cracks and grooves on the left lead to a large orange corner.
4) 6b+, 25m. Climb the groove above with difficult moves over the mid-height bulge. Continue to a ledge on the right to belay.
5) 5, 30m. Either climb the chimney above; or, scramble left to join the last pitch of *Diedro Gallego*.
FA. Chema Ramirez, Manolo Pomares 1982

Murcia
Alicante
Benidorm
Calpe
Xaló Valley
Gandia
Sella
Puig Campana
Ponoch
Echo Valley

DIEDROS MÁGICOS AREA

The right-hand side of the huge south face contains the classic long groove of '*Magic Corners*' and other routes which are only slightly less worthy. The rock is excellent and the aspect sunny. The long approach keeps the crowds away.

DESCENT (For the long routes) - There is an abseil line in between *Diedros Mágicos* and *Rompededos*. From the belay at the top of *Diedros Mágicos* make a 45m abseil to the ledge below. (This is where *Angalada/Cerdá/Gallego* joins). Make three 45m abseils from here down the line of *Rompededos*.

① Diedros Mágicos
. . ▢▢▢▢ [____] **6a (E1)**
A great mountain route. Start below the long groove which goes the full length of the face.
1) 5, 25m. Climb the corner to a cave which has a bolt belay.
2) 5, 25m. Continue up the corner to another bolt belay.
3) 5+, 30m. Follow the corner to a peg. Move right across the wall (a devious move) to a good ledge and bolt belay.
4) 4, 25m. Move up then follow grooves and cracks leftwards to belay back in the main groove.
5) 6a, 50m. The crux. Climb up to another ledge and a possible belay. Move up to the roof above then a hard move right leads into a corner. Up this, then left to another corner which leads to the top. Abseil off from here or the pillar above leads to the top in four more pitches (grade 4).
FA. H.García Gallego 1980

② Asesina a tu vecina ▢▢▢▢ [____] **6b+**
30m. A sparsely equipped sport route to the right of the corner of *Diedros Mágicos*. Run-out and/but excellent.
FA. C.Ramírez, Q.Barberá 1980s

③ Rompededos . . ▢▢▢▢▢ [____] **6c**
Another great route up the fine wall to the right of *Diedros Mágicos*. The first two pitches are fully-equipped. Take a rack of wires for the last two pitches. The name means 'Break Fingers'!
1) 6c, 45m. Climb easy rock and then a small bulge. Up by the fine face until a tough sequence leads to a 'left-handed' finger flake and more hard moves (crux) gain a good ledge. Enter the shallow groove above (hard for the short) and follow this past spaced bolts to a small stance, 11 bolt runners.
2) 6b+, 30m. Climb up then left to the top of the large perched flake, (old thread) then climb the wall passing a useful tree (peg and bolts) until harder climbing and then one very thin move gains easier terrain with a stance to the right.
3) 5+, 34m. Follow the groove (loose blocks to the left) behind the stance passing a bulge (bolt) before trending right then back left (old peg) over a small bulge to a short smooth groove to reach stance on the left. Abseil from here or:
4) 6a, 30m. Traverse right to a ledge and follow the old bolts up the wall to a new bolt. Lower from this or follow easier rock to the belay of *Diedros Mágicos*.
FA. A and F.Bayonas, B.Durán, J.Rodríguez, M.López 1983

④ Anglada/Cerdá/Gallego . ▢▢▢ [____] **5+ (E1)**
A worthwhile route, which takes the right arete of the wall. The name isn't very catchy! Start well right of *Diedros Mágicos*, below a pillar of broken rock.
1) 3, 15m. Climb the pillar to a ledge just right of a groove.
2) 5+, 45m. Climb the slab until level with a crack. Move right to the crack then step left into another flake/crack. Follow this past a large ledge to another ledge.
3) 4, 45m. The groove on the right leads back left to the top of a pillar. Follow the groove on the left to a large ledge and tree.
4) 4+, 45m. Climb the grooves above to a corner (peg). Move right to another corner and climb this to a groove on the left. Continue to the large ledge above.
FA. M.Anglada, Cerdá, M.A.Gallego 1979

Further right is a triangular wall with two shorter routes on it.

⑤ Tricolomanía . . . . ▢▢▢▢ [____] **6b+ (E3)**
The left-hand side of the wall has some poor rock. Take a rack.
1) 6b+, 45m. Climb a groove then move left to a bolt. Move back right to a bolt line and struggle up this to the belay.
2) 6b+, 45m. Continue up past a peg then move back right past some more bolts to a steep finish.
FA. Q.Barberá, R.Llí 1984

⑥ Cleptomanía . . . . . ▢▢▢▢ [____] **6b+ (E3)**
The right-hand line also needs a small rack.
1) 6a+, 40m. Climb the wall past 2 bolts, then move back left to a peg belay above a pillar.
2) 6b, 26m. Move right and climb the wall (4 bolts).
3) 6b+, 24m. Move across right to below a roof. Pull over the roof to finish.
FA. C.Ramírez, M.Pomares 1982

Simon Blagdon and Rich Mayfield on the 2nd pitch of *El Diamante* (6a+), Aguja Encantada, on the Puig Campana (*page 187*) one of several worthwhile and long outings on this fine tower. Photo: Mark Glaister

Murcia

Alicante

Benidorm

Calpe

Xaló Valley

Gandia

Sella

Puig Campana

Ponoch

Echo Valley

PONOCH

The Ponoch is the massive face of rock that overlooks the town of Polop. It is often stared at from the motorway in awe and wonder, but few people venture onto these extensive walls. The face has many trad routes and a few fully-equipped sport routes on a bigger scale than most in the area. Routes here can be run-out, exposed and affected by signifi-

cant rockfall from the huge face above. Rockfall should be expected at all times, as the often easy upper pitches of the meandering trad routes follow loose ledge systems. A helmet is essential when climbing here. If you enjoy these then you could try getting hold of a copy of the local guide to the mountain - *Guía de Escalada del Ponoch* by Carlos Tudela (1998) which list over 60 more climbs on these spectacular faces.

Bernia from Ponoch, at sundown.

CONDITIONS

The enormous south face of the Ponoch is exposed to any sun that is going - great in the cooler winter months but desperate in the heat since there is little shelter. If there is much of a wind blowing then it will be really wild up here!

APPROACH
(area map page 151)
From the A7 drive towards Polop (signed Callosa d'en Sarrià and Guadalest) you will soon see the large hulk of the Ponoch on your left. 9km from the A7, by a roundabout with an industrial estate, turn left (signed 'Guadalest') on to the ring-road. At the third roundabout on this road (after 1.5km) turn left into

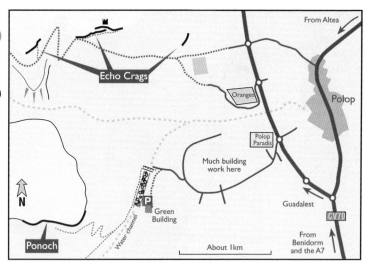

the new Urbanisation Polop Paradis and drive up to parking by a large yet discreet green building at the high point of the road. Walk up the dry stream bed then scramble out of the gorge on the right (cairn) and follow a path which zig-zags up the terraced hillside beneath the crag, aiming for an open bay. This is to the left of an obvious pinnacle, whose profile comes into view as you near the base of the crag. Don't linger at the base if there are parties above, since there is plenty of loose rock up there!

Dwarfed by the immense scale of the cliff a climber is (just) visible on pitch two of *Gorillas en la Roca* (6c+) on Ponoch - *page 197*. Photo: Sherri Davy. Inset: Mike Appleton the crux pitch of *Gorillas*, 6c+.

Murcia

Alicante

Benidorm

Calpe

Xaló Valley

Gandia

Sella

Puig Campana

Ponoch

Echo Valley

Mont Ponoig 1181m

Tozal de Levante

Ponoch

Echo 2

Echo 1

Echo Playa

Lots of sun

20 min

Multi-pitch

Windy

Valencianos escape route

Agulla del Frare

Bottom of wall hidden behind ridge

❶ Héroes del silencio . . . 🔲🔲 ▭ 6c+

An excellent, fully bolted route, giving sustained, fingery climbing on perfect rock. Start beneath the line of new bolts up a non-descript wall in the next bay to the left of *Valencianos*.
1) 6a, 45m. Follow the bolts up the wall to a good ledge.
2) 6a+, 25m. Climb the concave wall and make a tough move around the bulge. A tricky pitch.
3) 6b+, 45m. The wall above has a fingery start and a desperate second clip. Things then ease considerably and enjoyable climbing leads to a stance in a break.
4) 6b+, 45m. Traverse left, then steeply past some holes to pull out at the base of a smooth slab. Thin climbing weaves around the bolts before easier ground and a shallow groove reach a calcite stance with an assortment of belays.
5) 6c+, 30m. Traverse left to a steep crack line. Follow this and make a desperate and blind pull onto the wall above. Move out right to easier ground, before another fingery shield, fortunately easier than it looks, gains easy ground and a belay.
DESCENT - Abseil down a new set of abseil stations off-line to the left of the route (facing in).
FA. Chiri Ros, Isabel Pagan, Manuel Amat Castill 1991/92

❷ Vía Valencianos . . . . . 🔲🔲 ▭ 6a (E1)

A fine, and huge climb up the centre of the face, the first line on the cliff, put up in 1972. The route has over 300m of climbing and a lot of rambling - even fast teams will want to start early. It starts at a scratched arrow below the left-hand end of the grassy ledge system cutting across the base of the face.
1) 3+, 55m. Climb rightwards to the ramp (possible stance) then ramble to a wire cable belay.
2 - 5) 2+, 140m. Scramble along the ledge, then up the steepening ramp passing belays at intervals.
6) 4+, 40m. Climb the steeping slab moving right at half-height to reach a small stance below steeper rock.
7) 6a, 45m. The crucial pitch contains plenty of fixed gear! Follow this up and left across the wall (passing an optional stance) to reach the base of an open groove.
8) 4+, 35m. Climb the groove to its end and a belay on the left.
9) 4+, 25m. Weave up the wall to a stance below easier ground.
10) 3, 40m. Trend right then up, the right again to the major ledge system that cuts across the upper part of the face.
11) 1, 50m. Follow the ledges right to below an open groove.
12) 4+, 30m. Up the groove to the higher ledge system.
NOTE: It is possible to escape right from here along the ledge system, to join the descent route. Care required.
13) 1, 50m. Scramble back left to where the ledge ends.
14) 3, 20m. Climb the ramp to a belay below a leaning groove.
15) 6a, 35m. Up the groove to its closure where exposed moves reach easy ground.
16) 4, 50m. Easier climbing trending slightly right reaches the top - at last!
DESCENT - See photo opposite. Walk uphill in a NE direction towards the top of the hill to a small col (cairns). A 40m abseil from a tree leads to open ground. Head down and left (cairns and white arrows) out onto the buttress to the north of the huge gully. On the end of this descend a ramp to locate the anchors. Two abseils (25m and 30m) lead to the foot of the face.
FA. J.Pi, J.Adalid, C.Torregrosa 1972

❸ Gorilas en la Roca . 🔲🔲🔲 ▭ 6c+

A fantastic route with contrasting climbing. There is some loose rock, so care is needed. The climb is fully bolted, though there is no belay at the top of the first pitch so take a couple of slings. Start at the back of the obvious bay, at the first easy ground to the left of the pinnacle/tower. *Photos page 195.*
1) 6a, 45m. Once you spot the new bolts, follow these negotiating a tricky bulge before the rock disappears and loose scrambling gains a big ledge. Belay by the scratched 'X' which shows the way and the start of the good climbing.

Gorillas en la Roco continued...
2) 6b+, 45m. Follow the rib, grooves and wall above by sustained, sharp gout d'eaux pulling.
3) 6c+, 40m. Climb boldly to a bolt, then on to a shelf beneath a leaning wall. After a tricky start this gives superb climbing up the shallow groove system running up its right-hand side. Pull out onto easier ground and continue to another good belay.
4) 6a+, 30m. No bolts are visible, but follow the ledges right for a couple of moves, before launching confidently upwards, whereupon the bolts do appear. Sustained and excruciating moves lead up the wall and rib to a belay.
5) 6b, 25m. Cautiously gain a loose alcove and try not to imagine what built the nest! Exit rightwards before enjoying the perfectly formed leaning wall above.
6) 6b+, 35m. Follow the wall leftwards, then back right before tackling the hanging groove. Trend back left via one tricky wall to reach a good belay.
DESCENT - Abseil carefully back down the route. When you reach the X ledge, scramble around the bay to the right (facing out) and descend a couple of steps to escape via an abseil station. This is above the batch of trivial single pitch routes on the wall to the left of pitch 1.
FA. Manuel Amat Castill, Antonio "Chiri" Ros 1989/90

❹ Viaje Espacial . . . . . . 🔲🔲 ▭ 6a+ (E2)

Reportedly a fine climb up the walls and ramps to the left of the easier ground taken by *Valencianos*. The route starts at the base of the *Valencianos* ramp and trends generally rightwards following the line of least resistance. Take a rack.
The pitches are **1) 5, 25m. 2) 5, 30m. 3) 5+, 35m. 4) 6a+, 10m. 6) 6a, 40m. 7) 6a+, 35m.** From the end of the climbing traverse right to an anchor and make three long abseils to gain easy ground near the bottom of the *Valencianos* ramp.

❺ Jack Daniels . . . . 🔲🔲 ▭ 6a+ (E2)

A bit of a wandering line between *Viaje Espacial* and the groove of *Valencianos*. The pitches are **1) 6a+, 45m. 2) 6a+, 40m. 3) 5, 30m. 4) 5, 30m.** Not marked on the topo.
FA. Chiri Ros, J.Sánchez, J.Matas 1983

❻ Rocinante . . . . 🔲🔲🔲🔲 ▭ 7b

A fully bolted sport route up the walls to the left of the tower of Agulla del Frare. The rock is excellent, the climbing sustained and the pitches long. **1) 7b, 50m. 2) 7a, 50m.** Take 20 quickdraws and double ropes for the descent.
FA. Chiri .Ros, P.Masip 1993

❼ Flor de Luna . . . . 🔲🔲 ▭ 6a+ (E2)

A popular climb, with an easy approach and descent (well relatively), on good rock, and not too long - at least when compared to the stuff further to the left! Start in the bay at the right-hand side of the face.
1) 4+, 40m. Trend slightly right up the side of the buttress.
2) 4+, 45m. Continue in the same line to a good ledge.
3) 6a+, 25m. Follow the right-trending wall and groove (crux) to easier ground an a little higher a belay on a good tree.
4) 5, 45m. Move easily right then climb to the right of the crest of the buttress before pulling back left to a stance.
5) 6a, 40m. Continue up the buttress (tricky but soon easing) then the groove on the right and up to a stance.
6) 5+, 40m. Climb a little higher then follow the ledge out left to its end and then climb a short exposed wall to more ledges.
7) 5, 45m. Originally the route finished up the grassy ramps than run up an left to reach the *Valencianos* escape route, though it is much better to trend right onto the rounded buttress and climb this to a sudden finish.
FA. J.Matas, J.Lorenzo 1978

ECHO VALLEY

The Echo Valley is the impressive rocky defile that cuts deep into the mountains behind the bulk of the Ponoch. The area is still relatively unspoilt which makes it a pleasant venue for those who are after a bit of solitude. There is much excellent high walking here though the state of the access road is rather off-putting. Much of the climbing on the longer routes here is 'traditional' requiring the carrying of a decent sized rack of gear and double ropes. Many of the harder routes were originally climbed using the Environmental Nut Placement system, or ENP, though this system has not proved popular - see page 20. Recently many shorter single pitch face climbs have been added to the lower walls; there is little doubt these will become popular. Further up the valley are several more huge cliffs that have also been developed with long traditional routes including Echo Placa, Col Lama and the Haunted Walls. These routes have not been included in this guidebook - check **www.compasswest.co.uk** or **www.rockfax.com** for more information.

CONDITIONS
Echo Playa is the lowest cliff and is sheltered; it goes into the shade in the afternoon. Echo One and Castillo both face south and get all the sun that is going. The lower walls are sheltered from the cold north winds. Echo Two is in the sun until mid afternoon, after this it can become chilly, especially in the winter. In hot weather it makes a good venue for late afternoons and evenings. None of the crags can be considered reliable wet weather venues but, if the wind is blowing from the west then the central section of Echo Two can stay dry.

APPROACH (area map page 151)
From the coast drive up towards Polop then take the new ring road (signed Guadalest). Turn left at the second roundabout after the one next to 'Polop Paradis'. The cliffs are arranged on the right-hand side of the track as you drive up the valley, Echo Playa, Echo One, El Castillo and Echo Two. Parking is tricky for Echo One and El Castillo - inevitably as these are the most popular cliffs.

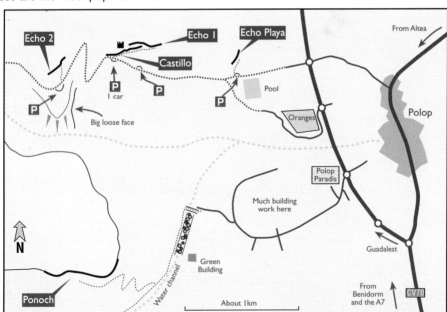

Samantha and Rich Mayfield climbing *Espolon Encantada* (5) on Echo Two - *page 205*.
The Echo Valley has many fine climbs on good rock, and across a range of styles, from
complete clip-ups to routes that require a full rack. Photo: Mark Glaister

Spanish Gold

Orion and Diedro Edwards

ECHO TWO - MULTI-PITCH ROUTES

This magnificent tall face has some great routes for the climber in search of something a bit more adventurous then the usual 'Costa clip-ups'. The routes described on this page are long multi-pitch undertakings which rely mainly on leader-placed gear. They should be regarded as full-day challenges so allow plenty of time, carry water with you and make sure someone knows what your plans are.

APPROACH - Continue underneath Echo One up the steep and twisty dirt road to parking opposite Echo Two which is 5 mins away up the slope.

DESCENT (Walking down from the summit) - From the summit walk south (left looking in) and scramble down the ridge, overlooking the climbs, to a broad ledge. Walk down a sloping scree ledge (right looking out) to an abseil point. A 25m abseil reaches the hillside. Walk down this making for the end of the crag which is visible on the left.

DESCENT (Abseil) - At the top of *Diedro Edwards* is a large boulder on the edge of the wall. There is a rope sling and chain on the wall to the right (looking out) of this. Abseil to the top of the pitch 4, then to the top of the tower. Next to the top of pitch 1 and finally to the ground.

GRADES - The routes are given sport grades but they have been given colour spots to reflect their overall difficulty. Most also have a British grade mentioned.

Murcia | Alicante | Benidorm | Calpe | Xaló Valley | Gandia | Sella | Puig Campana | Ponoch | Echo Valley

1 Espolón de Echo . . . . . 🎵🪕 [____] **3 (VDiff)**
(VDiff) 120m. The left-hand arete of the wall which has many variations. Start in the gully behind the left-hand side of the crag. Climb the steep wall rightwards to get onto the ridge and follow this easily to a large step. Climb the ridge on the left to the summit in two or three long pitches.
FA. R.Edwards 1998

2 Vía de Polop . . . . . 🎰🎵🪕 [____] **5+ (HVS)**
Start at the top of the slope, below a long overhang 10m up.
1) 5, 25m. Climb up to a short crack on the left and onto the slab. Trend right and then up to blocks below the roof. Traverse left to the end of the blocks and then up to a belay.
2) 3, 10m. Follow the shallow groove to a large ledge.
3) 4, 28m. The pillar on the right then move around into a cave.
4) 5+, 25m. Climb the wall on the right into a small cave. Climb left and up the narrow gully to a good ledge.
5) 5+, 40m. Climb the short wall and overhanging groove above. Traverse right onto the slab and then up to a crack. Up this and the short walls above.
DESCENT - Walk off as described to the left.
FA. R.Edwards, M.Esslinger 1999

3 Through the Looking Glass
. . . . 🎰🎵🪕 [____] **6a (E1)**
A good introduction to the style of climbing. The start is loose. Start at the top of the slope below a leftwards slanting fault.
1) 5+, 25m. Up the fault and follow this to a hard move round the arete to a crack. Up to a small roof and over this to a belay.
2) 5, 25m. Traverse along the break to the next bay and follow the line below the overlap (peg), pull over a wall to a groove which is followed. Move right to a good ledge and bolt belay.
3) 6a, 30m. Climb the steep wall on the right (2 threads) to follow the fault line right to a steep corner. Move up, then left, and climb direct to a small ledge (thread/nut belays).
4) 6a, 45m. Climb the steepening slab and a short crack. Up this to a ledge and tree. Head up left to below the top wall.
5) 4+, 45m. Climb up and right to the slanting overhang. Follow this then move out right to the slab . Cross to cracks on the right and up these to a ledge. Climb short walls to the top.
FA. R.Edwards, C.Morton, B.Rynne 2001

4 Capricorn Encounter 🎰🎵🪕 [____] **6a+ (E2)**
Start below a scoop with a glued and bolted flake at its base.
1) 6a+, 25m. Climb into a scoop then left to a hard move up and right (2 bolts). Continue direct then move right and climb the steep arete above a small pillar. Make some difficult moves up the arete and follow a crack to a good ledge and belays.
2) 5+, 25m. As for *Looking Glass.*
3) 6a+, 30m. Go up right then back left to a faint crack. Follow this and head left onto a slab. Up to a belay in a corner.
4) 5, 50m. Climb the small pillar left of the tree and continue up a slab to an overhanging block. Climb past this then over ledges to a larger ledge below the headwall.
5) 6a+, 35m. Climb the wall then traverse right and up to below a small overlap. At its end climb direct to a good ledge and finish up a short wall.
FA. R.Edwards, M.Edwards and D.Whitley (P5) 2000/1

5 El asesino y redención . 🎰🎵🪕 [____] **7a (E4)**
A long route with interesting climbing and exciting positions. Start up the slope below a groove with a ruined wall at its base.
1) 7a, 20m. The Assassin. This pitch can be done on its own. Climb into the overhanging crack and up to the roof. Climb out over the roof and onto the left wall, follow a thin crack and pockets to a niche and bolt belay.
2) 6a, 18m. The Redemption. Follow the groove (loose) and climb left to the middle of the wall to bolts in a small cave.
3) 6b, 28m. Traverse left to a ledge below an overhanging wall to a large hole (thread). Climb this to a ledge then the over-hanging wall above, trending right, to reach a ledge with trees.
4) 5+, 50m. Climb left and then up to a couple of steep walls. Up these to a good ledge, then traverse left to ledge and belay.
5) 5+, 45m. Climb the shallow groove and, at its top, traverse left onto a ledge. Continue to the top of the crag or,
5a) 6b, 45m. Climb the wall direct passing a bolt to reach a good ledge. Climb direct to the top of the crag.
FA. P1 M.Edwards. 1999. The rest - R.Edwards, M.Esslinger 1999

6 Andromeda . . . 🎰🎵🪕ENP [____] **7c (E6)**
A direct route, from which retreat would be difficult after P3. The route has several SENPs which will be replaced with bolts some time in the future. Start in the middle of the face, just left of a ruined wall and below an overhanging crack.
1) 6a, 20m. Climb into the crack from the right and follow this to a hanging belay. An excellent pitch in its own right!
2) 7a, 25m. Climb right onto the overhanging wall and up this trending rightwards to a hidden pocket on the right. Climb direct to a hole then move left to reach a steep, wide groove. Climb this to reach a belay on the right.
3) 6a, 25m. Climb the groove on the left and continue left to a slab. Climb this to a traverse line going left. Follow this to some small caves and climb through these to another larger cave.
4) 7c, 38m. Climb over the roof on the left and then straight up to a 'bolted' flake. Climb straight up to the roof above (threads) over this and onto the ramp which is followed for a short way. Climb the wall direct to a small ledge and belay.
5) 6a, 35m. Climb left and then straight up the steep slab to a good ledge and belays.
6) 6a, 40m. Climb rightwards into a depression then left into a short groove. Go right to another groove and follow this finishing up a slab at the top. Block belays.
FA. R.Edwards, M.Edwards 1999

7 La gloria escondida 🎰🎵ENP [____] **7a+ (E5)**
A route tackling the full length of the wall. Start below a right-wards-slanting roof 20m up. The *Rock 3-ENPs* on this route may be replaced with bolts in the future.
1) 6a+, 20m. Climb up friable rock to a thread. Pull over the overlap and follow the line of 3 ENPS to a ramp going left. Follow this to the bay below the roof.
2) 7a, 25m. Climb the steep groove, swing left onto the leaning wall and climb on pockets to ledge then left to a belay.
3) 6a+, 48m. Move right up a groove past a tree. Continue up the shallow groove to an ENP, traverse left along a ramp to a groove. Up this then move left to a cave stance.
4) 7a+, 30m. Climb right along the ledge then swing round into a corner. Go up (thread) to the leftward-sloping ramp. Follow this steeply (3 ENPs) to a roof. Move right (ENP) and pull over the roof, difficult, and move left to bolt belays.
5) 6a, 25m. Climb directly up the wall then traverse left to a long crack. Up this then traverse left into a cave and bolt belay.
6) 6a, 28m. Climb right out of the cave to a thread. Go up then left to a small ledge. Climb the steep wall above and then the groove to a ledge on the left by a bush.
7) 5, 35m. Move along the ledge to the left and climb the slabs, walls and ledges to the top of the crag.
FA. R.Edwards, M.Edwards 1998

ECHO TWO - SINGLE-PITCH ROUTES

The lower section of the tall wall of Echo Two consists of a very steep band of bulging red and grey rock. This is covered with loads of excellent routes, which are mainly in the higher grades. Some are fully bolted, and others require leader-placed protection.

APPROACH - Continue underneath Echo One to parking below Echo Two which is 5 mins away.

GRADES - The routes are given sport grades but the trad routes have been given colour spots to reflect their overall difficulty. Most have also been given a British grade.

❶ Hi Flyer . . . . 🔧🔨 ⬜ **6c (E4)**
28m. Start below a scoop with a glued and bolted flake at its base. Move up right (thread and bolts) to a fault going left. Move left then up onto a slab and climb the crack to a lower-off.
FA. R.Edwards 2001

❷ Secundo Veces . . . . . . 🔧🔨 ⬜ **6c+**
28m. Fully bolted. Climb a steep wall into a niche. Pull out left onto a fine wall. Climb fairly direct up the fine wall, ignoring the confusing bolts to the left and right.
FA. M.Edwards, R.Edwards 2001

❸ Stone Roses . . . . . 🔧🔨 ⬜ **7b**
28m. Fully bolted. Climb the crack-line up left into the niche. Make a very hard move up right to gain a long crack which leads to the belay. *Photo page 217.*
FA. M.Edwards, R.Edwards 2001

❹ Route 4 . . . . 🔧 ⬜ **(7a/b)**
30m. A fully bolted pitch through the bulge and up the wall.

❺ Chilling Out. . . . . 🔧🔨 ⬜ **8a (E7)**
14m. A tough pitch which may be extended upwards.
FA. M.Edwards 2001

❻ Route 6 . . . . 🔧 ⬜ **(8a)**
14m. A short and steep pitch which is fully bolted.

❼ The Assassin. . . . . 🔧🔨 ⬜ **7a (E4)**
20m. The first pitch of a much longer route. Follow a steep crack, over a bulge to a belay in a niche.
FA. M.Edwards 1999

❽ Spanish Gold . . . . 🔧🔨 ⬜ **7a (E4)**
20m. The first pitch of a multi-pitch project.
FA. M.Edwards, R.Edwards 2001

❾ The Long Stretch . . . . . 🔧🔨 ⬜ **6b (E3)**
Start right of *The Assassin* below an overhanging crack.
1) 6b, 20m. Climb the wall on the left to a thread and make a long reach right into a groove. The steep crack in the right wall is an alternative. Climb past two holes and make the long reach right, then continue right to a ledge and chain belay.
2) 6b, 18m. Climb the groove to a ledge and belay.
DESCENT - Abseil off.
FA. M.Edwards, R.Edwards 2000

❿ The Dawning. . . . . 🔧🔨 ⬜ **6b (E3)**
20m. An easier start to *The Long Stretch*. Start to the left of a large chimney below a steep wall with a good horizontal break. Climb to the break and make a long reach left. Continue direct, and then slightly right and up, to a good pocket. Trend slightly right to a lower-off.
FA. M.Edwards, R.Edwards, M.Hesslinger 1999

⓫ Indigo . . . . . . 🔧🔨 ⬜ **8a+ (E8)**
15m. A short but powerful climb. Start from the left end of the terraced wall, just right of a chimney, below a pocketed crack. Enter the crack and follow this with increasing difficulty to its end. Climb the overhanging wall above (2 bolts) and then make powerful moves onto the hanging slab (bolt) and then on to the lower-off.
FA. M.Edwards 2000

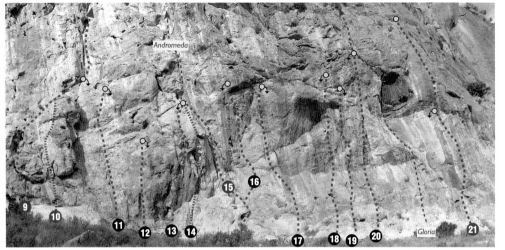

Murcia · Alicante · Benidorm · Calpe · Xaló Valley · Gandia

Sella · Puig Campana · Ponoch · Echo Valley

⑫ Millenium . . . . 🔲 **8a**
15m. A fully bolted route up the very steep wall. Start up the overhanging flake and then use crimps and a pocket to negotiate the short wall above to the lower-off.
FA. M.Edwards 2000

⑬ Death Pulse 🔲 **8a+ (E9)**
20m. A strenuous and overhanging route which is poorly protected. Start below the steep overhanging wall left of *Andromeda*, and below a slabby loose section of rock. Climb the loose rock below the wall up to the first large pocket in the overhanging wall above. Enter this and make a very dynamic move rightwards to a shallow scoop. Climb past this then continue strenuously up large pockets to the final headwall. Climb a thin crack to its end and make difficult moves to gain the belay of *Andromeda*.
FA. M.Edwards 2000

⑭ Asteroid Storm 🔲 **7c+ (E7)**
20m. Less technical and with larger holds than *Death Pulse*. Large cams are useful. Start as for *Death Pulse*. Climb the loose rock to the steeper section and pull up powerfully into the large pocketed overhanging wall. Climb to the crack and continue to a large under-cling. Pull up powerfully to join *Andromeda* which leads to the belay.
FA. M.Edwards 2000

⑮ Andromeda (pitch 1) . . 🔲 **6a (E1)**
20m. Pitch 1 of this huge route makes a nice little climb on its own at a reasonably friendly grade compared to the other routes hereabouts. Climb into the crack from the right and follow this to a lower-off. The rest of this route is much harder!
FA. R.Edwards, M.Edwards 1999

⑯ Shelter . . . . 🔲 **8a**
20m. A fully bolted pitch up the steep wall right of *Andromeda*.
FA. M.Edwards

⑰ Super 'G' . 🔲 **8a (E8)**
20m. A powerful line taking the cracks and flakes in the overhanging wall right of *Andromeda*. Surmount the lower bulge onto the slab (thread) and climb this to the overhanging wall. Pull over the first bulge to a sloping ledge (thread) then onto the overhanging wall and a thin crack. Follow this (bolt and peg). Climb strenuously up the flake /crack to its top and exit on right to large pocket (peg). Pull strenuously up to a small ledge and belays.
FA. M.Edwards 1999

⑱ Iratika . . . . . . 🔲 **8b**
20m. A fully-bolted route with a hard finish crossing the imposing roof on its right-hand side.
FA. M.Edwards

⑲ Path of Excess Power . . 🔲 **8a+**
25m. A hard and unrelenting line of tufas up the steepest part of the overhang which is now fully bolted. Follow the steepening line to reach crucial climbing leading up the overhanging wall by dynamic moves to a large hole. Climb out over the final bulge and then continue on easier rock to a ledge.
FA. M.Edwards 1999

⑳ Mad Dog . . . . . 🔲 **8a (E7)**
25m. A strenuous crack climb. Start below a overhanging crack, to the left of *La gloria escondida*. Climb bulges either on the right or left and then the slab which leads to the base of the overhanging crack. Follow the crack then move left to a large flake. Climb right up the overhanging wall to a lower-off.
FA. M.Edwards, R.Edwards 1999

㉑ Dreammaker . . . . . 🔲 **6b (E2)**
Exciting climbing on more exciting rock! Start to the right of the overhanging wall of *La gloria escondida* and just to the left of *Voyage to Orion*, below a very shallow open groove.
1) 6a+, 15m. Climb the steep wall to a block protruding from the wall. Go over this and enter the shallow groove on the right. Climb this to reach a small ledge and belay. Lower off or:
2) 6b, 35m. Climb the groove then move right to gain a good hold below the roof. Climb over this and up the crack above, to the base of a steep slab. Climb this to a large niche. Go over this to a small ledge and bolt belays.
FA. R.Edwards, M.Edwards, M.Jones

PLACA INMACULADA

To the right of the main bulk of Echo Two is an impressive groove capped with a roof. Right of this is 'the immaculate face' and round right a slabbier wall.

APPROACH - Placa Inmaculada is the huge corner and wall to the right of the main bulk of Echo Two.

DESCENTS - It is possible to abseil off most of the routes on twin 50m ropes.

GRADES - The routes are given sport and UK grades. They have colour spots to reflect their overall difficulty.

Placa Inmaculada - Right

❶ **Diedro Edwards** . . . 6b (E3)

Start 5m left of the right edge of the wall. The route has 2 original *Rock 3-ENPs* on the last pitch.

1) 4, 25m. Climb the overhanging crack and then move left across the wall to the base of a groove. Up this to the overlap and pull right into the groove above. Follow this to a good ledge on the left. Bolt belay.

2) 5+,25m. Climb the groove into the first cave. Pull over this and continue up the groove to belay in a second cave.

3) 4, 25m. Follow the groove to the top of the tower, bolt belay.

4) 6a, 20m. The steep groove to the top of the pillar, bolt belay.

5) 6b, 45m. Climb to the roof and move up and left. Continue to the small overhang, move right then left up cracks to slabs which are followed to the top. Block belays.

FA. R.Edwards, S.O'Rouke and 'Patty' 1997. Pitches 1 to 3 had previously been climbed by some local climbers.

❷ **Voyage to Orion** . . . 6c+ (E4)

A big route with great positions. Start as for *Diedro Edwards*. The route has several of the *Rock 3-ENPs*.

1) 6a, 30m. Climb the crack and traverse left to a groove. Move left again across a steep section into another groove. Climb this to the roof, pull over and swing up and right to a ledge. Climb the thin crack to a ledge and a junction with *Diedro Edwards*.

2) 6c+, 45m. Climb the shallow depression above to a sling. Continue up the trending slightly right to a small cave. Move left and climb the overlap step right and climb the rough wall to a shallow bay. Climb over the bulge to a good ledge.

3) 6b, 30m. Move left into a cave, pull over the roof and into a groove on the right and onto a ledge. Climb the steep juggy rock, move right into a groove, then up this to a bolt belay.

4) 6b, 30m. Climb the short, steep wall left of the ledge and make a spectacular traverse left until you can climb direct (thread) to a recess. Move right then back left to follow cracks and grooves to the top of the route. Thread belay.

FA. R.Edwards, J.Toms, V.Leuchsner 1998

❸ The Silent Sleeper . . . . 🎭🎽⬜ 5 (VS)
40m. A good easier route. Start on the right of the crag, at the lowest point, just to the left of a large boulder. Climb the slab past an old iron spike and ascend leftwards to a steep slab. Up this and move right into a corner. Go up this for a short way, to a old bolt, then climb directly up the wall to a ledge. Climb the steep wall into a shallow depression which leads to a wide bay with a thread belay. Abseil off from belay high up.
FA. R.Edwards, E.Edwards 1997

❹ Sea of Dreams . . . . . . 🎭ENP⬜ 6a+ (E3)
48m. This one has a hard finale. Start in a recess below a thin flake in the centre of the slab. Climb up to the flake then continue direct to the slab above. Up this (*Rock 3-ENP*) and the groove above to a recess and bolt belay. Abseil off.
FA. R.Edwards 1998

❺ The Sickle . . . . ENP⬜ 6a+ (E2)
50m. Start just left of the groove of *Cumple años 61st.* at a narrow rib. Climb the rib and the wall above (2 *Rock 3-ENPs*) to a steep black wall on the left, thread. Climb the slab above to a steep groove, then up this to the large recess and belay. Abseil off.
FA. R.Edwards 1997

❻ Cumple años 61st.. 🎭⚡ENP⬜ 6b (E3)
Some dramatic positions. Start left of *Diedro de Naranja*.
1) 6a+, 45m. Climb the groove and the curving crack then pull right past the overhang (thread). Climb the crack to a slab, up this (*Rock 3-ENP*) to a groove on the right then climb to a small ledge and large recess. Abseil off or:
2) 6a+, 35m. Climb the slab on the left to a large slot, continue left onto the steep wall and follow a line of holes and cracks to reach a ledge and bolt belay on the wall above (3 *Rock 3-ENPs*).
3) 6b, 45m. Climb the steep wall on the left to a thread then right into a shallow groove. Up this past some threads then climb a steep wall and move right onto a ramp. Follow this to a steep crack which leads to the top (2 *Rock 3-ENPs*).
DESCENT - Make 3 abseils to the ground. It is easiest to swing left onto the *Diedro Edwards* abseils as soon as possible.
FA. R.Edwards, P.Milton 1998

❼ Diedro de Naranja . 🎭🎽ENP⬜ 6b (E3)
A sustained route up the big orange groove.
1) 6a+, 25m. Climb slabby rock then the groove proper as it steepens. Follow the groove by climbing direct on its left-hand side, and then direct again (thread). Belay in a recess (thread).
2) 6b, 25m. Climb the orange slab on the right and follow the ramps rightwards (3 *Rock 3-ENPs*) to some threads. Move right again then up into a cave. Traverse right into the centre of the slab and follow this to the good ledge and belay. Abseil off.
FA. R.Edwards, M.Bonesteel, E.Revs Vilapiana 1997

❽ The Prayer to the Raven and the Crow
. . . . 🎭🎽🏞🎷⬜ 7c
A great climb. Start below the line of bolts through the scoop right of *Diedro de Naranja*.
1) 7c, 18m. Enter the scoop and follow it direct, passing a large pocket/hole, to a good ledge. Bolt and thread belay.
2) 8a, 28m. Step right below the line up the steep crack of *Going Nuts*. Climb this then move left to a flake, climb to a small overlap and trend diagonally right then up the wall to a horizontal break. Climb direct again to easier rock and continue up to the belay below *Solstice*.
FA. M.Edwards, R.Edwards 1999

❾ Solstice 🎭🏞🎽🎷🗝🎽⬜ 8a (E8)
20m. A hard direct finish to *Prayer to the Raven*. Swing boldly up left into two large holes (threads and an SENP) Climb up and follow pockets to a groove which leads to a ledge.
FA. M.Edwards 1999. Later climbed without the SENP by M.Edwards.

❿ Naranja Directa . . . . . . 🎭ENP⬜ 7a (E4)
A variation finish to *Diedro de Naranja*.
1) 6a+, 25m. As for *Diedro de Naranja*.
2) 7a, 25m. Climb to the cave then move out left onto the overhanging wall (*Rock 3-ENP*). Climb direct to a ledge on the right and then follow a series of pockets to the top.
FA. M.Edwards, R.Edwards 1999

⓫ Going Nuts . . . 🎭🏞🎷🎽⬜ 8a
50m. A sustained route on perfect rock. The original ENPs have been replaced by bolts. Start below a bulge in the wall. Climb the slabby depression to the bulge and through this to a sloping ledge. Up the overhanging flake and into to a scoop then onwards with difficulty to an easing of the angle. Move rightwards to enter a shallow scoop and up this with difficulty to easier ground. Continue up the wall (wires) past a thread to belays on the large ledge. Abseil off.
FA. M.Edwards 1998

⓬ Midnight Runner . . 🎭🎷🎽⬜ 7a+ (E5)
45m. Sustained and technical. The ENPs have been replaced by bolts but it is not a sport route. Start just left of a flat-topped boulder. Head for a bulge in the rock on the right then climb direct and follow pockets to a blanker section. Continue direct to a good ledge on the right. Climb the narrow slab above and then trend right to a belay. Abseil off.
FA. R.Edwards, M.Edwards 1998

⓭ Children of Laughter . . 🎭🎽⬜ 7a+ (E5)
50m. A long pitch with good protection. Start from a flat boulder and climb rightwards into a scoop, follow this to a move left to a chain (a 5 to here). Go left and then back right to a thread and continue direct (thread) to a slab. Climb the steep slab trending right and then direct to a belay. Abseil off.
FA. R.Edwards, E.Edwards 1998

⓮ Espolón Encantada . . . . 🎭🎽⬜ 5 (HVS)
A wandering line with good climbing. Start at the lowest point of the wall, where a series of small cracks trends up leftwards.
1) 5, 25m. Climb the cracks then right to a small arete. Climb this and then head right to a good ledge and thread belay.
2) 5, 40m. Climb the crack on the left and at its top move right to a ledge. Step right past a thread then continue directly before trending right up a slab. Keeping left of the vegetation to a small stance and belay. Descend by a 50m abseil.
Photo page 199.
FA. R.Edwards, E.Edwards 1998

⓯ Vía los palmeras . . . . . 🎭🎽⬜ 5+ (HVS)
Start 3m to the right of *Espolón Encantada*, below the palm.
1) 5+, 20m. Climb left across the slab and then back right and climb direct to the palm tree. Move left below this to reach ledge above. Belay.
2) 5+, 35m. From the ledge, climb right and then direct. Follow the left-hand side of the slab (thread on right) to a narrow pillar. Up this and through broken blocks to a belay and abseil point.
FA. R.Edwards, E.Edwards 1998

Murcia · Alicante · Benidorm · Calpe · Xaló Valley · Gandia · Sella · Puig Campana · Ponoch · Echo Valley

Murcia

Alicante

Benidorm

Calpe

Xaló Valley

Gandia

Sella

Puig Campana

Ponoch

Echo Valley

PLACA INMACULADA RIGHT

The final section of Echo Two is a huge dome-shaped wall of perfect light grey rock. This has a number of long and technical wall climbs mostly with sparse protection. The grades given may not look to tough but really this wall is more for the experienced trad climber.

APPROACH - Continue around the corner from the main corner and wall of Placa Inmaculada.

DESCENT - Abseil from the belays at the top on twin 50m ropes.

GRADES - The routes are given sport grades but they have been given colour spots to reflect their overall difficulty. Most also have a British grade as well.

❶ The Visionary
.... 🎯🎿🐚🔧☐ **8a (E8)**

25m. A superb, bold climb tackling the black wall. Start below the black streak. Take a full rack including a range of cams. Climb the slab towards the black streak (threads) then move right to a pocket. Continue up the wall to then leftwards to a shelf. Move up leftward to a shallow groove (thread) then climb the wall above (run-out) trending towards a right-facing flake. Continue direct by less-steep rock, and an easy wall, to the roof then through this to the belay.
FA. M.Edwards, R.Edwards 2000

❷ Dust to Victory
.... 🎯🎿🐚🔧☐ **7a (E6)**

25m. An eliminate up the narrow wall and black streak left of *Rock Dancer 2*, joining *Rock Dancer 2* to finish.
FA. M.Edwards

❸ Rock Dancer 2
.... 🎯🔧☐ **6a (E1)**

40m. A popular pitch on good rock and with good protection. Start below a slabby wall with two threads high up. Climb the short corner to the slanting crack and follow this then traverse right and climb directly up the slab until it steepens. Climb up to the left of a thread then move right. Continue up and slightly right following a thin crack. At its top, move left and then continue up slabs to a ledge. *Photo opposite.*
FA. R.Edwards, E.Edwards 1999

❹ Taurus
.... 🎯🐚🔧☐ **6a (E2)**

50m. A route with solid but spaced protection. Start in a small recess with a slim groove on the left. Climb the groove then straight up to the steeper rock above. Climb left then back right before heading straight up the slab using good hidden holds. Aim for the groove in the middle of the headwall, up this then the wall on the right, to reach a ledge. Abseil off.
FA. R.Edwards, E.Edwards 1999

❹ Kfour
.... 🎯🎿🔧☐ **6c (E4)**

45m. A route with good moves, though it is tricky to protect. Start as for *Taurus*. Climb up the vegetated slab on the right towards the right-hand side of a white stain on the wall. Climb left onto the stained rock and make hard moves onto a good hold. Climb leftwards to a ledge then go up to a shallow groove on the left and surmount the overlap on its left-hand side. Climb up to steeper rock and finish up a groove. Abseil off.
FA. R.Edwards, M.Edwards 1999

❺ Yes to Dance
.... 🎯🔧☐ **6b+ (E4)**

45m. Another worthwhile slab climb. Start at the right-hand side of the wall, below a rib of rock, where the rock ends and the vegetation starts. Climb the rib to a slab, up this to a steep black wall then left to a series of pockets leading out left. Climb direct into a shallow crack and groove, then up the wall to the leaning rib above. Climb this on the right to the top. Abseil off.
FA. R.Edwards 1999

Paul Cox climbing *Rock Dancer 2* (6a/E1 5b) on Placa Inmaculada, Echo Two - *opposite*. A fine route on perfect rock with plentiful trad gear placements. Photo: Mark Glaister

BANDS OF THE 80s WALL

The Castillo stretches down to the track. The lower left section has been developed with the most popular sport routes in the whole valley, equipped by unknown climbers. The first thirteen routes are on the short wall just above the track - not surprisingly they are popular.

APPROACH - Park by the cliff (1 car) or a little further down the hill leaving room for vehicles to pass.

NOTE - Despite being described in print for several years no names have been forthcoming for these climbs. We have taken the liberty of naming them, so no letters please - unless of course you know their true identities!

1 Duran Duran **6b**
14m. The short sharp wall on the far left - stay left of the bolts.

2 Kajagoogoo. . . . . **6b+**
14m. Tricky moves lead past the orange patch, which is approached from the right. A bit of an eliminate but at least it is better than it looks.

3 Everything but the Girl . **6a**
14m. The blunt rib in the centre of the face is delicate and sharp, leading to a butch finish over the juggy roof.

4 Rick Astley . . . . **7b+**
14m. The blank face is desperate but at least it's not chipped!

5 Spandau Ballet . . . . . . **7a+**
14m. The right side of the smooth face gives excellent technical climbing despite the drilled holds that make it possible.

6 Teardrop X-plodes **7b**
14m. Desperate climbing up the broccoli covered wall - a real tip shredder.

7 Kate Bush . . . . **6b+**
14m. The steep groove just left of the small tree leads leftwards to crucial moves up and right into its continuation.

8 New Order **6b**
14m. The steep tufa and sharp rib grey rib above.

9 Swing Out Sister **6b**
14m. Climb the wall past a tiny tufa to a tricky mantel out right.

10 Morrisey. **7b**
14m. A depressingly desperate height-dependant dyno for stuck-on hold leads to easier climbing up the face above.

11 Adam Ant . . . . **7a+**
14m. Climb the pocketed wall into the grey scoop then the goutte covered wall above. Excellent but hard

12 Wham . . . . **5+**
16m. Grotty rock leads to the juggy crack and then the left-trending ramp above. Accessing this is the crux.

13 George Michael. . . . . . **5+**
16m. More (or the same) grotty rock leads to a short wall then two sets of juggy bulges.

Lots of sun | **2 min**

16

12 **13** **14** **15**

11

10

2 3 4 5 6 7 8 9 17

1

MONSTERS OF ROCK WALL

A fine grey wall with a clutch of good sharp routes.
APPROACH - 100m from the road and reached by a short scramble up past the routes described opposite.
NOTE - OK, you guessed, we made these names up too.

① The Darkness . . . . 🔲 **6a**
20m. Climb cracks leftwards then through a pair of bulges.

② AC/DC . . . . 🔲 **6b**
20m. The grey rib then right at the bulge and up a groove.

③ Deep Purple . . . . 🔲 **7a**
18m. Zig-zag cracks lead rightwards to a groove, then up the wall on the left. Long reaches over the final bulge.

④ Led Zeppelin . . 🔲 **7a+**
18m. The best line on the wall. Climb the steep brown pillar. Avoid the right-hand crack for a harder finish.

⑤ Black Sabbath . 🔲 **7a**
18m. The centre of the orange wall is good and hard.

⑥ Ozzie . . . . 🔲 **7a**
18m. The right-hand side of the lower slab and then up pale grey streaks and a short diagonal crack.

⑦ Scorpions . . . . 🔲 **7a**
18m. Fingery climbing up the grey wall on the right.

⑧ Motorhead . . . . 🔲 **6c**
26m. A long pitch crossing a ramp at mid-height and with a steep finish. Worthwhile. *Photo page 217.*

⑨ Iron Maiden . . . . 🔲 **6a**
26m. An easier route with a tricky lower section. Trend left to join the previous climb for a worthwhile finish.

⑩ Judas Priest . . . . 🔲 **4+**
16m. The last offering on the wall is the easiest route here. Cross the break and climb the rib to the lower-off.

⑪ Anthrax . . . . 🔲 **6a**
30m. Just right of the tree-filled gully and the face above.

⑫ Megadeath . . . . 🔲 **6b**
30m. A similar line just to the right. The crux is the roof.

The wall to the right has three unknown routes.

⑬ Route 13 . . . . 🔲 **?**
20m. The centre of the wall passing the diagonal break.

⑭ Route 14 . . . . 🔲 **?**
14m. Follow the water streak to a lower-off just below the bush.

⑮ Route 15 . . . . 🔲 **?**
16m. The right-hand line on the smooth wall.

⑯ Route 16 . . . . 🔲 **6b**
34m. A diagonal crack line leads to a single bolt belay on *Route 15*; it is 5 to here. Continue direct past a line of four more bolts.
DESCENT - Lower-off carefully or abseil.

⑰ Route 17 . . . . 🔲 **6a**
1) 6a. Can be done on its own.
2) Scramble across easy ground to the base of the upper wall.
3) 5. A vertical wall leads to another ledge.
4) 5. One more pitch to the top.
DESCENT - By abseil.

Murcia

Alicante

Benidorm

Calpe

Xalo Valley

Gandia

Sella

Puig Campana

Ponoch

Echo Valley

Adjoining

CASTILLO - WASP AREA

A pleasant place to climb that features some of the easiest trad routes in the area. In addition to these short trad climbs there are some longer offerings that get well above the ground. Most of the routes are slab and/or crack climbing with plentiful protection from wires and Friends. Higher up on the wall is a very steep section of orange rock that has a set of harder routes some of which may have been bolted.

APPROACH - From the parking follow the track uphill passing under the face until the bay of *Little Bootie*, with its diagonal cracks, is reached. The first multi-pitch routes are located just to the right. To reach the upper climbs continue round to the right of the buttress and follow ledges back out to the left to the base of the soaring chimney line.

DESCENT - The easiest descent for the long routes here is to locate the top of *Scorpion* and abseil down this line using its belays - double ropes needed.

① **Little Bootie** .... 4 (Sev)
14m. Climb the short wall and then the left crack. Lower-off.
FA. R.Edwards 1998

② **Big Bootie.** .... 4 (Sev)
14m. The other crack to the same lower-off.
FA. R.Edwards 1998

③ **Árbol Directo.** .... 4+ (HS)
Start directly below the small bush.
14m. Climb the slab then move right to a crack just above the tree. Follow this to the lower-off.
FA. R.Edwards 1998

④ **Domingo negra** ... 6a+ (E2)
12m. As for *Abol Directo* to below the tree. Move right (ENP) then climb direct before trending right up a crack to a lower-off.
FA. R.Edwards 1998

⑤ **Vino tinto** 6b (E3)
12m. A bold route. Start below a overhanging groove. Climb the corner and then follow the steepening-slab leftwards. Make some hard moves past a jammed wire and continue up the slab.
FA. M.Edwards 1998

⑥ **Salir por encima** .. 6b+ (E3)
14m. A strenuous, well-protected roof. Climb the corner to an overhanging crack. Up this and the crack above to a lower-off.
FA. R.Edwards 1998

⑦ **Strongbody** 6a (E1)
14m. Climb the right arete of the groove.
FA. R.Edwards 1998

⑧ **The Wasp** .... 4+ (VS)
Some pleasant climbing with a spectacular finish, and quite popular. Start below a steep slab at the left edge of the wall.
1) 4, 45m. Climb to and up a steep groove, step into the groove on the right, and up to large block (belay possible). Climb the wall trending right then direct to a ledge, chain belay.
2) 3, 15m. Traverse easily leftwards along ledges to reach a large bay at the foot of an arete.
3) 4, 45m. Climb the arete into a slanting groove. Go up this and move right at its top to a ledge (belay possible). Move left and climb the slab rightwards stepping left at the top onto a good ledge and trees.
4) 4+, 20m. From the left end of the ledge climb direct to the steep wall above. Follow the exposed leftwards-slanting fault line which leads to the top.
DESCENT - Abseil back down the line.
FA. R.Edwards 1998

Lots of sun | 5 min

Photo: Rowland Edwards

Castillo - Upper Wall

9 Mosca . . . . **3 (VDiff)**
24m. Start right of *The Wasp* below a wide crack. Climb the short wall and enter the wide crack on the left. Follow this to a large block. Climb the wall behind and trend right over slabs and blocks to reach the belay.
FA. R.Edwards 1998

10 Mosca derecha . . . . **3 (VDiff)**
24m. Start by the left side of a large bush. Climb the slab until you can traverse left to a crack. Follow this to a ledge and then continue direct to the belay.
FA. R.Edwards 1998

11 Mosca directa . . . . **4 (VDiff)**
24m. Start down and left of the bush. Climb the slab, move slightly left and then direct to a ledge. Climb the corner on the right and then more broken rock to the belay.
FA. R.Edwards 1998

12 Scorpion . . . . **4+ (HS)**
A long route with a spectacular finish. Start to the right of some large bushes growing 10m up the face.
1) 4, 45m. Climb cracks and grooves to the right of the tree then continue direct up a thin crack. Follow this, and the broken rocks, to a belay on the left.
2) 2, 20m. Climb the short wall onto the vegetated slab and head left to the base of the slabs on the left.
3) 4, 30m. Climb the slab and then the slanting corner to a recess. Go rightwards up the diagonal arete then a short wall. Move left and right, past a bush, to a good belay ledge.
4) 4+, 30m. Climb the crack to the head-wall and traverse left to the base of the steeper section. Climb the fault-line and move right to a good flake. Pull over the roof and climb the slab to a belay. The easier finish of *The Wasp* is just to the left if needed!
FA. R.Edwards 1998

13 A Game of Two Halves . . . **6a**
30m. The short, bolted direct finish to *Scorpion*.
FA. R.Edwards, M.Bradley 2001

CASTILLO - UPPER WALL

The higher walls contain some striking lines. The left-hand side has some well-positioned long sport routes on a good wall of rock. In the centre are three long crack climbs and on the right 2 more delicate routes up a pillar.

APPROACH - Scramble up left from below The Bay (see opposite) to the ledge below the wide crack in the middle of the wall.

DESCENTS - Many of the routes have lower-offs or can be abseiled down. There is also a good abseil line down *The Wasp*.

The Wasp Scorpion

Approach from The Bay

Photo: Rowland Edwards

The first 3 routes are started from a ledge which is reached by a short shared pitch below All Aboard!

❶ The October Sessions
.... 7b+
25m. The left-hand bolt line gives excellent and fierce climbing on perfect rock.
FA. M.Edwards 2001

❷ Revelation . . . 7b
30m. Start up an easy groove, stepping right to clip the first bolt. Follow the red wall above direct past some scoops.
FA. M.Edwards 2001

❸ All aboard! . . 7c
30m. A magnificent long pitch forcing its way up the central head wall with some sustained climbing.
FA. M.Edwards, R.Edwards 2001

❹ Route 4 . . . . (7a+)
30m. A long fully-bolted line on the right-hand side of the red wall.

❺ The Cut 6b (E3)
A trad route with three contrasting pitches. Start below a thin crack, 4m left of the huge deep chimney.
1) 6b, 40m. Climb the slab direct to a thin crack. Follow this until it ends then climb up the wall (bold) to an old thread and continue up easier rock to a belay ledge.
2) 6a, 36m. Climb left (old thread) to a rising traverse which leads to a ramp. Climb this to its end and continue to a short groove. Climb direct over a block and traverse left to a belay.
3) 5, 10m. Break out left and then pull through the bulge on the right. Continue steeply to the top.
FA. M.Edwards, H.Lee 2000

❻ Cosmic Messenger 6a (E1)
An interesting climb through the overhangs at the top of The Castillo. Start left of the wide chimney of *Force of Nature*.
1) 5+, 40m. Climb a crack on the left of the wide chimney to a sloping ledge. Go left to a thread belay on *The Cut*.
2) 5+, 32m. Climb right to a sloping fault. Climb this then direct to below the tree. Pull over the overhanging block to reach a good stance and belays just above the tree.
3) 6a, 20m. Climb up then left into the slanting crack-line and follow it in a spectacular position across the headwall.
FA. R.Edwards, M.Edwards 2001

❼ Force of Nature 7c (E6)
An unbalanced climb which tackles the large overhangs at the top of the face after an easy start up the big chimney.
1) 5, 40m. Climb the chimney and follow the right-hand branch where it forks to a ledge on the left.
2) 5, 30m. Follow the crack slanting left and then head directly up a crack to reach a belay above a tree. This is shared with *Cosmic Messenger* which provides an easy escape.
3) 7c, 20m. Gain an off-width on the right and follow this to below the roof crack. Climb this with great difficulty.
FA. M.Edwards 1999

❽ The Edwards-Lee Pillar 6a+ (E2)
1) 6a, 25m. Start below the left-slanting crack on the front face of the pillar. Climb the wall past the tree to a recess. Move out left to enter the crack and follow this until it is possible to break out right and climb direct to the belay.
2) 6a+, 25m. Climb the slanting crack on the left then break out right below a block and climb direct up the slab (thread) to the belay above. A 50m abseil reaches the ground.
FA. M.Edwards, H.Lee 2001

❾ The Mark of Zorro 6b (E3)
The harder alternative to *The E.L. Pillar*. A bold first pitch.
1) 6b, 25m. Start as for *The E.L. Pillar*. From the recess, break out right following the thinner left-slanting crack. Where this fades, climb the bold slab until the crack re-emerges. Follow this to the belay of *The E.L. Pillar*.
2) 6b, 25m. Move out right to a shallow groove (thread). Continue to a thin crack above until this joins *The E.L. Pillar*. Finish up this.
FA. M.Edwards, H.Lee 2002

Steep approach scramble

Murcia
Alicante
Benidorm
Calpe
Xaló Valley
Gandia
Sella
Puig Campana
Ponoch
Echo Valley

ECHO ONE - THE BAY

High on the left-hand side of the main bulk of Echo One is a wide depression known as The Bay.

APPROACH - From the parking follow the track uphill past the Wasp Area. Continue along the base of the cliff until the clean wall of the Bay is visible above you. An easy scramble leads up to the base of the wall.

DESCENTS - Use the abseil from the top of *Mistaken Identity*. Those with long ropes (60m or more) can lower-off from *Pictures of Perfection*.

❶ Mistaken Identity . . . . . 🗝️ 🔲 **5 (VS)**
Climbs the left edge of the wall, starting at a thin rib.
1) 3, 20m. Climb the rib and walls to a bush-covered ledge.
2) 5, 30m. Climb the wall on the right and follow the well-spaced line of bolts to a sloping ledge. Up the steep slab to the roof and trend right to the top. **DESCENT** - Abseil off (50m).
FA. R.Edwards, E.Edwards 1997

❷ Vía Carob . . . . 🔲 ENP 🔲 **6b+ (E3)**
48m. Start in a small bay right of a bush-filled groove. Climb the groove to ledge and lower-off (possible stance) then climb up right and up the steep wall and slab (3 ENPs).
FA. R.Edwards 1998

❸ Cracks for Angels . . . . . 🔲 ENP 🔲 **6b (E3)**
1) 6a, 30m. Start as for *Vía Carob* up the rib and then head right along either of diagonal cracks. Weave past the small roof and climb the crack to a bolt belay on top of a flake.
2) 6b, 25m. Climb the crack on the left to an ENP. Trend leftwards up the steep slab to the top. Belay and abseil point.
FA. R.Edwards, M.Edwards 1998

❹ The Pod . . . . 🔲 🔲 ENP 🔲 **6b+ (E3)**
A route with contrasting pitches.
1) 6a, 25m. Climb the pod until it closes and make a bold swing left on a slab. Go right and climb a steep crack (2 ENPs) to a bolt belay.
2) 6b+, 25m. Climb onto the right wall and go up this (3 ENPs) to the steep slab above. Follow this to the top.
FA. R.Edwards, M.Edwards 1998

❺ Prophesy . 🔲🔲🔲🔲🔲 🔲 **8a (E8)**
30m. Start up *The Pod* then break right level with a small tree and climb up to a large pocket (thread). Make a long reach right to a flake-crack, climb this direct then move left on sharp pockets. Moves back right and follow a thin crack and make hard moves up to the left. Step back right and make bold moves to a hanging flake-crack and then powerful moves direct to a thread. Climb direct then move left (peg) to continue boldly, directly to the chain lower-off.
FA .M.Edwards, H.Lee 2002

❻ Pictures of Perfection . . 🔲 ENP 🔲 **5 (HVS)**
30m. Start below a large scoop. Follow the crack past an old tree then right (2 ENPs). From here, move rightwards into a groove. Follow this until it steepens then move right again into a good flake crack. Follow this to a good ledge.
FA. R.Edwards, E.Edwards 1997

❼ Rock Factory . . . . 🔲 ENP 🔲 **6a+ (E4)**
30m. A bold route! From the last ENP on *Pictures of Perfection*, climb up a steep slab to a roof on the left, over this and up the groove to a belay.
FA. R.Edwards, M.Edwards 1998

ECHO ONE

This impressive dome-shaped cliff dominates the lower end of the valley. It is clearly visible from Toix West if you know where to look! There is plenty of good climbing here, but a decent rack is needed along with nuts to use the ENP system on many of the climbs. Fully bolted these would be popular major classics! Suggested UK grades have been offered.

APPROACH - From the parking follow a variety of tracks up and right then contour horizontally out right, across a wide gully to the foot of the face - 10 mins from the car.

DESCENTS - For the routes on the left a 50m abseil from above *Mistaken Identity* (see previous page) is the easiest way down. For those which reach the top of the crag, abseil directly down the centre of the face via the fixed belays.

❶ Diamond Solitaire 6a (E1)
Start below a cave at 16m, perched above slabbier rock.
1) 5+, 22m. Climb the slab and then move left to the cave. Leave this onto a good ledge and belay (peg and nuts).
2) 6a, 20m. Climb the steep groove on the right and the crack above to a ledge. Move left into a recess and belay (nuts).
3) 5+, 20m. Climb the crack in the wall above to a roof. Pull over this and trend rightwards into a bay with thread belay.
4) 4+, 34m. Climb onto a block on the right, move back left and continue straight up the steep slab and easy groove to the top.
FA. R.Edwards, M.Bonesteel 1997

❷ Diedro Edwards . . . . . . 6a+ (E3)
A route with a bold third pitch. Start below a leftward-facing groove about 14m up.
1) 6a, 28m. Climb the wall and into the groove. Up to a recess.
2) 6a, 20m. Climb the main groove to a large ledge above.
3) 6a+, 24m. Follow the depression in the centre of the orange wall then right to a wide crack leading to a ledge.
4) 4, 30m. Climb the wall behind the belay to the top.
FA. R.Edwards, M.Bonesteel 1997

❸ Movimiento mágico . . . 6a+ (E2)
Start below a diagonal orange scoop.
1) 6a+, 24m. Climb the slab to the steeper section (ENP) then up to the overlap. Trend right and up to a ledge.
2) 6a+, 24m. Climb across the wall on the right to the arete (ENP), go right then up cracks to a ledge and belay bolts.
3) 6a, 34m. Climb right up the steep wall, 2 ENPs. Take cracks and then trend right to a ledge, then up the crack above.
4) 3, 20m. Climb the arete easily to the top.
FA. R.Edwards, D.Golding, W.Kersten 1998

❹ The Wizard 6b (E3)
25m. Start below a detached block and crack. Climb the crack then reach right and clip a jammed Friend on the ledge. Move left and climb direct to a scoop. Climb the scoop then move up to the right and climb direct to the large flake-block. Climb over this and on to the steep slab and direct to the lower-off. It is also possible to finish leftwards into *Movimento magic*.
FA. M.Edwards, H.Lee 2002

❺ El murciélago 6a (E1)
24m. Worthwhile and quite exciting. Trend left up the slab to ledges then climb the delicate shallow groove (avoidable ENP) to a huge perched flake. Pull steeply up to gain the shallow groove and follow this on improving holds to twin bolts.
FA. R.Edwards, D.Golding, W.Kerston 1998

❻ St Valentine's . . . . 6b+ (E3)
1) 6b+, 35m. Climb to a recess then straight up to the steep wall. Climb the pocketed wall (ENP) to a ledge then move left into a groove, up this to a bolt belay.
2) 6b, 50m. Up the slabby arete to the wall above. Step right onto the leaning wall (2 ENPs) and move up and right to broken cracks. Follow these then up the slab on the right the arete to a crack. Follow this past a tree to a recess.
3) 3, 20m. Either abseil from here or continue up *Vía Esther*.
FA. P1 - R.Edwards, D.Goldy P2 - R.Edwards, M.Edwards, F.Beith 1998

❼ Initiation . . . . 5+ (E1)
24m. A route with a strenuous finale. Begin under some slanting slots in the slab. Up these rightwards then back left to a steep crack. Climb this to a tricky exit. Single bolt lower-off.
FA. R.Edwards and students 1997

❽ Second Blood . . . . 5+ (HVS)
30m. Follows the steep groove right of the prow. Climb to some broken cracks and continue to below the prow. Climb up left then follow the steep crack to the roof. Go over this into a groove and finish up the wall on the left.
FA. R.Edwards 1998

❾ Rough-Rider . . 6c (E4)
30m. Start as for *Second Blood*. Follow the slots to the base of the steep rough wall on the right. Ascend rightwards (ENP) and make a long reach up to a thread. Move up right into a shallow groove and follow this to a belay. Abseil off.
FA. R.Edwards, G.Cater, S.Nuttal 1998

❿ Deception 6a (E1)
24m. Better than it looks - hence the name! Climb the left-hand side of the pinnacle then move right into a cave. Above this climb the crack/groove to its end and make a steep exit past threads. There is a lower-off just above.
FA. R.Edwards, M.Steel 1997

⓫ Vía Diagonal . . . . 5+ (HVS)
30m. An alternative start to *Rincón De Placa*.
FA. R.Edwards, E.Edwards 1996

⓬ Design and Form 6a (E2)
30m. A counter line to *Vía Diagonal*.
FA. M.Edwards, S.Nuttal 1998

⓭ Un Rincón de Placa . . . 4+ (HS)
A wandering route with some interesting positions. Start below a groove to the left of the arete of the cliff.
1) 4, 30m. Climb the groove then a steep wall to a gully. Belay here or cross over left to reach the belay ledge of *Deception*.
2) 4, 35m. Climb the slab behind the belay and then the left arete. Traverse down and left to reach a good ledge.
3) 4+, 25m. Climb the groove to a large recess.
4) 4+, 28m. Finish as for *Diamond Solitaire*.
FA. J.Brown 1980s

⓮ Vía Esther . . . . 4+ (HS)
A worthwhile outing up the right arete of the crag. Start below the arete. A rough descent down to the right is possible.
1) 4, 25m. Climb across the short steep slab by a left slanting crack then move across right onto a slab. Up this and then climb short grooves to a small stance and thread belays.
2) 4+, 20m. Climb the wall and move right into grooves which lead to a good ledge. Swing right and climb the short wall onto a good ledge with thread belays.
3) 4+, 40m. Climb left of the belay then head up and right to a crack. Go up this then move right onto the arete. Climb direct then move left onto a good ledge and thread belays. Possible abseil descent from here.
4) 3, 20m. Climb the wall behind the belays and go direct to the top. A short scramble leads to the summit.
FA. R.Edwards, E Edwards 1995

Murcia

Alicante

Benidorm

Calpe

Xaló Valley

Gandia

Sella

Puig Campana

Ponoch

Echo Valley

① Espolón Izquierda ...... 🎲🔲 4+
14m. The left arete of the cliff has a tricky start and steep finishing moves on huge jugs to clip the lower-off.

② Er nu .... 🎲🔲 5+
14m. A tricky first move reaches easy romping to a sharp finish up a short leaning rack.

③ Pituland .... 🎲🔲 6a
14m. Start at the red 'no 8' and climb the sharp rib to easier ground then a good finish on the final tower.

④ El diedro. .... 🎲🔲 5+
14m. Enter the groove awkwardly from the right, then a short steep layback leads to a ledge. Finish up the tower just right.

⑤ El pilar .... 🎲🔲 6a
16m. Climb through the bulges at a nice collection of tufas then continue up the rib above, passing just left of a large tree to a steep but juggy finish.

⑥ Rad .... 🎲🔲 5+
16m. Start from the cave. Pull over the roof then climb easier rock to a rugged slab. Up this - sharp and sustained - to a discreet multi-strand lower-off tucked under the overlap.

⑦ Olla ora .... 🎲🔲 5
16m. Climb the rib with occasional use of the left arete, then cross to jugs on the right. Step left and finish direct. Spaced bolts and harder if done direct.

⑧ Coco .... 🎲🔲 6a+
30m. A lower section left of a shrubby groove (name) leads to a roof. Pass this then climb easily to the final tower which gives a good, well protected finale.

ECHO PLAYA
Situated down the hill from the imposing towers of Echo One and Echo Two is a smaller crag with just over a dozen climbs in the 'orange' zone. The fact that it is only two minutes from the car, and that the routes are fully-bolted, will ensure its popularity. The rock is rough, and there is still some loose material around. There is also quite a lot of vegetation on some of the climbs - a little traffic would certainly help.
The names of these routes have mostly been made up.
CONDITIONS - It is in the sun until early afternoon.
APPROACH - Following the route into the Echo valley the cliff is clearly visible on the right. Park on the right-hand side of the road in a dirt pull-out just before wire gates on the left. Cross the terraces to the cliff.

⑨ Torre alta ...... 🎲🔲 6a
30m. Start up a big left of a big boulder. Climb the rib and weave through a bulge to a slab below the upper tower. Pull over on small pockets and finish with difficulty. Worthwhile.

The next three routes start of a flat block below a grey slab.

⑩ Variante .... 🔲 6a
20m. Start in the centre of the slab as for the next route but step left as soon as possible and climb to twin bolts on the lip of a ledge. Leave a crab or better step right and finish as for:

⑪ Placa áspera .... 🎲🔲 6a
24m. Climb straight up the slab to a break, then onto a second. Steeper rock leads to a lower-off on the rim.

⑫ De un cerdo .... 🎲🔲 5+
24m. Climb rightwards to the overlap then up the slab leftwards on 'surprising' pockets. A steep section - crux, easier on the right leads to easier rock and the feature of the route's name. Pity whoever put the bolts in did not do a better job.

⑬ Torre .... 🎲🔲 6a
28m. Climb right of the grotty gully and the face above to a nice finish high on the tower.

Alan James contemplating the stopper move on *Stone Roses* (7b) on Echo Two - *page 202*.
Inset: fingery climbing on *Motorhead* (6c) on the lower walls of the Castillo - *page 209*. Photo: Sherri Davy.

A wildly spectacular position on the superb rock of the classic blunt arete of *Tai Chi* (6b+) at Olta - *page 259*. The view out from the cliff towards Calpe, the salt-pans and the Peñón is one of the very best in the area. Large areas of this extensive cliff remain undeveloped.

Calpe

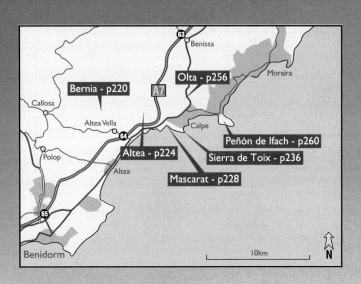

Bernia - p220

Olta - p256

Callosa

A7

Altea Vella

84

Calpe

Peñón de Ifach - p260

Altea - p224

Sierra de Toix - p236

Polop

Altea

Mascarat - p228

65

Benidorm

10km

N

Benissa

63

Moraira

BERNIA

The Bernia Ridge is the spectacular rocky crest that runs from east to west, a short distance to the south of Calpe. It rises to 1126m at the western summit and is often described as the Costa Blanca's version of the Skye Ridge, and indeed it does have a passing resemblance to its northern sister. The crest of the ridge offers a spectacular and arduous day out, though care is needed as there have been both benightments and fatalities here. The developed climbing area consists of several sport and trad routes which pick lines out from the good bits of rock along the southern flank of the ridge. The sport routes tend to be in the higher grades and include the classic *Magic Flute*. In contrast the trad routes tend to be easier, generally following cracks and all the ones listed here end at lower-offs. There is still much scope for new route development, though the sharp vegetation can be off-putting.

CONDITIONS

The Bernia Area faces south west and get loads of sun but is exposed to any wind due to its altitude and aspect. Progress along the foot of the cliff can be a painful affair due to the coarse vegetation; the occasional animal track helps. The routes are generally quick-drying and the outward views toward the Ponoch and Echo areas are excellent.

APPROACH (area map page 219)

From the N332 coast road at Olla de Altea, take the road inland towards Callosa d'En Sarrià. Go through Altea Vella and 1.8km from the leaving town sign, turn off to the right, before a sharp right bend marked with chevrons (there is a turn off a short way before this as well). There is a well-hidden grey utility box here with 'Pirri' spray painted on it, as well as purple and black arrows. Drive uphill passing through the centre of a farm and past some gates on the right with 'Costera Blanca' on them. Continue climbing up the winding road until after 5kms you arrive at some 'Casitas' (small cottages) high above the coast. Park here, or at the small picnic area a little further on the right. From here you can see the jutting ships prow of the 'Sphinx' on the cliff above and to the left. To reach the climbs follow the steep concrete road up to the highest buildings and walk round behind these to locate a good track that cuts across the hillside, descending slightly as it goes. All the routes can be accessed from this path by cutting directly uphill to the base of the routes though scratchy vegetation may be encountered.

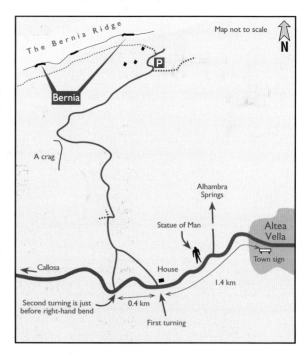

Ian Parsons tackling the superb tufa of *The Magic Flute* (7b+) at Bernia – *page 222*. Recent new routes on Bernia have dropped into two very different categories; a set of short and fairly scrappy pitches near the parking, and several magnificent hard routes on the walls to either side of the *Magic Flute*. Photo: Neil Foster

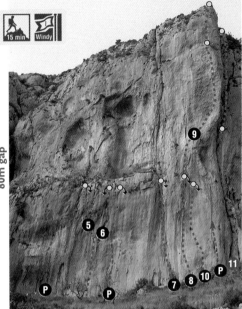

MAGIC FLUTE AREA
Left of *The Magic Flute* is a steep wall with four routes, no precise details are known however they are all hard and good. The first line is a project above a man-made pool.

⑤ Route 5 . . . . [____] (7c/8a)
25m. Climb a blank wall then branch left up cracks and tufas.

⑥ Route 6 . . . . [____] (7c/8a)
25m. The right-hand variation finish to the last route.

The next line is still a project. Beyond this is;

⑦ Tufa Groove . . . . . [icons] [____] 7b+
25m. The stunning tufa-draped groove.

⑧ The Magic Flute . . [icons] [____] 7b
25m. Brilliant climbing. Gain the beckoning tufa using pockets and then climb it to a lower-off. Head down or continue up.....
Photo page 221.

⑨ The Sphinx . . . [icons] [____] 8a
50m. The exposed and spectacular prow gives a long and demanding pitch. From the upper belay a **6a+** pitch leads to the top. The bolts and other fixed gear on both pitches are very old.
FA. Mark Edwards, Rowland Edwards 1990s

⑩ Route 10. . . . . [____] (7c/8a)
25m. Pockets and slots lead up the improbable wall.

Right again is yet another project and the the major line of;

⑪ The Grand Diedre . . . . [icons] [____] 6c
The big corner to the right of the prow.
1) 6c, 2) 6b+
FA. Rowland Edwards, Mark Edwards 1990s

BERNIA - LEFT
One of the most striking features on this side of the Bernia Ridge is the huge ship's prow of *The Sphinx*. This is home to one of the best routes in the area - *The Magic Flute*. To the left and right of this are more excellent hard pitches and further left again is a huge arete and a steep wall.
APPROACH - There is a vague path running up from the traversing path to the base of the wall, which runs leftwards as far as The Magic Flute Area. Beyond this you need to bush-wack about 80m further left to reach the first routes described below.

The routes are described starting at the tall arete.

① The Immaculate Arete . [icons] [____] 7b+
30m. A superb route up the huge arete starting up a grey slab.
FA. Mark Edwards 1990s

② Jayne's Project . . . . . . [icons] [____] 6c
25m. A slab leading to an overhanging wall with pockets.

③ Paradise Lost . . . . [icons] [____] 7a
25m. A slabby start but steeper above.
FA. Mark Edwards 1990s

In between routes 3 and 4 are two projects.

④ The First and Last . [icons] [____] 8b
25m. Start up a rugged slab to reach the steep crack splitting the soaring grey wall.
FA. Mark Edwards 1990s

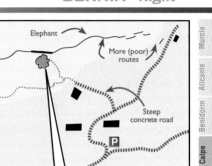

BERNIA - RIGHT

The first routes you arrive at are much less impressive than the magnificent challenges further along the ridge. However, they are at a friendlier grade and are very near the car.
APPROACH - From the parking, continue up the track until a steep concrete road appears on the left. Walk up this and continue to the crag which has a huge tree in front of it.

About 100m to the left of the first wall is a slab with a diagonal crack on its right-hand side.

⑫ Secrets . . . . 🔧🔖🛠️ ☐ **7a+**
35m. The slab direct. Take a small rack.
FA. Mark Edwards 1990s

⑬ The Diagonal . . . . . . 🔧🛠️ ☐ **6c**
35m. The crack itself in one long pitch. Some fixed gear but take a full rack.
FA. Mark Edwards 1990s

⑭ Mark in Time . . 🔧🔖🔩🛠️ ☐ **8b**
35m. A big route up the steep, double curving wall 50m to the right. Lots of pockets.
FA. Mark Edwards 1990s

This is the first wall you arrive at, tucked behind the huge tree.

⑮ Pobrecito . . . . ☐ **6a**
14m. An ugly route up the blocky groove and short crux wall.

⑯ Ranura . . . . 🔧🔖 ☐ **5+**
20m. Nice climbing (after the shrubby start) up the technical groove on the left, and over the roof above the 'bergschrund'.

⑰ Pedazos . . . . 🔧🔖🔩 ☐ **6a+**
22m. Climb the rib then the left slanting crack, taking care to avoid the big loose flake. The upper wall is better

⑱ Bloque! . . . . 🔧🕸️🔖 ☐ **7a+**
10m. The rib right of the wide crack leads to the double overhangs, the first is easy the second a real stopper.

⑲ Brevemente . . . . 🔧🕸️ ☐ **5+**
12m. The short left-hand line has the odd good move.

⑳ Bajo de estatura . . . . 🔩 ☐ **5**
12m. The right-hand line. Short, sharp and a bit loose.

There are more routes further up right (steep and hard), round the arete (short and slabby) and near the track (just tiny).

Murcia | Alicante | Benidorm | Calpe | Xaló Valley | Gandia | Bernia | Altea | Mascarat | Sierra de Toix | Olta | Peñón de Ifach

ALTEA

Two contrasting cliffs, both in superb settings. Altea Col is steep, imposing and recently developed with some majestic long routes. The location high above Mascarat, with fine views to towards Calpe and the Peñón, offers dramatic isolation in sharp contrast to the immense development passed on the approach drive. The clean slab of Dalle d'Ola was one of the first crags to be developed

Alan James in the huge corner of *Ja Mama, 6b+* Altea Col - *page 226*.

for visiting climbers and has become infamous amongst Costa Blanca devotees from the 1980s and early 90s. Whilst it is a bit tired and very much old wave, the slab consists of immaculate rock and the main routes give excellent climbing as well as providing you with a great view of all the luxurious apartments far below.

APPROACH (area map page 219)

The crags are situated at the top of the extensive Altea Hills estate which overlooks the town of Altea. Turn off the N332 at the big 'Altea Hills' entrance and follow the road uphill, across the motorway, to a complex junction by a large hotel. Turn right (without attracting the security guard's attention) and continue around the fountains and head off rightwards up 'Avenue de Europa'. Follow this road as far as 'Ave. Gran Bretange' on the right.
For Dalle d'Ola - Take the left-hand branch and continue for about 200m until the crag appears on the right.
For Altea Col - Turn right up 'Ave. Gran Bretange' then take the next left 'Ave. Gales'. Drive up here to a sharp bend by a concrete pumping station where a dirt track leads up the hill. Park here and pick up a well-cairned path which leads rightwards from 100m along the track, to the crag which can be clearly seen.

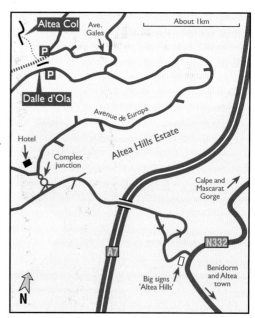

Left margin tabs (top to bottom): Murcia, Alicante, Benidorm, Calpe, Xalo Valley, Gandia, Bernia, Altea, Mascarat, Sierra de Toix, Olta, Peñón de Ifach

ALTEA *Dalle d'Ola*

Murcia | Alicante | Benidorm | Calpe | Xaló Valley | Gandia | Bernia | Altea | Mascarat | Sierra de Toix | Olta | Peñón de Ifach

DALLE D'OLA

A compact face of good rock, equipped with fat chain-link bolts and only seconds from the car. The locals call the cliff Canyelles, though its usual name comes from the German climber who placed the bolts and named it after his dog! The cliff is basically a broad flat wall with a small subsidiary buttress to the left. We have continued to use the coloured names though much of the paint has faded away.

CONDITIONS - A superb suntrap which makes it good for the winter months but keep well away when it is warmer. It is well-sheltered from the wind.

DESCENT - There are three lower-offs at the top of the slab. Care is needed on the routes on the right unless you have a 70m rope.

To the left of the main wall of the crag and the slanting rake is a subsidiary buttress split by a red groove; the first three routes are here. They are not especially sparkling.

① Left-hand Blue Bolts . . . . ☐ **5+**
16m. On the far left, climb the pleasantly slabby wall.

② Left-hand Red Bolts . . . . ☐ **5**
28m. Right of the red corner follow a thin crack to a ledge with bolts (possible belay). Finish up the short steep wall behind.

③ Left-hand Yellow Bolts . . . . . ☐ **5+**
28m. The right-hand bolt line to the same finish.

The rest of the climbs are on the main sheet of rock, the first four being reached by scrambling up a shrubby ramp.

④ Black Bolts . . . . . . 🔲🔲🔲 ☐ **6b**
22m. An unbalanced climb with a sharp crux low down.

⑤ Orange Bolts . . . . 🔲🔲 ☐ **6a**
24m. A boldish start leads to easier climbing above.

⑥ Green Bolts . . . . . 🔲🔲🔲 ☐ **6a+**
30m. Start from a large block and make difficult moves to reach the first break. Continue up a smoother section to an easy finish.

⑦ Yellow Bolts . . . . 🔲 ☐ **5+**
32m. A good climb, quite stiff for the grade early on but then easing with height.

⑧ White Bolts . . . . . 🔲🔲🔲🔲 ☐ **6b**
32m. Another good one. Steep moves gain the slab then climb up this to the final bulge which is taken at its left edge.

⑨ Blue Bolts . . . . 🔲🔲 ☐ **6a**
34m. A steady lower section leads to the crucial bulge just below the cliff top.

⑩ Pink Bolts . . . . 🔲🔲 ☐ **5+**
34m. A good introduction to the cliff with a low crux and easier climbing above, then a delicate finale.

⑪ Red Bolts . . . . . . 🔲🔲🔲 ☐ **6b+**
30m of climbing. Disjointed! The right-hand line on the lower wall leads to a traverse right (stance) and a tough crack finish.

⑫ Firenza . . . . 🔲 ☐ **6c**
10m. A short stiff pitch located to the right of the top pitch of the previous climb gives the hardest moves hereabouts.

Murcia / Alicante / Benidorm / Calpe / Xaló Valley / Gandia / Bernia / Altea / Mascarat / Sierra de Toix / Olta / Peñón de Ifach

ALTEA COL
A fine east-facing cliff that is clearly visible dead ahead, from just south of the Maryvilla entrance when heading south from Calpe. The cliff is beautifully situated, easy to get to, has a good set of existing routes and plenty of potential for new ones.
APPROACH - The approach path takes you to the left-hand sector. Short scrambles are needed to reach some of the starting ledges. For the right-hand sector, drop down and follow a faint path around under the crag and around the corner.
CONDITIONS - Both sections face east and get the sun in the morning. They will give good shade in the warm months but may be cold in winter since they are very exposed to the wind.

The first climbs are in a small bay just left of the main wall.

① Route 1 . . . . **6a**
14m. The short left-hand line is not very good!

② Lion . . . . **6c+**
16m. A thin vertical wall on small edges is short on bolts. Technically not too bad but a bit scary.
FA. D.Lyon, D.Dutton, C.Greatwich 1990s

③ Witch . . . . **6c+**
24m. The right-hand wall of the bay past tufas and holes has 'broccoli' rock at present but will improve with traffic.
FA. D.Dutton, D.Lyon, C.Greatwich 1990s

④ Wardrobe **6b**
28m. A big pitch up the left-hand edge of the main wall.
FA. D.Lyon, D.Dutton, C.Greatwich 1990s

⑤ Tschook du ? . . . . . **6b+**
30m. A tricky start and sustained wall is good all the way.
FA. Jens Muenchberg 1990s

⑥ Leo . . . . **6a+**
28m. The easiest route on the wall with a gentle start. It gets a bit technical above but is never desperate.
FA. Jens Muenchberg 1990s

⑦ Route 7 . . . . **?**
28m. An unknown line.

⑧ Entre dos tierras . . . . . **7a+**
24m. A poor, unbalanced route which has a desperate start and then much easier climbing above.
FA. Jens Muenchberg 1990s

⑨ Walking the Milkyway . **6c**
28m. Another hard start with an easier (6a+) wall above.
FA. Jens Muenchberg 1990s

⑩ Soft and Huggy . . . . . . **6a+**
28m. Despite the name there are some sharp holds and well-spaced bolts. Move right to the shared lower-off.
FA. Jens Muenchberg 1990s

⑪ Kuscheltiger **7a**
28m. Start as for *Soft and Huggy* but traverse right. The slab higher up provides the fingery crux.
FA. Jens Muenchberg 1990s

⑫ Ja Mama . . . . **6b+**
28m. The huge groove is harder and less good than it looks. *Photo page 224.*
FA. Jens Muenchberg 2003

⑬ Salva mea **8a**
24m. The tufa streaks give an excellent pitch. *Photo on cover.*
FA. Jens Muenchberg 2000s

⑭ Suse 4711 . . . . . . **6b+**
24m. The exposed arete (worth belaying) around the corner from the start of *Salvea mea*. The bolts are spaced!
FA. Jens Muenchberg 1990s

⑮ Dark Reign . . . . 🔲🔲🔲 **7a+**
24m. A fine route up the face left of the huge roof. Scramble up to a belay in a small cave. Move left around the arete and climb the bulging wall to good holds. Continue up the wall and finish up a tricky hanging groove.
FA. Richard Davies 2001

⑯ Elliea . . . . 🔲🔲🔲 **7b**
35m. A superb pitch but rope drag can be a problem. Scramble up to the left then and climb the wall on pockets to good holds. Continue up and leftwards until a long reach gains a good flake. Move rightwards through the bulge on poor holds and pull over to a belay point (25m). Follow the crack leftwards until a pull right through the bulge is reaches the belay (35m). Care needed with the descent.
FA. Richard Davies 2002

⑰ El Paso Blanco . . . 🔲🔲🔲 **7c+**
20m. Start as for *Baby Born* to the pod. Exit from the left and climb the steep blank white wall above. Make a hard move to gain a one-finger pocket and then attack the wall above and slightly to the left. This eases quickly.
FA. Richard Davies 2002

⑱ Baby Born . . . . 🔲🔲 **6c**
14m. Start below the right-most side of the big roof at an orange streak. Climb up to a diagonal pod and exit right. Continue up the wall above to a chain belay and lower-off.
Baby Obsession Link, 7a - *Baby Born* to the top of *Pure Ob*.
FA. Richard Davies 2001

⑲ Pure Obsession . . . 🔲🔲🔲 **7c**
24m. Climb a short groove, pull right to a hole and up to better holds. Head steeply up and leftwards to a good rest then continue up the steep wall, which soon eases, to reach a lower-off.
FA. Richard Davies 2001

⑳ Slabazonic . . . 🔲🔲🔲🔲 **8a**
20m. A well-bolted, steep, sharp and fingery wall. Pull through the roof of the cave then climb the wall above. Not very slabby!
FA. Richard Davies 2002

㉑ Crimpo Fantasia . . 🔲🔲🔲 **6c+**
25m. Start down the slope and climb the slab to below the roof. Step right through this and ascend the wall on tiny holds. Finish up the steep rib to a lower-off.
FA. Richard Davies 2002

㉒ Snake Country . . . . 🔲 **6a**
20m. Climb the wall on mostly-excellent holds to a bulge. Pull over this and go easily up the slab to a flake and final wall.
FA. Richard Davies 2002

㉓ Snake in the Sack . . . . . . 🔲 **6b+**
20m. Start below the corner crack part way up the wall. Climb past this, up the easy slab, to a final steep wall.
FA. Richard Davies 2002

㉔ Monsters Inc. . . . . 🔲🔲 **6c+**
25m. The slab to the right leads to a steep fingery wall. Up this to a good hold in a scoop and pull up onto the slab. Continue through the bulge on to a ledge and up the wall above (large thread on left) then head straight up to the lower-off.
FA. Richard Davies 2002

㉕ Adder Basher . . . . 🔲 **6c**
18m. Climb the slab rightwards and then up the wall to the hole. Follow the flake steeply up the wall.
FA. Richard Davies 2003

MASCARAT

Often gazed at in awe from the car as you whip through the tunnels on your way some-where else, the towering walls of the Mascarat provide some fine long routes in a weird and exciting setting. The road and traffic noise dominate the atmosphere a bit, although this is of little significance on the South West Face, and in the gorge. Several of the long routes have become established classics on the Costa Blanca hit list with *Llobet/Bertomeu (Vía UBSA)* being one of the more popular long and relatively easy routes around. Others are seldom climbed by visiting climbers but are worthwhile none-the-less. The hard routes on the Hambre de Mujer wall and Cleoplaca wall are all superb and quite popular.

CONDITIONS

The tall walls give shady climbing on many of the routes and a cold wind can whistle down the gorge in winter. This makes it a good place to head for in very hot weather but conversely a dreadful place if it is at all chilly. The longer routes on the South West Face are much more exposed to the sunshine and should all be considered as major full-day undertakings. Make sure you are well equipped with an appropriate rack of gear and take plenty of water and sun screen.

APPROACH (area map page 219)

The Mascarat is the bit with all the bridges, tunnels and huge towering walls of orange and grey limestone on the N332, just to the south of Calpe. Some of the routes start from the road level, and some start from the base of the gorge. The problem is what do you do with your car? By far the best option for the routes which start at road level is to persuade someone to drop you off although there is parking (robbers!) in a lay-by just uphill from the turning to Pueblo Mascarat. For the gorge routes, turn off the N332 about 250m south (downhill) from the lowest tunnel signed towards 'Pueblo Mascarat'. Follow this road down past a bridge on a bend (the track up the gorge leads off from this bridge) and either bump up the kerb (get well off the road) or continue to a T-junction, turn left and drive around to park on the latest urbanisation development. Don't leave anything in your car.

NOTE - this area is being built all over so it is possible that these parking spots may become inaccessible in the future - check **rockfax.com** for update details.

To get to the routes which start in the gorge, walk up the cobbly bed of the dry river. The routes at road level can be reached by slogging up the steep bank on the left (looking up the gorge) to arrive by the small tower.

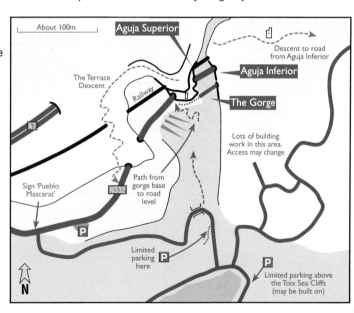

Paul Cox climbing the fine groove on *Llobet/Bertomeu (formerly Vía UBSA)* (5+) on the South West Face of Aguja Superior - *page 230*. This photo sums up climbing in the Mascarat Gorge; fine positions, in spectacular scenery, and with the different generations of road far below you. Photo: Rich Mayfield

❷ Espermació . . . . . . 🔲🔲🔲🔲 6a (E1)

A seldom-climbed line up the right-hand side of the pillar.
1) 5+, 40m. Climb the wall just right of *Las Tetas* ....
2) 5+, 45m. Move up to gain a left-trending crack. Follow this to the left edge of the pillar, then climb another crack to a stance on top of the pillar.
3) 6a, 40m. Move right then climb the wall to a grassy ledge. Escape rightwards from here to the ridge.
FA. Salvador Guerola, Emilio Perales 1986

❸ Llobet/Bertomeu . . 🔲🔲🔲🔲 5+ (HVS)

An old and popular climb long known as *Vía UBSA*. The route was fully bolted briefly but some of the gear has since been removed - carry a light rack. Although there is only one hard pitch, it is a fairly committing undertaking. Start by the steps opposite the old electricity house, by the old bridge.
1) 3, 44m. Follow the pillar leftwards to a 'netting' belay .
2) 4, 44m. Up the rib above to where the ridge levels out.
3) 2, 50m. Scramble easily up the ridge to a grassy terrace and cross this to a peg belay below and left of a groove in the wall.
4) 4+, 46m. Climb up right (bolt) to the groove, and climb it for 3m then pull onto the right edge. Follow a line of cracks up the wall to threads and traverse right for 10m to a stance.
5) 5+, 36m. Climb the polished groove (pegs and a bolts) and continue in the same line to belay on threads and an old bolt.
6) 4+, 20m. Climb the wall left of the belay (bolt) to a short wall. Trend right (pegs) to a slab and an exposed stance.
7) 4, 36m. Continue traversing right to a groove, climb this and slabs above to the top.
From here use the Terrace Descent (described opposite) or continue to the top. There are two more pleasant easy pitches, a scramble and a ridge walk across the top. To descend, traverse the ridge until you reach houses, descend through this then head back across the mountain to the Terrace Descent. *Photo page 228.*
FA. G.Llobet, J.Bertomeu 1974

AGUJA SUPERIOR

The south side of the Mascarat Gorge has two huge faces split by a ridge which runs down to the disused road bridge. This ridge is the start of one of the more popular long routes in the area - *Llobet/Bertomeu*. The other routes are on the side walls and have complex approaches and descents. They are in an atmospheric setting and provide some memorable adventures.
GEAR - The routes tend to have pegs or bolts by the hard bits, and on the stances, but a rack is advisable.

SOUTH-WEST FACE

APPROACH (Routes 1 and 2) - Cross the road just below the middle tunnel and gain the scree slope crossed by the railway. Slog up past this until you can scramble up a band of rock on the right. The start of Route 1 is marked by a scratched cross.
TERRACE DESCENT - The routes top-out on a ledge system. It is possible to continue to the top or there is an easy escape off left along the terrace. Cross this to a rock step, climb over this then descend open slopes on the left, skirting above the railway tunnel. This leads down to the road. Take care not to descend before the rock step.

❶ Las Tetas de mi Novia 🔲🔲🔲🔲 6b+ (E3)

A good route on the left-hand side of a huge pillar, high up on the south west face of the buttress. A full rack is needed.
1) 6b+, 36m. Climb the wall below the groove past a variety of fixed gear. Hard moves lead left into the groove to belay.
2) 6b, 44m. Climb the groove above until forced left into another groove. Climb this until moves back right gain a good crack (pegs) leading to a stance.
3) 6a, 20m. Traverse easily rightwards until you can climb a short awkward wall past a peg to gain an exposed stance.
4) 6a+,45m. Climb directly above the stance trending rightwards to the ridge. *Photo page 5*
FA. Roberto Lli, Quique Barber 1984

SOUTH-EAST FACE

The rest of the routes start on the south east wall, but they top-out at the same place as *Llobet/Bertomeu*. Despite the enclosed atmosphere, the situations are superb. One slight draw back is the incessant traffic noise.
APPROACH - Climb over the railings on the middle road bridge then move up right to a ledge. Rope up here!
DESCENT - Use the Terrace Descent.

❹ El Pajarón . . . . 🔲🔲🔲🔲 6a (E1)

The old classic of this wall. The approach is a bit scrappy, but after that it is solid and excellent. Full rack needed.
1) 3+, 55m. Scramble leftwards up vegetated rock to below a groove in the clean upper wall.
2) 6a, 38m. Bridge up the groove then move up and right into the continuation groove. At its top, trend left to a small ledge.
3) 5+, 34m. Step right and climb up then move right again into a hidden groove (pegs) which leads to a good ledge.
4) 5+, 30m. Move up behind the stance into a slabby groove and follow the crack above to a stance out on the left.
5) 5, 30m. Follow the red corner (no fixed gear) and a flake on the left followed by cracks to a ledge.
6) 5, 20m. Continue to join *Llobet/Bertomeu* before its last pitch then finish up it or climb the steep groove on the left to the ridge (5).
FA. Salvador Guerola, Emilio Perales 1986

CONDITIONS - The vast south west face is exposed to the sunshine and the wind which can make it a good place on calm winter days. The routes are all major undertakings. Make sure you are well equipped with an appropriate rack of gear and take plenty of water and sun screen.
The south east face gets shade from midday but can be bitterly cold if there is a wind blowing down the gorge.

Descend along the terrace

Murcia · Alicante · Benidorm · Calpe · Xaló Valley · Gandia · Bernia · Altea · Mascarat · Sierra de Toix · Olta · Peñón de Ifach

❺ **Finis África** . . . . . . 🔲 **7b+**
50m. A huge and desperate pitch from the large grassy terrace, to the big cave at the end of pitch 3 on *Sylphara*. Abseil off.

❻ **Sylphara** . . . . . 🔲 **7a (E4)**
This fine climb originally started from the base of the gorge (see Hambre de Mujer Wall - route 4) but a storm altered the start, so nowadays it is best to begin at bridge level. Full rack needed. The crux pitch is substantially harder than the rest of the route.
1) 5+, 36m. From the right-hand end of the ledge, climb up a slab then traverse across rightwards to the cave.
2) 6a, 40m. Leave the cave by its left edge and climb up the long rib above to another cave.
3) 6a+,36m. Step left from the bottom of this cave and climb a left-trending groove to its top.
4) 7a, 36m. The big one and it's not really aid-able! Follow the arduous curving groove above to a good ledge at the top.
5) 5+, 20m. Climb a corner then move right to belay.
6) 5, 40m. Climb a short groove to a pillar. Belay at the top.
7) 4, 45m. Move up then left to join *Llobet/Bertomeu* to finish.
FA. Ernesto López, Koke Pérez, Enrique Barberá 1979

❼ **Vuelo del águila** . . 🔲 **6a+ (E2)**
A long and exposed climb taking the right arete of the steep face overlooking the gorge. Start as for *Sylphara*.
1) 3, 45m. Traverse right on ledges to a long cave.
2) 6a, 30m. Climb slabs right of the cave to 2 bolts. The crack on the right leads to shallow grooves and a cave. Bolt belay.
3) 6a, 50m. Slabs on the left lead to a crack (bolt, ignore pegs going left). Climb the chimney on the right, past overhangs, to a groove. Move left below a roof then up a groove to a ledge.
4) 5, 36m. Climb the right-slanting groove then just right of the arete to a ledge.
5) 4, 40m. Continue just right of the arete until you can step on to it. Climb the slab to a good ledge.
4a) 6a+, 36m. Alternative pitch. Climb the groove above and pass a small cave on your left. Go direct to a cave.
5a) 5, 45m. Climb into another cave on the left (nest) then up a groove to follow slabs and a chimney which lead to the arete. Follow this to a good ledge.
6) 4. 25m. Follow the arete to a belay (peg).
7) 4+, 30m. Follow the arete to a good ledge.
8) 4, 25m. Climb the arete to ledges and the walk off.
FA. Unknown. P4 and P5 - Rowland Edwards, Mark Edwards 1985

Murcia · Alicante · Benidorm · **Calpe** · Xaló Valley · Candia · Bernia · Altea · Mascarat · Sierra de Toix · Olta · Peñon de Ifach

GEAR - The single pitch routes are fully bolted with lower-offs. The long routes have some gear but a rack is advisable.

Afternoon · 15 min

Descent

AGUJA INFERIOR

The 'Smaller Pinnacle' is the tower on the opposite side of the gorge to the main Mascarat walls. It has a striking, clean, triangular wall, which is obvious when driving north on the N332 - this is the home of *Cleoplaca*. There are also several other short hard climbs on this wall, plus several long routes.

APPROACH - Almost all the routes start at road level so you will either need to slog up the hill from the Sea Cliffs parking or be dropped off at road level.

DESCENT - For the routes which top-out, follow the ridge towards Toix Oeste and get onto the road which leads down to the base of the gorge.

Access to Gede

Multi-pitch · Windy

The first route takes a long and exciting line, up the left-hand side of the pinnacle. It is not marked on the topo.

❶ Boulder Terminar.. 🔼📷🪝 ☐ 5+ (HVS)

An impressive route with some exciting positions above the road. The first three pitches are fully bolted and descent is possible from the top of pitch 3 but the upper section does have some good climbing, including the crux pitch. Start by abseiling from the left-hand side (looking uphill) of the new road bridge, to a small ledge above the base of the gorge.

1) 5+, 40m. Climb across to a detached pillar, then move up a wall and make a delicate traverse left until you can reach a cave.

2) 4+, 36m. Pull steeply into the groove and follow it to ledges.

3) 3, 20m. Scramble easily up a corner behind and onto a big ledge. You can escape leftwards here, back to the road, or scramble up the ramp to below a big red groove.

4) 5+, 40m. Climb the groove (easier than it looks) until you are forced left across a slab to a stance.

5) 4, 30m. Move left then climb up another groove, past a hole. Some big flakes lead to a stance with a tree, below a crack.

6) 5, 20m. The crack is awkward but soon eases and leads to a rather sudden finish. A more direct finish is **6a**.

FA. Javier Motes, Moises García, Enrique Barberá, Ernesto López 1970s

Above and right of the road tunnel are two more long diagonal grooves. The next route follows the left-hand of these.

❷ G.E.D.E. . . . . 🔼📷🪝 ☐ 6a+ (E2)

The line is easy at the bottom then intricate and wild at the top. The route is fully-bolted except for the last easy pitch. The best approach is to walk below the *Cleoplaca* wall and follow the little tunnels through the cave to emerge just above the road. You can get at it directly from the road but it's not as much fun.

1) 4+, 36m. Climb the groove above then traverse left to a small stance in the base of the second groove.

2) 5, 36m. Follow the next groove then move left onto a ledge.

3) 5+, 36m. Above the ledge is the big corner of *Boulder Terminar*. Climb the wall to the right of this to a small stance.

4) 6a+, 34m. Climb a steep flake behind the stance (pulling on a bit of gear reduces this to **5**) then move around the pinnacle and continue to a well-positioned ledge.

5) 3, 30m. Scramble easily to the top.

FA. G Llobet, Calleja, Sanchez 1975

❸ Cuevas . . . . 🪝 ☐ 6b+

14m. A curious little route on the road side of the cave down and left of the *Cleoplaca* wall. It is just inside the cave and has a lower-off in space. Take care getting to the start.

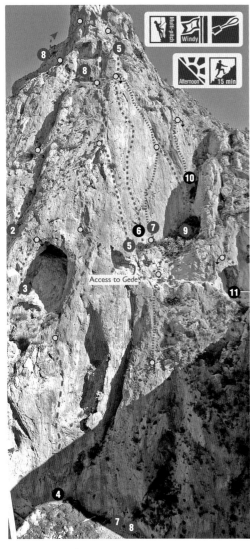

Access to Gede

Botella/Montesinos continued...
3) 4, 18m. Traverse directly across the slab on the right to the *Cleoplaca* belay. The sensible option is to abseil from here but:
4) 4+, 50m. Climb the grooves above taking care with the rock.
5) 4+, 50m. Follow the flakes to the left of the grooves then step back right to easy ground. Belay on the crest. Be careful not to knock rocks onto the road from these upper pitches.
FA. Juan Montesinos, Rafael Botella 1970s

6 Cleoplaca . . . . 🔲🖐🤚✒️ ▭ **7b**
48m. One of the best technical challenges in the area up a magnificent shield of rock - *the Queen of walls!* The climbing is very sustained and hard on the fingers with no respite. Rope-drag can be a problem at the top where the holds are so small that a tiny bit of extra drag can make all the difference, so don't attempt it in one long pitch unless you have double ropes. If you have a single rope, take a hanging stance on the flake after a tricky initial section.

7 Vía Aurora . . . . 🔲✒️ ▭ **6a (E1)**
A long route starting in the base of the gorge, between the two road bridges, and continuing up the right-hand edge of the *Cleoplaca* wall.
1) 6a, 38m. Climb the lower wall leftwards. then direct as possible. eventually via a flake to a stance (pegs) on the right.
2) 5+, 10m. Move left and make a hard move to reach the terrace below *Cleoplaca*. Belay on the bolts below the wall.
3) 6a, 30m. Climb awkwardly to gain a right-trending ramp line which is followed with difficulty (spaced peg runners) to a crack and stance on the right.
4) 6a, 25m. The crack above leads to the bolt belay at the top of *Cleoplaca*. Most folks abseil off from here (45m). However if you do need that summit sensation then continue up *Montesinos* which goes up the grooves directly above.

8 Triple Direct . . . . 🔲✒️ ▭ **6a (E1)**
210m. An excellent combination is the lower section of *Aurora*, the middle bit of *Botella/Montesinos*, a short section of *G.E.D.E.* and the final grooves of *Boulder Terminar*. This provides a nine pitch outing at a sustained 5+/6a which spirals up the buttress from the depths of the gorge to the ridge crest high above.

The next routes are fully bolted with lower-offs.

9 La Carabela . . . . 🔲🗲 ▭ **6c+**
24m. Start up the gully on the right then trend left and climb steeply to the belay on *Aurora*.

10 Bridge of Spies 🔲🗲🤚✒️ ▭ **7c**
32m. A magnificent, if slightly manufactured, route up the large curving arete and hanging tufa fin to the right of the main wall.

11 Espinaca Please Olive . . . 🗲 ▭ **7b**
10m. A ugly route above the tunnel entrance.

To the right is a short wall above a grassy terrace.

12 To Be in England . . 🔲🗲 ▭ **7a (E5)**
24m. A wire is needed at the start then follow the bolts rightwards across the face.

13 Crazy Ingleses. . . . . . . 🖐✒️ ▭ **6b+ (E3)**
20m. One peg and one thread protect scary climbing up the scoop on the right-hand side of the face. Very bold.

4 Route 4 . . . . 🔲❓ ▭ **?**
The only details known about this route are that it is fully-bolted and it starts in the base of the gorge. The first pitch looks hard (**7a/b**) but above that the climbing appears to be much easier (**6a/b**) and the finish up the tower looks spectacular.

5 Botella/Montesinos 🔲🗲🔸 ▭ **6a (E1)**
Another long route with two good lower pitches but it eases with height and the finish is a bit scrappy. Start from the old road bridge and walk across underneath the *Cleoplaca* wall. Scramble up a flake to the ledge under the wall, bolt belays.
1) 6a, 34m. Move left to gain the groove-line, which bounds the face on its left. Climb this, past a deep hole, and belay on a small ledge on the left.
2) 5+, 24m. Pull back right into the crack and follow it up the edge of the wall to a stance below steeper rock.

Murcia
Alicante
Benidorm
Calpe
Xaló Valley
Gandia
Bernia
Altea
Mascarat
Sierra de Toix
Olta
Peñón de Ifach

50m gap

THE GORGE
Deep in the gorge which cuts through the towering walls of the Mascarat, are a couple of compact walls with a few routes between them. The atmosphere is enclosed and the area is liberally strewn with debris which has either been washed down the river (usually dry) or chucked off the bridges. However, the climbing is good, especially on the *Hambre de Mujer* wall.
APPROACH - From the parking above the sea cliffs walk back down the road to the little bridge. From here an indistinct path leads off up the bouldery bed of the gorge.

HAMBRE DE MUJER WALL
The steep wall directly under the lower bridge gives fine climbing slightly reminiscent of Huntsman's Leap in Pembroke.

1 **El sherifico** . . . . . . 🔲🔲🔲 **7b**
24m. A superb route with a hard, reachy move near the bottom and a sustained and pumpy finish.

2 **Hambre de Mujer** . . . . . 🔲🔲🔲 **7a**
26m. A great route which gives a full body pump! It follows the superb snaking groove with just enough holds and some well-spaced bolts. It doesn't really have a crux but there aren't many easy moves either. Save some energy for the final bulges.

3 **Hambre Variación** . . . . 🔲🔲🔲 **6c+**
24m. By starting up *Hambre* ... it is possible to miss out the really hard bit of *Que Dios reparta suerte* and finish up its good, and more reasonable, top section.

4 **Que Dios reparta suerte** . . 🔲🔲🔲 **7c**
24m. The start is often wet, and always desperate. This is actually the first pitch of the original start of *Sylphara* on the South East Wall. This start was altered after a particularly savage storm removed the bottom 5m of boulders leaving some very blank rock.

5 **Lubricante vaginal en uno.** 🔲🔲🔲 **7a**
14m. A short route with one hard move past the pocket.

Further up the gorge, where it narrows, is one last weird route.

6 **Abedul** . . . . 🔲🔲🔲 **7b**
24m. Start up a slabby pillar and then swing around the corner where it starts to get steep. One more hard move leads to a rest before the final bulge with the lower-off above.

THE SOFT ROCK WALL
Just before the first bridge is a smooth wall on the right. Its sunny aspect and easy access means that this is the most popular wall in the whole of Mascarat, but it isn't the best.

7 **Mujer Contra Mujer** . . . . . 🔲🔲🔲 **6a+**
22m. The left-most route on the wall, which goes through a small hollow. From this (thread) exit right and climb the steep slab to the lower-off.

8 **Marica el última** . . . . 🔲🔲🔲 **6a+**
22m. The wall between the two holes has two variations (both about the same grade) and a hard move off an undercut. The first bolt is quite high.

9 **Auntie Bolt** . . . . 🔲🔲🔲 **6a (HVS)**
22m. Climb up through the right-hand cave. The first bolt is above the cave, so take some gear, then clip the bolts on the previous route.

10 **Soft Rock** . . . . 🔲🔲🔲 **6a (HVS)**
38m. The wall right of the cave has lots of threads but needs a bit of gear as well. It improves with height. Abseil off or walk left to the bridge and abseil down from below *Cleoplaca*.

11 **Pobre cito** . . . . 🔲🔲🔲 **4+ (HS)**
40m. A poor line up the wall to the right. Descend as for the previous route.

12 **Brother Wolf** . . . . 🔲🔲🔲 **5+**
16m. Pulling through a small bulge is the crux. Then trend right to the lower-off.

13 **Sister Moon** . . . . 🔲🔲🔲 **6a**
16m. The right-hand side of the wall. The last bolt may be missing making it a bit bold and wires won't help!

Murcia

Alicante

Benidorm

Calpe

Xaló Valley

Gandia

Bernia

Altea

Mascarat

Sierra de Toix

Olta

Peñón de Ifach

The roadside attraction of *Plata* (6a+) on Toix Este - *page 239.*

The Sierra de Toix forms the impressive ridge that juts out into the sea overlooking Calpe to the north and Benidorm to the south. The rock outcrops on the ridge are virtually continuous but only some sections have been found worthy of development and, although some of the routes are not particularly outstanding, it does have an important role in the climbing available in the Costa Blanca. The crags are extremely accessible with many good routes especially in the easier grades and it will probably be visited at least once by most visiting groups. The wide choice of routes available and the 360° aspect means that it is almost always possible to find something to do here whatever the weather.

There is a wide variety of climbing on the ridge from 5m five-bolt slab climbs to serious trad routes on the harsh sea cliffs. If you are after tough trad climbing experience then head for the Candelabra del Sol which is home to some amazingly-positioned trad routes which will doubtless give a memorable day's outing. The best sport climbing is in the 5 to 6b range, but there are also some excellent harder routes on Toix TV and Toix Norte. The recent developments on Toix Placa have added a host of new, easier climbs and these have already proved very popular.

Many of the routes have become established classics over the years and inevitably some are beginning to get a bit polished. Since this was one of the first areas to be developed on the Costa Blanca, the original 'chain-link' bolts are now looking a bit old (though still feel pretty substantial) and it may be a good idea to carry some wires with you.

The older routes on Toix Oeste and Este were bolted in the mid 1980s by Erika and Pel, two Swiss climbers. Toix TV was developed by Mark and Rowland Edwards in the mid to late 80s. The same pair also developed the wild routes on the Candelabra del Sol. In the late 1990s father and son Muenchberg and others rebolted some and added many more routes to Toix Placa.

CONDITIONS

One of the main attractions of the Toix area is the many mid and lower grade climbs it offers and the fact that climbing it possible in most weather conditions. If it is raining inland - not totally unheard of in winter - then it is often dry here. Conversely, when the sun is beating down, it is possible to find some shade. Obviously Toix Norte is in the shade, but for easier routes Toix Oeste in the morning and Toix Este in the afternoon are both worth considering. Its exposed position mean that it can be windy, especially on Toix Oeste and Toix TV. For detailed conditions notes, see the yellow boxes with each buttress.

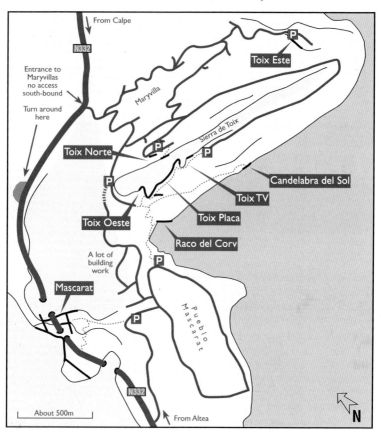

APPROACHES (area map page 219)

The Sierra de Toix is the rocky ridge to the south of Calpe. Most of the various buttresses described here are reached from Maryvilla - the sprawling collection of holiday villas on the northern slopes of the ridge. The Maryvilla's turn-off is well-signed on the N332 to the south of Calpe, just north of the Mascarat Gorge (Note: entry is not allowed south bound, continue a couple of hundred metres to where a lay-by allows an about-face). Once you are in Maryvilla it is very easy to get completely lost in the maze of roads which zig-zag up the hillside but stick to the approach descriptions listed with each crag and you should be okay. If you are driving up from further south, then take the Altea turn off (junction 64) and drive through the Mascarat Gorge on the N332 to find Maryvilla on the right.

Chris Craggs enjoying *Semi Dulce* (5+) on Toix Placa - *page 248*. The slabby south-facing walls of the Sierra de Toix have been extensively developed over the last few years with many excellent fully-bolted, mid and low-grade routes. Photo: Sherri Davy
Inset: Dave Gregory on pitch 3 of *Omar Sus* (5) Toix Placa - Lower *page 246*

TOIX ESTE

Toix Este is a popular roadside crag with glorious views over Calpe and the Peñón. The climbing varies from good long routes with fingery cruxes, to short little polished things on crusty rock. The gear is much the same as elsewhere on Toix, with the odd manky bolt and lower-off, but you shouldn't need wires for most of them. This is a good airport day crag since it is easy to keep an eye on your gear.
APPROACH - Turn off the main road from Calpe, into Maryvilla then branch left, branch right, middle of three, branch left, road joins from left, keep going and hey presto, there's a crag! Turning is possible 200m further on.
DESCENT - Many of the routes are more than 25m long so please take great care when lowering off.

The far left-hand section of the crag is reached via a small path which leads up to the face from the road directly below.

❶ Hetti 4
40m. The line is marked by arrows and threads. There is an optional stance at 25m if required.

To the right is the name Solar Energy painted on the rock. There are some old threads but no grade is known.

❷ Fluida Conexión Izquierda. 6b
28m. The left-hand branch out of the next route. Either lower-off the threads or continue to the top.

❸ Fluida Conexión . . . . . 6b+
28m. An interesting initial section up the steep wall. Move right to gain a groove on the upper slab. The gear and belay are old.

❹ Borro el toro . . . . . 7a+
28m. A very fingery slab with one chipped hold.

❺ Edward's Slab 6c
24m. Teeter up the edge of the slab with difficulty.

❻ La tonta del bote . . 6b+
30m. A devious variation though with good moves. Start up *Vía de los fakiros* and traverse across to *Edward's Slab.*

❼ Vía de los fakiros. . 6b+
24m. Climb up the right-hand side of the small roof, then step left and make a hard moves up above (tricky clip for shorties).

❽ Hannah . . . . 6a+
28m. A long route which follows the grey rib. The start is hard.

❾ Purpúreo . . . . 4+
28m. The slab starting just left of a cave is pleasantly-sustained.

The next routes can be can be reached by a prickly scramble along the base of the main wall, or from below by the parking spot.

❿ Spölli. . . . . 4+
40m. Climb the cracks, the crux bulge is at 20m. There is a poor lower-off at 25m and another higher up.

⓫ Winter 6a
28m. A good route with a hard start up the slab continuing up steep rock above. Take care when lowering.

⓬ Verde. . . . . 5+
28m. There is a thin start then jugs above as things steepen up. The line is marked by paired bolts. Take care when lowering.

⓭ "P" 5
30m. A line of red marks up a thin crack. Finish up *Verde.*

Murcia
Alicante
Benidorm
Calpe
Xaló Valley
Gandia
Bernia
Altea
Masarrat
Sierra de Toix
Olta
Peñón de Ifach

⑭ Vía la fina . . . . 🔲🔲🔲 5
1) 4+, 20m. Climb the scoop to a stance in the cave.
2) 5, 20m. Tough moves gain the groove above. Exit left.

⑮ Plata . . . . 🔲🔲🔲 6a+
24m. Another technical slab climb which crosses *Vía pyramid*. The start is the crux (slippery), above that it is sharp!
Photo page 235.

⑯ Vía pyramid . . . . 🔲🔲🔲 5
The long diagonal line which splits the face. Take a rack.
1) 4+, 20m. Follow the groove - a bit floral - to the cave.
2) 5, 20m. Pull through the bulges then trend left to the arete.
2a) 4+, 18m. Traverse the rugged slab for an easier escape.

⑰ Sol y bon tiempo . . . . . 🔲🔲🔲 6b+
24m. A fingery section at mid-height gives the difficulties.

⑱ Vía yuyuba Directa . . . . 🔲🔲🔲 6c
22m. Continue direct from where the parent route moves right.

⑲ Vía yuyuba . . . . 🔲🔲🔲 6a+
24m. The excellent central line has a hard move rightwards to reach the groove left of the roof.

⑳ King Cucudrulu . . . . 🔲🔲🔲 7a
24m. Only one teeny weeny little hard move, but what a move!

㉑ El oso y el mandaron . . . . 🔲🔲 6a+
24m. Another popular roadside route which has a fine lower wall and a tricky roof to finish. Escape leftwards is possible.

㉒ Verde dos . . . . 🔲🔲 5+
20m. A slippery start leads to the groove but break leftwards up the wall for steep sustained finish.

㉓ La ramuna arenosa 🔲🔲🔲 6a
20m. The big corner is followed, then step left onto the wall for a finish that is a bit of a shocker.

㉔ Going Solo . . . . 🔲🔲 6c+
14m. A polished technical nasty that has had too many ascents.

㉕ Graphic Whore . . . . 🔲🔲 6c+
14m. The rib is friable low down but has a good finish over the bulge. Photogenic.

To the right are a couple of unnamed 6a routes that climb the worst rock on the crag. They have not proved popular!

㉖ Amarillo . . . . 🔲 5+
12m. The line of yellow bolts is slippery, technical and balancy. The old lower-off is shot, either use the last bolt or top out.

There are a few more lines to the right but they are very poor. However on the far side of the road is a pair of bolts which are the abseil station to:

㉗ Adiós Dalí . . . . 🔲🔲🔲🔲 7c+
18m. A sustained and technical slab route which has been described as being similar to slate climbing.

Murcia · Alicante · Benidorm · **Calpe** · Xaló Valley · Gandia · Bernia · Altea · Mascarat · **Sierra de Toix** · Olta · Peñón de Ifach

TOIX NORTE
The northern side of the Toix Ridge is clearly visible from Calpe and is continuous for most of the length of the ridge, however only two small sections have so far been developed. The largest, and most impressive, section is Pared Blanca, the large white wall towards the right-hand end. Pared de la Tuberia is a shorter wall above the approach road.

TOIX NORTE
APPROACH - Turn off the main road from Calpe, into Maryvilla, then take the following sequence of turns; right by the telephone, branch right at next junction, take next road on the left, continue straight past two other junctions (up to this point it is the same approach as for Toix TV) then turn sharp right at the next. The road then leads up the hill and doubles back under Pared de la Tuberia. Park further up the road.

PARED BLANCA
... is the huge white wall above you!
The routes are fully-bolted, but the bolts are far apart.

❶ Route 1 . . . . 🏋️🏃🧗 ☐ **7b**
26m. The left-hand line passing an old thread and a tree at half-height, then continuing over a roof.

❷ Por quien doblan . . 🏋️🏃🧗 ☐ **7b+**
26m. A blank line which contains the odd chipped hold but is still very impressive. Start at the painted name and trend right to the crucial central section. Above this things ease - a little.

❸ Route 3 . . . . 🏋️❤️🧗 ☐ **7a+**
28m. The best route on this wall is sustained and pumpy with three cruxes. The last crux is at the top and the other two are well above the new bolts which protect them. A grade of **E5 6a** gives the right impression.

❹ S.S. . . . . 🏋️🏃🧗 ☐ **7b**
26m. Another superb route up the pocketed seam to the right of the brown-streaked groove. Steep sustained and pumpy, especially on your right arm!

PARED DE LA TUBERIA
This is the uninspiring wall above the road. On first acquaintance it seems a bit short and insignificant but the routes pack a lot in and the rock is exceptionally rough.

❺ La Niña . . . . 🏃 ☐ **6b+**
10m. Pull through the undercut base to reach a diagonal crack and exit rightwards with difficulty. Sprint to the belay.

❻ La Novia . . . . 🏃 ☐ **6b**
10m. A direct line to the lower-off. Pull into a scoop then exit rightwards and then finish direct up the wall.

❼ La Viuda . . . . 🏃🎗️ ☐ **6c**
10m. The start is fierce and sharp though things soon ease.

❽ Piñón . . . . 👐🏃 ☐ **7a**
12m. Climb to the big hole then exit leftwards and follow spaced holds to a final tricky move.

The last two routes look a bit better than the others but are extremely painful and fingery at the top. The bolts are a bit 'tinny' as well.

❾ Route 9 . . . . ⚡🏃👐 ☐ **7b**
20m. Start left of the scoop and pull right to a hole and a spidery crack. Above this are desperate finishing moves through the bulges.

❿ Route 10 . . . . ⚡🏃👐 ☐ **7a+**
20m. Juggy climbing leads to a tricky scoop. Up this to the break then trend leftwards across the steep upper wall.

Sylvia Fitzpatrick contemplating the tricky finishing moves of *Monkey Wall* (6c) on Toix TV - *page 250*. This magnificent natural amphitheatre is one of the best sun-traps around and a fine place to enjoy sunsets over Benidorm and the mountains to the south. Photo: Rich Mayfield

Murcia
Alicante
Benidorm
Calpe
Xaló Valley
Gandia
Bernia
Altea
Mascarat
Sierra de Toix
Olta
Peñón de Ifach

TOIX OESTE

The most popular climbing on the Sierra de Toix is found at Toix Oeste. The routes here are one of the reasons for coming to the Costa Blanca - bolted winter-sun climbing at an easier grade than is usual available elsewhere. Some of the bolts on this crag are now rather old although some are being gradually replaced.
APPROACH - Turn off the main Calpe road (N332) at the junction signed to Maryvilla, north of the Mascarat Gorge (not allowed south-bound). Follow signs for Castellete de Calpe and park at the end of the road.
DESCENTS - It is possible to lower from some of the routes. On the longer ones you can abseil on double 50m ropes, wtih a single rope two abseils can be made.

From mid morning | 2 min | Multi-pitch | Windy

❶ Amarilla . . . . . 5+ (E1)
The left arete of the wall has little fixed gear.
1) 4, 24m. Take the easiest line up the left arete of the bay.
2) 5, 24m. Follow the steep wall (run-out) to a belay. It is possible to abseil off from here in one (44m).
3) 4, 20m. Follow the left-hand rib to another stance. There is a direct variation on this pitch at **5**.
4) 30m. Follow easy ground up the ridge.
DESCENT - Traverse east to the first notch and abseil down *Lofi* (Toix Placa page 246) on the south-side of the ridge. 4 short abseils on a 60m rope, or two long ones with double ropes.

❷ Zorro Veloz . . . 6b
42m. A fine climb up the left-hand side wall of the bay with sustained climbing and spaced bolts. It can be split.
FA. Tono Quintana 2004

❸ Plata 6a
1) 6a, 20m. A steep pitch up the left-hand side of the bay.
2) 5+, 24m. Move right to gain the shallow groove and follow this as it curves back left to a stance.
DESCENT - Abseil (45m).

❹ Green Route I . . . . 6a+
A popular route which can be done in one huge pitch.
1) 6a+, 20m. Climb direct to the prominent stance. Strenuous.
2) 6a+, 24m. Finish directly up the steep wall.

❺ A Black Route 7a
24m. A technically interesting route via the orange orifice and some fingery undercutting. The hardest hereabouts.

❻ Red Route Directa 6c
24m. The steep wall to the right. Lower off the belay of the previous route or continue up the next route.

❼ Red Route I . . . . . 6a+
44m. This long, single pitch is one of the most popular routes on the crag (hence it is a bit polished). Take a lot of quickdraws. The start is the crux but the thin slab above provides an interesting finish. Descend by abseil (45m).

❽ Black Route . . . . . 6b+
45m. Start in the same place as the last route but climb the slab to its right. It is possible to miss out the hard bit by climbing the groove to the right at a more balanced 6a.

❾ Green Route II 5
50m. A good climb which finishes up the prominent flake of *Espolon Limaban*. The gear is of mixed vintage but there is plenty of it. The pitch can be split at a mid-height stance just after the slab and before a tricky move onto the upper wall.

❿ Espolón Limaban 5
A fine route up the impressive flake crack high on the face. The original route of the crag, put up in June 1977.
1) 4, 32m. Climb the wall just right of the groove with deviations to the left as and when needed. Belay by a tree.
2) 5, 30m. Climb cracks then a short tricky wall to the layback flake. Up this - easy but spooky - then continue to higher ledges and a choice of belays. Descend by abseil.

On the next section four routes have recently been added amongst the older classics rather confusing things on the central section of the face. They are equipped with a mixture of gear including 8mm bolts instead of the usual 10mm and have new paint spots. Pick your colour and go!

⑪ Dedi - UBSA . . . . 🔳🪢 [ ] 6a

The first of the newer offerings is easily spotted!
1) 5, 26m. Follow the black and pink spots and assorted fixed gear past the tree and over the overhangs to a good stance.
2) 6a, 30m. Climb easy rock then overhangs by a powerful move to easier ground and ledges. Abseil off.

⑫ Red Route II . . . . 🔳 [ ] 5+

One of the older classics that runs up the centre of the buttress in two pitches. The original red paint has almost gone.
1) 5, 28m. Start at the 'V+' and follow the faded red paint to a ledge and stance. The second clip is a bit run-out, care needed.
2) 5+, 30m. The easier upper section heads up a couple of corners to finish left of the bulges. The new routes get in the way!

⑬ Del Plas . . . . 🔳 [ ] 5+

1) 5+, 26m. Follow the black marks up the centre of the wall and through the overhangs above to good ledges. On the crux moves, avoiding the *Blue Route* is tricky.
2) 5+, 30m. Up the wall trending right then through the overhangs via parallel cracks and one stiff pull. Abseil off or:
3) 3, 26m. Easy ground follows the black spots to the last wall.
4) 5+ 28m. The final bulging wall set high above everything!
DESCENT. Abseil back down the route or traverse the crest and make a 40m abseil down the line of *Lofi* (p246).

⑭ Carlos . . . . 🔳🪨 [ ] 6a

1) 6a 28m. Take pink/black spots up the right-hand side of the face by sustained and fingery climbing
2) 6a 26m. Continue following the spots, passing the bulges with difficulty to reach easier ground and abseil anchors.

⑮ Blue Route . . . . 🔳🪢 [ ] 5+

1) 5+, 28m. The faded blue paint and chain-link bolts show the way up the wall and through a bulge.
2) 5+, 30m. The bulging corner-crack has an exposed exit leftwards in a good position. A pitch with a plethora of fixed gear.

⑯ Posi . . . . 🪨 [ ] 6a

1) 6a, 26m. The line of pink spots paralleling *Dire Straits*.
2) 5+, 26m. Tackle the bulges above, barely independent.

⑰ Dire Straits . . . . 🔳 [ ] 5+

26m. The large name has faded. Trend right up the rib (old orange spots) then climb the steep bulging wall to ledges.

⑱ Espolón Gris . . . . 🔳 [ ] 4+

An excellent fully-bolted, easier route up the right arete.
1) 4+, 32m. Climb direct from the lowest point of the buttress with a jig left and right to pass the initial bulges.
2) 4, 30m. Continue up the flaky groove following the bolts all the way to the double bolts. Abseil off.

Two old bolts in the rib to the right mark the lower section of a route that never gets done!

TOIX
Toix Oeste

Benidorm Alicante Murcia

① Método tradicional. 🪢 4 (HS)
20m. The blocky corner and grooves has no fixed gear. Pleasant enough though not really what you came to Spain for!

② Red Route III. 6a
20m. Another red one! Climb the steep slab into a groove then up this and the rib to its right. Can also be started from the left (easier) and the right (harder).

③ Renov 5
An excellent climb, often overlooked because of its recessed position. It gets all the sun that is going.
1) 4+, 22m. From a block trend left to enter a pleasant groove and follow this to steeper moves and a good stance on the left.
2) 5, 28m. Follow great rock up the slab right then left to reach a short groove. Up this, then trend right to a belay.

④ Green Route III 6a
This route follows the wall left of the curving groove.
1) 6a, 25m. From a pedestal climb the steep wall and groove (pegs) to a belay in a niche.
2) 5+, 20m. Climb direct to a belay above. Alternatively, a better finish can be made leftwards across the wall but a few wires are needed.

⑤ El Menú de Día 5+
45m. The curving groove. Where it becomes blank, pull out right or continue direct at **6b+**. Both variations join and finish up the groove of the *Green Route III*.

⑥ Black Route II 5
36m. The long rib right of the scooped groove is a fine pitch. There is a stance at 14m and a steep finish up the groove.

The rock to the right is taken by **Chabito 4+, 5**. *Currently the fixed gear is not up to Toix standard so avoid it.*

TOIX OESTE - RIGHT
Just beyond the toe of the main buttress of Toix Oeste is the lower section of a long wall which stretches up eventually to Toix TV. The first section has a characteristic scoop right of a short wall and is home to 6 routes.

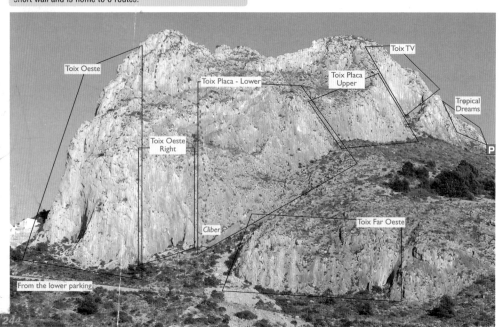

From Toix Oeste

TOIX FAR OESTE

To the right of the main Toix Oeste cliff is a gully and beyond this is a short wall with a number of easy bolted routes. None of these is a mega-classic but they are amongst the most popular in the whole area. The numbers along the base of the cliff don't correspond to the route lines. The names, originally made up by Chris Craggs, appear to have stuck!

APPROACH - Head down rightwards from the main buttress of Toix Oeste.

CONDITIONS - The wall gets the sun from mid-morning and is more sheltered than some of the buttresses higher up.

① La roja una 3
18m. Start by the number 1 and climb the groove then fluted slab to a lower-off above the top block.

② Asombroso . . . . 3+
16m. The rib gives a pleasantly-sustained pitch

③ Costilla . . . . 4+
16m. Good climbing just to the right of the groove with awkward final moves. Becoming polished.

④ La roja dos 4
18m. A worthwhile pitch on good rock. Start by the number 2 and weave around a little to keep it easy.

⑤ Bella ruta 4
18m. The centre of the steep slab is sustained at the grade.

⑥ Ocho fixe 4
18m. Climb the steep white slab following the line of 8 bolts, then trend right to the lower-off.

⑦ La roja tres 5
16m. Easy rock leads to the 1st bolt and then tricky and polished moves are needed to gain the niche. Finish easily

⑧ La roja quatro 3
16m. The slab is the easiest route here and maybe anywhere!

⑨ Senor Jones 4
16m. The last of the easy routes is the least worthwhile due to the ease of avoiding the difficulties.

⑩ Presto . . . . 5+
14m. The 'blank' slab left of the big fallen block has a tricky rock-over then easier climbing past a huge dubious flake and a steep finish.
FA. Tono Quintana 2004

Further to the right is a recess with a couple of steeper routes and some more slabby ones.

⑪ The Whole of Creation . 6b+
18m. Ape up the tufa on the left-hand side of the bay then continue up the easier groove above.

⑫ Enérgico . . . . . 6a+
18m. The steep line in the back of the bay up the spaced pockets then the wall and roof above. Exit left.

⑬ La roja seis . . . . 5+
12m. The short slab to the left of the '6'.

⑭ El endo 4
12m. The right-hand side of the slab.

245

The Black Route
Toix Oeste

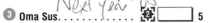

TOIX PLACA - LOWER

This extensive wall has a number of popular well-bolted easy routes. Some of them cross sections of scrappy ground but most also feature plenty of good climbing.
APPROACHES - The approach from below is the easiest since it leaves a down-hill walk out. From the Toix Oeste parking, scramble under the main buttress and up the loose gully on the far side to ledges below the face.
GEAR - Most of the routes have adequate fixed gear in the shape of pegs, bolts and bleached threads. Carrying a light rack, including a selection of slings, might be a good idea.
WARNING - The amount or loose rock on the ledges here means a helmet is a good idea - both when climbing and when sitting at the bottom of the crag!

① Gliber............ 5+
Despite some grotty terrain this is worthwhile route, well equipped where it matters. Start right of the *Black Route*.
1) 5, 36m. Climb the rib trending slightly rightwards to the first bolt then up the buttress passing a small roof to a good stance.
2) 5+, 14m. Continue up the slanting crack splitting the wall (4 bolts) then head leftwards past the arête to a stance.
3) 4, 30m. Straight up slabby rock, passing ledges to a bay.
4) 3, 30m. A scrappy pitch. Climb to a ledge at 5m then trend left (red arrows) to a stance below a groove.
5) 4+, 40m. Up the steep corner/groove (bolts) and then continue more easily to a finish up the right arete.
DESCENT - Traverse 40m east (red arrows) to the notch. A 30m abseil leads to the tree on *Lofi*, then make two (46m and 15m) or three (30m, 16m, 15m) abseils down *Lofi*.
FA. Hannelore and Kurt Krentzenbeck 2000s

② Ruwa............ 5
Pleasant and low in the grade.
1) 5, 44m. Climb the runnel in the wall below the ramp to a possible stance, then continue straight up the fine slab. It can be approached more easily up the ramp from the left.
3) 3, 30m. The shrubby ramp leads to a large ledge system.
4) 5, 44m. Climb the rib to a small overhang, then trend left to a short wall. Up this then follow a crack before trending right.
5) 5, 44m. Climb a short crack in a groove before trending right up easier ground to an exit up a shrubby gully.
DESCENT - as for *Gliber*.
FA. Hannelore and Kurt Krentzenbeck 2000s

③ Oma Sus............ 5
Next yea' '08
A route with a fine top pitch. Start in the gully at the name.
1) 4, 26m. Take the line of threads and bolts to a good stance.
2) 3, 34m. Continue up slabs (threads) to the mid-height ledge.
3) 4, 30m. Up for 4m then trend rightwards up the weakness.
4) 5, 30m. Follow the line of the rightward-trending ramp with well-spaced bolt protection and great positions.
Photo page 237.
FA. Hannelore and Kurt Krentzenbeck 2000s

The next routes start at the top of the steep section of the gully. Scramble across to a bay on the left (with names) to start.

④ Lofi............ 4+
A direct line heading towards the tree below the ridge.
1) 3, 20m. Easy climbing on the left (threads) to a big ledge.
2) 4+, 30m. Step left to where threads and 3 bolts protect a short groove (loose blocks) and better wall to a good ledge.
3) 4, 24m. Up a short wall then follow the threads to the tree.
DESCENT - Abseil from the bolts by the tree.
FA. Hannelore and Kurt Krentzenbeck 2000s

⑤ Lara............ 4+
1) 3+, 20m. Easy climbing to the same ledge.
2) 4+, 20m. Trend up and right to a two bolt belay in a groove.
3) 4+, 34m. Continue right across a delectable slab passing bolts and threads to a finish on the right.
DESCENT - Abseil off the shared belay (34m and 30m).
FA. Hannelore and Kurt Krentzenbeck 2000s

Murcia · Alicante · Benidorm · Calpe · Xaló Valley · Gandia · Bernia · Altea · Mascarat · Sierra de Toix · Olta · Peñón de Ifach

Mnday?

From mid morning | 10 min | Multi-pitch | Windy

Murcia
Alicante
Benidorm
Calpe
Xaló Valley
Gandia
Bernia
Altea
Mascarat
Sierra de Toix
Olta
Peñón de Ifach

⑥ **Anto** . . . . 🔳 **5**
Starting from the right-hand side of the ledge.
1) 3, 30m. A direct line up the slab following threads and bolts.
2) 5, 40m. Up the wall direct then trend slightly up and right. An excellent pitch, worth the effort involved.
DESCENT - Abseil off the shared belay.
FA. Hannelore and Kurt Krentzenbeck 2000s

⑦ **Maria** . . . . 🔳 **3**
30m. A discreet line of fixed threads and pegs marks a beginner's route leading up low-angled rock to the stance of *Ana*.
FA. Hannelore and Kurt Krentzenbeck 2000s

⑧ **Ana** . . . . 🔳 **4+**
A great second pitch.
1) 3+, 28m. Pleasant climbing trending leftwards up walls and grooves to a stance and two bolt belay.
2) 4+, 34m. Climb direct then right, following the arrows all the way to a twin-bolt belay. Take a dozen clips.
DESCENT - Abseil off the shared belay - to the ground in two!
FA. Hannelore and Kurt Krentzenbeck 2000s

⑨ **Hewa** . . . . 🔳 **5**
54m. A fine long pitch up the slab to a groove. Continue up the rib (crux) then move out left and then trend right behind a pinnacle to a pair of abseil bolts. Protected by threads, bolts and a jammed knot!
DESCENT - Abseil to the left (looking down) - 34m to the deck.
FA. Hannelore and Kurt Krentzenbeck 2000s

⑩ **Route 10.** . . . . 🔳 **6a+**
50m. An old route, the 1st on the buttress, that is effectively a right-hand start to *Hewa*. Protected by a peg and a couple of chain-link bolts. Rarely done nowadays.

⑪ **Mushu** . . . . 🔳 🔳 **6a**
22m. Good climbing up the steep left-hand side of the tower passing a huge white scar, to a lower-off on the rim. Glue-ins.
FA. Hannelore and Kurt Krentzenbeck 2000s

⑫ **Ghost in the Shell** . 🔳 🔳 🔳 **6b+**
22m. The right-hand line up the steep tower is fingery and sustained in its upper part giving fine climbing protected by some of the biggest glue-in bolts around.
FA. Hannelore and Kurt Krentzenbeck 2000s

⑬ **Jan** . . . . 🔳 **4+**
34m. Climb the pillar with a couple of tricky moves early on and then the grooves leftwards to a lower-off above a jammed block. Excellent rock though still a touch scruffy, it should tidy up nicely. Despite what is says on the rock at the start of the route, this length is correct.
FA. Hannelore and Kurt Krentzenbeck 2000s

⑭ **Los Urbanos** . . . . 🔳 🔳 **5**
32m. Tackle the nicely-sustained rib trending slightly leftwards onto easier ground then continue direct by juggy climbing to the lower-off on the crest of the wall.
FA. Hannelore and Kurt Krentzenbeck 2000s

⑮ **Anbea** . . . . 🔳 **4**
34m. Climb the right-hand arete of the face (threads and bolts) to just below where the angle eases then traverse left just below the top of the cliff to the lower-off used by *Los Urbanos*.
FA. Hannelore and Kurt Krentzenbeck 2000s

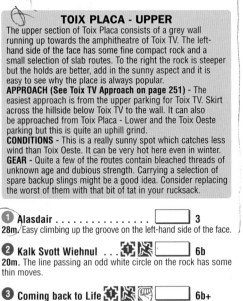

TOIX PLACA - UPPER

The upper section of Toix Placa consists of a grey wall running up towards the amphitheatre of Toix TV. The left-hand side of the face has some fine compact rock and a small selection of slab routes. To the right the rock is steeper but the holds are better, add in the sunny aspect and it is easy to see why the place is always popular.

APPROACH (See Toix TV Approach on page 251) - The easiest approach is from the upper parking for Toix TV. Skirt across the hillside below Toix TV to the wall. It can also be approached from Toix Placa - Lower and the Toix Oeste parking but this is quite an uphill grind.

CONDITIONS - This is a really sunny spot which catches less wind than Toix Oeste. It can be very hot here even in winter.

GEAR - Quite a few of the routes contain bleached threads of unknown age and dubious strength. Carrying a selection of spare backup slings might be a good idea. Consider replacing the worst of them with that bit of tat in your rucksack.

1 Alasdair . . . . `[____]` **3**
28m. Easy climbing up the groove on the left-hand side of the face.

2 Kalk Svott Wiehnul . . . `[icons]` `[____]` **6b**
20m. The line passing an odd white circle on the rock has some thin moves.

3 Coming back to Life `[icons]` `[____]` **6b+**
20m. A hard first clip, desperate moves past the bolt and sustained thin climbing make this one (very) high in the grade.

4 Thalia . . . . `[icons]` `[____]` **6b+**
20m. A safe taxing move early on leads to romping above.

5 No Name . . . . `[icon]` `[____]` **6a+**
20m. Amazing! The right-hand side of the slab is indeed called *No Name* - strange.

6 Pegasus . . . . `[icons]` `[____]` **6a**
28m. There are 2 bolts at the start. Climb direct (**6a+**) or easier to the right, then trend right again to climb the line above the lower section of *Cicky Bugger*.

7 Cicky Bugger . . . . `[icons]` `[____]` **5+**
28m. Start at the name then step right to climb the steep wall in the back of the scoop.

8 Heaven Is... . . . . `[icons]` `[____]` **5+**
28m. Nice balancy climbing up the rounded rib then move out right for more of the same.

9 Johanna . . . . `[icons]` `[____]` **5**
28m. Lots of pockets and spaced bolts make this one memorable (or carry a few wires to plug the gaps).

10 Heti . . . . `[icon]` `[____]` **4+**
30m. The line of jugs and threads although on the crux it is possible to clip a bolt on *4 You*. Many of the threads are badly faded, consider replacing some of them, if only temporarily.

11 4 You . . . . `[icons]` `[____]` **6a**
26m. The wall to the right of the threads of *Heti* is good and hard at the start with a tricky clip for shorties.

12 Semi Dulce . . . . `[icon]` `[____]` **5+**
30m. Climb the wall left of the grotty groove to jugs then make awkward moves onto the slab. Move out right then climb direct on pockets to an easier finish. The middle section shares bolts with *4 You*.
Photo page 237.

13 Steinbeisser . . . . `[icon]` `[____]` **6a**
30m. Climb the rib right of the scruffy groove on good rock, then when the rib narrows step left and continue leftwards to a belay just right of *Semi Dulce*.

Murcia
Alicante
Benidorm
Calpe
Xaló Valley
Gandia
Bernia
Altea
Mascarat
Sierra de Toix
Olta
Peñón de Ifach

⑭ Fantasia . . . . 🔆▢ **6a**
22m. Climb the clean rib with difficulty for 12m then more easily to a lower-off where things turn grassy.

⑮ For my son Jens . . . . . 🔆▨▢ **6b+**
30m. A pleasant rib following the glue-in bolts leads to a big ledge - a worthwhile **5** this far. It is probably worth belaying here if you want a go at the deceptive scoop lurking above.

⑯ Aladdin . . . . ▨▨▢ **6c**
30m. Easy and scruffy climbing leads to a hard finish (one-move-wonder) up the right-hand side of the leaning scoop.

⑰ Hafa . . . . 🔆▨📷▨▢ **4+ (VS)**
1) 4+, 40m. Climb the cracked face directly for 20m (lots of ancient threads) then head right (the little arrows sure help) and then direct to a stance in a red niche. A worrying pitch.
2) 4, 36m. The second pitch heads out left (pegs and threads) but it isn't much cop - better to abseil off.

⑱ Hova . . . . 🔆▢ **4+**
1) 4, 30m. The clean, slabby rib leads past threads and bolts to a two-bolt belay below steeper rock. A pleasant pitch.
2) 4+, 22m. Bolts and threads mark the line, which soon trends left. It is a bit bold to start. *Noldis* goes right off this pitch.
DESCENT - Abseil off.

⑲ Noldis . . . . 🔆▨▢ **5+ (HVS)**
1) 4, 22m. Follow the numerous threads up the clean rib below and left of the amphitheatre to a good stance.
2) 4+, 22m. Climb the wall (threads and bolts) then trend right (arrow) to a multi-bolt stance on the right below steeper rock.
3) 5+, 20m. Head up and right into the exposed groove and finish up this, two bolts and not much else - carry a few wires.
DESCENT - Abseil with care, the middle pitch is diagonal.

TOIX TV - AMPHITHEATRE

The best routes at Toix TV are in a huge tufa-laced amphitheatre perched at the very top of the Toix ridge.

APPROACH (See Toix TV Approach opposite) - From the upper parking spot follow the left-hand (lower) path marked with red dots. Drop under Tropical Dreams wall and continue around a scruffy spur until the amphitheatre is above you. Scramble steeply up to it.

CONDITIONS - The amphitheatre is one of the finest suntraps you will find anywhere. It is an ideal venue for a cooler days when you can stop up here and watch the sun set over Benidorm which proves to be a curiously attractive sight.

❶ Scorpion. . . . . 🗿🗿🗿🗿 ▭ 7a+
1) 6c, 30m. A seldom-climbed pitch due to the sparingly-placed bolts. Start it from *Cobra* if you don't like the height of the first one and the flaky rock. Pitch 1 is worth doing on its own.
2) 7a+, 20m. Up the steep groove to the top.

❷ Cobra. . . . . 🗿🗿🗿 ▭ 8a
A magnificent long route which follows the main features of the wall. Pitch 1 is often done on its own.
1) 7b, 20m. There is a complex right-hand variation at the bottom which avoids some of the harder moves but feels safer.
2) 7c, 16m. Up into the cave.
3) 8a, 20m. A superb (but chipped) finale in a great position.

❸ Short and Sweet . . . . . 🗿🗿 ▭ 5+
22m. A short but worthwhile route up the middle of the wall, shaded by the big roof. It has a fine selection of holds.

The next two routes require a 60m rope to lower off. Alternatively lower to the base of Mongoose.

❹ Monkey Wall . . . . 🗿🗿 ▭ 6c
30m. A magnificent route up the left-hand tufa system with the crux bulge at the top. The gear is sparse low down.
Photo page 241

❺ Painted Wall . . . . 🗿🗿 ▭ 6b+
30m. A good, sustained tufa climb with a great finish.

❻ Max Headroom 🗿🗿🗿🗿 ▭ 7c+
20m. Fierce face climbing - just where are the holds?

❼ Mongoose. . . . . 🗿🗿🗿🗿 ▭ 7c
20m. More fierce face climbing, technical and sharp.

❽ Dynosaurus . . . 🗿🗿🗿🗿 ▭ 7b
18m. This one has a reach-dependent crux and also is harder than it used to be since it lost a hold.

❾ Gripper. . . . . 🗿🗿 ▭ 6a+
20m. Link the two bulging scoops on the left or right.

❿ Chain Lane . . . . 🗿 ▭ 6a
20m. A good easier route though with some old bolts.

⓫ Nut Route . . . . 🗿 ▭ 5 (HVS)
20m. There is no fixed gear on this one and it doesn't see much attention - no surprises there then!

⓬ Chunkies . . . . ▭ 4+
18m. Homemade bolts but at least there are plenty of them!

Murcia
Alicante
Benidorm
Calpe
Xaló Valley
Gandia
Bernia
Altea
Mascarat
Sierra de Toix
Olta
Peñón de Ifach

Murcia · Alicante · Benidorm · Calpe · Xaló Vall·y · Gandia · Bernia · Aliea · Mascarat · Sierra de Toix · Olta · Penón de Ifach

Not a good crag! Rock loose.

TOIX TV - TROPICAL DREAMS

A short wall in an lovely position. The routes are pleasant and there is certainly a day's entertainment here for most.
TOIX TV APPROACH - Turn off the main road from Calpe, into Maryvilla, then follow the signs for 'Toix Mirador'. This takes you on the road which rises up the hillside towards the seaward end of the Toix ridge. Follow this to the bend at the very edge of the world (fantastic views of the Penón), and continue to a small parking spot below the TV transmitter, at the road end. Try to leave turning space. From the parking follow the rough path across the hillside to the crag which is above and right of you as you approach it.
CONDITIONS - The wall faces south and gets plenty of sun. It isn't quite as well-sheltered as the Amphitheatre but it can still be very warm here.

The first routes are on the far left of the wall. Scramble up from the central gully via the fixed rope to reach the starts. Most of the route names are painted on the rock.

① Daddycool 6a
16m. The glue-ins up the flat wall on the far left. It is nearer 6a+ if you do it direct.

② Terminator . . . . 6c+
20m. Climb past a thread then up the left-hand side of the scoop to a finish up the steep slab.

③ Follow Me . . . . 7a+
20m. Powerful moves lead through the centre of the scoops. If it proves too much the maillon will come in useful!

④ Salida 7a
20m. A good and varied route, strenuous to start and then delicate above, with 'interesting' moves through the bulge.

⑤ Gaudi Max 6b
22m. The prickly wall above the left end of the fixed rope.

The next two routes start from the gully below the left-hand side of the face - reached from the right by a fixed rope.

⑥ Cloud No.9 . . . . 5+
22m. Climb into the scoop and press on past the scar.

⑦ El baile . . . . 4+
24m. The crinkly rib above the fixed rope has spaced bolts.

⑧ UB40 . . . . 6a
22m. Up the right side of the rib then the cracks trending right.

⑨ Tropical Dreams . . 6a
22m. The best route here with a steep start and crimpy upper section and on superb rock throughout.

⑩ Dear Renate 6a
22m. Climb pockets (old peg, thread and bolts) and then the wall. The move around the small tree is a bit tricky.

⑪ Verlassen + betrogen . . . . 4+
22m. The old name has been crossed out. Climb the short wall into the well-cleaned white groove, then the walls above.

⑫ Banana Joe . . . . 5+
14m. The wall and groove above the left-hand side of blocks.

⑬ Universal 6a
20m. The wall and overhanging rib then slabbier rock above.

⑭ Gufelwufel 5
22m. Climb to and through the small cave, then on up the pleasant wall above. There is a little loose rock below the cave.

⑮ Seduction 6a
22m. From a red dot (wot no name?) climb the flat wall, passing to the right of a bush.

RACO DEL CORV

Directly below Toix Oeste, a magnificent wall of exotic rock rises out of the sea. This is home to several sport and trad routes most of which are classics.

The beach below this wall is a pleasant spot to swim or sunbathe and rarely has anyone on it.

APPROACH - The best approach is from the parking for the Mascarat Gorge (see page 228). From here, walk down to the beach. It is also possible to walk down here from below Toix Oeste but this is steep and nasty, especially on the return.

CONDITIONS - The wall is well-sheltered and gets the afternoon sun. The rock can be greasy in the mornings if it is humid.

DESCENT - The most common descent from these routes is to traverse the prominent grassy break at two thirds height, to a bunch of threads at its left-hand end. Make one diagonal abseil from here to another ledge below, then make one more 50m abseil to the beach. It is also possible to climb to the top of the crag and walk down, but there is no fixed gear on the upper section of the cliff.

GEAR - A full rack of gear is required for routes 5, 6, 7 and 8. Just a small rack of wires is needed for routes 3 and 4.

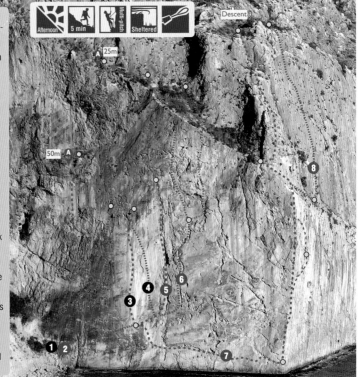

❶ **Clive's Redoubt** . . . . . . 🔲🔲 ▭ **7a**
50m. A full 50m pitch up the line of abseil building to a steep finish at the top.
FA. D.Dutton, D.Lyon

❷ **Isla de encanta** . . . . . . 🔲🔲 ▭ **6b**
80m. A two pitch outing, both pitches are 6b and 40m.
FA. Tono Quintana 2000

The next 6 routes share a common first pitch. Take the easiest line across the wall to a belay on the prominent sloping ledge.

❸ **Sombre** . . . . . 🔲🔲🔲 ▭ **7b**
25m. A sustained and technical route. It is a bit chipped at the top, on the section shared with *Müne*. Take some small wires to supplement the spaced bolts.

❹ **Müne** . . . . 🔲🔲 ▭ **7b**
25m. A created route which joins *Sombre* near the top.

❺ **El Dorado 1** . . . . 🔲🔲 ▭ **6a+ (E2)**
A brilliant climb on magnificent rock, best enjoyed on New Year's Eve for the full effect.
1) 6a+, 35m. From the sloping ledge make a diagonal traverse out right until you are below a wide crack. Swarm up this to a hanging stance above.
2) 6a+, 30m. Climb steeply leftwards then finish up the slab above, past a few bits of fixed gear, to the diagonal grassy break. Belay a long way up left along the sloping ledge.

❻ **Ven Corada** . . . . 🔲🔲 ▭ **6b (E3)**
Another good route although not quite as good as *ED 1*.
1) 6a+, 25m. From the ledge, traverse right until next to the hanging rope. Climb up some scoops then go diagonally rightwards to a small stance below a bulge.
2) 6b, 40m. Climb up slightly leftwards past some well-featured rock to the grassy break. Belay a long way back.
There is a poorer alternative right-hand pitch 2 at bold **6b**.
FA. A Gómez 1987

❼ **Vía Missing Link** . . 🔲🔲🔲 ▭ **6b+ (E3)**
A magnificent route up the arete which needs a full rack of gear.
1) 6a+, 35m. From the sloping ledge move right then carefully down-climb, to gain a low traverse line. Follow this awkwardly, staying just above the water (difficult to protect) until it is possible to climb diagonally upwards (don't climb up too soon) to a scoop which leads to the hanging stance on the arete.
2) 6b+, 45m. Power up the arete above, first on the left, then on the right. From the diagonal break, either traverse left to gain the grassy ramp, or climb up the rib above to the top (50m, 5).
Variation - Luces Nocturnas, 6b
2a) 6b, 25m. Just after the route swings around the arete, traverse right to a cave to belay.
3a) 6a+, 25m. Pull up above the cave and climb back to the arete above. Only a bit easier than the original and less good.

❽ **Le Galleon** . . . . 🔲🔲 ▭ **6a (E1)**
35m. A good pitch that can be done on its own with an abseil approach, or as an extension to *Missing Link*. Start from a belay below the slab and climb the centre of the slab (possible stance at half-height).

'The old team' on *Missing Link* (6b+) on Raco del Corv at Toix - *opposite*. It is a different photo but a similar image to the evocative cover of Chris Craggs' first guide to the Blanca which was captioned "New Year's Day 1988 - where were you?". Photo: Sherri Davy

Murcia

Alicante

Benidorm

Calpe

Xaló Valley

Gandia

Bernia

Altea

Mascarat

Sierra de Toix

Olta

Peñón de Ifach

Photos: Rowland Edwards

CANDELABRA DEL SOL

The southern side of the Toix headland forms a continuous cliff up to 80m high. Several routes have been developed giving atmospheric climbing. Most of the routes on this section are only part-bolted so take a full rack of gear. The old SENPs should have been replaced.

APPROACH - Follow the track beneath Toix Oeste and continue on a rough path to where a well-cairned path leads for about 1km across the hillside, dipping into a wide gully at one point. Shortly after this, there is a smooth wave of rock on the left and the path drops down to the cliff edge. Some ancient ladders can be found which lead to ledges above the sea. Descent (or ascent) of the ladders without a rope, is E8 2a, so it is best to abseil.

CONDITIONS - The wall is well-sheltered and gets the afternoon sun. The rock can be greasy in the mornings if the air is humid.

❶ Rowland's Promised Land 🖼️💧 [____] 6b (E3)
An expedition; allow 5-6 hours for the trip. Start as for *J to X*.
1 to 6) 105m. As for *Journey to Xanadu*.
7) 2, 18m. Cross the gully to ledges and traverse to a belay.
8) & 9) Traverse left at either of two levels for 50m; the lower is harder (**4,4+**) and can be damp; higher is easier (**3, 3+**). The stance here can also be reached by two long abseils.
10) 3+, 20m. Move left into the next groove and climb the left-hand side of the pillar to a thread belay.
11) 6b, 30m. Climb to the top of the pillar and then move right and climb direct. Continue leftwards to a thread and on to a hanging stance. Bolt belays.
12) 6a, 25m. Head left past a pocket then go direct to a ledge.
13) 6a+, 45m. Climb the wall on the right to a leaning buttress then climb the front of the this to slabs and a short wall to finish.
FA. R.Edwards, M.Edwards, R.Mayfield, T.Phillips 2000

❷ Journey to Xanadu . 🖼️🖼️💧 [____] 6c (E3)
A committing extension to *MMT.*
1) to 3) 55m. As for *MMT.*
4) 4, 20m. Traverse round a pillar and across a slab to a bay.
5) 25m down. Enter the narrow cave and abseil from the thread to just above the sea.
6) 5, 30m. Move left to a narrow cleft and traverse (choice of levels) to its far side and a stance below a steep crack-line.
7) 5, 20m. Climb the crack to the first cave and a good stance.
8) 6a+, 25m. Move left onto the wall and climb to a slab. Up the crack and left to a ledge. Climb the wall to a belay.
9) 6c, 20m. Climb up and right into a bay and then right again Continue up a thin crack to a cave and thread belay.
10) 6a, 30m. Climb into the roof of the cave then left onto the wall. Up this (thread) and over the roofs on the left to the top.
FA. R.Edwards, Mark Edwards, Michael Esslinger 1999

❸ Kubla Khan . . . . . . 🖼️💧🖼️ [____] 7b (E5)
The overhanging crack right of *Journey to Xanadu*. Steep and sustained but not technically too difficult.
1) to 6) As for *Journey to Xanadu*.
7) 6a, 35m. Climb the crack to the first cave (belay on *Journey to Xanadu*), then continue up the crack into the next large cave.
8) 7b, 40m. Climb the wall on the left and bridge up the wide crack. Continue (threads) to a leaning wall and climb this to a small ledge and belay. Can be aided at **6b+/A0**.
9) 6b, 20m. Up a steep corner on the right and the slab above.
FA. R.Edwards, M.Hesslinger 1999

❹ Dimage . . 🖼️🖼️💧🖼️💧 [____] 6b+ (E4)
A good route with some fine positions.
1) to 3) 55m. As for *MMT.*
4) 6a+, 25m. Climb left onto a loose pillar then move left onto the steep wall, up this boldly to a ledge and bolt belay.
5) 6b, 25m. Climb right up the steep wall to a ledge then climb the short wall and a shallow groove on the left.
FA. R.Edwards, M.Edwards, M.Jones 2000

Murcia
Alicante
Benidorm
Calpe
Xaló Valley
Gandia
Benita
Altea
Mascarat
Sierra de Toix
Olta
Peñón de Ifach

⑤ Magical Mystery Tour . . 🔲🔲 ENP 🔲 5 (HVS)
A popular trip. There is some fixed gear, including ENPs (see page 20) to mark the line but take a full rack. Approach by walking west from the ladders. Competent climbers will find the first 2 pitches solo-able however, if unsure, rope up.
1) 3, 25m. Traverse left to the arete and then left again, descending into the *Candelabra del Sol* cave.
40m. Walk/scramble left across ledges to the left edge of the left and step around left onto a good ledge.
2) 3, 10m. Climb the wide crack on the left to a ledge then drop down left into a hollow.
3) 4, 20m. Traverse left (old peg) to the arete and climb round into scoop (poor bolt). Pull up over the overlap into a larger scoop. Belay on old bolts and/or ENPs.
4) 4, 25m. Traverse right to the arete (old bolt) and climb this, trending right at the top, to a ledge with 2 ENPs; or continue traversing right into the next cave, poor bolt and gear to belay.
5) 5, 40m. Climb right and up into the next cave then left onto the arete (poor bolt) and go direct to a good ledge. Move right and climb the groove, moving right at its top.
FA. R.Edwards 1986. Climbed solo, bolts placed later.

The next two routes have old and unsafe bolts.

⑥ Raptured Dreams. . 🔲🔲🔲🔲 7a (E5)
50m. The route is a touch loose at the bottom and a selection of large wires are needed for the final crack.
FA. R.Edwards 1980s

⑦ The Flame . . . 🔲🔲🔲🔲🔲 7b
50m. A fine pitch up a tufa. Take some wires to protect the moves to the first bolt, and for the short second pitch (**6a**). The crux heave onto the tufa requires commitment.
FA. R.Edwards 1980s

⑧ Candelabra del Sol 🔲🔲🔲🔲 8a
50m. An impressive route. Follow the steep back and side wall of the cave in one huge pitch. There is a 2nd bolted line which follows the back of the cave, via a belay. This alternative is **7b+**.
FA. M.Edwards 1980s

⑨ Goliath . . . . . . 🔲🔲🔲🔲🔲 8a
45m. A hard route up the bug tufas left of the ladders. Climb the left side of the pinnacle then move onto the arete. Follow this then climb up to a crack and enter the chimney between the tufas. Continue boldly up the headwall to a ledge. Finish up the steep groove.
FA. M.Edwards, R.Edwards 2000

⑩ Lady in Space . 🔲🔲🔲🔲 6b (E3)
Start below a steep crack to the right of the ladders.
1) 6b, 27m. The gear is mostly fixed but big cams may help. Climb the crack to a ledge in the roof and continue to the lip. Swing onto the steep wall on the right then bridge out and climb trending right then left into the wide bay to a ledge.
2) 6b, 30m. Climb the wall on the right then cross onto the opposite wall. Traverse this and make hard moves up into the roof (threads). Continue out to the lip of the cave and climb the short wall to the top.
FA. R.Edwards, M.Edwards, R.Mayfield 2001

⑪ Malice Aforethought 🔲🔲🔲 6b (E3)
1) 6b, 27m. *Lady in Space* pitch 1.
2) 6a, 28m. Climb the right wall to a ledge (thread), move up right to the arete and finish up this. Belay well back.
FA. R.Edwards, D.Golding 2000

OLTA

The impressive ridge of rock which overlooks Calpe has a few routes dotted around although the best are centred on an impressive arete and the walls on either side of it. The rock is excellent and the views over Calpe are stunning with the Peñón making a magnificent backdrop for photographs of the superb arete of *Tai Chi* (see page 218). The other major classic is the *Super Tufa Groove* which is one of the best 6b+ routes in the area.

The rock is quite sharp and a day here tends to take its toll on your finger tips. Some of the harder routes have improved or fully-created holds which spoil the experience a bit, but mostly the moves and climbing are excellent. Hopefully one day more routes will be climbed up on this ridge since the potential of the much larger right-hand end hasn't been touched yet.

CONDITIONS

The crag faces south east and catches plenty of sun although in winter the sun goes off the crag in the early afternoon. It is high and exposed to any wind.

APPROACH
(area map page 219)

The crag should be approached from Calpe. First you need to get onto the road to the 'Estacion F.C.' which leaves the N332 from the main Calpe junction. This is awkward if you are approaching from the south; either turn off into Calpe and go around the first roundabout to come back under the N332, or over-shoot the junction and turn around so that you are coming south on the N332. Drive past the station across the tracks, following the brown signs steadily uphill to 'Monte Olta' and 'Zona de acampada' and park by the (free) camping site. Head up the hill to a track, turn left and follow this past a big zig-zag, and then a chain and on to a large water tank on the right. A rough track leads behind this, up the steep hillside to the crag.

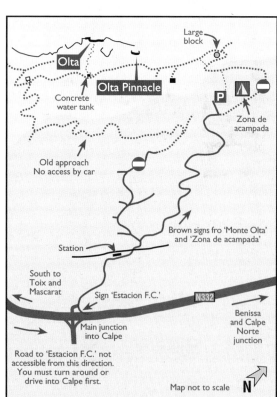

Murcia · Alicante · Benidorm · **Calpe** · Xaló Valley · Gandia · Bernia · Altea · Mascarat · Sierra de Toix · Olta · Peñón de Ifach

'El Cap' going up and lowering off the *Tufa Groove* (6b+) at Olta - *page 258*. Not photographed as often as its near-neighbour *Tai Chi*, but the *Tufa Groove* is probably a better route; a fine steep line on great rock.

Murcia
Alicante
Benidorm
Calpe
Xaló Valley
Gandia
Bernia
Altea
Mascarat
Sierra de Toix
Olta
Peñón de Ifach

OLTA

The largest feature of the crag is the huge white groove on its left-hand side. To the right the walls and ribs are smaller but contain a good set of worthwhile routes.

There are two buttresses near by which have been developed with routes.

OLTA SOUTH - This is tall narrow tower above the track to the left of the main crag which can be approached direct from the below. The names are written on the rock but the grades here are guesses.
Learning to Fly, 6a
Ham in Pan, 6a
Unknown, 5c
Living on the Edge, 6c

OLTA PINNACLE - This is the pinnacle below and right of the main crag (see photo on page 256). It can be approached direct from the track below, by a rough scramble from the second font. The names are written on the rock.
Nido de Condores, 4+
Panamericana, 4+

❶ Lost in Flight. . ⬚⬚⬚⬚ ▢ 7c
28m. Start left of *Tufa-Groove* and climb the easy slab to a bolt. Enter the hanging-crack and climb this to a big block at its top. Stand on this to get started on the wall then reach left to get a good flake and move left. Climb the middle section of the wall. It is crying out for a direct start.
FA. Richard Davies 2002

❷ Si Maria . . . . . ⬚⬚⬚⬚ ▢ 7c
28m. Climb *Lost in Flight* until established on the top wall and then continue direct to the belay.
FA. Richard Davies 2002

❸ Tufa-Groove . . . . ⬚⬚ ▢ 6b+
28m. Stunning climbing with less helpful holds than you expect though it is never too desperate. Follow the groove - steep for the grade - look where you end up on the lower-off!
Photo page 257.
FA. Jens Muenchberg 1990s

❹ Tao . . . . ▢ 6a
18m. The crack leading to a wide chimney then exit left to a lower-off. A real oddity which is seldom climbed.
FA. Jens Muenchberg 1990s

❺ Wings of Freedom . ⬚⬚⬚ ▢ 7a+
20m. Cross the initial bulge with difficulty then continue up the sustained wall above.
FA. Jens Muenchberg 1990s

❻ Ki . . . . ⬚⬚⬚ ▢ 6c
24m. From blocks, a hard start leads to deep pockets. Step left onto the wall before looping out further left then back right to a final steepening.
FA. Jens Muenchberg 1990s

❼ Mulan . . . . . . ⬚⬚⬚⬚⬚ ▢ 7a+
24m. A thin eliminate up the centre of the face with a reachy crux and some very sharp holds.
FA. Jens Muenchberg 1990s

8 Tai chi . . . . 🔳🔳 ⬜ **6b+**
26m. The superb and photogenic arete. It is probably **6c+** if you climb direct past the second bolt although most folks go right. *Photo page 218.*
FA. Jens Muenchberg 1990s

9 Spanish Eyes . . . . . . 🔳🔳 ⬜ **6b**
20m. Right of the arete, easy rock leads to a bulge, passed leftwards with difficulty. Easier cracks above.
FA. Jens Muenchberg 1990s

10 Fantasía encanto . . . . . 🔳🔳 ⬜ **7b+**
20m. From blocks, climb to a crimpy slab then on up the technical and chipped wall above. An inverted 'mono' is obligatory!
FA. Jens Muenchberg 1990s

11 Ninja . . . . 🔳🔳 ⬜ **7c**
20m. Climb to and up the big white tufa then tackle the leaning wall above on poor (chipped) holds.
FA. Jens Muenchberg 1990s

12 Hillside Avenue . . . . ⬜ **6c**
20m. An artificial line with a chipped finish. Climb the side wall of the lower rib then a step left and pull though a bulge. Continue up the rib and final pocketed bulging wall.
FA. Jens Muenchberg 1990s

13 Halt Mich . . . . ⬜ **6c+**
20m. Another line-less chipped route with a tough finale. Climb past a thin in-situ thread then trend left into a groove (drilled thread) before attacking the crucial bulging wall.
FA. Jens Muenchberg 1990s

14 Hola Olta . . . . 🔳🔳 ⬜ **6c**
20m. The gradually-steepening slab and wall that crowns it give a good but rather sharp pitch.
FA. Jens Muenchberg 1990s

15 Vamos . . . . 🔳 ⬜ **5+**
22m. A hard start leads up the slab then move right above.
FA. Jens Muenchberg 1990s

16 Best of '95 . . . . 🔳🔳 ⬜ **5**
22m. A good pitch with awkward moves early on - use the crack to the right if needed. There is pleasant climbing above.
FA. Jens Muenchberg 1990s

17 Du Darfst . . . . 🔳🔳 ⬜ **5**
24m. The best of the easier stuff here. Start at the name and follow the sportingly-placed bolts up the steep slab.
FA. Jens Muenchberg 1990s

18 Turrón . . . . 🔳 ⬜ **5**
24m. A bit close to the next climb though the moves are good. It has an odd assortment of bolts with everyone being different. Join *Du Darfst* at the thread to finish.
FA. Jens Muenchberg 1990s

19 Das Buch der 5 Ringe . . . . ⬜ **5+**
22m. The bulging crack-line is tricky early on, then it eases. The bolts are a bit spaced.
FA. Jens Muenchberg 1990s

20 Touch Me Softly . . . . . 🔳🔳 ⬜ **5**
22m. The corner is awkward to enter and the hand-crack at mid-height is fun. Finish up the head-wall or sneak right.
FA. Jens Muenchberg 1990s

21 Christmas Dreams . . . . 🔳🔳 ⬜ **5+**
12m. A very short wall on positive holds and a thin upper part. Pleasant but short-lived.
FA. Jens Muenchberg 1990s

22 Breakthrough . . . . ⬜ **5**
12m. Spaced pockets and a steep bulging finish.
FA. Jens Muenchberg 1990s

There may be one more route on the right - no details known.

PEÑÓN de IFACH

Murcia
Alicante
Benidorm
Calpe
Xaló Valley
Gandia
Bernia
Altea
Mascarat
Sierra de Toix
Olta
Peñón de Ifach

The most striking landmark in the whole of the Costa Blanca is the stunning 332m high tower of the Peñón (or Peñyal d'Ifach as it is often known nowadays) which towers over Calpe. The subject of the majority of the area's postcards must surely attract every climber's eye and those who have attempted routes here will know that the climbing does not disappoint.

The South Face of the *Peñón* is the more extensive of the two main climbing areas. This huge, vertical, orange wall rises up above an approach slope to a top half riddled with caves, overhangs and groove systems. Many long routes find their way up the complex face and weave through this complex rock architecture and finish satisfyingly on the summit of the Peñón.

There are a number of low-to-mid-grade challenges which are popular classics requiring an early start and a decent rack of gear; *Valencianos* and *Vía UBSA* are the prime examples. The really big ticks are the superb, fully-bolted classics like *Costa Blanca, El Navigante, Puto paseo ecológico* and *Nueva Dimensión*; there are few sport routes to compare with these anywhere in the Costa Blanca. The other face described here is the North Face which faces inland and overlooks the park's Visitor Centre and is a useful venue when the weather is hot although it does have a seasonal climbing restriction usually from 1 April to 30 June because of nesting birds.

The rock is of variable quality; the smoother orange rock can polish to a high sheen and there is some loose material especially on the lower pitches. It is worth wearing a helmet, especially on the easier and more popular routes, since there is a lot of loose rock around. A top-tip to avoid rock fall is make sure you are on the mountain early so that there are fewer people above you! Of course this also means that it is vital to be careful when climbing here since there may well be teams below.

All the routes are long and can require up to 5 hours or more for a leisurely ascent although there are reports of people taking as long as 11 hours on *Gómez-Cano*. Despite this, climbers who are well organised should manage to reach the summit in 3 hours or less.

GEAR

The fully-bolted routes are well-equipped with double bolt belays making an abseil descent possible (on a single 60m rope with care) should things turn against you. The older classics are more sparsely equipped, with fixed gear of variable quality. On these routes a small rack is mandatory. The pitches tend to be long so it is advisable to take twin 9mm ropes to help with rope drag.

CONDITIONS

The main climbing faces south west and is full in the sun from mid-morning onwards. Its exposed position means it can get breezy, but the heat is likely to be more of a problem. If you are a slow climber, carry lots of water and sun cream. The North Face is a different proposition since it is in the shade except on summer evenings.

APPROACH (area map page 219)

If you are based in Calpe, you will know where the Peñón is! If you are driving up from further south, then take the Altea turn off the A7 (junction 64) and drive through the Mascarat Gorge on the N332. Soon after, turn off right into Calpe. Drive down the main road towards the Peñón ahead. When the road veers around to the left, turn right (signed 'Peñón'). Keep going to where the road forks and take the right-hand branch. Drive down here to the harbour side and park. See route pages for approaches from here.

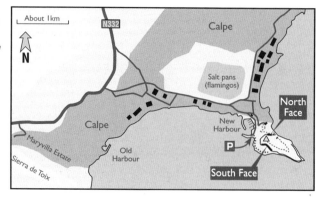

Mike Appleton and Colin Binks on the majestic final pitches of *Costa Blanca* (6c+) on the South Face of the Peñón - *Page 267*. This route is typical of a number of routes on the face that have spectacular and exposed finishing pitches on a superb band of steep rock that runs across the wall from *Les Miserables* to *Nueva Dimensión*.   Inset: the Peñón from Calpe.

THE NORTH FACE

This is the large white face which overlooks the town. The section close to the path has been banned on occasions in the past - check the situation at the Visitor's Centre if in doubt. There are four shorter climbs on the left and three longer routes based around the big buttress to the right.

ACCESS - No climbing from 1 April to 30 June because of nesting birds.

APPROACH - Follow the main summit path up from the visitor centre. This path zig-zags up the hill eventually swinging back left and running close to the cliff. Just before this a little track leads up rightwards into a bay where *Roxy* and *Pany* are located.

DESCENT - For the climbs on the left an abseil descent is possible. For the rest, top out and walk down the main path which leads back through the slippery tunnel below the North Face.

❶ Verde esmeralda . . 🔲🔲🔲 **6a+ (E2)**
An interesting trip through some weird and wonderful rock.
1) 4+, 30m. Climb through bushes to a groove. Up this to a comfortable grotto stance.
2) 6a+, 20m. Move right and tackle the bulges above to reach easier ground. Move up then left below the bulges to a good stance below a groove.
3) 5, 35m. The crack and corner system above are followed to a stance short distance from the ridge.
4) 4, 10m. Finish easily.
DESCENT - Down the slope on the left to reach the tunnel.
FA. Goly, T.Nuñez

Next is a fine white wall above the path. This has been banned on occasions, check the situation at the Visitor's Centre.

❷ Vampiro . . . . 🔲🔲🔲 **6c**
A fine route with a difficult and sustained second pitch.
1) 6b+, 24m. A tricky start passes an overlap, then steeper rock taken on good holds leads to a small stance.
2) 6c, 30m. Climb the ramp then head up the wall (sustained) to tricky moves into a shallow niche. Tough laybacking up a flake system leads to better holds and stance on the right.
3) 6c+, 30m. Step right and follow the bolts with more difficulty to a slab and very substantial tree belay.
FA. Jorge García Tejada

❸ Asignatura pendiente . . 🔲🔲🔲 **6b**
A great route following the centre of the wall giving three contrasting quality pitches.
1) 6b, 25m. Cross the overlap then climb left to reach a crack that slants to the right through the bulges. Up this until an awkward pull gains the easy groove leading to a good stance.
2) 6b, 30m. Step right and climb the shallow groove until difficult moves lead up and left to better holds. Continue up and left to a long flake crack that leads to a small stance.
3) 5, 24m. Climb up until forced left into the chimney. This has an awkward exit then climbing leads to the big tree belay.
FA. E.López 1985

❹ Taberna del puerta. 🔲🔲🔲 **6c+**
A taxing couple of pitches. Start under the groove in the right edge of the face.
1) 6b+, 30m. Climb the groove then move left to a slanting crack. Up this then straight up the wall on spaced holds. More difficult moves lead to easier rock. Move left to the stance.
2) 6c, 30m. Climb up right to bolt line running up the crest of a blunt rib. Continue straight up following this with great difficulty to a small stance and multi-bolt belay.
FA. Jorge García Tejada

The next routes start by a chimney near the right-hand side of
the bay, left of a large buttress dropping from the summit.

❺ Vía Roxy . . . . 🔆 🧗 ✏️ ▭ 6b (E3)
A scrappy first few pitches lead to an excellent finish high on
the wall. Take a full rack with some large stuff.
1) 5, 30m. Climb leftwards from the chimney to a crack. Follow
this past a bulge to a ledge on the left.
2) 5, 20m. Head up the corner above.
3) 5, 30m. Climb the wall to the ramp which crosses the face.
Descend rightwards to belay in a corner.
4) 5+, 30m. Wander up the wall above then move right into the
main groove corner and follow this to a ledge.
5) 6b, 25m. Traverse left in a good position then move up and
back right to the soaring crack. Hard moves lead to a tiny stance.
6) & 7) 6a, 50m. Follow the groove and crack upwards to an
easing in angle. Easy climbing remains to the summit.
FA. A.Ballard, J.M.Gonzalez 1981

❻ Diedro Botella . . . . . . 🔆 ✏️ ▭ 5+ (E1)
An interesting outing that links the start and finish of *Vía Pany*
with the central groove of *Vía Roxy* producing a good direct line
up the face. Start at the chimney of *Vía Pany* and carry a rack.
1) 4, 25m. As for *Vía Pany*.
2) 3, 45m. As for *Vía Pany* until it is possible to follow a ledge
leftwards to a stance at the foot of the imposing corner.
3) 5+, 30m. Climb past a tree and move right to a corner. Climb
this (pegs) to a steeper corner which is bridged past a wooden
wedge. A short distance above is a ledge and bolt belay.
4) 5, 25m. Continue up the groove which gradually eases eventually arriving on top of a tower and a junction with *Vía Pany*.
5), 6) and 7) 4, 60m. As for *Vía Pany*.
FA. A Botella 1960s

❼ Vía Pany . . . . 🔆 🧗 ✏️ ▭ 5 (VS)
The most popular route on this face has a fair bit of shrubbery
although the climbing higher up is worthwhile. Take a full rack.
The stances are mostly geared.
1) 4, 25m. Climb the chimney in the right-hand side of the bay,
then move right over a bulge to a good ledge on the right.
2) 3, 50m. Bush-bash up to the top of the buttress on the right.
3) 3, 20m. Climb the rib above then traverse 8m left to a belay.
4) 5, 35m. Climb straight up the chimney to a ledge and
continue to a stance on the top of the second buttress. Take
great care with loose rock on this pitch!
5) 4+, 30m. Step around the corner to the right and up an easy
low-angled broad ramp to the top of the buttress.
6) 4, 30m. Climb the slab slightly leftwards to reach a crack
falling from the summit. Follow this in a fine position to a
stance and belay about 15m up the crack system.
7) 4+, 30m. Follow the crack - it is awkward low down but
the angle and the difficulties ease as height is gained. Where it
becomes vegetated pull out left onto the rib (bolt) and follow
this eventually moving left into another groove that leads to the
cliff top and a belay on easy ground.
FA. Panyella, Salas 1955

Murcia · Alicante · Benidorm · Calpe · Xaló Valley · Gandía · Bernia · Altea · Mascarat · Sierra de Toix · Olta · Peñón de Ifach

THE SOUTH FACE
The main area of interest for climbers is the towering South Face with its many superb, long and intricate climbs. The more popular routes are all frequently climbed and reasonably well geared, though there is still much loose rock. A helmet and plenty of caution is advised for the routes which start up *Valencianos* and the corner of *Diedre UBSA* since both these routes form large natural funnels channelling rock onto the lower pitches. Another good idea is to be on the route by 8:30am then you will be above most parties and may be able to finish the route in the shade.

Diedre UBSA

Diedre UBSA

PLEASE TAKE GREAT CARE
WHEN CLIMBING THESE ROUTES
NOT TO DISLODGE ANY ROCK.

Afternoon   20 min

Murcia
Alicante
Benidorm
Calpe
Xaló Valley
Gandia
Bernia
Altea
Mascarat
Sierra de Toix
Olta
Peñón de Ifach

APPROACH - From the harbour walk around the flat road along the waterfront to just before the end of the track. Scramble steeply back leftwards along the base of the cliff. The open-corner of *Valencianos* is obvious.
DESCENT - From the summit follow the well-built footpath which zig-zags downhill and through a short tunnel, to emerge below the North Face, just above the visitor centre. This takes around 20 minutes.

❶ Same . . . . 🔲🔲🔲 ☐ **6a (E1)**
This route follows the diagonal ramp below the huge dome leading to the prominent ridge at the top of the *Valencianos* slab. The climbing is good and the chimney is an 'experience' but the route is spoilt slightly by the line. Start by a ramp between the cracks. There are some bolts but take a small rack.
1) 5, 20m. Gain and climb the ramp to the right-hand crack and follow this to a stance on the right.
1a) 6b, 30m. The left-hand crack gives a fine strenuous pitch.
2) 5+, 34m. The long, awkward and wide crack above.
3) 5, 20m. The wide continuation now in the main groove.
4) 4, 30m. Wander easily up and right to below a chimney.
5) 6a, 40m. Climb the scoop and crack into the chimney and continue up this to an enclosed stance.
6) 5, 16m. Continue up the chimney until it opens out.
7) 4, 50m. Follow the slab to the ridge. Join and finish up the last three pitches of *Valencianos*.
FA. J.L.Moreno, Jordi Palas, Santi Llop

The shared start of routes 2 to 9 is in the centre of the bay, at the highest point of the approach slope. The name Vía Valencianos is painted on the rock to the left in huge red letters.

❷ Vía Valencianos . . 🔲🔲🔲 ☐ **5+ (VS)**
The classic and popular easy route up the face. Although it is a big expedition, it is possible to retreat by abseil if things turn against you. There are some bolts and pegs but take a full rack.
1) 3, 35m. Climb first rightwards then back left and on to the base of the big white slab. Belay bolts on the left or right.
2) 3, 36m. Walk leftwards past bushes to gain a ledge running back right above the slab and belay directly above your second.
3) 5+, 30m. Climb the corner at the right end of the ledge then the slippery slanting crack past various fixed/jammed gear (crux - polished). Move left to belay below the upper slab.
4) 4, 20m. Climb left onto the slab to a bush belay.
5) 4, 44m. One long pitch leads to a superb belay on the ridge.
6) 4+, 30m. Walk along the ridge then traverse to the left and climb a flake/crack to a bulge. Belay on bolts a little higher.
7) 20m. Climb rightwards by the easiest line. Belay in a notch.
8) 30m. Easy climbing leads to the summit.
FA. A.Martí, M.Gómez, A.Botella, A.Tebar 1958

❸ Direct de UBSA . . . 🔲🔲🔲 ☐ **5+ (HVS)**
1) 4, 30m. Follow the first pitch of *Valencianos* but move left to a bolt belay below the centre of the slab.
2) 5, 16m. Climb direct up the slab, with plenty of protection, to a small stance and belays below a short wall in the middle of the easy traverse on *Valencianos*.
3) 5+, 20m. Climb steeply to gain a fine slab that leads to belays.
4) 5, 34m. Trend right up the right-hand bolt line up the steep wall passing occasional fixed gear to gain the great slab. Climb directly up this to a belay on *Valencianos*. Either continue up this - 75m with moves of 4 - or make three abseils to the ground.

❹ Polvos mágicos . . . 🔲🔲🔲 ☐ **6a+ (E2)**
A direct version of *Valencianos*. It is possible to escape onto *Valencianos* at several points on the route should the going get too tough. Take a full rack of gear.
1) 2+, 35m. Pitch 1 of *Valencianos*.
2) 6a+, 25m. Climb the sustained and slippery corner direct. The final section is the hardest.
3) 5+, 30m. Pitch 3 of *Valencianos*.
4) 4, 20m. Meander up easy ground to gain the right edge of the upper slab, beneath the steeper headwall. Belay in a recess.
5) 5, 30m. Follow the pleasant corner above to the ridge.
6) 4, 20m. Climb a groove to the ridge and then move left to easy ground.
7) & 8) 50m. The last two pitches of *Valencianos*.
FA. Pablo Rosa, Miguel Devesa, Roy de Valera 1960s

❺ Sensacion de vivir . 🔲🔲🔲 ☐ **6b+**
A worthwhile bolted line finishing up the left-hand side of the *Valencianos* slab. Take a small rack of wires for the start.
1) & 2) 6a, 60m. As for *Polvos Magicos*.
3) 6b+, 40m. Move right and tackle the left-hand of two bolted cracks. Trend left to a stance.
4) 6a+, 50m. Climb up and onto the slab, and follow it by sustained climbing all the way to the ridge.
DESCENT - Either abseil off, or continue up *Valencianos*.
FA. Jaime Arviza, José Juan Quesada 1991

❻ Virginia Díez . . . . . 🔲🔲🔲 ☐ **6b**
A short, bolted direct finish to *Polvos Magicos*. It is well-positioned but a lot of effort is required to get there.
1) to 4) 6a+, 110m. As for *Polvos Magicos*.
5) 5, 25m. Follow the twisting groove in the steep wall.
6) 6b, 25m. Continue steeply to finish up the prominent upper groove and watch out for the snake!
DESCENT - Either abseil off, or continue up the ridge to the top.
FA. Jaime Arviza, Miguel Díez 1991

❼ Pilar López de Sancho . 🔲🔲 ☐ **6c**
A spectacular line up the great tower which hangs over the *Vía Valencianos* slab. It shares the same slow start as the last route but the finish is worthwhile. Take a few wires for the start.
1) & 2) 6a, 60m. As for *Polvos Magicos*.
3) 6b, 40m. Move right and tackle the right-hand of two bolted cracks in the steep wall under the great slab
4) 6c, 50m. Move easily back right and upwards and climb superb hanging groove onto the slab above.
5) & 6) 6b+, 80m. Continue in 2 pitches to the top via the groove and then the bulging arete.
Vía Pilar Lopez de Pancho, 7b+ - A hard left-hand variation pitch parallel to pitch 5.
DESCENT - Either abseil off, or continue up the ridge to the top.
FA. Miguel Diez, Jaime Arviza 1990s

❽ Piratas . . . . 🔲🔲🔲 ☐ **5+ (HVS)**
One of the original lines on the wall. It has good climbing but doesn't see much traffic. Some of the rock is loose. Take a rack.
1) to 3) 5+, 105m. As for *Valencianos*.
4) 4+, 25m. Climb up a corner then follow a ramp rightwards to a belay around an arete.
5) 4+, 25m. Follow the corner (peg) to a cave belay - threads.
6) 5, 20m. Exit the cave to the right - high thread - then climb up a crack to a pedestal belay.
7) 4, 25m. Climb the corner past some bushes to a belay.
8) 4+, 20m. Surmount the final bulge by bridging and continue to the ridge. Escape more easily to the summit path.
FA. Armand Ballard, J.M.Gonzalez 1979

❾ Los miserables . . . . . . 🔲🔲 ☐ **6c+**
A good set of pitches with the drawback of all the rambling it takes to get to the last two pitches. A two-star alternative is to substitute pitches 3 and 4 of *Pilar López de Sancho*, moving right below the hanging groove to the base of pitch 5. Take a few wires for the start.
1) to 3) 6a+, 90m. As for *Polvos Magicos*.
4) 6b, 20m. An aimless pitch. Climb up and left, then back right to a ledge below the corner of *Piratas*. Now things improve.
5) 6c+, 40m. Climb the wall just right of the corner past one short hard section (easily by-passable by climbing the corner on the left at 6b). Trend up and right to a ledge belay.
6) 6b, 30m. The first of two superb pitches heading straight up the final wall to a small stance.
7) 6b, 50m. More great climbing through some steep bulging caves provides a stunning finish. Belay on wires then scramble off.
FA. Jaime Arviza , Emilio Perales 1991

Murcia | Alicante | Benidorm | Calpe | Xaló Valley | Gandia | Bernia | Altea | Mascarat | Sierra de Toix | Olta | Peñón de Ifach

Murcia
Alicante
Benidorm
Calpe
Xaló Valley
Gandía
Bernia
Altea
Mascarat
Sierra de Toix
Olta
Peñón de Ifach

Gómez-Cano

A

Routes 1, 2 and 4 all have stances behind the pinnacle

Línea Mágica

Tunnel

5

1

Scramble

2

3

4

6
7

Gómez-Cano

DIEDRE UBSA AREA
One of the most prominent features of the South Face is the tall slim tower which forms a long corner on its right-hand side - *Diedre UBSA*. The front of this pinnacle has been developed with two superb, fully-bolted mega-routes which give a great day out for those who demand a bit more from their 'clip-ups'.
APPROACH and DESCENT - See previous page.

❶ Costa Blanca..... 🔳🔳🔳 ⬜ **6c+**

A brilliant route which is one of the best the area. The climbing is superb and independent and the finish is breathtaking. It is fully equipped. Start as for *Vía Valencianos*.

1) 15m. Move up then right along a ledge to belay below a slab.

2) 6b, 40m. Climb onto a slab and make some thin moves up leftwards. Easier climbing leads up and right to a belay.

3) 6b, 35m. Climb directly up the wall and grooves above.

4) 6a, 35m. Continue to a stance on the edge of the pinnacle.

5) 6b+, 32m. Step down and across the gully onto the wall behind. Surmount a small overhang and continue up the wall above with some sustained moves and long reaches.

6) 6b+, 20m. Straight up the wall to the large upper cave.

7) 6c+, 30m. Swing wildly out of the cave and grind to a halt at thin move. After a rest another hard move, involving a blind reach, gains easier ground and the top.

6a) & 7a) 6b, 50m. A good way of avoiding the hard last pitch is to traverse the ledge of *Diedro UBSA* to join and finish up *Los miserables* - a three star alternative at **6b+** for the whole route. *Photo page 261.*

FA. Jaime Arviza, Salvador Guerola 1993

❷ Puto paseo ecológico .. 🔳🔳 ⬜ **7a+**

This fully-bolted 7-pitch monster has atmospheric and intimidating climbing. Start midway between *Costa Blanca* and *Diedre UBSA*, below a line of bolts in the centre of the huge pillar.

1) 7a+, 30m. Climb into a crumbly cave. Pull out right and up a leaning, compact wall (crux!). Easier climbing to a belay.

2) 6c+, 20m. Climb up past a rock scar, make a scary move leftwards onto a flake. Climb overlapped walls above to a belay.

3) 6b+, 30m. Climb a worrying bulge then easy ground to a big steep jamming/layback crack which leads to a belay.

4) 6c, 20m. A technical and exposed hanging arete leads to a belay on big ledge on top of the pinnacle.

5) 5, 25m. Step down across the void to gain lovely, easy and smooth jamming cracks. A very pleasant respite.

6) 6c+, 30m. A brilliant, big overhanging pitch up a band of perfect rock. Make ever-steeper moves up the big corner to a tricky capping roof. Completely wild!

7) 7a, 40m. Bolts lead left to a thread in a pocket, but there are no holds. Stretch left to clip a bolt out on the wall, then reverse back to base. Drop down and traverse underneath a perfect top-rope left to pockets in the leaning wall. Lever up these to the aforementioned thread and follow the thin corner above, past the odd chipped slot, to easy ground and the top. There may be a higher method of doing the traverse.

FA. Roy de Valera, Miguel Cebrian 1999

❸ Me estoy
quedando sin yemas .... 🔳🔳 ⬜ **7a**

There is another line of bolts on the right-hand side of the pillar.

1) 7a, 30m. Use 2 points of aid to get started, then follow the pleasant wall to a stance.

2) 6c, 20m. The excellent groove-line to a junction with *PPE*.

The long groove to the right of the large pinnacle provides the substance of one great old trad route and also the start of one of the major clip-ups of the crag.

❹ Diedro UBSA..... 🔳🔳🔳 ⬜ **5+ (HVS)**

A classic expedition which takes the groove to a belay behind the pinnacle and then continues to reach the large cave high up. From here the route escapes by spectacular abseil to gain a ledge and corner on the left which leads to the top. The route is slightly spoilt by the looseness of the first few pitches. Take a small rack although you may only place a couple of runners since there is plenty of fixed along the length of the route. Start left of the base of the groove by a large cactus bush.

Diedro UBSA continued...

1) 15m. Scramble up any line (loose) to belay left of the base of the groove.

2) 4+, 30m. Climb awkwardly right to the groove then up to a stance in a chimney.

3) 5+, 30m. Continue bridging up the groove, past a possible stance just before a harder section.

4) 5, 25m. Another pitch up the corner.

5) 4, 30m. Move right onto a slab and then back left and climb up to a shady stance behind a pinnacle.

6) 5+, 25m. Climb up to a jammed block and make a long move around this onto the wall above. Climb up and rightwards into a chimney to belay.

7) & 8) 25m up, 8m down. Scramble to the top corner of the cave (stance) and abseil off the large clump of tat onto a ledge below, swinging slightly left to the twin bolts.

9) 4, 30m. Traverse into the corner and move up to belay.

10) 4+, 35m. Climb the corner to gain the ridge. Easy rock leads from here to the summit.

FA. Luis Riguez, Jose Guerrero, Pedro Oliva 1960s

❺ El navigante .. 🔳🔳🔳🔳 ⬜ **7a**

A magnificent route which is of the same calibre as *Costa Blanca*, if not even better. It follows a very steep and direct line up the centre of the face to reach a fine position high on the wall. A wire or two may be needed for the section shared with *Diedro UBSA* which also contains some loose rock.

1) & 2) 4+, 45m. As for *Diedro UBSA*.

3) 5+, 15m. Continue up the corner but step right and climb onto a small black glacis. Belay at the right end of this.

4) 6b, 28m. Climb straight up the vertical rubble on some weird and wonderful holds (scary) and then smoother rock above.

5) 6b, 30m. Another long pitch leads left then back right and up an area of flowstone. Juggy climbing reaches a crack which leads to a belay shared with *Gómez-Cano*.

6) 6c, 20m. Tackle a short steep arete (scary) or groove to the left (technical).

7) 6a, 30m. Move left awkwardly then climb the groove and then the crack on the left (strenuous) to a good stance.

8) 7a, 30m. Climb the overhanging face above via the crack on the right with one hard move (or aid). Continue on steep rock via a crack then swing left to a niche. Exit rightwards then climb a groove and slab. Scramble up easy rock to the summit.

FA. Salvador Guerola, Emilio Perales, Juan Terradez, Jaime Arviza 1991

❻ Manuel...... 🔳🔳🔳🔳 ⬜ **6b (E3)**

A long route with a fine first pitch but overshadowed by its neighbours above that. The upper sections have little quality fixed gear and there is much loose rock. Tack a full rack and prepare for an adventure! Start below the red flowstone wall.

1) 6b, 30m. Follow the tatty gear up the steep wall to a lower-off where the angle changes.

2) 6a/A1, 30m. Move up to reach a big flake then climb up this. At its top reach a bolt ladder. Aid up this to a stance about 5m above.

3) 6a, 45m. Make a diagonal traverse up right to a groove and followed this to the base of the first big cave on *Gómez-Cano*.

4) 4, 45m. Pitch 4 of *Gómez-Cano* but continue to the ledges above and move right through an arch to a bolt belays.

5) 5+, 40m. Follow either of two ribs above to a slab which leads up leftwards to a stance. The tempting bolts to the right of this pitch are on *Linea-Magica*.

6) 5+, 35m. Climb the chimney above then make hard moves out right. Climb the crack above and belay in a corner.

7) 4, 30m. The crack and arete on the right to easier ground.

8) 3, 30m. Easy ground leads to the top.

FA. Manfred (solo) 1970s

❼ Manuel Pitch 1 ...... 🔳🔳 ⬜ **6b**

30m. The superb first pitch is often done in its own right and has just enough fixed gear too be considered a sport route.

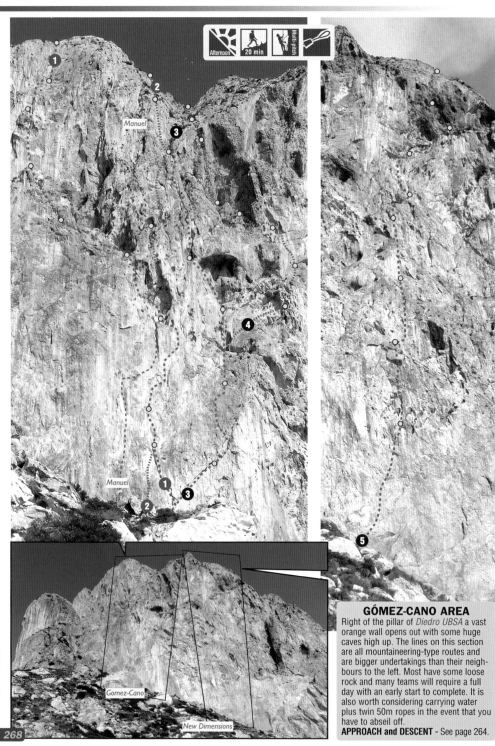

PEÑÓN de IFACH *Gómez-Cano Area*

Manuel

GÓMEZ-CANO AREA

Right of the pillar of *Diedro UBSA* a vast orange wall opens out with some huge caves high up. The lines on this section are all mountaineering-type routes and are bigger undertakings than their neighbours to the left. Most have some loose rock and many teams will require a full day with an early start to complete. It is also worth considering carrying water plus twin 50m ropes in the event that you have to abseil off.

APPROACH and DESCENT - See page 264.

Gomez-Cano

New Dimensions

Murcia | Alicante | Benidorm | Calpe | Xaló Valley | Gandia | Bernia | Altea | Mascarat | Sierra de Toix | Olta | Peñón de Ifach

❶ Vía Gómez-Cano 🔲🔲🔲🔲 6b (E3)

A massive mountaineering classic which takes in some incredible rock at a reasonable grade. It follows a long sweeping diagonal line through the series of huge honeycomb caves high on the wall. Take a full rack of gear including some foot slings for the aid pitch. The upper pitches are not well protected. Start below the diagonal crack at the name painted on the rock.

1) 6a, 30m. Climb the crack up rightwards then move onto a flake which comes back left. Make a tricky move out right, past a bolt, to a sloping stance.

2) 5+, 15m. The groove above is awkward.

3) 7b+ or A0/5+, 40m. Climb up a groove then move rightwards onto the wall. Head up here towards a diagonal crack. Either climb smoothly up the crack, or swing around like a baboon on the pegs. 1 wire is needed on the peg ladder. Belay in the base of the start of the huge caves.

4) 4, 30m. Climb to the top left-hand corner of the cave and pull around into a large bay. Scramble across left and make some exposed moves on a short rib around into another cave system and two threads for a belay.

5) 3+, 40m. Walk leftwards to a belay on the edge of a cave.

6) 20m. Scramble up spikes and flakes to the foot of a groove.

7) 5+, 30m. Follow the corner then make tricky moves into the crack above. This leads to a stance in a chimney.

8) 6b, 40m. Squirm up the chimney and the grooves above until you are forced right onto a ramp and an exposed belay.

9) 6b, 40m. Climb up into a corner and follow this to a bulge. Move around this on undercuts and follow a corner above to easier ground. Scramble to the top from here.

FA. Miguel Cano, Migeul Gómez 1970s

❷ Línea Mágica 🔲🔲🔲🔲 6c+

Another long modern route which gives superb climbing and positions. A small rack is need for the section shared with *Gómez-Cano.* Start just left of *Gómez-Cano.*

1) 6b, 30m. Climb the bolt line to join *Gómez-Cano.* It is possible to continue in one 45m pitch to the next stance.

2) & 3) 7b+ or A0/5+, 55m. As for *Gómez-Cano.*

4) 6b, 20m. Climb straight up a corner then through the roof of the cave in a position of some excitement! Belay on the ledge.

5) 6a, 40m. Traverse around a rib to a bolt ladder in the next bay (possible belay). Move up left through a bulge, then rightwards to a groove. Climb this then escaping right at a thread on the arete.

6) 6c+, 35m. Climb up a wall to reach a steep section then pull through this (hard) to easier ground.

7) 5, 40m. Scrambling remains.

FA. Jaime Arviza, Esteban Clemente 1991

❸ Anglada Gallego 🔲🔲🔲 6c (E4)

This long route follows the centre of the main face between the two huge cave systems. It is not popular featuring some suspect rock and old fixed gear. Also the climbing is a bit unbalanced with all the hard stuff at the bottom. Start down the slope from the crack of *Gómez-Cano.* The name is on the rock.

1) 6b, 35m. Follow flakes up right, then climb direct to the start of a prominent slanting crack-line. Follow the crack and belay at small foot ledges.

2) 6c, 40m. Continue along the crack for a few moves, then move up onto the compact wall above. Follow the gear up and slightly leftwards to reach a narrow ledge. Move easily right past a peg to gain an easy groove-system leading to a stance.

3) 20m. The corner leads easily to a great cave.

4) 5+, 40m. Strenuous corners on the left lead to a recess.

5) 5, 25m. Follow the groove above to a junction with the well-bolted line of *Línea Mágica.*

6) 5+, 40m. Traverse right into a corner and climb it with difficulty at its top. Step left to another *Línea Mágica* belay.

7) 8) & 9) 120m. Scramble easily up the gully to the col between the two summits of the Peñón.

FA. J.M.Anglada, M.Angel, G.Gallego

❹ Mistela......... 🔲🔲🔲 6c (E4)

A pair of spectacular, fully-bolted pitches high on the crag are reached by a lengthy approach on more traditional ground.

1) 6b, 35m. As for *Angalada Gallego.*

2) 6c, 30m. As for *Angalada Gallego.*

3) 5, 45m. Climb the groove and enter an open bay with a thread on the left. Walk right to a pocketed archway on the right wall and climb up into this. Step out right and climb the slabby wall to a ridge overlooking another open bay. Walk across this to a bolted stance up on a shelf on the far side of the bay.

4) 6a, 25m. Climb an easy, brittle rib to ledges. Move right onto better rock and climb up past a thread. Move right, passing a peg in a small groove, then direct, exiting onto ledges below a long overhang. Nut belay, or a bolted alternative out right.

5) 6b+, 15m. Climb the converging cracks past the odd peg and wooden wedge. Big thread belay out left on the next ledge.

6) 3, 25m. Traverse left around the corner to enter another large bay. Walk up this to a bolt belay below a short wall.

7) 4, 25m. Climb the wall then easy ledges. Belay beneath the bolt ladder.

8) 6a+, 25m. Follow the bolts leftwards up the overhanging brown wall to a well-bolted stance in a niche. A brilliant pitch on a band of rock which serves *Nueva Dimensión* and *Puto paseo ecológico* equally well.

9) 6c, 15m. Follow the bolts up and left, negotiating a bush on the lip, to arrive at a well-bolted stance back on *Angalada Gallego.* Hanging on to clip all the bolts probably constitutes the crux of this pitch.

10) 40m. Easy scrambling remains.

FA. Miguel Cebrián, Roy de Valera

❺ Nueva Dimensión 🔲🔲🔲 7b

This amazing route up the awe-inspiring right-hand side of the vast South Face of the Peñón. After a very hard first pitch it relents and then builds again to a superb climax on the headwall. Take a small rack for the three easier pitches, which shouldn't be underestimated, and prussik loops in case you fall off pitches 8 or 9. The easier middle pitches are loose.

1) 7b (7a min to frig, E5 6b) 35m. The line of black bolts is harder than it looks. The crux in the middle leads to a hands-off rest. Take a good breather here since the upper section is tough. A final hard move gains the belay - phew!

2) 7a, 35m. Climb straight up the wide crack behind the stance and follow the line over two awkward bulges above. The line of bolts out to the left of the stance is an enjoyable alternative **6c** pitch which gets a bit lost higher up by a thin slab.

3) 6b+, 50m. A huge long pitch, take lots of clippers.

4) 6c+, 40m. The short hard wall then easy ground to a belay on a big ledge below a hanging seat - a good spot for lunch.

5) 5, 20m. Step right around the corner past a peg. Follow the loose groove and step right onto a belay above a pillar.

6) 5+, 30m. Teeter left (peg and bolt). Continue into a bay then left to a thread. Squirm back up (bolt) right to a ledge.

7) 5+, 35m. Meander up to a rib towards a solitary bolt and belly-flop onto the next ledge. Walk right and pick your jaw off the ground after you have seen where the next pitch goes.

8) 6c, 25m. Enjoy the position as you tip-toe up the groove, then launch up the big holds to grab the blobs. Pray they don't break off and clip all four bolts at the belay. Take a deep breath and stare downwards for 10 seconds.

9) 6c, 40m. Follow the hanging groove to a thin pull (smallest holds on the route?) onto the wall above. Continue past a couple of ledges to a good stance.

10) 40m. Scramble off rightwards past two grooves then double back left to reach the top.

FA. Roy de Valera, Juan Carmelo Merino 1991

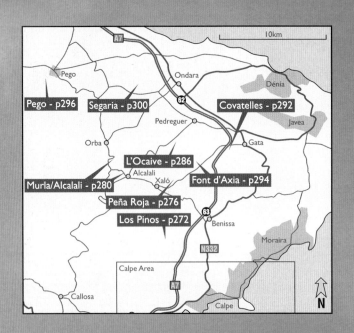

Pego - p296
Segaria - p300
Covatelles - p292
Murla/Alcalali - p280
L'Ocaive - p286
Font d'Axia - p294
Peña Roja - p276
Los Pinos - p272

Xaló Valley

Route 9 (7b+) on Alcalali - *page 280*. This excellent little roadside crag gets all the sun that is going. At the moment there are only a handful of routes here but several of these climb superb featured rock and are worth calling in for.

LOS PINOS

This recently developed crag is in a pleasant location and offers fine views down towards the coast. It is an easy 20 minutes drive from Calpe, conveniently situated next to the road and with a good set of well-bolted routes. All the ingredients for lasting popularity you may think - however the angle of the rock and subsequent grade range means that it is only of any real interest to those operating in the 7s and 8s - pity really!

The routes aren't that long but the climbing tends to be steep and sustained with powerful moves, packing a lot into their diminutive length. Sector Pinturas is dominated by steep roof-climbs whereas Sector Casa tends to be more sustained walls. There is still scope for some new routes so expect more developments here.

APPROACH (area map page 270)

Travel north from Calpe along the N332 towards Benissa and take the signed left turn towards Xaló/Jalón. If you are coming from further south then use the A7 and leave at junction 63, then turn south and drive through Benissa to reach the same junction. Immediately after turning towards Xaló/Jalón take the road on the left, signed to the village of Los Pinos. After 5km there is a pronounced right-hand bend (great views from the mirador) where the Sector Pinturas is immediately above you. Park on the bend for this buttress or travel 500m further along the road, round a left-hand bend, to reach the restricted parking for the Sector Casa. In both cases the routes are only a few minutes from the car.

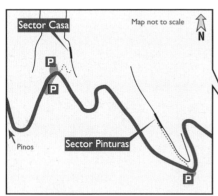

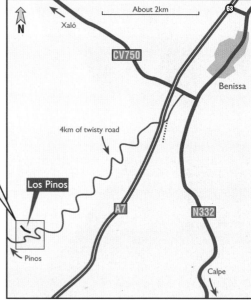

CONDITIONS

Los Pinos generally faces south west and both sectors are in the sun from mid-morning onwards. They are not very exposed to the wind and in the Sector Pinturas the roofs give some protection from rain. Sector Casa dries quickly and is a good venue after heavy rain though after prolonged wet periods there will be the inevitable seepage from the tufa systems.

Richard Davies on his own route *Espresso* (7a) at Los Pinos - *page 274*. Richard has been active in the Xaló and Calpe areas over the last few years adding a number of fine new routes to crags like Los Pinos, Murla and Altea Col. He publishes his new route information on his own web site **www.freewebs.com/costablancarock** Photo: Neil Foster

Murcia

Alicante

Benidorm

Calpe

Xaló Valley

Gandia

Los Pinos

Peña Roja

Murla/Alcalali

L'Ocaive

Covatelles

Font d'Axia

Pego

Segaria

❶ Let's Get Started . . . . 6a+
12m. Start up a shallow groove on the left and continue up the stepped, grey wall.
FA. Richard Davies 2004

❷ The Mediator 7a
12m. Climb a short groove then make a hard move right to gain the easier upper wall.
FA. Richard Davies 2004

❸ Tasha Basher . . . . 6b+
18m. The leaning corner and wall to final bulge.
FA. Richard Davies December 2004

❹ Penny Pinching . . . . 6b+
12m. Pass a small roof and gain a shallow groove which leads to a lower-off. The continuation is a bigger at **7a+**.
FA. Richard Davies December 2004

❺ Algo más? . . . . 6b+
18m. A shallow groove that is steeper than it looks.
FA. Richard Davies 2004

❻ Espresso 7a
18m. Climb to a flake and pull steeply up until established in a groove. Exit from this and climb pockets to the belay.
Photo page 273.
FA. Richard Davies 2003

❼ Algoda . . . . 6c+
18m. Climb the corner/flake line to the bulge. Move right and climb up to the belay.
FA. Richard Davies 2003

❽ Jingo . . . . 7a+
15m. Start right of an old tree. Climb past a hole to a good hold below the overhang. Pull up and then move rightwards to finish up *Bubble Trouble*.
FA. Richard Davies 2004

❾ Bubble Trouble . . . . 7b+
15m. Climb to a flat hold then make hard moves up and right to reach a thin flake. The upper section is much easier.
FA. Richard Davies 2004

SECTOR CASA
A steep sector with a good set of hard routes. In the shade until mid-day and sheltered from the wind and light rain.
APPROACH - Scramble from the sharp bend up to the crag on the right-hand side of the valley.

❿ 2004 . . . . 7b
15m. Climb to a small roof, pull over and climb the shallow groove. Move right (hard) to gain a crack and finish up this.
FA. Richard Davies 2004

⓫ Stormbringer . . . . 7a+
15m. A very hard start leads to technical climbing to gain a flake high in the wall. Continue up the crack-line.
FA. Richard Davies 2003

⓬ Eso Picante 6c
18m. Start below the hanging corner/flake and climb to this then pull steeply right and up to the belay.
FA. Richard Davies 2003

⓭ Tirade . . . . 7c+
18m. Start up pockets to the bulge, then make a hard pull on small holds onto the sustained upper wall.
FA. Richard Davies 2004

⓮ Batacazo 7c
18m. Tackle the central line linking a series of pockets and cracks to a belay just below the top. Sustained.
FA. Richard Davies 2003

⓯ Final Destination 7c
18m. The line to the right finishing at the hole.
FA. Richard Davies 2003

⓰ Summer Rain (Project) . . . . . . ?
18m. Will be around **8a+**.

⓱ Poca Lizard 7b
18m. Start off the wall and climb pockets to reach the steep pocketed crack-line in the top wall.
FA. Richard Davies 2003

⓲ Gothika . . . . 6c+
15m. Start inside the stone-walled enclosure and pull to good holds then move left to gain the easier upper wall.
FA. Richard Davies 2003

SECTOR PINTURAS

This steep crag is about 15m tall and has a prominent roof running along it for most of its length. In the developed section the roof relents somewhat to allow a few relatively easier routes but, for the most part, this is Black Spot territroy. There is a loose band of rock at the base of the crag which has prevented greater development.

As to Pinturas, if you can spot any cave paintings, you are a better man than me!

APPROACH - Park on the long lay-by on the outside of the bend, cross the road and you are there! From the parking spot the view back towards Calpe is rather fine.

The climbs are up the steep rock to the right of the iron railings around the 'invisible' cave paintings. 500m further on there are two further lines although no precise details are known.

A further 30m lead to the Pinturas protected by an enclosure. Just past this
is a leaning wall.

❶ Child for the Wicked..... 7c
12m. Start by a flake and move right to a hole. Climb past the tufa to eventually gain better holds. Move left to finish.
FA. Richard Davies December 2004

❷ The Core............. 7c
12m. From the start of *Child for the Wicked* climb straight up.
FA. Richard Davies December 2004

❸ The Reaper........... 7c+
12m. 2m left of *The Core*, a hard start leads to a very hard move to gain reasonable holds. More tricky moves then it eases to the lower-off.
FA. Richard Davies December 2004

❹ Project 1............... ?
15m. The roof will be about **8b+**!

❺ Jog Jog 8a
10m. Climb to a tufa then somehow gain a large jug out in the roof. Move right to good holds and make a long reach to finish.
FA. Richard Davies 2003

❻ Route 3 .... 7a+
15m. Climb the flake-line up the edge of the wall to a belay.

❼ Route 4 .... 6b+
15m. A worthwhile line and the easiest route here.

❽ Route 5 .... 6c
10m. Climb steeply through the bulge to a low belay.

❾ Paprika 7b
15m. Undercut to reach a hole at the break in the roof. Pull steeply to better holds and climb the wall above.
FA. Richard Davies 2003

❿ Paella is Waiting.. 7b+
12m. Climb to the hole in the roof. Pull right and make fingery moves to better holds.
FA. Richard Davies 2003

⓫ The Destroyer 8a
12m. Climb left of *Blob Face* and traverse the shelf until it is possible to pull right across the lip.
FA. Richard Davies 2003

⓬ Blob Face 7c
12m. Climb to the wide roof. Straight across this with increasing difficulty on the hanging tufas.
FA. Richard Davies 2003

PEÑA ROJA

Peña Roja (also know as Lliber after the local town) is probably the best of the crags in the Xaló Valley. The routes are generally vertical or gently overhanging and some of the rock is quite hard on the fingers though the worst of the 'broccoli' rock has had its sharp edges knocked off over the years. The setting is tranquil and there is a good collection of mainly-tough wall climbs, though there are a few slippery routes of a lesser grade for climbers with lower aspirations, especially on the grey slab at the left-hand edge of the cliff.

Prickly Pears are abundant in the valley, a good indicator of the climate here. Surprisingly they are edible, but only after removing the prickles!

CONDITIONS

In poor weather the crag makes a good venue being very well-sheltered and steep enough to stay dry in light rain. The bowl shape of the cliff means that it can be very hot though fortunately it does go into the shade by mid-afternoon making it ideal for slow-starters on hot days.

APPROACH (area map page 270)

The crag is situated about 20km north of Calpe. From Benissa, follow signs towards Xaló. On entering the town, turn right towards Lliber then right again at a roundabout. Just before entering Lliber, make a sharp left turn down a ramp which leads into the concrete water channel. Drive down here and cross the ford. Continue towards the crag and park by the almond groove. Don't be fooled by the huge red cliff that you can see from the road, it is loose and full of birds.

NOTE: it has been known for the water channel on the approach to suddenly fill with water, independent of any rain. Keep an eye out since you won't be able to get your car out if this happens.

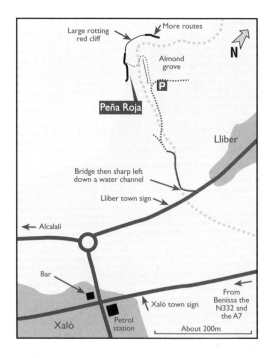

An unknown climber on the most popular route on the crag, the cleverly-named *Lliberpool* (6b) on Peña Roja - *page 279.* Polish has made it a bit harder than it used to be but it still represents a fine challenge.

PEÑA ROJA

PEÑA ROJA

On the far left is an attractive grey slab though sadly this is polished. To the right are some grooves then a steeper side-wall with a collection of better, but much harder, climbs. The fine right-hand wall is much steeper with little for those operating in the 6s although *Lliberpool* is worth calling in for. Climbers honed from a winter on the wall should love the place, but they may find the grades tough!

1 Como un loco . . . . 🔲 **6a**
12m. The balancy left-hand side of the slab via a low bulge.

2 Sansón sin pilila . . 🔲🔲🔲 **6a**
16m. The sustained centre of the slab keeping right of the bolts via a vague flake. Trending right up easier ground. Polished.

3 Sansón y dalila . . . . . . 🔲🔲 **6a**
16m. The right-hand line climbs the face left of a left-facing flake and can be quite hard if you do it all direct. Tricky 1st clip.

4 La desarrugada . . . . 🔲 **6b+**
12m. Climb the right edge of the slab and cross the bulge rightwards on sharp holds.

5 Agárrate como puedas . 🔲🔲 **7a**
14m. Use the glued-on blob at the start to gain better holds above, usually via a dyno. Impossible for the short perhaps?

6 Puta hila. . . . . 🔲🔲 **6c+**
16m. Just to the right up the blunt rib, starting from a small cave. The rock on this one is particularly sharp.

7 Toro salvaje . . . . 🔲🔲 **7a**
14m. Start behind a big tree and climb the red scoop.

8 Hall 9000 . . . . . . 🔲🔲🔲 **6c+**
14m. Direct through the niche on small painful holds.

9 El pasa de la dende . . . 🔲🔲 **6a**
20m. The corner-crack and butch roof (tricky clip on the lip) lead to scrappier herbal ramblings above to a distant lower-off

Round to the right is a steep wall left of an open groove. Take care with a loose flake high on the next two routes.

10 Through the Magic Door . . 🔲 **6a**
22m. Climb the wall right of a corner starting from a big boulder to a roof and a finish leftwards up the hanging grey slab.

11 Soca una igualita. . 🔲🔲🔲 **6b**
22m. Climb the fingery grey wall then, when the angle eases, trend left to finish at the same lower-off as *Magic Door*.

12 Techno manía . . . . 🔲🔲🔲 **7a+**
16m. The wall behind the tree has a fingery start and a tricky finish over the roof, though it is easier to go left here.

13 Tarzan de las monodedos . 🔲 **7b**
16m. Climb directly up the grey wall - hard and sustained.

14 La bella . . . . 🔲🔲🔲 **7b**
16m. The best route on the side wall. Reach the prominent large pocket and continue to the small overlap via the crux moves. Climb more easily rightwards to reach the lower off. Superb climbing but nearly impossible for the short.

Murcia

Alicante

Benidorm

Calpe

Xaló Valley

Gandia

Los Pinos

Peña Roja

Murla/Alcalalí

L'Ocaive

Covatelles

Font d'Axia

Pego

Segaria

⑮ La bestia . . . . . . 🗺🤚💧[____] **7b+**
16m. Good climbing but too close to the corner for comfort.

⑯ Sulacco . . . . ⚙💧🤚[____] **7a+**
18m. Climb the grey streak 2m right of the corner keeping left of a tall orange perched flake. Mild at the grade.

⑰ Fisura Yablonski . . . . 🗝🗺[____] **7a**
18m. The centre of the red wall with a tricky bulge to start then thin face climbing above, trending right to a final hard move.

⑱ Caballo loco . . . . 🗝🗺[____] **7a+**
18m. The crinkly red wall starting up a left-facing groove. A strenuous start and technical mid-section lead to a good finish.

⑲ Muévete un huracán. . . ⚙💧[____] **6c**
18m. The fine arete left of the groove. Another tricky start with a hard third clip. Trend left to finish.

⑳ Siempre en alguna parte . 🗝[____] **6c**
18m. The wall right of the corner is good if you can avoid the leftward temptation. Name at the bottom.

㉑ Lliberpool. . . . . 🗝💧[____] **6b**
20m. Great name, fine climb! It is sustained but never desperate and is becoming polished. Start below a floral pocket and climb the steep wall before moving right to jugs in a niche. Pull left onto the wall and finish direct. Excellent! *Photo page 277.*

㉒ Le Baton. . . . . ⚙🗺[____] **7b**
18m. A hard move at half-height, either dyno for a blob or climb to the left of it.

㉓ El desafio . . . . 🗝🗺💧[____] **8a**
18m. The bulging arete above a hole is desperate, and very steep. Previously given 7b+ by mistake.

㉔ Pan y circo . . . . . . ⚙🗺💧[____] **7c**
18m. Awkward, technical and sustained.

㉕ Sin tarjeta de presentación 🗝[____] **7a**
18m. Superb climbing with a tricky finish to a strange hold. The lower section is also hard.

㉖ Route 26. . . . . ⚙🗺💧[____] **7c+**
16m. A hard route over the narrow roof.

㉗ Route 27. . . . . ⚙🗺💧[____] **7b+**
16m. The wall and roof on tiny holds then the blunt arete.

㉘ Rockadictos . . . . ⚙💧[____] **6c**
16m. A hard move near the bottom and sustained higher up.

There are five more routes to the right of the rotten red cliff which are of questionable quality. This section faces west and receives the sun until much later in the day.

The first is **El Ultimo Huracán, 6c**, *to the right is* **Sir Lawcelot, 7a+**. *Above these is a short pitch starting from a ledge,* **La Corrida, 6a+**. *Further right and below are two more routes,* **Arthur Conan Doyler, 6a+** *and* **Gangrejos a Gogo, 6c**.

MURLA/ALCALALÍ

Murla is a short steep edge of rock on the southern rim of the Serra de Seguli above the town of the same name. Alcalalí is an eastward extension of the same outcrop, also above its eponymous settlement. The former faces west and has a large collection of Black Spot routes, and is a great destination for those in search of short, steep and hard climbing! Alcalalí faces south and although it is only home to a small collection of climbs some of these are well worth the effort especially considering the roadside setting. There remains much scope for development on both cliffs so expect routes to appear between those listed here.

APPROACH (area map page 270)
The crags are situated about 20km north of Calpe. If you are on the N332, drive north towards Benissa and take the CV750 signed to 'Xaló/Jalón. Drive through here and on for 3km to the town of Alcalali. At the T-junction in town turn left then immediately right (signed 'Pego'). Continue down here for about 1km until the Alcalalí crag can be seen, on the right, above a bend in the road - parking for 3 cars. To get to Murla, continue along the CV750 from Alcalali bearing right at a crossroads towards Orba. A couple of hundred metres after the junction is a right turn into a new urbanisation (the crag can be seen up and right). Drive up to the highest road and park just after a sharp left-hand bend with concrete block-house (the water supply). Pass behind this to locate a narrow scratchy path that rises towards the left-hand end of the cliff, five minutes away.

CONDITIONS
Murla faces west getting plenty of afternoon sun and Alcalali south which means it is an all-day sun trap. Alcalali is sheltered, Murla much less so, and the latter is a great retreat on hot days. It will also provide dry climbing in the rain, at least until it starts to seep!

Pete (PODSACS) O'Donovan enjoying a bit of tufa-wrestling on the roadside crag at Alcalalí - *page 285*.
A small crag but with several worthwhile climbs, on great rock, that see little attention.

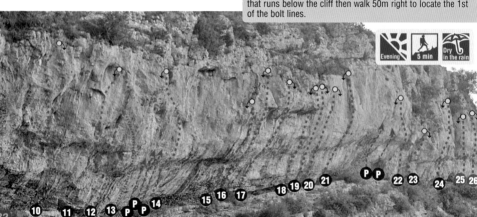

⑦ Route 7 . . . . 7c+?
14m. The roof and bulges above.

⑧ Route 8 . . . . 7c+
12m. The elegant open groove.

⑨ Route 9 . . . . 7c
10m. The steep arete. Possibly a project.

SECTOR EMPINADO

⑩ Route 10 . . . . 8a+
15m. The line of pockets.

⑪ La Chaqueta hidraulica. 8a
15m. Start from the plinth then go!

⑫ Route 12 . . . . 7c
15m. A hard start (cheater stones?) to a painful pocket-line.

⑬ Route 13 . . . . 8a+
15m. Pockets up the steep wall above the block.

The next three lines are all very hard projects.

⑭ Bailando.. . . . . 7b
15m. Four bolt-on holds mark the line. Artificial but fun.

There is then a gap of 10m before the next routes.

⑮ Route 15. . . . . 8a
15m. Plough up the tufas.

SECTOR IZQUIERDA
The section of rock nearest the parking is steep but less so than the stuff futher to the right!
APPROACH - From behind the concrete block-house, follow the track to a short scramble up to the left edge of the crag.

① Route 1 . . . . 6c+
7m. A steep line on sharp pockets. Pull leftwards.

② Route 2 . . . . 7a
10m. Start as for the last route but trend right.

③ Route 3 . . . . 6c
14m. A hard start.

④ Route 4 . . . . 6c+
14m. An even harder start.

⑤ Route 5 . . . . 6c
14m. Climb the corner.

⑥ Holds? What Holds? 8a
10m. A hard start leads to an impass on the bulge.
FA. Richard Davies 2003

SECTOR EMPINADO
The 'Steep Sector' is well-named with its daunting collection of fiercely-overhanging and technical offerings.
APPROACH - Scramble up to the left-hand edge of the ledge that runs below the cliff then walk 50m right to locate the 1st of the bolt lines.

Photo: Richard Davies

20m gap

⑯ Route 16. . . . . 8a+
15m. More tufas and a broken hold.

⑰ Route 17. . . . . 7c+
15m. A steep bulging tufa-line above a hard start. Excellent.

⑱ Route 18. . . . . 8a
15m. The steep wall and the right-hand side of the roof.

⑲ Route 19. . . . . 7c+
15m. Very fingery and technical wall climbing.

⑳ Route 20. . . . . 7c+
15m. Possibly still a project.

㉑ Route 21. . . . . 7c+
15m. Climb the bulge, black streak and the groove above.

Next is a gap before 2 very hard projects.

㉒ Route 22. . . . . 7c
15m. Pockets through a bulge. Move left and up to the belay.

㉓ The Last Bicep . . . . . 7b+
10m. A steep start, to the right of the bolt, leads into the hanging groove. Finish up the right-hand crack.
FA. Richard Davies 2004

㉔ Tendonator 7b
14m. Start 10m right of *Bicep* at a shallow corner. Make a hard move to better holds then pull through the roof to jugs. Climb up rightwards then straight up the wall.
FA. Richard Davies 2004

㉕ Route 25. . . . . 6c+
14m. A hard start (**7a** on the left) leads past a hole and into a chimney/groove. Follow this to finish.

㉖ Route 26. . . . . 6c+
8m. Climb a short wall and then pull through the bulging rock above to finish.

SECTOR CRAZY, CRAZY
Two tiny walls that get all the sun that is going.
APPROACH - Continue under all the crazy steep stuff and round the arete to two more-amenable pieces of rock.

㉗ Scary Movie . . . . 6a+
8m. The left-hand line up the centre of the wall.
FA. Richard Davies 2004

㉘ Via Segunda 6a
8m. The central line is easier if you keep right of the bolts.

㉙ Via Primaria . . . . 5+
8m. The right-hand line on the wall.

A further 20m along the path is another clean wall just left of a small cave.

㉚ Route 30. . . . . 6a+
10m. The wall just right of the flake/corner.

㉛ Route 31. . . . . 6b+
10m. Direct up the barrel-shaped slab.

㉜ Crazy, Crazy. 6c
10m. A fine climb through the low bulge and easier wall above.
FA. Richard Davies 2003

㉝ Spanish Holiday . . . . 6c+
10m. Start as for *Crazy, Crazy* then move right and climb up to a hole. Finish by moving back left to the lower-off.
FA. Richard Davies 2003

㉞ Atchata. . . . . 7b+
10m. The final line on the wall has one desperate move through the bulge. The rest is about 6c.
FA. Richard Davies 2004

SECTOR MAJOR
There are two more hard routes (around 7c) about 500m to the right. These can be reached by following the vague path below the crag. The path actually continues towards Alcalali.

Murcia · Alicante · Benidorm · Calpe · Xaló Valley · Gandia · Los Pinos · Peña Roja · Murla/Alcalali · L'Ocaive · Covatelles · Font d'Axia · Pego · Segaria

Murcia
Alicante
Benidorm
Calpe
Xaló Valley
Gandia
Los Pinos
Peña Roja
Murla/Alcalalí
L'Ocaive
Covatelles
Font d'Axia
Pego
Segaria

The first climbs are about 100m left of the parking and are reached by a short diagonal ascent.

❶ Route 1 . . . . 3+
14m. A short route on the left (first bolt is a chain-link) leading to an old belay; move right for a better one.

❷ Ainée . . . . 4+
26m. The right-hand of the easier routes has an awkward start and a short extension pitch (4+) although it can easily be done in one long pleasant pitch.

❸ Stohlwitter 6a
14m. Start at the name and climb the steep red groove to the bulges. Climb direct, or improvise out right, then past a big perched flake to a lower-off below the steeper rock.

❹ Windle Poons . . . . 6c+
15m. The tufa and wall left of *Elendigliches*.
FA. Richard Davies 1 January 2005

❺ Elendigliches . . . . 6a+
26m. Start at the (huge!) name and climb rightwards to the pocket line. From the top of this, climb the crux wall to good ledges then step left and head up the final wall which is awkward to start. A climb worth calling in for!

ALCALALÍ
This small crag is a continuation of the edge that runs down the hillside from Murla. It has a good set of hard routes on the right and some new easier ones on the left and is worth a look for a short day. Some time here can easily be linked with a visit to Murla, Peña Roja or even L'Ocaive.
APPROACH - From Xaló/Jalón drive to the T-junction in Alcalalí, here turn left then immediately right (signed 'Pego'). Continue down the twisty road for about 1km until the crag can be seen on the right, above a bend in the road. There is parking for about 3 cars.
CONDITIONS - The crag faces due south, gets very hot because of its recessed position and can seep after heavy rain. We have no route names for many of the climbs, but most of the grades have been confirmed.

Murcia
Alicante
Benidorm
Calpe
Xaló Valley
Gandia
Los Pinos
Peña Roja
Murla/Alcalalí
L'Ocaive
Covatelles
Font d'Axia
Pego
Segaria

Twenty metres to the right are two harder routes, which are based around the broad arete up and left from the parking.

❻ Route 5 . . . . 🔲🔲🔲⬚ **6b**
26m. Start behind the cactus forest, on left-hand side of the bowl. Climb the sharp grey rock then trend right up steeper terrain. Looks a bit unlikely at the grade!

❼ Heaven Can't Wait . 🔲🔲🔲⬚ **7b**
26m. Climb the rib above the right-hand side of the prickly pear then the left-slanting groove to a steep finale.
FA. Rich Mayfield 2004

The rest of the routes are to the right of the short valley directly above the parking.

❽ Route 7 . . . . 🔲⬚ **6b**
44m. The left-hand side of the main wall is climbed by this mega-pitch. It has always been described as a poor route, but it has to be admitted it looks pretty good. There is a mid-height stance/lower-off.

❾ Project 8 . . . . ⬚ **?**
30m. This will be hard when completed.

❿ Route 9 . . . . . 🔲🔲🔲🔲⬚ **7b+**
30m. A sustained start leads to a technical and fingery upper wall following the long pale streak. There is a bee's nest in one of the holes near this route. Keep away if you see bees buzzing around the crag. *Photo page 270.*

⓫ Route 10 . . . . 🔲🔲🔲⬚ **6b**
32m. Climb the rib and trend right to a cave. Bridge out of this and follow cracks to an impass. Direct here is a desperate **7b** but you can grope right into a cave (threads and summer-time bee's nest) and move back left above the hard section for a steep finish and a more balanced route.

⓬ Route 11 . . . . 🔲🔲🔲⬚ **7b**
22m. The stunning central tufa direct via some fat pinch-grips. A good **7a+** variation runs up the wall to the right of the mid-height tufa. Often wet once the rains start. *Photo 281.*

⓭ Route 12 . . . . 🔲🔲⬚ **6b+**
16m. The lower section features brilliant pulls between big pockets to a finish up the groove.

⓮ Route 13 . . . . 🔲🔲⬚ **6c**
14m. The short one, finish above a little cave. Low in the grade.

⓯ Route 14 . . . . 🔲🔲🔲⬚ **7a**
20m. A hard start up the elephants trunk which is very hard if you climb direct (there is a right-hand variant). Fine climbing up the wall above with another tricky move by the 5th bolt. This upper move can be by-passed bringing the whole route down to **6c+.**

L'OCAIVE

Murcia
Alicante
Benidorm
Calpe
Xaló Valley
Gandia
Los Pinos
Peña Roja
Murla/Alcalalí
L'Ocaive
Covatelles
Font d'Axia
Pego
Segaria

L'Ocaive is the prominent rocky tower to the south west of the small towns of Ondara and Pedreguer. It is a large and rather vegetated looking crag which still has scope for further development, both trad and sport. Most of the existing routes on the main face are in the lower and mid-grades, giving pleasant climbing on steep pocketed slabs. Recent developments have concentrated on the most impressive feature of the crag, a large overhanging bay high on its right-hand side, and this has increased the number of hard routes considerably.

APPROACH
(area map page 270)

L'Ocaive is situated south west of the small town of Pedreguer, which is just off the A7 to the north of Benissa and Calpe. Turn off the A7 at junction 62, signed 'Ondara', which takes you onto the N332. Turn right towards Gata, then right again towards Pedreguer. On the edge of Pedreguer turn right (inland) at a small roundabout towards Llosa de Camancho and Alcalali. As you head up this road, and 50m after you pass the 7km post, turn left up a short road to park at the first level area.

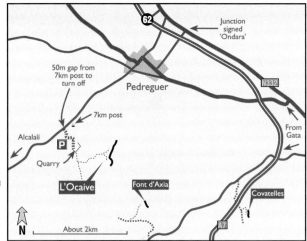

Walk up the steep track on the left to a grotty flat area (sometimes used for shooting). From the right-hand corner of this follow a good path up the hill bearing right heading for the gully beyond the cliff until a steep scrambling and scratchy path lead leftwards to the foot of the face, arriving below the Sector Maniaticos. More direct approaches are horribly sharp and best avoided.

An alternative to trying to negotiate Pedreguer is to approach from Alcalalí. This is also logical if you are combining L'Ocaive with one of the other Xaló Valley crags. Just keep an eye on the km posts and turn right 50m before the 7km post.

CONDITIONS
A fine north-west-facing tower of a crag that is in the shade until mid-afternoon and thus is an ideal venue on hot days. Most of the cliff dries quite quickly but it is exposed to the wind.

The lower section of the two pitch route *Plac Mania* (6a+) on L'Ocaive - *page 289*.
Although the crag looks vegetated from a distance, this shot reveals how much
good clean rock there really is here.

SECTOR PLACAS TOCHAS
The left-hand side of the main slabby face has a handful of routes which pick out the clean quality rock.
APPROACH - Walk leftward from Sector Mantiaticos where the crag approach path arrives.

Sector Maniaticos - 50m

Routes 1 to 3, Hidden Rock - 200m

SECTOR HIDDEN ROCK
The first routes are on a scrappy little leaning block above an animal enclosure down and left of the main cliff. There are three bolt lines in the cave, two on the back of the leaning block and the opposite wall, all look hard and no grades are known. The 3 routes described are on the less-impressive front face.

❶ Lagarto cachas . . . . . . 7b+
8m. A powerful but poor boulder problem on tiny holds on the edge of the wall. Start at the painted name. 4 bolts.

❷ Signs of Life 6c
10m. Short-lived and difficult climbing up the black tufa.

❸ The Fly 6a
8m. To the same lower-off as *Signs of Life*.

SECTOR PLACAS TOCHAS

❹ El bordillo de ilustro 4
12m. A short pitch (3 bolts) to a good stance at the base of more impressive rock.

❺ Cuerpo de mujer 6a
18m. The excellent left-hand line off the stance, tricky early on then again approaching the lower-off.

❻ La esquina asesina . . . 6a+
18m. From the same belay as the previous route, step right and follow the long rib with the crux moves reaching the lower-off.

❼ Route 7 . . . . 4+
20m. The long twisting chimney/groove is pleasant and mild.

❽ Aluncina con la esquina 5+
20m. A good pitch. Start up the chimney but climb the steep juggy wall to its right via a series of ring bolts.

To the right are 3 shorter routes with faded names on the rock.

❾ Si ta cais ta codos 6a
12m. Start on the ramp at a hollow and follow the ring bolts.

❿ No m'aclara 6a
12m. The blunt rib is reached via a tricky start and followed with interest.

⓫ El grajo del carajo 6b
18m. Start at the right-trending ramp and climb the slab on small pockets and edges to a tricky bulging finish (ring bolts).

Sector Cuevas

SECTOR MANIATICOS

The best of the easier routes on the crag are on the tall central wall. This appears to be vegetated and grassy from a distance but the routes pick out the good rock and most are better than they look. Most of the routes have their names painted at the base of the wall.

① Plac Manía . . . . 6a+
1) 6a+, 20m. Climb the pocketed wall and pass a smooth section to a lower-off. Trickier (**6b+**) if you stay direct although the groove on the left is hard to avoid. Hanging stance.
2) 6a, 26m. Continue by sustained climbing up the face above. *Photo page 287.*

② No t'as veras 6a
16m. Trend slightly right following twisting cracks up the smooth wall. Good climbing.

③ Ampárate, no me toques . 6a+
16m. Climb crozzly rock to start then smoother scoopy stuff above. More excellent sport.

④ Hombres de papel 6a
18m. Start below an orange streak high up. Good climbing leads to a lower-off above and left of a cave.

There is an old route to the right with pegs and threads - no grade known.

The next routes are to the right of a prominent vegetated gully.

⑤ El medio de Icaro . . . 6c+
1) 6a, 18m. Start up a rib and climb a long and rather rambling pitch to a small stance.
2) 6c+, 12m. The thin wall high up provides the technical crux.

⑥ 96 octanos . . . . 6a+
1) 6a+, 18m. Follow the long, sustained and excellent rib.
2) 6a, 18m. The extension pitch up bubbly rock and a tufa, then a series of holes, is very good and quite hard.

⑦ Piel de gato . . . . 6a+
20m. The face with new bolts is sustained and quite bold due to the spaced nature of the bolts.

Up the slope are three routes on the buttress where the wall swings round towards the huge red cave system.

⑧ El Incrédulo 6a
14m. Start behind a large fallen block, climb past a rock scar and bush, then on up a white rib before stepping back left to a big lower-off in a bay.

⑨ Corazón salado . . . . 6a+
14m. Up a pillar, then a narrow right-trending ramp and finally a crack-line before moving right to the belay above the ledge.

⑩ Ella la araña . . . . 5+
18m. A reasonable low grade route. Climb over a boulder and on up the groove to its end then swing left at the top to reach the lower-off of the previous route.

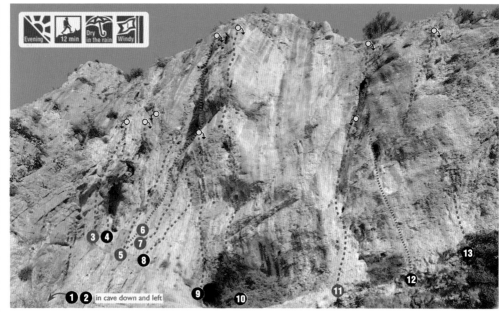

SECTOR CUEVAS

The right-hand side of the crag is dominated by a huge orange cave which has a series of desperate hard pitches on some great rock formations.

APPROACH - Either approach from the Main crag or, if you are coming straight to this section, then continue on the crag approach path up the hill, bearing right, heading for the gully. Keep going away from the crag until close to some trees where the (very good) path makes a 'U' turn. The path then splits in front of the cave and heads down past the routes. Don't try and approach directly.

The first two routes are on either side of a smaller cave down and left of the main Sector Cuevas.

❶ Pib. . . . . 🔲 7c
24m. Climb the slabby rib to enter the wide groove. Follow the left-hand side of this.

❷ Basket Case . . 🔲 7b
18m. Climb to a big hole then swing right on good holds before making a final tricky pull to reach a big flake. Very Steep!
FA. Richard Davies 2002

The next routes are on the left-hand side of the main cave.

❸ Route 3 . . . . 🔲 6b+
20m. The left-hand edge of the cave to a steep finish.

❹ Project . . . . 🔲 ?
20m. The line just inside the left edge will be good when completed. Currently it is 7b to the last move.

❺ Route 5 . . . . 🔲 7a
20m. A line of tufas left of *Los primos* gives a great pitch.

❻ Los primos . . . . 🔲 6c+
1) 6c+, 20m. The line of cracks and pockets leads to a cave. A bit of a one move wonder but good climbing.
2) 6c+ 26m. Climb just right of the overhanging crack system on crumbly orange rock. Spectacular!

❼ Route 7 . . . . 🔲 7a
20m. The flaky line to the right running up to join *Los Primos*.

❽ Route 8 . . . . 🔲 7b
24m. Very good climbing direct up a steep tufa to reach the *Los primos* cave. The difficulties lie in reaching the good pockets in the steep bulge, after which the climbing eases.

❾ Route 9 . . . . 🔲 8a
25m. Start in the cave entrance and the leaning groove. Follow the tufas up the much steep upper wall. *Photo opposite.*

❿ Project 10 . . . . 🔲 ?
40m. Start just right of the previous route and follow the bolts which lead up the fantastic arete.

⓫ Route 11. . . . . 🔲 6c
1) 6b+, 25m. The crack-line makes an excellent single pitch.
2) 6c, 18m. Good climbing up the wall after the initial glued-on hold. You can just get down with a 70m rope. *Photo opposite.*

⓬ Route 12. . . . . 🔲 7c
25m. Start 3m right of a groove and climb through a bulge (hard) and the easy wall above. Continue to belay of *Route 11*.

⓭ Route 13. . . . . 🔲 7b+
35m. A steep start and smooth wall using glued on holds.

⓮ Route 14. . . . . 🔲 6c+
A loose line above a bush right of *Route 13*.

Clare Reading, in magnificent evening light, on the first pitch of *Route 11* (6b+) on L'Ocaive - *opposite*. Photo: Neil Foster
Inset: Richard Davies on the stunning *Route 9* (8a) - *opposite*. Photo: Davies Collection

COVATELLES

Murcia · Alicante · Benidorm · Calpe · **Xaló Valley** · Gandia · Los Pinos · Peña Roja · Murla/Alcalalí · L'Ocaive · **Covatelles** · Font d'Axia · Pego · Segaria

This long low outcrop of limestone can be seen from the motorway (on the right when travelling north). Despite this proximity, it has a secluded feel about it and is worth a visit (perhaps combined with Font d'Axia which is only fifteen minutes away) if you fancy somewhere different. The crag looks quite scrappy, and to be honest it is, but at least the locals have had the bright idea of only developing the best bits of rock here. As probably the worst crag in the book it is not worth a visit from afar!

APPROACH (area map page 270)

From Gata de Gorgos, take the Lliber road for 3km, passing under the motorway. After the 3km marker post, cross a bridge then 200m further on turn left onto a narrow tarmaced road, signed Cami dels Gorgos. Drive down this to a river-bed and turn right at the T-junction. Swing left through the left-hand storm drain under the motorway (past the 'Danger of Flooding' signs!!) and park where the road heads up and right out of the river bed, 700m from the tunnel. From the parking walk along the stream bed

The short-lived groove of *El coloso* (5+) at Covatelles. *Opposite.*

for a hundred metres or so, looking out for a red arrow on a rock pointing leftwards into the bushes. Follow a series of these arrows until number twelve (also C16 painted on the rock) and scramble another 10m or so before heading left along a terrace for a couple of hundred metres to a small stand of pine trees. Climb up one level then walk back right to the start of the climbing. Heading straight up the gully from the last red arrow is possible for thick-skinned and well-clad individuals; all others are strongly advised to follow the route as described above.

CONDITIONS

Sheltered and rapid drying, the place is worth considering when the weather is misbehaving. It faces west and gets plenty of afternoon sun.

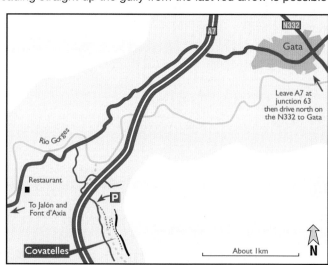

Murcia · Alicante · Benidorm · Calpe · **Xaló Valley** · Gandia · Los Pinos · Peña Roja · Murla/Alcalalí · L'Ocaive · **Covatelles** · Font d'Axia · Pego · Segaria

COVATELLES

The cliff runs diagonally up the hillside as a long narrow band of rock. All of the best bits of rock here have been developed, the stuff in between is really poor.

❶ La prima . . . . 🔲 6a+
12m. Pull over the substantial roof and then step right to pass a small overlap to reach a lower-off. Crusty.

❷ Dedos de metal . . . . 🔲 7a+
12m. The leaning wall is tackled by using a large lump of rock bolted on to the face, then sprint for the chains. Avoiding bridging into the corner on the right is a major problem.

❸ El coloso . . . . 🔲 5+
12m. The main red-streaked slanting corner gives a pleasant but short-lived pitch, trending right before leaning out left to clip the lower-off of the previous climb. *Photo opposite.*

❹ El beso de la muerta 🔲 6c
12m. The grey, tilted wall is harder than it looks and it looks pretty blank! The climbing is sustained and fingery. Five bolts protect very well.

Across the gully to the right is a scrappy wall with a huge fallen block in front of it and to the right of this a long low cave.

❺ Jabón serrano . . . . 🔲 5
12m. The clean slab on the extreme left is well bolted.

❻ The Jump Kill . . . . . . 🔲 6b+
14m. A killer of jump to start (leap for the orange pocket) or a large cairn for aid, then press on up the sustained wall.

20 metres further right and behind some huge blocks is a shrubby slab with a pedestal at its foot and a solitary bolt.

❼ Golpe de gracia . . . . 🔲 5
16m. Climb the right rib of the slab on good rock to a lower-off just below a tree at the top of the cliff.

❽ Triki, el monstruo . . . . . . 🔲 6a+
14m. The best route here? Start at the name and climb straight up the pleasantly-sustained pocketed wall.

Up the ramp to the right, past a hole, are two routes up a wall behind a flat rocky ledge.

❾ Izquierda . . . . 🔲 6b+
14m. The left-hand line has a tough sustained lower wall, trending rightwards through a small niche to a halfway ledge, and a much easier upper section.

❿ Derecha . . . . 🔲 6a
14m. A direct line with a couple of tricky moves up the initial wall and then pleasant climbing to the shared lower-off.

Towards the right side of the cliff are a series of large caves. The next routes start just to the left of these.

⓫ El gusano franciscano . . . . . . 🔲 6a
14m. Climb the white wall via a shallow groove to a lower-off above a big broken flake. Six bolts. Name on the rock.

⓬ Bodido babe . . . . 🔲 6a
18m. Head up a steep juggy wall, through a bulge then up a slab to a lower-off at the top of the cliff. Quality rock.

⓭ Chico listo . . . . 🔲 6b+
18m. A much harder right-hand start to *Bodido babe* joining it at 10m then finishing up the slab.

⓮ Samuray . . . . 🔲 6b+
16m. To the left of the large cave are smaller twin caves. This starts at a belay bolt on the ledge below these. Pull rightwards out of the right-hand cave then swing back left to climb the wall above.

The large roofs and caves to the right are home to at least one project - La babosa musculosa - though after glueing the first three blobs on the locals appear to have lost interest!

FONT d'AXIA

A small but pleasant crag in an idyllic and remote-feeling setting, despite only being a short walk from the road. There is only a small number of climbs here but, as a good percentage of them are in the lower grades and are well-bolted, the place is ideally suited to the newcomer to sport climbing who wants to get the feel of the game without being too closely scrutinised. There are a couple of mid-grade offerings for any lost hot-shots, though the active bee's nest in the caves at the centre of the cliff can make access to these difficult. The place can conveniently combined with a visit to Covatelles which is only fifteen minutes away.

Approaching the big flake on *Zapatelles* (5+) at Font d'Axia.
Opposite.

APPROACH (area map page 270)

From the minor road between Lliber and Gata de Gorgos, 200m west of the 5km post and opposite a large white house with a turret, is a track that runs north. Follow this as it bends right then crosses a dry riverbed. Continue (dirt and concrete in various proportions) keeping left at the only significant junction to a point where a dirt track branches back hard right. This is opposite a parking area in the bushes (ideal for keeping the car cool) and is about 2km from the road. Leave nothing in the car. Follow the track out and up onto a plateau then climb up a couple of terraces and cross over to the base of the cliff by looping round the head of the dry valley.

CONDITIONS

The crag has a sunny aspect and is sheltered from north-easterly winds making it a good choice on blowy days. The rock isn't the best around, though it is okay with care.

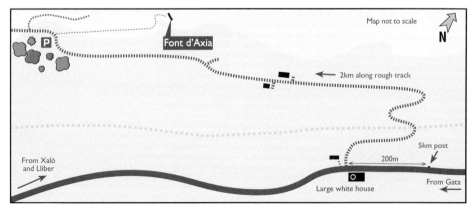

Map not to scale

N

Font d'Axia

P

2km along rough track

5km post

200m

From Xaló
and Lliber

Large white house

From Gata

BEWARE of bees nests

① Izquierda ruta . . . . 🔲 3+
14m. Straightforward climbing up the slab on the left gives a pleasant introduction to climbing on either end of the rope.

② BVD . . . . 🔲 4 (HS)
14m. The groove with an assortment of fixed tat - take wires. Trend left to the lower-off used by the last route.

③ Winne . . . . 🔲 5 (VS)
26m. The long rib sprouting threads galore - take wires. At the last thread, move right to a lower-off on the ledge.

④ El paval . . . . 🔲 4+
26m. Start below a long crack and follow it on great rock. Pleasant moves and good gear ensure its popularity.

⑤ Cilla . . . . 🔲 5 (VS)
26m. Another line of of fixed oddities up the face to the right. Take some wires and beware the wooden nut!

⑥ Savina . . . . 🔲 4
18m. Start at the black painted square and follow clean rock directly before trending away to the left.

⑦ Perell el cacaolat . . . . . . 🔲 5+
20m. A route with pleasant climbing but spaced gear. The final section is easier but some of the rock requires care.

⑧ Innominate . . . . 🔲 6b
10m. Pull over a bulge (hard for the short) and climb the crinkly wall to ledges and a solitary bolt lower-off with a maillon.

⑨ La ley del canteo . . . . . 🔲 6c
20m. Start at the name. The lower section is straightforward (a pleasant **4+** to the half-height lower-off) then things turn tough. A left-hand finish is a touch easier but the bolts are old.

⑩ El drak . . . . 🔲 5
24m. Perhaps the best route on the cliff. Start by a niche and trend slightly left to a potential lower-off after 12m (indifferent beginners route, **4+**) then back right up the rib following pink spotted bolts. Step right into the groove, or finish direct up the face on good rock at **5+**.

⑪ Les zapatelles del pastor . 🔲 5+
24m. The left-trending groove is followed, then make steeper moves up an orange-streaked groove past a large semi-detached flake. A couple more moves lead to easier ground.
Photo opposite.

⑫ Frizer se transforma 🔲 6b
16m. Climb the right-hand side of the bay following black bolts up a broad fingery rib and into a hollow, then pull over a roof on finger pockets.

PEGO

This pair of recently-developed buttresses lie on the outskirts of the town of Pego. The lower wall is very accessible but gives rather indifferent climbing. The upper wall is 15 minutes from the road and has much more to offer. Both crags have proved very popular since they were developed and it looks like there is plenty more rock in the area just waiting for some attention.

APPROACH (area map page 270)

The crag lies just to the south east of the town of Pego in a steep rocky ravine - the Barranc de les Coves. Navigate a way to the southern end of the town (through the middle via the church taking streets that allow you to go forward or left - or round the outskirts) to where a newly installed dual-carriageway road (the extension of the Passeig Cevantes) with small cypress trees down the centre, runs towards the hills. This soon turns into a minor road and just before it crosses a river-bed there is a left turn (signed to the climbing). Follow this for

Xaqueta d'Ocasio (6a+) on Sector d'Iniciacio, Pego. *Page 299.*

0.3km then branch left onto a dirt road. This leads in another 0.3km to parking on the left for two or three cars, 20m from the Sector d'Iniciacio. The path to the Sector Placa del Sol starts in front of the cliff and rises a short distance then runs along disused terraces for 10 minutes then rises more steeply again to a pleasant flat area at the foot of the face.

CONDITIONS

Both of the developed cliffs face just east of south and are in the sun until mid afternoon. The recessed nature of the valley means that they are sheltered from the worst of the weather. The lower cliff dries rapidly although the upper one can suffer from seepage after heavy rain due to the extensive hillside behind the crag and the preponderance of tufas.

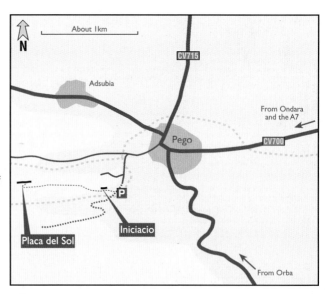

Fine rock and interesting climbing are the hallmarks of the recently-developed Sector Placa del Sol at Pego.
The shot illustrates the lower section of the classic *Quimera* (6c) - *page 298*.

Lots of sun | 10 min | Sheltered

Lower sections obscured

SECTOR PLACA DEL SOL

A fine sunny face with a series of excellent climbs which are well worth the slightly longer walk in.

❶ Forats negras . . . . 🔲 🔲 6a
24m. The left-most route starts off the ramp. It has a poor start but raises its head nicely for a steep sharp finish.

❷ Cabra loca . . . . . 🔲 🔲 🔲 6b
20m. The line of big pockets on the left-hand side of the main section of the cliff. A hard move gains the sharp stuck-on holds required to pass the crucial section. A bit shoddy!

❸ Borrego volador . . . 🔲 🔲 🔲 6b+
20m. The steep wall to taxing moves onto easier-angled rock.

❹ La fila de ta tia . . . . . . 🔲 🔲 6c
20m. From the name, climb the steep and slightly crusty wall.

❺ Muca muca . . . . . . 🔲 🔲 🔲 7a
24m. Start in the same place as *La fila de ta tia* but trend to the right onto the steep central section of the face. It is a cracker.

❻ Teto . . . . 🔲 🔲 🔲 7a
24m. The impressive centre of the face left of the cave.

❼ Anaconda . . . . 🔲 🔲 🔲 🔲 7c
24m. Approach the hole from the left and pass it steeply. Continue up the sustained face above.

❽ Quimera . . . . 🔲 🔲 6c
24m. Spectacular and excellent climb up the tufas to the right of the cave entrance. A pumpy piece of exercise.
Photo page 297.

❾ Garguller . . . . 🔲 🔲 7a+
22m. The scooped wall is climbed centrally with difficulty.

❿ Route 10 . . . . 🔲 7b
22m. Poor eliminate up the narrow gap. Avoid *Mística*.

⓫ Mística . . . . 🔲 🔲 6c
22m. The rib on the right-hand side of the scooped wall.

⓬ Route 12 . . . . 🔲 6c
22m. The pinkish scoop steepens with height and has crucial moves exiting left onto *Mística*.

⓭ Plat combinat . . . . 🔲 5+
22m. The best of the easier routes on the cliff.

⓮ Rafelet . . . . 🔲 5
22m. The easiest line on the face is worth doing.

⓯ Caldetes . . . . 🔲 5+
22m. The last line here and not the best.

Murcia
Alicante
Benidorm
Calpe
Xaló Valley
Gandia
Los Pinos
Peña Roja
Murla/Alcalali
L'Ocaive
Covatelles
Font d'Axia
Pego
Segaria

SECTOR D'INICIACIO

This isn't a great crag but since it is only 20m (that's metres not minutes) from the car and has a sunny aspect, you can forgive the locals for squeezing a few too many routes in. Ticking them all gives a good couple of hours sport - a suitable warm-up for the Sector Placa de Sol perhaps? The short, sharp nature of the climbs means the grades feel a bit harsh on many of them.

① **El Diedro** . . . . ☐ **5**
10m. The short-lived groove on the left gives a couple of steep bridging moves after a scruffy scramble approach.

② **Placca** . . . . ☐ **5**
12m. The route on the side-wall has difficulty staying out of the greenery in the gully.

③ **Plaqueta** . . . . 🔲 ☐ **4**
12m. The clean rib. Pleasant with a steep start and useful tree.

④ **Mosquera** . . . . ☐ **5**
12m. The wider cracks in the front of the buttress with a left-ward exit to the lower-off of *Plaqueta.*

⑤ **Ximet** . . . . 🔲 ☐ **5**
12m. The thinner cracks have a steep start and an awkward set of holds. Quite sustained.

⑥ **Fortas** . . . . 🔲 ☐ **5+**
12m. Climb the centre of the wall on surprising holds. A good pitch.

⑦ **Xaqueta d'Ocasio** . . . . 🔲 ☐ **6a+**
12m. The steep cracks in the right-hand side of the face give sustained interest. Probably the best route here.
Photo page 296.

⑧ **Salt del Jauar** . . . . ☐ **6b**
12m. The steep rib on the right is too close to the gully.

10m to the right are a pair of short routes arranged around an open groove.

⑨ **Perro Flaco** . . . . ☐ **5+**
10m. The steep groove until it is possible to escape out right.

⑩ **Hace Calor** . . . . ☐ **5**
10m. The wall right of the corner.

SEGARIA

The Serra de Segaria is the long rocky range of hills that bounds the northern side of the valley running inland, to the west of Ondara. When travelling north on the A7 the cliff is clearly visible indeed the eastern end of the crag virtually overhangs the motorway. Almost the whole of the southern flank of the mountain (a conservative estimate puts it at 4km long) is rocky, much of it is of good quality and, because of its distance from the road, it is much bigger and more complex that first appearances might suggest. The small selection of routes that have been done so far are the work of expat Brit Al Evans and friends. The routes have been done ground up, using a standard trad rack and a bunch of pegs - these are definitely not sport routes. The best of the routes are very good and the climbing here offers something a little different for the standard Costa Blanca fayre. However the compact nature of the rock means that climbing (both the route finding and locating decent gear) is a serious affair and many of the routes are very run-out. Add in the distance from the road and the strenuous approach and it becomes clear that this is a place that requires a little care.

APPROACH
(area map page 270)

The developed section of the cliff is reached from the Segaria Park (a picnic area) which is a little tricky to find on first acquaintance. It is most easily reached by turning west off the N332 just south of Vergel and 1.5km north of Ondara. Currently the road is not signed and to add to the confusion there is building work going on close by the motorway. Follow the road under

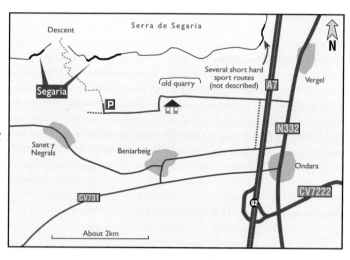

the motorway, running parallel to the hills, round a couple of right-angled bends, then just before it turns into a dirt track the parking place is to be found on the left. A tarmac track leads to some (holiday?) cottages then a cairned-path leads leftwards up the hill heading for the prominent gully that splits the cliff. The routes described are located to either side of this.

CONDITIONS

The crag faces south and offers little shelter from the sun (or perish the thought, inclement weather). Bring plenty of water, the 25 minute approach to the crag is steep and hot work.

Al Evans, local activist, on the 1st ascent of *Peter Pan* (6a/E1) - *page 302*. Photo: Trent Rosenbaum.
Inset: Serra de Segaria, the latest Costa Blanca Crag X goes on for miles and MILES!

SEGARIA

Walk descent

Lots of sun | 25 min | Multi-pitch | Windy

SOUTH FACE - LEFT

① The Ticking Crocodile . . . . ⬜ 5 (HVS)
Start at a slab with bulges.
1) 5, 35m. Follow the slab on the right side of the overhangs (2 pegs). An awkward bulge leads to easier climbing and then on to a big ledge with a tree.
2) 3, 15m. Scramble to the top of the ledge and traverse horizontally right to the ledge at the start of *Peter Pan* and *Wendy*.
FA. Al Evans, Carol Mc Tavish 2004

② Smee . . . . ⬜ 3 + (HS)
15m. Climb the left-hand wall of the blunt buttress. Go left at the ledge at two thirds height up a crack. You can easily walk off from the top or continue up one of the upper routes.
FA. Al Evans (solo) 2004 The first route put up here.

③ Wendy . . . . ⬜ 4 (HS)
1) 4, 20m. Start from the ledge and climb up, keeping left of the overhanging block, to a belay shared with *Peter Pan*.
2) 4, 15m. Move up and left under the bulge to a ramp, follow this and belay on the right.
3) 30m. Regain the ramp and trend left to a V-groove. Climb this then trend right to the abseil station on *Peter Pan*.
FA. Rob Lillywhite, Chris Lilley, Trent Rosenbaum 2004

④ Peter Pan . . . . 🔧⬜ 6a (E1)
1) 5, 20m. Climb the slabby wall right of the prominent overhanging block and belay on the large ledge above.
2) 5+ 20m. Climb through the bulge passing a 'horn' on the right, trend right to easier ground and a belay in a niche.
3) 6a, 30m. Step left onto the lip of the overhang, pull through the bulges and trend right to a slabby rib. Up this then right through another bulge and right into a crack system that leads to a ledge and two peg abseil station at the top of the rib.
Photo page 301.
FA. Al Evans, Adrian Bates 2004

SEGARIA SOUTH FACE

The recent developments here are on the 100m high face above and left of Segaria Public Park, and the rock across the gully to the left. A good cairned path leads from the car park to the foot of the crag in about 25 minutes. The rock quality is very good but generally the protection is rather sparse. Spanish and UK grades have been used but the latter are more appropriate. The routes have their names painted at their bases.
DESCENT - There are some fixed abseil stations (55m double ropes are needed) check route descriptions. The alternative is to ascend the rough ground above the crag and head left or right to the col where a marked-path leads back to the foot of the crag. Follow the white paint.
NOTE - These descriptions and grades have not been checked. These are not sport routes, fixed gear is thinly spread - take a full rack, double ropes, a helmet and great CARE!

⑤ Tinkerbelle . . . . ⬜ 5 (HVS)
1) 4, 20m. Climb the slab 5m right of *Peter Pan*, on the right of the bulge. Move left to a good ledge with peg and nut belays.
2) 5, 20m. Move right onto the face and continue straight up to a huge ledge and thread belay. At present abseil off from here but a contuation up the rib on the right is inevitable.
FA. Adrian Bates, Al Evans, Claire Allen 2004.

SOUTH FACE - RIGHT

All routes on tthis section of the crag have their names written discreetly at the bottom. The route are described using the 4-trunked tree of I Have A Cunning Plan as a reference point.

⑥ Time Team . . . . ⬜ 6a+ (E2)
18m. Start 35m left of the 4-trunked tree at a blunt buttress with a thin crack on its right-hand side. Climb up to a hard move round the bulge on its right which leads to easier ground and a good belay ledge. Scramble off left to gain the path.
FA. Al Evans, Rob Lillywhite 2004

⑦ Kate . . . . ⬜ 5 (VS)
1) 5, 20m. Start up the blunt buttress left of *Bob*. Climb this on its left-hand side, then cross easier ground to tree belays.
2) 3+, 15m. Move down and right to gain a leftward-sloping ramp, follow this and the wall above to the large ledge. Walk right to the tree abseil of *IHACP*.
FA. Adrian Bates, Trent Rosenbaum 2004

⑧ Black Adder . . . . ⬜ 4 (VS)
35m. Start 15m left of the 4-trunked tree at the start of *I Have a Cunning Plan* in a shallow bay. Take the vague rib on the right of the bay to a bulge. Now climb diagonally left through the bulges to the huge ledge. Abseil off.
FA. Al Evans (solo) 2004

⑨ Bob . . . . ⬜ 4 (HS)
40m. Start 2m left of *IHACP*. Climb the ramp, step right, then left under the bulge and follow the ramp finishing left up a rib. Go across to the tree abseil descent of *IHACP*.
FA. Rob Lillywhite (solo) 2004

⑩ I Have a Cunning Plan . . . . . . ⬜ 3 (S)
40m. Start at a slabby rib behind the 4-trunked tree and climb the centre of the buttress past a bulge to a ledge. Step across the gully and climb a slab, then traverse left past a cactus to a tree belay on a good ledge. Descend by abseil from the tree.
Direct Finish 5 (HVS) - Instead of stepping across the gully cross the bulge direct.
FA. Al Evans (solo) 2004. Direct - Carol McTavish 2004

Murcia | Alicante | Benidorm | Calpe | Xaló Valley | Gandia | Los Pinos | Peña Roja | Murla/Alcalai | L'Ocaive | Covatelles | Font d'Axia | Pego | Segaria

Descent

to the descent gully

11

A

6   7   8 9   10   12   13   14   15   16

4-trunked tree

Lots of sun | 25 min | Multi-pitch | Windy

---

⑪ The Baldrick Extension . . . 🔋 ▭ **5+ (E1)**
1) 40m. As for *I Have a Cunning Plan* to the tree belay.
2) 15m. Straight through the bulges then trend to the right to a small ledge and good peg and thread belay. Not well protected!
3) 30m. Head straight up the slabby wall to a good ledge and peg. Nut and thread belay below a left-slanting groove.
4) 20m. Steeply up left (peg) into the groove (a bit loose) then up this to good thread belays below the scree. Either abseil down to *IHACP* (two 55m ropes required), and then abseil from the tree belay to the bottom; or slog up and descend via the col.
FA. Al Evans, Catherine Rolfe 2004

⑫ A Senior Moment. . . . . . . 🔧 ▭ **5 (HVS)**
On the main face, just right of centre is the groove of *Last of the Summer Wine*. Start on the rounded rib left of this.
1) 25m. Climb through the bulges to a ledge with peg belay.
2) 25m. Take the wall on the left (poor protection) more or less direct to another stance and peg belay.
3) 50m. A fine pitch up the headwall with exposed climbing on magnificent holds following the crest of the buttress.
FA. Graham Rawcliffe, Al Evans 2004

⑬ Last of the Summer Wine . 🔧 ▭ **5+ (E1)**
1) 25m. Climb the slanting groove, mainly on its right, to below a vegetated ledge, then take the wall on the left to the belay of *A Senior Moment*.
2) 20m. Traverse out right to the blunt white rib, climb this and the wall above to a three peg belay. A fine pitch.
3) 55m. Climb the crozzled wall left of the belay to an overlap, move right and make a difficult move round its end, past a bush. Continue up past cracks and corners until it is possible to step left onto a fine white slab. Delicate climbing leads to good holds and a fine exposed finish.
FA. Al Evans (p1), Graham Rawcliffe, Mick Ward (p2 and 3) 2004

⑭ Unconventional Lives . . . . ▭ **5+ (HVS)**
The big wall right of the main buttress up its left side.
1) 25m. Climb up the depression to a ledge on the left, then head right across the slab to a peg belay below the bulges.
2) 50m. Climb up and left through the bulge, then up the slab to a ledge and thread and peg belays. Either abseil from here (head down to a good ledge below an overhang with a hidden thread for the next abseil) or scramble to the top and walk off.
FA. Al Evans, Helen Taylor, Annabelle Ison 2004

⑮ No Pockets in Shrouds . . . . . . ▭ **5 (HVS)**
A line through the overhangs at a break on the right.
1) 25m. Climb easily up to the weakness at the right end of the roof, pull through and continue to a ledge. Peg and nut belays.
2) 15m. Move up and left through a bulge, then step back right and climb straight up to a good ledge. Peg and Friend belay.
3) 25m. Trend left up the slabby bulges then go direct to a ledge and a beefy thread belay at the cliff top.
4) 10m. Traverse easily left to a fixed abseil point as for *UL*, or scramble to the top and descend via the col
FA. Gavin Roberts, Al Evans, Graham Rawcliffe 2004

⑯ Days of Wine and Roses. . . . . ▭ **5+ (HVS)**
Start 15m right of *No Pockets in Shrouds*.
1) 40m. Climb the easy slab and rib on the right to a small overhang. Move easily up left to a belay before the overhang.
2) 20m. Move up right through the bulges, then left on an obvious traverse line and up to belay as for *No Pockets in Shrouds*.
3) 20m. Move right then follow discontinuous cracks, then right to a flaky crack in head wall. Up this then the short wall above to a flake and thread belay.
4) 15m. Traverse easily left to a fixed abseil point as for *UL*, or scramble to the top and descend via the col.
FA. Roger Whetton, Graham Rawcliffe (alts) 2004

Gandía

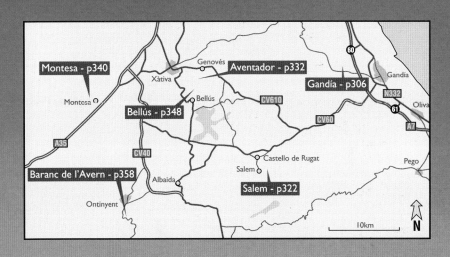

Montesa - p340

Aventador - p332

Gandía - p306

Bellús - p348

Baranc de l'Avern - p358

Salem - p322

Genovés

Xàtiva

Montesa

Bellús

Gandía

Oliva

CV610

CV60

Castello de Rugat

Salem

Pego

Albaida

Ontinyent

10km

N

60

N332

61

A7

A35

CV40

GANDÍA

Sitting in the middle of a broad valley, the main crag at Gandía looks rather small on first acquaintance but there are many fine climbs here on near-perfect rock formations and in a gorgeous setting. The grade range is good and, although it isn't the best area for people leading below 6a, there are enough easier routes dotted around the crag. The real attraction is in its steep bulging tufa-routes in the harder grades and it is an essential destination for those operating at around 7a/7b. Some of the harder routes are a bit chipped but the best bits tend to be swinging around on the natural holds on the steeper lower sections. The easier climbs are mostly on grey slabs and walls featuring fingery and technical climbing and are all of a high quality and not filler-in routes.

The routes here are the work of Club Alpi de Gandía; Juan Carmelo Merino, Pep Ginestar, Miguel Cebrián, Xavi Calabuig and Albert Monzó. They have been climbing here since the 1980s and have done a great job maintaining the bolts, lower-offs and paths. The grades in this book are the same as used by the locals and are at the upper end of their ranges.

ACCESS - There have been occasional access difficulties and bird nesting restrictions in the past, especially at weekends - please observe any signs.

CONDITIONS

The crag faces south, catches all the sun going and is sheltered, it can be here hot even in the middle of winter. The steeper areas suffer from seepage after rain when many of the hard tufa climbs become impossible. However if the water hasn't had a chance to seep through, then you will should find something dry, though it may be pretty tough! El Bovedón stays dry in the rain but the routes are hard.

APPROACH
(area map page 305)

Drive north on the toll A7 to junction 61 - Oliva. Exit at here and turn left towards Gandía at the next junction. Drive through Bellreguard (s-l-o-w) to the new roundabout and take the second exit signed to 'Valencia'. Once on the bypass take the 'Barx' exit. Turn left under the N332 and under the motorway. Take the first major right, signed 'Raco de Tomba' and park below the crag. For those with less time and more cash it is faster to drive to the next junction on the motorway then head back south to the roundabout on the ring road. This adds about 10km onto the journey and knocks 15 mins off. The current access route crosses the dry river bed just 'up-stream' from the parking. See page 320 for approach to El Bovedón.

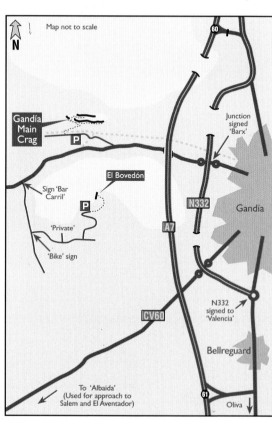

N — Map not to scale

Gandía Main Crag — P

Sign 'Bar Carril'

El Bovedón — P

'Private'

'Bike' sign

Junction signed 'Barx'

N332

Gandía

A7

N332 signed to 'Valencia'

CV60

Bellreguard

61

Oliva

To 'Albaida' (Used for approach to Salem and El Aventador)

60

SECTOR CRITIC
At the far left-hand side of the crag is a buttress separated from the main crag by a steep, narrow gully. This receives the sun later than the main crag - cool in the mornings, warm in the evenings.
APPROACH - Walk left from where the approach path hits the crag, underneath the cave in Sector Hidraulics.

① Margarita, quan pixa . . . . [ ] **6a+**
8m. Short, sharp and unremarkable. Two bolts.

② Esperó groc. . . . . [ ] **6b**
14m. Start behind the big tree and climb the white wall to large pockets, then up sharp grey rock above.

③ Diagnosis superficial . . . . [ ] **6b**
14m. Take the previous climb to the level of a large flake on the right. Step onto this then climb the wall and thin crack above.

❹ Pasando de poli . . . . [ ] **7b**
14m. Start on the right of the tree and climb up to a flake. Head up the wall past a small overlap. A very thin finish remains.

❺ Voldria morir. . . . . [ ] **7a**
14m. Start up *Pasando* but move right into *Ja estic mort*. The combination is probably the best way up the wall.

❻ Ja estic mort. . . . . [ ] **7a+**
14m. The smooth wall just to the left of the big red corner.

❼ Gran Diedro . . . . [ ] **5+**
18m. This route has been rebolted and is still excellent.

The next 3 routes are based on the arete and wall to its right.

❽ Selectiva . . . . [ ] **6c**
18m. Start at a large vertical pocket. Up this then the bulges above. Continue (past a thread) into a shallow groove until it is possible to exit round to the right.

❾ Espolón "why" . . . . [ ] **6c**
18m. From below the right side of the arete climb the leaning wall on spiky pockets. Continue close to the arete passing a thread and peg to more difficult moves until things ease.

❿ Megaloceras . . . . [ ] **7a**
18m. A desperate, polished crux involving a pull on some miserable sloping pockets. "A 7c move on a 6b route".

To the right is a sheet of grey rock with two prominent flake cracks and a nice collection of mid-grade routes.

⑪ Águilas . . . . [ ] **5 (VS)**
18m. A fine route with no fixed gear! Gain the base of the flake and follow it steeply on jugs and finger jams. At the top of the flake move up to a belay on a higher ledge.

⑫ Piccolissima . . . . [ ] **6a**
18m. The face between the two flakes has a prominent bolt. Gained this direct (or via a ramp) and pass it via tricky moves (5+ for the tall). Jugs lead to the chains of the previous route.

⑬ Tierra Lliure . . . . [ ] **5+ (HVS)**
18m. Gain the base of the right-hand flake from *Piccolissima* and follow it into a corner. Belays are located on the left, or better, in the right wall of the corner above.

⑭ P.S.A.N. . . . . [ ] **6b**
14m. Climb the smooth wall past a prominent bolt. Move left to the finish of *Terra Lliure*.

⑮ Beniarrés no em diu res . . [ ] **5**
20m. Pleasant climbing up the wall, starting at the left side of an alcove/groove and then continuing up the corner above.

⑯ Tallà . . . . [ ] **5**
20m. The open groove with bolts in the right wall is followed throughout, then continue up the wall above. Pleasant.

To the right are three old climbs that have fallen into disuse.

⑰ Placa Simond . . . . [ ] **4**
12m. To the right a short rib with bolts. The start is steep.

The bulge and arete of the wall contain several old pegs!

⑤ Rincón y costilla . . . . 🔲2🔲 3+
18m. The best beginner's route on the crag, the pleasant lower wall and groove leads to a mildly-exciting traverse out left to the reach the lower-off.

⑥ Erupción . . . . 🔲🔲 5
34m. An odd and exposed route that traverses rightwards above lip of caves to the belay above *Blaniulus guttulatus*.

From the lower-off above Erupción there are two ways on:

⑦ Pagaras amb costo . . . . 🔲 6a
16m. The left-hand line above the lower-off.

⑧ S'estrena en la trena . . . . 🔲 5+
28m. The line just to the right and trending to the right.

⑨ Coral bajilla . . . . 🔲🔲🔲 5+
16m. Start at the left edge of the cave and climb the slippery and technical rib rightwards then easier juggy ground above.

⑩ Monsters of rock . . . . 🔲 7a
12m. Hand traverse pockets in the lip rightwards. Strenny!

SECTOR HIDRAULICS

The appropriately-named large cave is to the left of where the approach path arrives at the crag. The routes are mostly hard, steep and polished and give great entertainment for both climber and spectator alike. To the left and around the arete there is a small collection of easier routes, they are short and unremarkable but pleasant enough for all that!

① Primera . . . . 🔲 3+
10m. A short distance up the gully that bounds the left side of the cliff is this pleasant offering. Short but on great rock.

② Secretos . . . . 🔲 4
12m. Up the wall trending left then pull back right to the belay.

③ Fe Ra . . . . 🔲🔲 4+
12m. Straight up the centre of the wall, steep but on good holds, then move left to the lower-off.

④ Dedos . . . . 🔲 5
12m. Trend right then climb the steep rib with one tricky move.

Fissura Tal

Murcia
Alicante
Benidorm
Calpe
Xaló Valley
Gandía
Gandía
Salem
Aventador
Montesa
Bellús
Barranc de l'Avern

11 Pequeño saltamontes. . . . 5
12m/28m. An odd route up the hole that blends climbing and caving! It eases as soon as you can get established in the tube. The best finish is to traverse out right above the overhangs and climb the short steep wall on good holds.
Photo page 313.

12 Assassí de vampiros . . 7a
12m. Follow the line of bolts straight up the wall and through the bulges to the cave with lower-off. Well strenny!
Photo page 317.

13 Negué Gorrak 8a
14m. Steep and desperate up the leaning wall.

14 Phythophthora cithrophthora 7b
14m. Climb broad blunt rib with a stubborn 'bloc' move early on, and jug hauling beyond. Start up this and finish up *Quien Molonda* for the best climbing.

15 Quien Malonda . . . . . . 7a+
14m. Gain the biggest cave from below using slippery holds then head out left onto the head wall. Step right and finish 'with gusto'. Polished pocket-pulling, but very good.

16 Parabólica Spherique. . 7a+
14m. Follow the previous route into the cave then exit to the right from this and finish across the roof. A great trip in upside-down-land with buckets all the way (except for one bit).

17 Kortatu. 7b
14m. Start just to the right of the fall line from the cave and climb direct, past a lower-off, to the finish of the previous climb using drilled pockets and some pretty poor tufas. A right-hand start is similar in style and grade.

18 Viatge a Cuba 7b
14m. Starting by 'SOSTRE' on the rock at ground level, this drilled offering runs straight up the leaning wall.

19 Blaniulus gluttulatus . . 7a
14m. Gain the right-hand cave from left or the right, then make difficult moves to reach the jugs round the lip and more hard moves to the lower-off. There is a hands-off rest in the hole.

20 Patatas a lo pobre . 7b+
14m. The steeply-tilted wall is climbed on tufas and then on pockets. Great climbing but often wet where it matters.

21 Asamblea de Mojaras . . . 8a
14m. A harder version of *Patatas* with smaller tufas and blobs.

22 Ostia coqueta . . . . . . 7a+
14m. Start just to the left of right-trending groove and climb the wall just to the left of the deep pockets of *Zucaricida*.

23 Zucaricida 6c
22m. Up the ramp for a couple of moves then swing left on to the bulging wall. Follow the line of pockets then continue direct to easier climbing up the wall to a high lowering point.

24 Leí del perrero . . . . . . 6c+
22m. Climb up the leaning wall immediately left of the slanting groove. Hard work and almost an eliminate!

SECTOR VICI

This impressive wall has a prominent red streak above a small cave. The routes here are amongst the best of their grade on the cliff, offering superb challenges which are a bit more vertical than elsewhere at Gandía.

APPROACH - Directly above where the approach path arrives at the crag just right of the Hidraulics cave.

❶ Fisura tal.. . . . . 6a+
22/30m. The open groove is entered steeply and climbed strenuously. At the top of the crack step right and climb the wall to reach the lower-off on the right or traverse away left.

❷ Pastor i porreta 6c
22m. A sharp eliminate up the bulges and rib. A blinkered approach is needed on the lower section.

❸ Niña de porcelana . . . . 6a+
22/30m. An old classic. Steep moves gain the first bolt then continue by varied climbing to reach a lower-off on the right. To convert the route into a two star offering step left to join the upper section of *Fissura tal* and head away left.

❹ Gora 7a
14m. A thin eliminate up the rib a short distance to the left of the thin crack that is the substance of *Pa roig*. Either lower off here or move right to have a go at the top pitch of *Asquerosa coincidencia* which improves the route a bit.

❺ Pa Roig 6b
14m. The thin pocketed crack-line gives good pocket-pulling with the crux moves at one third height where the crack closes and some smaller pockets are used for progress.

❻ Asquerosa coincidencia . . 6b+
24m. Steep moves on big holes/holds then a couple of difficult moves gain more excellent pockets and a lowering point. Push on past this to climb the tough roof (crux) on the rib above.

❼ El sol . . . . 6b+
24m. Magnificent climbing up the left-hand edge of the red streak with a tricky finish over the left side of the top roof.
Direct Finish 6c+ - pull direct over the roof - 2 drilled pockets.

❽ Kin mal d'ous 7b
10m. A silly (and hard!) climb out of the cave.

❾ Escorreguda precoç . . . 6c
22m. An awkward start either side of the cave leads past the lower-off of the last climb. Head up the wall and over the bulge.

❿ Peiote de bote. 6b
22m. Climb the shallow groove to a large hole from where better holds lead up the wall to the horizontal roof. Cross this centrally, with difficulty.

⓫ Valentet de València . . . . 6a+
24m. An excellent pocket-pulling pitch - easier than it looks. From the tree in the recess, head up the wall. As the climbing eases, move right to a recess then battle with the bulge above this, first left then right, to reach a lower-off just above.

⓬ Placa de Ulaca . . . 6b
24m. This fine fingery pitch up the grey wall. Climb up to the right edge of hollow with the tree then the wall until forced rightwards and then back left to reach the lower-off.

⓭ Muricana 6b
24m. Climb the left edge of cave and step right onto the wall. Power through the central bulges on sharp holds, before a small zig-zag is required to reach the lower-off.

SECTOR FUNDICIO LEFT

This steep sector has some long easier routes on its left-hand side.
APPROACH - Walk right from where the approach path arrives at the crag.

Lots of sun | 10 min

⑭ Nació . . . . 🔲🔳🔲 **6b+**
24m. Climb the wall just right of the cave past a set of conspic-uous hole/ds and up streaky rock. Sustained and excellent.

⑮ Madarikatuak . . . . 🔳🔳🔲 **6c**
14m. Start right of a flake and climb the wall ("bloody bushes") to a series of large bulges which are passed on their left (crux).

⑯ Chiqui . . . . 🔳🔲 **6c**
14m. Start where a diagonal crack reaches the ground and climb slabby rock to an alcove and steeper rock above, passing a broken flake.

⑰ Fes-te-ho . . . . 🔲 **6a+**
14m. Begin below an orange alcove at 10m. Head up a shrubby slab and follow rather broken rock via a left-facing corner above to reach the bright golden lower-offs.

⑱ En Falles no folles . . . . 🔲 **6b**
30m. A scrubby start leads to where the routes split. Climb the left-hand line up a grey wall and over a small roof. People with short ropes beware when lowering off.

⑲ Capitán Manchego . . . . 🔲 **6a**
30m. The right-hand line has an optional lower-off at two thirds height. Alternatively, join and finish as for the previous route.

To right the lower section of cliff is slabby and shrubby and there is a wide white rock platform at its base. The next route is left of a chimney flake with a tree growing behind it.

⑳ Kaya . . . . 🔳🔳🔲 **6b+**
24m. Starting at the left end of the rock platform, pass between bushes then climb slightly rightwards up the steep wall above.

SECTOR FUNDICIO - LEFT

㉑ Sense opció . . . . 🔲 **6b**
22m. Easy rock leads to steeper things, and a substantial roof, which is the main meat of the pitch.

㉒ Nupcias . . . . 🔳🔳🔲 **6b+**
20m. A slabby start and long open groove lead to bulges which are climbed leftwards on good holds (apart from at the start).

㉓ Milan Kundera . . . . . . 🔳🔳🔲 **6a+**
20m. Start behind a carob bush. Climb either of two lines up easy slabs then a groove with a flake in the back and a bulging crack. Avoid the tendency to move right if possible.

㉔ Chitiri, chitiri . . . . 🔳🔲 **4+**
22m. The central line here with a conspicuous bolt on a bulge low down and an open groove full of holes above. Very pleas-ant, one of the best easy routes here. The last move is steep.

To the right is a steep slab with two lines that share a belay.

㉕ La insoportable . . . . 🔳🔲 **6a**
14m. The left-hand line is quite taxing if tackled direct though the hardest moves are easily avoided.

㉖ La levedad . . . . 🔳🔳🔲 **5+**
14m. The central line is tough for a couple of moves.
Photo page 313.

㉗ El ser . . . . 🔳🔲 **6a**
14m. A short route just left of the fall line from a tree at 12m. It features a steep start and some rather odd rock.

Murcia | Alicante | Benidorm | Calpe | Xaló Valley | Gandía | Gandía | Salem | Aventador | Montesa | Bellús | Barranc de l'Avern

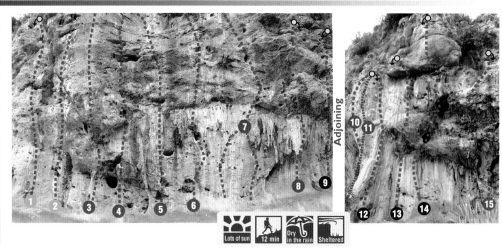

Lots of sun | **12 min** | **Dry in the rain** | **Sheltered**

SECTOR FUNDICIÓ

This steep sector has an impressive bulging wall in its centre with some great juggy routes. To the right of this is a pillar and a cave which promise more than they deliver.
APPROACH - Walk right from where the approach path arrives at the crag for a minute or so.

① Bombero gorilero. . . . . 🔲🔲🔲 **5+**
14m. Start at the left-hand end of the wall and make a few steep pulls before the angle and difficulty eases. Move left to a lower-off shared with the routes to the left.

② Tamborinaes 93. . . . . 🔲🔲 **6a**
22m. A better route then *Bombero* starting where the cliff becomes really steep. A strenuous start past bulges, then cross a groove and go up a rib to a pull over another tricky bulge.

The next wall gives the best climbing in this sector - steep juggy pocketed walls where power pays dividends.

③ Puntín d'Ernestín . . . . . 🔲🔲🔲 **7a**
14m. The line of bolts up the pillar gives a challenging route if taken direct. Unfortunately it is rather too easy to keep escaping rightwards onto the next route, which is more like **6b**.

④ El Rigio . . . . 🔲🔲🔲 **6b+**
14m. From a recess with hole at head height, bridge up and right, then swing back left rapidly to big holds and an awkward finish. The last bolt is badly placed.

⑤ Pepestroika. . . . . 🔲🔲🔲 **6b**
14m. Climb up to the hanging 'dong' at 4m. Layback up this and then press on to easier-angled rock. The lower-offs are most easily reached by looping left and leaning back right.

⑥ Última Albertència. . . . 🔲🔲🔲 **6c**
14m. Climb the orange streak to a hole, then the pocketed wall above to a rest before finishing up the bulging wall above. Hard for the grade but excellent.

⑦ Amarrada al pilló. . . . . 🔲🔲🔲 **6b**
22m. Follow a series of large and usually well-chalked pockets (choice of starts) then trend right then back left with a tricky move just before things eases. Continue in the same line up great rock.

⑧ Pere. . . . . 🔲🔲🔲🔲 **6c+**
14m. The big white tooth of a tufa is reached awkwardly. Shin up it to pass the bulges, then step right and make a huge reach over the roof to easier ground.

⑨ Route 9 . . . . 🔲🔲🔲 **7b+**
14m. A steep and powerful climb up the back right-hand corner of the bay, weaving through the bulges.

⑩ A mi no m'afecta . . . . . 🔲🔲🔲 **6c**
12m. Start up the pillar but trend left to seek out difficulties! Short sharp and hard for the grade - the local guide gives it 6b!

⑪ S'ambossa . . . . 🔲 **6c**
12m. A right-hand finish to the previous route continues direct.

⑫ Espanya no m'apanya. . 🔲🔲🔲 **7b**
12m. The right side of the pillar is steep, strenuous and technical, and includes a very short and intense crux.

⑬ En médium . . . . . . 🔲🔲🔲🔲 **7c**
12m. Right again is this offering where the rock is at its very steepest. Short but action-packed and sharp as well.

⑭ Día de borratxera. . 🔲🔲🔲🔲 **7c**
14m. The back of the bay via a hole and then on with greater difficulty over the roof and up the 'smooth' wall above with a disappointingly technical finish.

⑮ Joc de manos . . . . 🔲🔲 **6c+**
12m. The very overhanging line on the right side of the bay is tackled on mostly-good but spaced holds.

An unknown climber on *La levedad*, (5 +) on Sector Fundicío at Gandía - *page 311*. The bulk of the routes at Gandía are in the higher grades but dotted around the crag are a number of quality easier routes which are well worth seeking out.
Inset: Chris Craggs taking his route checking too seriously on the bizarre *Pequeño salta-montes* on Sector Hidraulics. Photo: Sherri Davy - *page 309*.

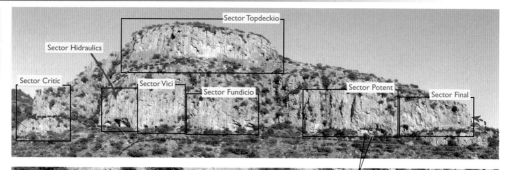

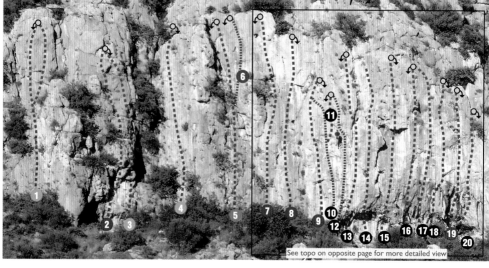

See topo on opposite page for more detailed view

SECTOR POTENT

Well named - those leading 7a to 7b will struggle to find a better wall than this in the whole of the Costa Blanca. The climbing and the rock formations are superb. Tick more than 3 routes here in a day and you will have earned your evening beer. On the left edge of the area are a few milder offerings for those in search of an easier time.

APPROACH - Walk right from where the approach path arrives at the crag for two or three minutes.

① Route 1 . . . . 5+
22m. Start in a bay and climb a sharp grey slab to shrubbery then the left-hand side of the tower above to a tricky last move. A right-hand finish is **6a** and pretty poor.

② Route 2 . . . . 6b+
20m. Climb through the white roofs with difficulty

③ Route 3 5
20m. A short wall then the steep groove on the left accesses the front of the buttress. Up this leftwards on sharp rock to the lower-off used by the previous route.

④ Novatillos . . . . 5+
22m. Start behind the bushes then climb the centre of the slabby grey wall by pleasantly-sustained climbing. Not too steep and well worth seeking out if you climb at the grade.

⑤ Route 5 . . . . 4+
28m. The long groove looks suspect but gives a fine, and long, pitch with an awkward bulge at two thirds height.

⑥ Route 6 . . . . 6c+
28m. The right-hand fork is tough and very unbalanced.

⑦ Maque, Popeye y la Sirla 6b
28m. Start from a big block and climb directly up the wall, then the rib above, into the trees. Slightly artificial in places.

⑧ Dónde hostias putas 6b
24m. The wall immediately to the left of the groove is tricky and gets gradually harder as height is gained. Escapable.

⑨ Joputa . . . . 6b+
22m. From the cave, climb steeply up the wall then cross bulges to get around onto the fine grey side wall. Up the centre of this, on surprising holds, to a thin move right at the very top.

Murcia

Alicante

Benidorm

Calpe

Xaló Valley

Gandia

Gandia

Salem

Aventador

Montesa

Bellús

Barranc de l'Avern

10 Star fort 7b
22m. Up the orange pillar following the left-hand branch to gain the hanging rib on the right of *Joputa*.

11 Tercer ull 7b
22m. Start as for *Star fort* but move right and climb easier rock to a lower-off on the right.

12 Muluk el targuí . . . 7a+
22m. Superb, intricate climbing with a big finish. Start around to the right of the pillar and climb the centre of the bulging wall with a very long crucial reach. Use the lower-off of *Tercer*.

13 Urbália Rurana 7b
24m. Start as for *Muluk* but keep to the right to pass the bulges with great difficulty and reach easier terrain on the grey face above.

To the right the cliff becomes continuously steep, festooned in bizarre tufas and is home to a collection of superb and hard climbs. After prolonged rain many of these tufas weep for a considerable time. Previous Rockfax guides had the names of these routes all jumbled up - sorry about that.

14 Sugar glass. . . . . . . 7b+
22m. The steep wall (conspicuous large ring bolts) has some excellent climbing. Climb past a hole with a bush and then press on up the front of the hanging pillar above.

To the right is a large right-facing flake starting 12m up and right again are two tufa systems about two metres apart, both offering superb climbs.

15 Botoia sakatu 7c
24m. Start steeply up the large black left-hand tufa system and eventually cross a roof high up the crag.

16 Enya . . . . 7b+
24m. The right-hand tufa system. Start at a small cave then trend right up the fine sustained and steep wall above. Steep and fingery climbing throughout. A hidden hole probably reduces the grade to **7b** but no-one finds it on the on-sight.

17 Baila al alba 7b
24m. A fine tufa system and with two roofs for good measure. The 4th bolts are paired. The crux is a bizarre move to get stood on a good ledge just below half height.

18 A la babilla . . . . . . 7a+
24m. Start just left a bush growing from the crag at head height. Climb up passing through a 'love heart' at 8m and then swing onto the trunk. It eases above. Superb!

To the right is the biggest tufa on this part of the cliff, it resembles an elephant wearing a ceremonial head dress - honest!

19 L'os 7a
24m. Start just right of the elephant-like tufa and press on up the pocketed seam and juggy wall above. Superb - again!

20 Dos super carrozas . . . 7a+
18m. Start by pulling over the bulge with difficulty. Continue up the tilted wall to a lower-off situated just below a tree.

21 Don Diego . . . . 7a+
18m. Another great route with a steep start. The climbing is okay if you don't think about it too much. Silver bolts trend left then right. All the pockets are good though some are spaced!

22 Jaque mate. . . . . 7a+
18m. A powerful start and a tricky finish, if you are pumped, which you probably will be. Trend slightly to the right to a large pocket above a tree and then on up the wall. Given 8a in the local topo for some reason!

SECTOR FINAL

The last section is relatively disappointing. The wall tapers and has less of the interesting formations Gandía is famed for. Having said that there are a few interesting wall and slab climbs in the lower grades and this area is usually quieter that the rest of the cliff.
APPROACH - Walk right from where the approach path arrives at the crag for three or four minutes.

❶ Solta el mos . . . . 🔁 ✂ ▭ **7a**
14m. Head slightly left up grey rock, then climb straight up the wall. More glorious pocket pulling.

❷ Galló de la Susanna Alba 🔁 ✂ ▭ **7a**
14m. Trend rightwards up the steep, pocketed rock. Much pumpier than it looks.

❸ Route 3 . . . . 🔁 ▭ **7a+**
14m. The left-hand line out of the cave.

❹ Route 4 . . . . 🔁 ▭ **7a+**
12m. The powerfully steep central line has one especially hard move to leave the glued flake. Poor.

❺ Groceries . . . . ✂ ▭ **7a**
16m. Trend leftwards up scoops and over a bulge. A pumpy pitch which was tough for the old grade of 6c+!

❻ Andreu i Papandreu . . . . 🔁 ▭ **6b+**
24m. Climb the centre of the orange-streaked wall, past a bulge early on, to reach more bulges. Then, depending how tired you are, make a choice - left or more direct (at **7a+**).

❼ A mano . . . . 🔁 ✂ ▭ **7a**
18m. This route runs up the left edge of the protruding buttress, protected by different generations of bolts. It is steep at the start and then continues up a flat wall above to a lower-off by a tree.

The next set of routes is worth seeking out by the lower grade climber. The first runs up a shallow corner.

❽ Bum bum ipaneme . . . . . . 🔁 ▭ **5**
14m. The shallow corner gives a pleasant pitch with a delicate move passing the second bolt and with the roof outflanked by a juggy left to right traverse.

❾ Beato Andrés Hibernon . 🔁 🔁 ▭ **6a**
14m. The wall right of the corner has a tricky rock-over to start. Hard if finished direct. Just about worth a star.

❿ Lleones . . . . 🔁 🔁 ▭ **5**
16m. An engaging grey slab climbed directly above the point where a diagonal break reaches the ground.

To the right are some good sunbathing ledges well away from the crowds that gather at the other end of the cliff.

⓫ Fetiche . . . . 🔁 ▭ **6c**
18m. Climb a scruffy slab up to a bay with a large roof and then power through the left side of this with considerable difficulty.

⓬ Abu Abd Allah Muhammad 🔁 ▭ **6b+**
14m. Star from an area of orange rock by climbing out of a cave and pressing on over the tricky roof.

⓭ Sense goma no conill . . . . 🔁 ▭ **6a+**
14m. Climb pleasant grey rock up the rounded rib in the lower section then the bulging arete above to chains on the lip of the roof (hint: these are most easily reached from the left).

Around the corner are the last two routes.

⓮ 3/4 d'hora . . . . 🔁 ▭ **6a+**
12m. The wall 3m right of the arete passing an unusual 'stuck-on' flake then up a bubbly rib and an overhanging groove.

⓯ Vergonya . . . . 🔁 ▭ **5**
12m. Climb up a scoop then trend left to the lower-offs of the previous climb. The Spanish grade as far as the first clip is mean; you have been warned!

Mike Lea and friends on *Assassi de vampiros* (7a) on Sector Hidraulics at Gandia - *page 309*. The crag offers some really fine short and powerful routes on some superb rock formations with plenty of tufas, pockets and even an elephant's trunk on one section!

SECTOR TOPDECKIO

The Upper Tier at Gandía gets far less traffic than the lower walls but has been described by some as the best sector at Gandía. It is situated above the lower walls and can be a bit cooler than the lower sectors if there is a breeze blowing.
APPROACH - It is best reached by the steep gully left of Sector Hidraulics. This gully is quite steep and requires some scrambling so take care. At the top of the gully head across rightwards to reach the routes. It can also be reached by the awkward gully between Sectors Fundició and Potent and also by a scramble from the far right-hand end.

There are two traditionally-protected routes up the pillar on the left, below a roof. Get them bolted!

① Pep Camarera 5
28m. Climb the fine grey slab to an overlap with orange staining below it. Pull through the overlap on its right side and continue steeply to the cliff top. No fixed gear.

② Golondrinas 5
28m. Another route with no fixed kit passing to the right of a large spike then taking a direct line to the top of the cliff.

Next is a fine grey slab with a diagonal line of overlaps rising across it from left to right. There are five routes here.

③ Eva Luna 6c
18m. Start off some blocks, step left onto the slab and climb it keeping to the right of a ragged crack line. Cross the bulges and press on slightly rightwards to chains below the final overlap.

④ Derribos Arias 6b
22m. Take a parallel line to *Eva Luna* tackling the bulges from right to left via a scoop. Finish at a lower-off above a ledge.

⑤ Sand Bag 7a
20m. Just right of the centre of the slab is a large hole at 4m, climb past this and then up some small tufas to the bulges. Head left with difficulty. The lower-off is on the ledges above.

⑥ Boca de grimpau . . . . . . 6b+
20m. The cop-out version avoids getting sandbagged by passing the bulges on their right-hand side.

⑦ Guatleta 6c
20m. Start up a vegetated ramp then tackle sharp and sustained climbing up steepening rock via a ragged crack splitting the smooth grey wall. The thread is the first runner.

⑧ Queferoset 6c
18m. The left-hand line on the pillar. Start behind a big tree and climb up the rib and press on through an overlap.

⑨ Rosarito 6b
18m. Start up a yellow groove and continue to the same lower-off as *Queferoset*. Just about worth a star.

There is then a gap of about 15m. The most obvious feature of the next section is a spectacular flying fin.

⑩ Esfínter dilatat . . . . 5+
20m. Begin at a cave and follow a line leftwards up pleasantly sustained and perfect rock via one harder move.

⑪ Sarcófago? . . . . . . 7b+
20m. The impressive block overhang is approached direct and then battled with.

⑫ Anatema maranata . . . 7b
20m. The roof right of the fin crossed on its right-hand side.

⑬ Celtas Cortos . . . . 6a+
22m. Just to the right thin dribbling tufas and finger pockets lead to the roof which is skirted at its right edge, with the lower-offs some distance above. A fine sustained pitch.

Murcia
Alicante
Benidorm
Calpe
Xaló Valley
Gandía
Salem
Aventador
Montesa
Bellús
Barranc de l'Avern

There is a gap with 15m of good looking rock. Considering that everything else here has been bolted, this section may soon sprout routes. The next wall is left of a gently bulging section.

⑭ Guirigay . . . . 🔲🔲🔲 **6a**
22m. Start under a right-facing groove in the upper part of the face. Climb through a bulge and up a pocketed white wall to a finish up the groove. Good climbing on sharp holds and no gift.

⑮ Route 15. . . . . 🔲🔲🔲 **6c**
20m. A straightforward lower section up the orange rock leads to hard moves up the shallow hanging groove on the right.

⑯ Tranquilizad . . . . 🔲🔲🔲 **7a**
20m. Climb directly up to the centre of the large grey bulge then trend rightwards through this to the open upper wall.

⑰ Route 17. . . . . 🔲🔲 **6b+**
20m. The right arete of the bulges is sometimes wet.

Right of the bulging area is a large hanging corner.

⑱ Descara . . . . 🔲🔲🔲 **6b+**
22m. The right wall of the deep corner is climbed trending rightwards and crossing the bulge with gusto.

Right again is another section of good rock without routes. The next routes are 10m further right.

⑲ Route 19. . . . . 🔲🔲🔲 **7a**
18m. Climb through the right-hand side of the red caves then make a hard move onto the wall above.

⑳ Boltxevique. . . . . . . 🔲🔲🔲 **6c**
18m. Climb the grey streak in the back of the bay passing right of a tree in a hole and continuing steeply. Impressive.

㉑ Vulcano . . . . 🔲🔲🔲 **6c+**
20m. Climb a slab with a prominent bolt then climb the pocketed wall just left of the tree to a technical finish.

㉒ Route 22. . . . . 🔲🔲🔲 **6c**
20m. The steep rock just right again is excellent.

㉓ Lo que sigui . . . . 🔲🔲 **6a+**
20m. Climb the pocketed wall and follow the diagonal crack then buckets lead through a roof into a scoop in the wall above.

㉔ Mal del tord . . . . 🔲🔲 **5+**
20m. Climb the low angle apron then continue straight up the wall passing to the left of the tree sprouting from the diagonal crack. The lower-offs are located where the angle drops back.

㉕ Kamari . . . . 🔲🔲 **6a**
20m. Climb right of the tree trending right via a central steepening then up easier rock above. Good holds and good climbing.

㉖ Cotó-en-pels . . . . 🔲🔲 **5+**
22m. Climb the steepening slab past a horizontal break and on up the face above. Very pleasant.

㉗ Route 27. . . . . 🔲🔲 **5+**
22m. The final line on the grey wall is pleasant.

EL BOVEDÓN

This cave gives some superb hard routes which should make the Costa Blanca more attractive to climbers operating in the upper grades.

APPROACH - Drive to Gandía. Continue past the turning for the main crag for 900m then turn left (signed 'Bar Carril'). Drive on for another 900m and turn left again. Drive down here for about 450m to the second turning on the left (which is a surfaced road just past a large green gate). Take this and drive to the end of the road. Park leaving room for cars to turn. Follow the path across a slope and back left to reach the crag (5 mins).

① Route 1 4
A scrappy route up the left-hand edge of the crag.

② Route 2 . . . . 6a

③ Route 3 . . . . 7b

④ Route 4 . . . . 6b
A reasonable little rib at far left-hand side of crag.

⑤ Route 5 . . . . 7a+
The 'broccoli' wall leading to steep bulge. A touch friable.

⑥ Route 6 . . . . 7b
The wall leading to a friable bulge.

⑦ Route 7 . . . . 7a+
A hard start up bulging wall then the easier rib above..

⑧ Route 8 . . . . 6c
This is the wall behind trees. Good climbing with a nice finish.

⑨ Route 9 . . . . 6c
Another good grey wall.

The next route starts in a cave where the crag begins to steepen up.

⑩ Route 10 . . . . 8a
Climb a tufa to powerful moves through the roof.

The next line is a project.

⑪ Trasnochando 8b
A direct line through the lower bulge, crossing *Ferrer*....

⑫ Farrear y corbardes 7b
Start up the block to the right and traverse left, then attack the steep wall to find a hard finishing move.

⑬ Perpetúan mobile . 7c
Climb direct to gain a left-facing flake. Leave this leftwards, then head back right to finish.

⑭ Larga, dura y caliente . 8a+
The long wall starting up a block.

⑮ Arcadia 7c
Climb the fine tufa to its top then break out right across the roof.

⑯ La Negra 8b
This may be the route breaking up left from the top of the tufa.

⑰ Abradacabra . . 7c+
At the steepening weave your way through various small caves that lead across the roof. *Photo page 7.*

⑱ Armando. . . . . 8a+
A long diagonal pitch crossing *Abracadabra* and *Arcadia*.

⑲ Route . . . . 8c?
Follow *Armando* but take the right-hand branch.

THE CENTRAL SECTION

The central section of the cave has several different lines which cross each other, there are also a number of projects and a number of link-up routes just to add to the confusion. The information about these routes has not been documented here but, if you find a local, I am sure they will advise. In amongst the routes somewhere is **Mestizaje, 9a**.

An obvious feature on the right-hand side of the main cave is a huge right-facing corner which has a project up it, and an 8b just to its left.

Route 20. . . . . 8b
The line right of the huge corner.

The next line is a project.

Route 21. . . . . . . 7b+
A fine long pitch. High in the grade.

Route 22 . . . . 7a
Start just left of the wall.

Route 23. . . . . 6b
A good long route which crosses the lip of the cave leftwards in a fine position. Start above the wall.

Route 24. . . . . 6b
Start as for the last route but continue direct.

Route 25. . . . . 7a+
The left-hand line of three shorter routes.

Route 26. . . . . 7a
The central line.

Route 27. . . . . 6c
The right-hand line.

CONDITIONS - This cave faces east and only gets a little bit of early morning sunshine. It makes a fine retreat in hot weather when it is shady for most of the day. The enclosed nature also means that it is well-sheltered from any wind and it is doubtful whether any rain has ever really had any impact on the main central routes. There could be seepage in places but even this is very limited.
GOATS - The local farmer has been known to use the cave to keep his goats in. When this is the case it is unbearably smelly.

Murcia · Alicante · Benidorm · Calpe · Xaló Valley · Gandía · Gandía · Salem · Aventador · Montesa · Bellús · Barranc de l'Avern

SALEM

Salem is a friendly crag with plenty of easily accessible and well-bolted climbing, and there is always sun and shade to choose from. The rock is generally good with water-washed limestone, covered in small solution pockets, on the right-hand side, and more featured walls on the left-hand side. As with many recently bolted crags, the gear and lower-offs are all solid and well-positioned though it has to be admitted that the over-bolting actually detracts from the climbing in a couple of sectors.

Many visitors here make the mistake of just climbing on the two sectors near the parking - Frigorific and Estival. Both these offer the odd good routes, especially in the easier grades, however they are not the best climbing here and you will get much more from the crag if you venture up onto the higher side walls and explore the place a bit.

Bolts have a habit of disappearing from the easier routes on Sectors Frigorific and Estival. Some people may find a small rack of wires useful just in case.

Salem has been mainly developed by Domingo Rus, Salvador Guerola, Emilio Perales and Lluis Ortiz. A local guide (with esoteric English!) is available from the bars in Castellon de Rugat.

APPROACH (area map page 305)

Salem lies 25km west of Gandía, just off the road between Castellon de Rugat and Muro de Alcoi. From Calpe the quickest approach to the crag is via Gandía. Follow the approach to Gandía described on page 306, until the first turn off on the ring road. This road is the CV60 signed to 'Albaida'. After 20km turn off towards 'Castellon de Rugat'. Turn of the main road (signed 'Castellon de Rugat/Salem') and drive round Castellon de Rugat, then turn right following the 'Salem' sign. After 2.3km, just before you enter Salem, turn left (signed 'Muro de Alcoy'). Follow a winding road until you see a large green factory (Font Salem water-bottling plant) on the right. The road swings around over a small bridge and you will see Sector Frigorifico just above the road. Park on the dirt track in front of a small substation. This all takes about 1 hour from Calpe.

CONDITIONS

The crags are laid out in a 'V' shape running into a deeply incised valley, sheltered from the wind. Extremes of temperature may be encountered as the crags on the right-hand side of the valley face north west and only get late afternoon sun, whilst the crags opposite face south and bask in the sun until late afternoon.

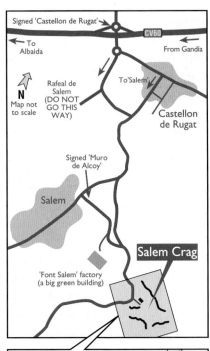

Left margin tabs: Murcia · Alicante · Benidorm · Calpe · Xaló Valley · Gandia · Gandia · Salem · Aventador · Montesa · Bellús · Barranc de l'Avenc

An unknown climber on the great rock of *Anonimo* (6c) on Sector Sol i Bon Temps at Salem - *page 326*. The shot shows that the fingery and technical symbols are deserved.

Lots of sun | Roadside | Sheltered

Sector Sol y Bon Temps

To the other south side Sectors

Access to Sector Estival

SECTOR ESTIVAL
Behind the pumping station is this small scruffy cliff with its set of mediocre, but popular, routes. Most of the routes start from ledges on the right, those on the left are reached by scrambling awkwardly around the right-hand side of the fence, please handle the fence with care.
CONDITIONS - A well-sheltered south-facing sun-trap.

1 Pal o'mine 4
16m. The rib on the far left is a bit shrubby.

2 Pal. 4
16m. The face just to the right also needs a brush-up.

3 Pal Santete 5
20m. The rib on the left then the face and a short tricky groove.

4 Pal Toni 6a
10m. From the end of the ramp the side wall is quite tough.

5 Acces denegat 6a
10m. From ledges climb the flat wall finishing over the bulge.

6 Farael tan guarro . . . . 6a+
12m. Across the roof on sharp holds.

7 R2 dedos . . . . 3+
12m. Climb a short steep rib which soon eases.

8 C3 pedos . . . . 4+
10m. Right of a bush climb a juggy crack and the slab above.

9 Boulder Rock 6c
10m. A nasty little number right of the ground-level cave.

10 Xeroki 4
14m. Climb a tricky 'crozzly' head-height crack, then the rib.

11 U2 . . . . 4+
14m. The clean rib has a steep start. It is one of the best here.

12 Mosca taca 4
16m. From the bay, step right and climb the grey bubbly rock.

13 Passeig dominical . . . . . . 3+
16m. Climb the low-angled gully/groove directly.

14 La brixa de Salem . . . . . . 4+
12m. Climb past a big useful hole and trend right at the top.

15 Negra neusl els set gigantes . . 4
12m. Climb past cleaned ledges and up the blunt rib above.

16 Naxcuda en lliure 3
12m. Right of the bushes climb the low angled rib.

SECTOR FRIGORIFIC

17 El kiki 6c
12m. Tricky moves past 3 bolts. Harder than it looks!

18 El gro 6b
12m. A slightly easier version of *El Kiki* on poor pockets.

19 Alaxuplala 6a
14m. Slink right past the 3rd bolt and trend right to finish.

20 Suc d'avespa 5
14m. Listed on the local topo but may not have its own bolts.

21 Xupla polen 5
14m. Start at a vague '14' and head up the scoopy corner.

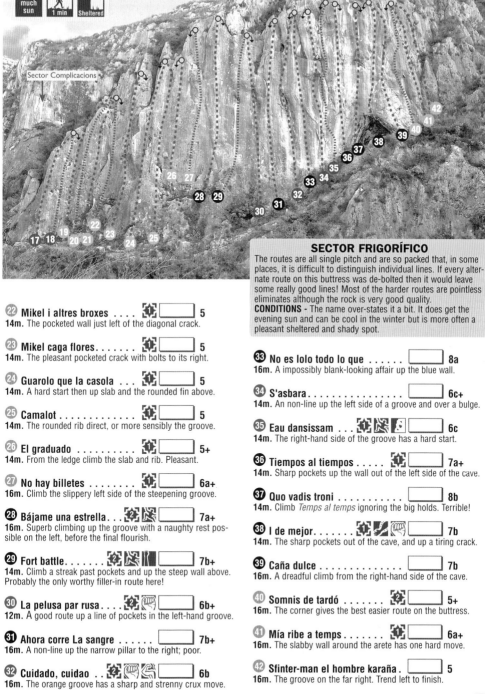

Sector Complicacions

Murcia
Alicante
Benidorm
Calpe
Xaló Valley
Gandia
Gandia
Salem
Aventador
Montesa
Bellús
Barranc de l'Avern

㉒ **Mikel i altres broxes** . . . . 🔧⬜ 5
14m. The pocketed wall just left of the diagonal crack.

㉓ **Mikel caga flores** . . . . . . 🔧⬜ 5
14m. The pleasant pocketed crack with bolts to its right.

㉔ **Guarolo que la casola** . . . 🔧⬜ 5
14m. A hard start then up slab and the rounded fin above.

㉕ **Camalot** . . . . 🔧⬜ 5
14m. The rounded rib direct, or more sensibly the groove.

㉖ **El graduado** . . . . 🔧⬜ 5+
14m. From the ledge climb the slab and rib. Pleasant.

㉗ **No hay billetes** . . . . 🔧⬜ 6a+
16m. Climb the slippery left side of the steepening groove.

㉘ **Bájame una estrella** . . . 🔧🏞⬜ 7a+
16m. Superb climbing up the groove with a naughty rest possible on the left, before the final flourish.

㉙ **Fort battle** . . . . . . 🔧🏞🎿⬜ 7b+
14m. Climb a streak past pockets and up the steep wall above. Probably the only worthy filler-in route here!

㉚ **La pelusa par rusa** . . . 🔧🎒⬜ 6b+
12m. A good route up a line of pockets in the left-hand groove.

㉛ **Ahora corre La sangre** . . . . . . ⬜ 7b+
16m. A non-line up the narrow pillar to the right; poor.

㉜ **Cuidado, cuidao** . . 🔧🎒📿⬜ 6b
16m. The orange groove has a sharp and strenny crux move.

SECTOR FRIGORÍFICO
The routes are all single pitch and are so packed that, in some places, it is difficult to distinguish individual lines. If every alternate route on this buttress was de-bolted then it would leave some really good lines! Most of the harder routes are pointless eliminates although the rock is very good quality.
CONDITIONS - The name over-states it a bit. It does get the evening sun and can be cool in the winter but is more often a pleasant sheltered and shady spot.

㉝ **No es lolo todo lo que** . . . . . . ⬜ 8a
16m. A impossibly blank-looking affair up the blue wall.

㉞ **S'asbara** . . . . ⬜ 6c+
14m. An non-line up the left side of a groove and over a bulge.

㉟ **Eau dansissam** . . . 🔧🏞🧗⬜ 6c
14m. The right-hand side of the groove has a hard start.

㊱ **Tiempos al tiempos** . . . . . 🔧⬜ 7a+
14m. Sharp pockets up the wall out of the left side of the cave.

㊲ **Quo vadis troni** . . . . ⬜ 8b
14m. Climb *Temps al temps* ignoring the big holds. Terrible!

㊳ **I de mejor** . . . . . . 🔧🔧🎒⬜ 7b
14m. The sharp pockets out of the cave, and up a tiring crack.

㊴ **Caña dulce** . . . . ⬜ 7b
16m. A dreadful climb from the right-hand side of the cave.

㊵ **Somnis de tardó** . . . . 🔧⬜ 5+
16m. The corner gives the best easier route on the buttress.

㊶ **Mía ribe a temps** . . . . 🔧⬜ 6a+
16m. The slabby wall around the arete has one hard move.

㊷ **Sfinter-man el hombre karaña** . ⬜ 5
16m. The groove on the far right. Trend left to finish.

SOL I BON TEMPS

A couple of open sunny walls high on the hillside above Sector Estival. With good rock and lots of well-bolted routes packed closely together, only the steep walk-in is preventing it from being a top convenience crag.

APPROACH - Walk past Sector Estival then zig-zag steeply up the hillside, over scree, to reach the base of the Sector. Continue left for the good stuff.

CONDITIONS - The wall gets lots of sun and is reasonably well-sheltered. It dries quickly after rain and doesn't seep.

❶ El lobo veloz . . . . ☐ 6a+
14m. A slight line up the grey slab left of a groove.

❷ Samurai . . . . ☐ 6b
14m. Climb the rib left of the groove, over a couple of bulges, then up the slab above. Hard for the grade.

❸ A tot ostia . . . . ☐ 6a+
24m. The shallow groove gives a good pitch with a low crux.

❹ Oferta explosiva . . . . ☐ 6b
24m. Parallel the groove up a crinkly wall (hard) then pass a hole and a small roof, before trending left to the previous climb.

❺ Super nova . . . . ☐ 6b
24m. From a small flowstone pillar at foot level, climb up the intricate wall, past white rock, before trending left more easily.

❻ Chinahauk . . . . . . ☐ 7a
22m. Start right of a hole at ground level and climb past some white rock - sharp and thin. It is steep but easier above.

❼ Paraboles lejanos . ☐ 7a
22m. From just left of a small vertical 'seam' at ground level, climb up a white streak and the rib above. Another technical route on little edges.

❽ Siniestro total . . . . . . ☐ 6c
28m. Start at some low-relief tufas and climb the bulging wall (scary clip) and sustained grey scoop above. Excellent.

❾ Tirante de roca . . . . . ☐ 6b+
28m. Just left of the cave, juggy climbing (sharp!) leads up the wall through a hole and then the scoop above.

❿ Seguix l'animal . . . ☐ 6b+
28m. Starting on the left edge of the cave is another cracker passing a diagonal cave/hole at one third height.

⓫ Azul marcia ilusión ☐ 7a
28m. Climb steeply out of the right side of the cave, following the gold bolts, until it is possible to join *Seguix* or *Anonimo*.

⓬ Anónimo . . . . ☐ 6c
28m. Follow the line of silver bolts up the steep white streak. *Photo page 323.*

⓭ Reposa celestial . . . . . ☐ 6c
28m. Start at a tufa with a prominent line of silver bolts and climb rightwards up the red streak past two holes.

⓮ La bola del nas . . . ☐ 7b
28m. From the small cave climb right and follow the pocketed seam past a deep horizontal slot. The third clip is desperate.

⓯ Reunión tumultuoso . . . ☐ 6b
30m. To the right of the cave, climb orange pocketed rock and a vague crack to and through a bulge, then up a sharp grey rib.

⓰ Las mollas de riglo . . . . . ☐ 6a
30m. A poor start and better finish. A grey rib leads into a grotty cave, escape upwards to find climbing on quality rock.

⓱ Vino Fino . . . . ☐ 7a+
30m. A right-hand finish also has the same grotty approach.

Murcia · Alicante · Benidorm · Calpe · Xaló Valley · Gandia · Gandia · Salem · Avenlador · Montesa · Bellús · Barranc de l'Avenc

The next routes are 10m further right, past a large bush.

⑱ Plan de choque . . . . . . 🔲🔲 ▭ 6b+
32m. Climb the floral rib between bushes. Trend left passing a white tufa and then up the left-hand bolt line in the head wall.

⑲ Paquete e medidas . . . 🔲🔲 ▭ 6c+
32m. A right-hand finish to *Plan a choque* up the sharp rib.

⑳ Que se mueran los feos 🔲🔲 ▭ 6c
32m. Right of the bush on the lower rib, climb steeply then pass a small tree growing out of a hole in the head wall.

The next three routes all share the same unsavoury start.

㉑ Tarugo . . . . 🔲 ▭ 6b+
30m. Climb the rib right of a large spiky palm plant, then left up a slab. Finish up the bulges on the left side of a large scoop.

㉒ Mabel's . . . . 🔲 ▭ 6a
30m. Climb the rib to reach the smart scoop then continue in the same direction passing tufas. Hard for the grade.

㉓ El cedro torre . . . . 🔲 ▭ 5+
30m. Start as for *Mabel's* but then move right and climb the right edge of the scoop.

㉔ El costilla roca . . . . 🔲 ▭ 5
26m. The sharp rib and better slab above. Beware the flake!

Down hill is a smaller, slightly scrappy section split by a horizontal roof. The next routes start from the ledge on the left.

㉕ Tovarich . . . . ▭ 6c+
14m. Climb out of the right side of a cave past three small 'stal' pillars and other flowstone features to a lower-off below a roof.

㉖ Tulukremlin . . . . ▭ 6c
14m. Start at a second small cave (at ground level) and climb straight up the centre of the wall passing a heavily 'adulterated' block to reach the same lower-off.

㉗ Con ibérica ya habrás volado . ▭ 5
14m. Start just left of a white scar and climb the rib before stepping left to use the lower-off of the previous climbs.

㉘ Pelut I pelat . . . . ▭ 6b
16m. Climb the wall to the right of the ledge, then take the left side of the shallow groove past a deep hole.

㉙ Síndrome de soledad . . 🔲🔲 ▭ 7a+
30m. Start below a hole at head-height and climb to the left side of the flat roof. Pull over it and continue up the rib above. The longest and best route on this sector (by quite a margin!).

㉚ Un montón de ostias . . . . 🔲 ▭ 7a+
16m. Climb the centre of the wall between the orange and blue rock to a lower-off away to the right beyond the roof.

㉛ Sarvachof . . . . 🔲 ▭ 6c
14m. Climb the rib on the right where the cliff starts to swing round direct to the lower-off to the right of the roof.

㉜ Culo flojo . . . . 🔲 ▭ 6a+
14m. The grey wall left of an easy groove gives a tricky pitch.

㉝ Esplonet . . . . 🔲 ▭ 4
26m. 30m to the right is this pleasant easy-angled rib which goes on - and on!

Murcia
Alicante
Benidorm
Calpe
Xaló Valley
Gandía
Gandía
Salem
Aventador
Montesa
Bellús
Barranc de l'Avem

SECTOR CHICA FÁCIL

The final section of cliff on the sunny side of the valley, is a big wall undercut at its base by a couple of caves. It is not as vegetated as it first appears and offers some fine two pitch routes, on good rock. If you climb these routes with a single 50m rope, it will take two abseils to descend. The locals call it Sol I Bontemps Barranc and have adopted the US idea of names for each individual pitch - so there are more ticks to be had!

APPROACH - Walk past Sector Estival and follow an indistinct path which contours across the hillside. It is also possible to drop down the hillside from Sector Sol I Bon Temps - rough!

CONDITIONS - Well sheltered and gets plenty of sun although it drops into the shade earlier than the other buttresses on this side of the gorge. It dries quickly and has little seepage.

1 Astisores perilloses 6a
20m. Climb the left rib of the cave and the wall above trending right to ledges and a belay (or lower-off!).

2 Dolche vitta . . . . . 5+
18m. Continue up the left side of the upper wall and over a small bulge to reach the chains.

3 Atmosfera. 7b
20m. Power through the centre of the large roof with difficulty then climb the wall to reach the same belay as above.

4 Bultaco entre las piernas 6a
18m. Continue up the centre of the wall above on excellent rock to reach a flake-crack, then trend left to join *Dolcha vitta*.

5 Honeymoon . . . . 6b+
20m. Climb the flake-crack that runs through the right-hand side of the roof to reach the central ledge.

6 Pasodobles. . . . . 6b+
20m. Climb the upper wall, trending slightly right, to a lower-off at the top of the cliff. With *Honeymoon*, this is a 3 star combo.

7 La fuerza del viento . . . . . **6a+**
24m. Climb left of a hole to a bushy break then straight up the centre of the slab on pockets to a lower-off. Or finish up -

8 Despedida de soltero **6b**
1) 6a, 24m. Oddly, this one has two pitches. Start left of a yellow corner then head straight up the rib above to a belay.
2) 6b, 22m. Continue up the bulging scoopy wall and the narrow tower above the belay to get the full tick.

9 Chica fácil **6a**
24m. Start just left of the tree and climb the slightly-loose yellow corner, a steep wall and then easier-angled better rock.

10 Es tinto basic **6c**
18m. It's a pity the extension pitch up the tower is harder.

11 Chapa charcos . . . . **6a+**
20m. Pull onto the wall left of the cave, step left and climb direct before moving back right to the lower-off.

12 Malas posturas **6a**
20m. Another looping pitch sneaking around the roof above.

13 Caza de brujas . . . **6b+**
20m. The left-hand side of the cave and shallow groove above.

14 La prolongacion **6a**
20m. Continue up the wall and power the roof to the belay.

15 El gordo de mi mesota . **6c+**
20m. Straight out of the centre of the cave and up the pocketed orange streak - strenuous.

16 Solo para aboyados **6c**
20m. Climb grey rock steeply then trend right just below easy ground to a belay on the right below the overhangs.

17 Mal de Cuerpo . . . . **6a+**
24m. Start from the belay above the last route. A mega pitch up the slanting groove then stepping right and climbing the fine exposed tower in a dramatic position.

18 Estreno duro **6b**
20m. The steep pocketed orange streak at right-hand side of the cave then rightwards just below easy ground.

19 No me toques rompo **6a**
20m. Straight up the grey rib that is directly under the belay.

20 No le toques la oreja . . **6b**
20m. The last route on the lower wall jigs right then left.

21 El demoño dojo . . . . **6b+**
30m. Start up *El principe* but move left onto the thin wall.

22 El principo del fin . . . . . . **5+**
30m. The rambling right edge of the buttress leads to a good finish up on the fin.

SECTOR INICIACIO

23 Langoliers **4**
14m. Climb the rib on the left then traverse above the vegetation to the lower-off on the right.

24 Gorro Andino **4**
12m. Straight up the steep lower wall then the grey slab above.

25 Solo con receta medica **4**
14m. Weave left then right to pass the bushes.

26 Semen retentum **5**
14m. Climb past a small overhang then trend right sticking to the cleaner rock.

27 Condenado a muerte **4**
14m. Pull over an overlap then trend right to the clean rib.

28 Tapa el forat **4**
14m. Climb the rib on the far right to ledges then trend left to reach the lower-off.

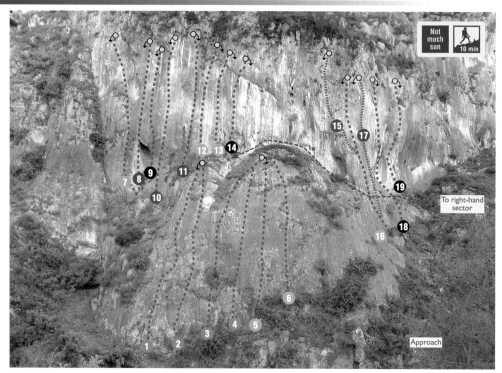

SECTOR COMPLICACIÓNS

This long and complex crag runs up the north-facing hillside. It consists of compact limestone covered in small pockets with rounded hollows and caves: the quality rock is a bit spread around. The base of the crag slopes making gearing up awkward and the lack of sun means the place can be freezing - or a welcome shady spot in hot weather.
APPROACH - Go past the end of Sector Frigorific and follow the path along the terraces up then up the hillside.
CONDITIONS - Shady, cool (and damp) or absolutely freezing depending on what time of year it is. Sheltered.

The first routes are on the slabby buttress. These are pleasant enough though after rain many of the pockets sprout greenery.

① Egipt Air . . . . 4+
24m. Start just left of the lowest point of the slab and go direct.

② Istambul . . . . 4+
24m. Climb left and right, then straight up the broad rib.

③ Peret i marieta . . . . 4+
20m. A wall leads through greenery to a ledge. Finish direct.

④ Sports Aitana . . . . 4+
20m. Straight up the rib from the vegetated ledges.

⑤ Borrul, Borrul 5
20m. From the right end of a ledge, climb the slab direct.

⑥ Si te Molla 5
20m. The climbing is okay but the approach is a bit grim!

The rest of the routes are on the walls above the slab. Approach by a devious scramble round, or one of the slab routes.

⑦ Jesuita bim bam . . . . 6a+
20m. Climb the rib to a ledge, then the scoops, trending left.

⑧ Estoy frito tres delicias . . . 6b+
18m. Fine climbing up the face just left of the tall cave.

⑨ Tbo negro 7b
18m. Desperately blank climbing up the wall above the cave.

⑩ No molla portar . . . . 6b+
18m. The smooth grey wall gives a good pitch on pockets.

The next four routes start on the ledge above the lower slab.

⑪ Chimpangali . . . . . 6b+
16m. The pocketed crack-line left of a rounded pillar

⑫ Viuda negra 6a
14m. The rounded pillar direct on good pockets.

⑬ Expolon 6a
12m. The orange streak above the cave - short and steep.

⑭ Semilla negra . . . . 🔲🔲 ⬜ **7a+**
12m. The steep bulge and grey wall just to the right of the cave.

⑮ Thu . . . . 🔲 ⬜ **7a**
26m. Start up the pillar but break left and side-step the wall.

⑯ Calvorotas . . . . 🔲 ⬜ **6a**
24m. A long route up the left edge of the hour-glass pillar.

⑰ Monomakina . . . . 🔲🔲 ⬜ **6c**
26m. The right-hand side of the pillar is entertaining.

⑱ Chupe pachá . . . . . 🔲🔲🔲 ⬜ **7a+**
22m. An excellent problem up the left side of the scoop.

⑲ Baja chocho . . . . 🔲 ⬜ **(7b)**
20m. The back of the scoop looks impossible to me.

⑳ Droga dura . . . 🔲🔲🔲🔲 ⬜ **7c**
18m. The pillar has more holds than the 7b!

㉑ Amiches . . . . 🔲🔲🔲 ⬜ **6a+**
26m. A stretch over the bulge gains the milder head wall.

㉒ Lluvia ácida . . . . . 🔲🔲🔲 ⬜ **7a**
18m. Climb through a bulge and up the fine grey slab beyond.

㉓ Marka pasos . . . . 🔲🔲🔲 ⬜ **7b**
18m. A huge undercut move gains vertical rock above.

㉔ Tu et punxes tio . . . . . . 🔲🔲 ⬜ **6c+**
16m. The clean, pocketed wall just left of the hole.

㉕ Pelas pa las pilas . 🔲🔲🔲🔲 ⬜ **7c+**
20m. A rather fearsome blank-looking wall above the hole.

Next are two projects Melodia de seduccion and Temblores.

㉖ Tómate un respiro . . . . . 🔲 ⬜ **(7b+)**
18m. The route up steep rock just left of the bulging roof was given 7a in the local topo - it may have lost holds.

㉗ Pedromina piruleta 🔲🔲🔲 ⬜ **7b**
14m. Spectacular moves on massive pockets over the roof.

㉘ El silencio . . . . . . 🔲🔲🔲 ⬜ **7c**
14m. A harder version of the last route. Powerful!

㉙ Con agua me cloroformo . 🔲 ⬜ **6b**
20m. Good climbing just right of the bulging roof.

㉚ Celtas cortos . . . . 🔲 ⬜ **6c**
22m. Branch right and climb the steep rock then a smooth wall.

㉛ Tírate al ruedo . . . . 🔲 ⬜ **6b+**
20m. The pillar leads to the open face above.

㉜ Les granotes minja . . . . ⬜ **6b+**
22m. The same start but move right to steeper rock.

㉝ Sed de libertad . . . . ⬜ **6a**
20m. The slab left of a flying arete.

Up around the corner to the right is a small cave.

㉞ Altamira . . . . 🔲🔲 ⬜ **7b**
16m. The left-hand end of the cave. A bit short.

㉟ Mierda en los dedos . . . . 🔲 ⬜ **7a**
14m. The right-hand end of the cave, up a short pillar.

㊱ Diedrosuro . . . . ⬜ **5+**
12m. Up the groove past three bolts.

㊲ Nicho para un bicho . . . . ⬜ **7a**
12m. Up the bulging arete to a 'middle-of-nowhere' lower-off.

Murcia · Alicante · Benidorm · Calpe · Xaló Valley · Gandia · Gandia · Salem · Aventador · Montesa · Beltús · Barranc de l'Avern

AVENTADOR

Aventador consists of a long wall of well-pocketed compact rock, with some good slabby face climbing and the odd steeper route, especially towards the left-hand end. The crag is situated in a secluded, sunny position and the river below provides swimming when it's hot. The lines are all pretty parallel, hence you can get the *"done one, done 'em all"* feeling with some of the routes however if you sample the different sectors there is plenty to keep you interested for a few visits. On certain sections the routes tend to get a bit mixed up with each other since there aren't many features and there are lots of bolts. It isn't uncommon to find yourself straying onto another route while climbing upwards in a straight line. It is also worth noting that the rock is very sharp and can take its toll on your finger tips especially if you try and cram a lot of routes into the day. On the plus side, many of the climbs feature fine long pitches and plenty of good climbing.

This historic crag was one of the first places in Spain to be developed for sport climbing in the early 1980s. This was principally the work of Salvador Guerola and Emilio Perales and their friends.

CONDITIONS

The crag faces south west, and receives the sun from mid-morning onwards. In summer it will be too hot for most but it is fine for the rest of the year. It is exposed to wind and there is not much shelter at the crag, though a few of the bigger bushes/smaller trees offer shade from the sun. The place is often infested with small (non-biting) flies in the spring - this may be associated with the nearness of the river.

APPROACH (area map page 305)

From the Calpe/Benidorm area the best approach is via Gandía. Follow the approach to Gandía (page 306) until the first turn off on the ring road. This road is the CV60 signed to 'Albaida'. After 12km, turn off this road towards Xàtiva on the CV610. After 18km always following Xàtiva signs is the town of Genovés. Continue towards Xàtiva, on the dual carriageway, and at the second roundabout double back and then take a right turn. Follow this road for 1.9km and turn left immediately after crossing the railway line, and after passing the fancy 'Alboy' sign. 400m further on is a T-junction; turn left and follow the road for a further 1.4km and park at a flat terrace on the right, just before the track winds uphill. From here walk up the track and break out rightwards to the crag which is now obvious on the hillside ahead.

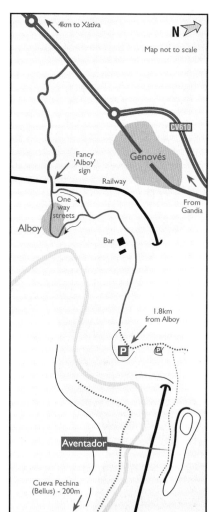

Chris Craggs on Pitch 1 of *Carbono 14* (5+) on Sector Caruso at Aventador - *page 335.*
There are many excellent two pitch climbs on this section of the cliff. Photo: Sherri Davy

SECTOR ALTO BRONX

At the left-hand end of the crag is a prominent steep cave. The first routes are located to the left of the cave. These routes have the attraction of staying in the shade a lot longer than the rest of the cliff, though they are mostly pretty tough although it is a great place for 6b+ leaders!

There are two old routes to the left. The first described routes start just left of a bush.

1 Placa cósmica . . . . 🔲 **6b+**
24m. A decent wall climb; the name is painted on the rock.

2 Spectrum . . . . 🔲 **6b**
1) **6b, 24m.** The same start as above but break out right.
2) **6a+, 14m.** The upper face on the right.

3 Fermín a pólito . . . . . . 🔲 **6b+**
1) **6b+, 20m.** Start immediately to the right of the bush and climb the bubbly wall, trending slightly leftwards.
2) **5, 20m.** Climbs slightly left and then straight up the wall to the ledge at the top.

4 Muertas est. . . . . 🔲 **6b+**
1) **6b+, 20m.** Follow the second bolt ladder to the right of the bush until it bears away to the right to a belay.
2) **5+, 22m.** Climb directly up the wall behind, keeping left of the shrubby groove, to ledges near the cliff top.

5 Falsos brutales . . . . . . 🔲 **6b+**
22m. Climb directly via a series of pale tufas and the occasional good pocket.

6 Panini di butifarras . . . 🔲 **6b+**
1) **6b, 26m.** Climb the wall directly then trend right (crossing the next route) to reach the belay above *Pedos de colores*.
2) **6b+, 18m.** Climb the steep wall trending right to pass a horizontal break then continue up the fine slab to the top.

7 Alterofilia copenguens . . . 🔲 **6b+**
1) **6b+, 24m.** From the left rib of the cave climb steeply, passing deep pockets, then trend left to a belay in a hollow.
2) **6b, 20m.** Head up the bulging rib on the right to a break and then trend right more easily to a lower-off/belay.

8 Pedos de colores . . . . . 🔲 **6c+**
22m. A good pitch up large holds and steep rock following the black streak. The crux is high up, just before the belay.

To the right is a steep cave which gives the hardest routes at Aventador. The first two lines are an old aid route Alto Bronx, and a forgotten old project.

9 Dale caña al mono. 🔲 **7b**
22m. Superb! The steep central line is marginally easier than it looks, with a crimpy slab to finish.

10 La reina de Africa . 🔲 **7c+**
20m. The fierce bulging wall left of a tufa starting at the name. The start is scary, then it's reachy, then the crimps go for miles.

11 Mayeutica. . . . 🔲 **7c**
20m. The wicked curving rib that forms the edge of the cave.

SECTOR CARUSO

12 Mesclaillos guerola . . . . . 🔲 **6b**
40m. A long direct line best split at a belay on *Antropía Afonica*.

13 Antropía afonica . . . . . 🔲 **6a+**
1) **6a+, 30m.** Start at the name and climb around the edge of the cave, passing left of the red tufa and ignoring the first belay in favour of a higher one at the right end of a good ledge.
2) **6a, 20m.** Trend left to enter the prominent right slanting corner that runs all the way to the cliff top.

14 Variation C . . . . 🔲 **6b**
22m. An upper pitch right of the corner of *Carbono 14*.

15 Trembolando estoy. . . . 🔲 **6b**
1) **6b, 24m.** A good direct line up the large red tufa and on directly up superb pocketed rock to the belay at the left end of the midway ledge system.
2) **6b, 16m.** Finish straight up the wall above the stance.

16 Astolfo hinkel . . . . 🔲 **6c**
1) **6a+, 30m.** Start behind the tree and climb up right of the prominent orange tufa then trend left below the left-hand lower-off on the ledge to eventually reach a belay below and left of the final groove of *Carbono 14*.
2) **6c 14m.** A hard finish up the smooth rib up and left from the stance or attempt the easier right-hand finish *Aisenkouen*.

⑰ Aisenkouen . . . . 🔧⬜ **6b**
14m. A slightly easier right-hand finish to *Astolfo*.

⑱ Karuso . . . . 🔧💗⬜ **7a**
1) 6a, 22m. An excellent pitch with a fluttery crux.
2) 7a, 20m. The fierce pocketed wall behind the stance is hard!

⑲ Extrema unción . . . 🔧2🪝🗺️⬜ **7a**
20m. A right-hand finish from the cable stance.

⑳ Carbono 14 . . . . 🔧3⬜ **6a**
1) 5+, 22m. Climb the steepening slab passing a bulge with a small patch of orange rock in it to either wire cable belay.
2) 6a, 22m. Traverse left and loop out left and then back right to enter and finish up the yellow right-slanting corner.
Photo page 333.

The next routes are very long single pitches from which you can't lower off without a 70m rope.

㉑ Vomitara óptica . . . . . . 🔧🪝🗺️⬜ **6c+**
34m. Start at the scratched name to the right of a white broken flake. Climb up the smooth wall between two read streaks and then rightwards to the lower-off under the bulges.

㉒ Vampiro . . . . 🔧💧🪝⬜ **7a**
34m. The left-hand finish to *Vomitera*.

SECTOR CARUSO

To the right of the cave is a tall smooth wall with some long 2 pitch routes. The routes here follow very complex lines and there are a number of direct variations which confuse matters. Also, some of the easier pitches are only sparsely bolted which makes picking the line out hard. Some of the names painted at the base, the prominent cable-belay shared by several routes and the finishing corner of *Carbono 14* are reliable features.

㉓ Asgarramenta Lumbar . . . 🔧⬜ **6c+**
34m. Starting at the vague name of the next route this is the left-hand finish leading to the *Vomitera* belay.

㉔ Astrokangrena bucólica . . 🔧⬜ **6b**
34m. Above the name, to an easier right-hand finish.

㉕ Aci em pegaras . . . . 🔧⬜ **6b**
30m. Climb the slab (new bolts) and a solitary tufa and then the wall rightwards.

㉖ Cristal pardo . . . . ⬜ **6b+**
30m. Trend left past a white flake on a ledge then up steeper rock. It shares its middle section with the previous route.

㉗ Calla pixorro . . . . ⬜ **6b**
32m. Start up a left slanting ramp behind a tree and climb poor rock passing the right edge of a ledge to better stuff above.

SECTOR MILI

The crag now turns slabby and the routes become less impressive, although there are some worthwhile easier challenges. The routes on the left all suffer from poor lower sections, though those on the right are better. A 60m rope is needed to lower-off most of these.

①　Trimomia . . . . 　6a+
30m. Start up *Mili* but continue up the left-hand line above where Mili heads off rightwards.

②　Guíeles marxoses . . . . . . 　6a+
30m. The right-hand line above the start of *Mili*.

③　Mili . . . . 　4+
A decent easy route with a poor 1st pitch but a better 2nd.
1) 4, 22m. Start behind the tree and climb the shrubby slab to a horizontal break. Follow this rightwards and climb a short corner to a good stance and variety of belays on top of a flake.
2) 4+ 20m. Step off the right end of the ledge and climb the fine slab on surprising holds diagonally rightwards before finishing up the left-facing flake crack.

④　Pepsiman . . . . 　6a
30m. Climb straight up the wall keeping right of the shrubbery, passing pegs and bolts to a possible stance. Take the left-hand line of fixed gear to a substantial chain.

⑤　Albomina . . . . 　5+
30m. A right-hand variation to the upper pitch of *Pepsiman*.

⑥　Cefalograma . . . . 　5+
28m. Start between the two left-hand bushes and trend leftwards to climb a broken white flake (possible stance on the left) before climbing the wall directly above.

⑦　Coconuts . . . . 　6a
32m. Start between the two bushes and climb the floral slab slightly leftwards passing a bulge at 10m and then on directly up the grey slab to a steeper finish.

⑧　Jorge negrete . . . . 　6a
32m. Start at the left side of the gap in the trees and trend left up the slab passing a horizontal break and on up clean white rock. Pass left of a bush and pull over a small overlap to finish just left of the corner that forms the exit for *Mili*.

⑨　OV . . . . 　6a+
30m. Climb the slab to the white triangular flake with a tree growing out of its left side. Step left and climb past a hole then head straight up the wall via a bubbly streak and pull over an overlap near the top of the face.

⑩　Coneiximent de mosquit . . . . . 　6b
30m. Start as for *OV* to the flake then climb straight up the bulging wall above to the lower-off.

⑪　Luis mariano . . . . 　6a+
30m. Start just right of the tree and climb leftwards up the lower slabs to a prominent white triangular flake halfway up the cliff. Step back right and continue directly up the wall above.

⑫　Collo que guai . . . . 　6a+
30m. Climb leftwards up the lower slab to reach diagonal ledges then head up the steeper wall above (crux) rightwards before climbing behind a bush and out right to the lower-offs.

⑲ Pepe Carvallo . . . . 🔲 **6a**
26m. Start at a 45° left-slanting flake and climb to the large vertical cave/slot two thirds of the way up the cliff. Up this then through the roof directly above.

⑳ Jerónimo . . . . 🔲 **6a**
26m. Start just left of an orange-tipped flake where the first bolt is visible above a short white streak. Head straight up the wall past a couple of ledges and passing under a bush at 20m. Finish as for the previous route.

㉑ Que asco que tusca . . . . 🔲 **6b**
26m. Begin at an small orange-tipped flake two metres off the ground. Climb straight up the wall passing to the left of bushes at 12m and climbing the final bulges via a ragged crack

㉒ Patatas de cargó . . . . 🔲 **6b**
26m. Start at a scratched arrow and just right of a bush 2m up the cliff. Climb straight up the wall and then pull through roof at large holes to reach the lower-off.

㉓ Cacau i tramas . . . 🔲 **6b**
26m. Start off a little flat ledge, the first bolt is above a diagonal crack and right of a large perched flake. Climb straight up pale streaks situated directly below the lower-off, then loop left and right to get through the overhangs as for the previous climb.

㉔ Pase milions . . . . 🔲 **6b+**
24m. Start at a 4m long, left-slanting crack. 'PM' is scratched on the rock. Climb the wall and cross the roof at a series of deep holes. Has a hard crux move and has been rebolted.

㉕ Blackmaster . . . . . 🔲 **6c+**
24m. Start at the hammered bits of lead and climb leftwards to, and then up, the hanging left arete of the corner of *Afrodita*.

㉖ Afrodita . . . . 🔲 **5+**
26m. Start at the name and climb up into the base of the prominent hanging corner high above. Bridge up, passing a huge perched flake early on, to reach a lower-off on the right.

㉗ Hermafordita . . . . 🔲 **6b**
26m. Start left of the square block and climb straight up the slab, passing left of the bushes. Finish up the right wall of the corner passing the right edge of a huge perched flake.

㉘ BA . . . . 🔲 **5**
22m. Start up the prominent flake and climb to tricky moves out left. Continue past a ledge (big ring peg - old stance) to a finish up the juggy right arete of the smooth wall.

㉙ Zapalastro . . . . 🔲 **6c**
22m. Start at the rounded rib to the left of a flake crack, right behind the square block. There is vague 'Z' is scratched on the rock. Climb the tough rib and pass to the right of the bushes. Finish leftwards across the final wall.

⑬ Mesinfoteles . . . . 🔲 **6a**
30m. Climb left of the large hole at 15m and pass the final overlap at the distinct yellow patch with difficulty.

⑭ Amadeus . . . . 🔲 **6a**
30m. Climb the shrubby slab and then the left arete of the prominent right-facing groove, before trending left up the wall to pull through the overlap just to the right of a yellow patch.

⑮ Pegamé en to el medio 🔲 **6a+**
30m. Climb past a tufa into the deep right-facing groove and bridge up this with increasing difficulty, exit right and continue on up the wall above. Beware a large loose block near the top.

⑯ Ala anem . . . . 🔲 **6b**
30m. Start right of a 2m high, grey tufa 'slug' with a hole in its top and climb up past the left side of a small overlap. Continue to the left of the red writing half way up the wall.

⑰ Has Cobrat? . . . . 🔲 **6b**
28m. Climb a rounded rib (peg) to ledges, where there is some large red writing, and continue directly to a lower-off hanging over the top of the cliff. Quite mild at the grade.

⑱ Tot es maneo . . . . 🔲 **6a**
28m. Begin at a vague rounded rib with 'PX' scratched on the rock. Climb the wall passing to the left of the cave/slot of the next route. Pull through the roof and use *Pepe's* lower-off.

BA and Zapalastro

Murcia · Alicante · Benidorm · Calpe · Xaló Valley · Gandia · Gandia · Salem · Aventador · Montesa · Bellús · Barranc de l'Avern

SECTOR NAVARRO
The right-hand end of the crag has some great steep slab climbs in the easier grades. Not surprisingly it is the most popular section of the cliff and some of the climbs are a bit polished. There are some good picnic spots here, just don't sit too close to the cliff.

1 Mortadela . . . . **5+**
22m. Start by a patch of white rock and head straight up the slab. It eases as you get higher.

2 Rompe techos . . . . **5+**
22m. The steep, sustained ragged crack right of the corner/flake leads to easier ground above.

3 Filemón . . . . **5+**
24m. Climb just to the right of twin blunt tufas and continue directly up the slab to lower-off on the head wall below a bush.

4 Carpanta . . . . **5+**
24m. Start at the name and climb between the bolt lines clipping one or the other!

5 Arcadia **5**
24m. The line left of the bubbly crack-line to steeper moves then a rightward finish. A good introduction to the cliff.

6 Vent **5**
24m. Trend right to reach and follow the discontinuous crack line by fine sustained climbing. Another good lower grade route.

7 Pepet . . . . **6b+**
24m. The fine sustained and fingery white rib directly above the bushes is reached from left or right. A bulge near the top proves problematical.

8 Navarro **6a**
24m. Start to the left of the flake and immediately right of the bushes. Step left to follow grassy cracks (new bolts, one of which is situated prominently in patch of white rock) to a lower-off on the left.

9 Asterix . . . . **5+**
22m. Start from the tip of the flake and climb through a small bulge and follow a pale streak to climb over the left edge of the overhang at the top of the cliff.

10 Obelix **6a**
22m. From just right of the tip of the flake climb up passing a black bolt early on head up the smooth grey slab and finishing over a substantial bulge just below the top of the cliff.

11 Idefix . . . . **5+**
20m. Start off the flake/ramp at head height, and climb straight up the slab, passing a bolt in a scar, and pulling over the right edge of an overlap. Well worth doing.

12 Rafa **5**
20m. Start just left of a bubbly crack-line and climb the slab to a lower-off on the left arete of a groove near the top of the cliff.

13 Pepe **5**
18m. From the name head up the rib, step left then trend right.

14 Dit **5**
18m. Climb direct from the toe of a short ramp, where '71' and an arrow are scratched faintly on the rock. Better than it looks!

15 La pelirroja ilustrada . . . . **6a+**
18m. The last line on the wall heads between the bushes and finishes up the detached pillar above.

To the right are some short steep routes - no grades known.

Fine fingery climbing on one of the tallest wall at Montesa *Sense titól* (6c+) on Paret de la Mola - *page 344*.
The rock here is a gritty limestone, with great friction and many surprising holds.

MONTESA

Montesa is a lovely little crag consisting of walls of good rough rock, in a splendid position. Many of the routes are quite short, however the climbing is continually interesting with plenty of good moves packed in. The rock is a sandy limestone with good friction, a pleasant contrast to the razor covered stuff by the coast. The crag has a range of features with face climbs aplenty, it even includes some cracks, chimneys and small overhangs. Included here are all the main buttresses. A full topo (which also includes the extensive bouldering) is available from Camil's Rock Bar in the town for the bargain price of €3. Funds from the sale of this topo are used to help pay for maintenance of the crag so, if you enjoy climbing here, please buy the topo.

The routes have been equipped by the local climber Ricard Jimenez. He is often found hanging around Camil's Rock Bar.

APPROACH (area map page 305)

Montesa is just west of the N430 between Albacete and Valencia. From the coast either head north to Gandía, and then drive inland on the fast CV60 towards Albaida and join the CV40 heading north (probably the fastest option), or from the Alicante area drive to and through Alcoi and again pick up the CV40 heading north. Once on the N430 dual carriageway, continue south (towards Albaceta) for a few junctions until you can turn off to Montesa. Follow the signs for the Castillo, turning right and go out of the town, steeply up around the back of the castle. Go over the top of the hill and park on the left close in against the wall, the crag is visible over your right shoulder. Walk down past the font and some picnic tables, the crag is two minutes up hill from here.

CONDITIONS

Most of the crag faces south and catches the sun. Although the setting is quite exposed it doesn't appear to catch the wind too badly. There is no shelter in the rain and non of the routes are steep enough to stay dry. Standing in front of the cliff, the block of Tormo Gros has a north-facing side which gives shade in hot weather. The routes on this wall are relatively friendly grades from 4 to 6a+ and with a couple at 6b+. The sunny south face is generally harder.

The short-lived but excellent *Pepe Blai* (6a+) on the Pedro Cristalino at Montesa. Fine rock, great moves in a pleasant setting; if only the buttress itself was just a few metres taller?! - *Page 347.*

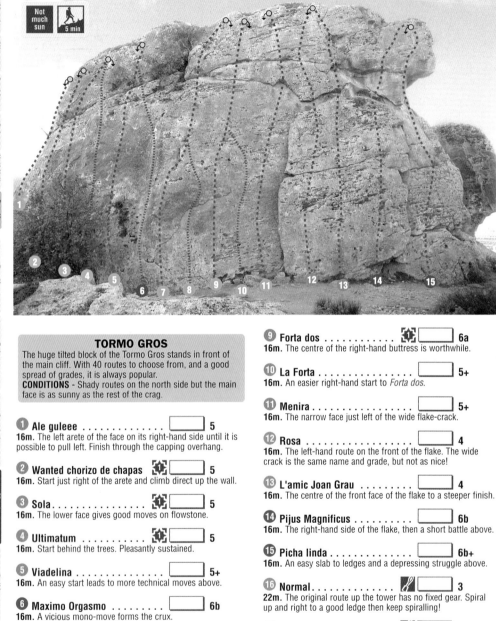

TORMO GROS

The huge tilted block of the Tormo Gros stands in front of the main cliff. With 40 routes to choose from, and a good spread of grades, it is always popular.

CONDITIONS - Shady routes on the north side but the main face is as sunny as the rest of the crag.

1 Ale guleee 5
16m. The left arete of the face on its right-hand side until it is possible to pull left. Finish through the capping overhang.

2 Wanted chorizo de chapas 5
16m. Start just right of the arete and climb direct up the wall.

3 Sola 5
16m. The lower face gives good moves on flowstone.

4 Ultimatum 5
16m. Start behind the trees. Pleasantly sustained.

5 Viadelina . . . . 5+
16m. An easy start leads to more technical moves above.

6 Maximo Orgasmo 6b
16m. A vicious mono-move forms the crux.

7 Selenta 5
16m. Climb just right of the water-streak and right of the gully.

8 Selenta dos. . . . . 6a+
16m. Technical climbing through the tricky bulge.

9 Forta dos 6a
16m. The centre of the right-hand buttress is worthwhile.

10 La Forta . . . . 5+
16m. An easier right-hand start to *Forta dos*.

11 Menira . . . . 5+
16m. The narrow face just left of the wide flake-crack.

12 Rosa 4
16m. The left-hand route on the front of the flake. The wide crack is the same name and grade, but not as nice!

13 L'amic Joan Grau 4
16m. The centre of the front face of the flake to a steeper finish.

14 Pijus Magnificus 6b
16m. The right-hand side of the flake, then a short battle above.

15 Picha linda . . . . 6b+
16m. An easy slab to ledges and a depressing struggle above.

16 Normal. 3
22m. The original route up the tower has no fixed gear. Spiral up and right to a good ledge then keep spiralling!

17 V.S.V. . . . . 6a+
16m. The short tilted wall and the little roof above the ledge.

18 C.B.S. 4
14m. A dark chimney to the ledge then exit as for *Normal*.

19 Free climbing 4
12m. The juggy wall and arete of the chimney. Exit to the right.

㉕ 7 anas1 . . . . 6b+
16m. The right arete of the tower, before the grotty gully.

㉖ Que fas? El porc 6a
18m. The centre of the pillar with a big bushy hole.

㉗ Poquet i bo . . . . 6a+
18m. The wall just left of the sharp hanging arete is exciting.

㉘ La cartera . . . . 6b+
18m. Climb to the pocket then left to the groove. Exit right.

㉙ Route 29 . . . . 6c
18m. The grey wall and edge of the roof above.

㉚ Route 30 . . . . 6c
18m. An alternative approach to the same steep finish of *Route 29*.

㉛ Lepones . . . . 6c+
18m. A wall and orange streak left of the niche to a steep finish.

㉜ Marti de Viciana . . . . . . 6c+
18m. The lower wall to a rest in the big chipped niche, then up its left arete and the wall above.

㉝ Mitja via . . . . 6c+
18m. The right arete of the niche approached direct.

㉞ Montesejos 6b
18m. The tricky lower wall to ledges then trend right.

㉟ Taxi bou 7b
18m. The desperately smooth rib to the right.

㊱ Xativeos-94 . . . . 6c
16m. Climb to a big hole then up the wall and rib.

⑳ Sherpa Pertemba . . . . . . 5+
12m. The centre of the wall through the scoop.

㉑ One Ticket for Kentucky 7c
12m. The rounded arete is very gritstonesque.

㉒ West 6c
16m. Move right from the slot and climb the slabby face.

The next three routes are on the side wall starting at a slightly lower level.

㉓ Ajetreos . . . . 6c+
16m. The slabby face gives a fine technical pitch.

㉔ Pin y Pon 7a
16m. The fine sustained centre of the slab.

Murcia
Alicante
Benidorm
Calpe
Xaló Valley
Gandia
Gandia
Salem
Aventador
Montesa
Bellús
Barranc de l'Avern

1 Milio . . . . 🔦⬜ **6b+**
14m. The left arete of the tower is the least worthwhile here.

2 Dagón . . . . 🔦🐛⬜ **6b+**
20m. Climb past the left edge of a hole then up the wall to a shake at the diagonal break. Cross the wall rightwards to finish.

3 Ningún Drama . . . . . . 🔦⬜ **6c**
20m. Climb past the hole and up the centre of the wall. Superb.

4 Sense titól . . . . . . 🔦🐛⬜ **6c+**
20m. A cracker up the right-hand side of the face. A sit-down rest can be had in the hole although this is above the crux.
Photo page 339.

5 La fura Deus . . . . 🔦⬜ **6b**
18m. The left-hand line on the east face of the tower.

6 Tuli-lola . . . . 🔦⬜ **6a**
18m. The arete of the tower steepens as it rises.

7 Fornicadores . . . . 🔦⬜ **4**
20m. A chimney route that goes off into the bowels of the cliff.

8 La bola del drac . . . . . . 🔦⬜ **4**
20m. Another chimney outing. Start on the left then cross the blocks to the chimney proper. Lower-off on the right or top out.

9 L'oratge . . . . 🔦⬜ **6b**
16m. The narrow rib is technical but feels escapable.

10 Diedro ecologic . . . . . . 🔦⬜ **5+**
16m. The groove with the tree, clip the bolts to the right or place nuts in the main groove. Exit through the roof on the left.

PARET DE LA MOLA
The main area at Montesa is the two buttresses behind the free-standing tower of Tormo Gros. These buttresses have many fine and long routes, on excellent pocket-covered rock.
CONDITIONS - This is a beautifully situated buttress which gets the sun until late in the day. There is no seepage and it dries quickly if there has been any rain.

Lots of sun | 5 min

11 Per aci Mixel no passa . . . . . . ☐ 6b
16m. Another of those funny pillar pitches.

12 Diedre güay . . . . ☐ 5
16m. The deepening groove is a good line. Top out or lower-off the bolts to the right.

To the right is a fine pocketed face. All the routes are easier than they look, especially for climbers trained on indoor walls.

13 Elo Deu del vent . . . . . ☐ 5+
16m. Fine climbing with a tricky move onto the slab.

14 Epiliano dels collons . . ☐ 5+
16m. More of the same. Every pocket is good!

15 Pic-pic . . . . ☐ 5+
16m. The flake-crack with big pockets has a steep start.

16 La colmena . . . . ☐ 6a+
18m. Climb the awkward groove past the bulging belly.

17 La Panxa . . . . . . ☐ 6b
18m. The belly indeed. A tough lower wall leads to the grooves.

18 Pepemite . . . . ☐ 6a+
18m. The right-hand side of the slab then the bulges above.

19 La lluita dels caps . . . . . . ☐ 6b+
18m. Pass the vegetation then climb straight up the steep face.

20 Xila . . . . ☐ 6a+
20m. The shrubby slab and steep rib directly above.

21 La Virgo . . . . ☐ 5+
20m. An excellent and varied groove with a tricky start.

22 Insubmissio . . . . ☐ 6a
20m. The blunt rib leads to the same finish as *Virgo.*

23 Qué morro! . . . . . . ☐ 6a+
20m. Climb the hard slab rightwards, then straight up the wall.

24 Te la mango . . . . . ☐ 6c
20m. The centre of the face is sustained and technical.

25 L'espectacul . . . . ☐ 6c
20m. A thin start up the wall. A left-hand start is **Speed, 6c+**.

26 Quan la lluna flora . . . . . . ☐ 6c
18m. The right arete of the wall is worthwhile.

27 Diedre de t'home dur . . . . ☐ 6b
20m. Climb the rib then head right up the face.

28 Galteta roja . . . . ☐ 6a+
20m. The pocketed face.

29 El nas de Roseta . . . . ☐ 6a+
20m. Right-hand side of the pillar is the last on this sector.

MONTESA *Pedra Cristalina*

PEDRA CRISTALINA

The short walls to the right of the central area of Paret de la Mola have a set of technical climbs on compact rock. The routes are very short but the rock is of immaculate quality. Remember - sometimes small is beautiful!

APPROACH - Follow the track out towards the bigger walls of the Paret de la Mola then cut back right across the rib to locate the left-hand end of the cliff.

CONDITIONS - This wall is south-facing and sunny like the Paret de la Mola.

❶ Estornuts . . . . ☐ 6b+
6m. Only 3 bolts to a lower-off.

❷ Llagrimes en la piedra . ☐ 7b
6m. Short and very fierce.

❸ Lo mas duro . . . . ☐ 7b+
6m. This is the one if you think you're 'ard enough!

❹ Baltario . . . . ☐ 6b
10m. The pocketed right side of the wall.

❺ Caxi-baxe . . . . ☐ 7a+
10m. The blunt arete and slabbier rock above.

❻ Quedara en tu memoria . . ☐ 7b
10m. A line up the hanging groove left of the corner.

❼ Me supura la fisura . . . . . ☐ 6a
8m. The corner and roof are usually an inelegant struggle.

❽ Ferrán JB . . . . ☐ 6c
8m. The white wall and roof right of the corner.

❾ La llumeneta . . . . ☐ 6c+
10m. The left edge of the brown streak is technical.

❿ Agárramela . . . . ☐ 6b+
10m. Up the rib just left of a big pocket.

⓫ Menir . . . . ☐ 6a+
6m. Only 2 bolts to the lower-off and hard to start.

⓬ ¡A la mili quillo! . . . . ☐ 6a+
6m. A reachy start leads to good pockets above.

⓭ Cristalina . . . . ☐ 6a+
8m. Another one with a hard start.

⓮ Colorines . . . . ☐ 6a+
10m. The well-named left arete of the groove.

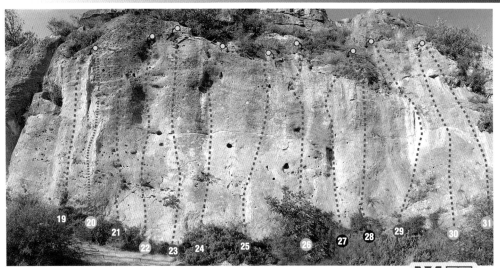

Lots of sun | **5 min**

⑮ Diedro besuco . . . . [　] 5
10m. The corner is the easiest on the cliff.

⑯ La teoría de la palanca . . . [img][　] 6a
10m. A one-move-wonder, the one move being the start.

⑰ Variante la teoría . . . . [img][　] 6a
10m. The name says it all.

⑱ El paso del embolo . . . . . [img][　] 6a
10m. The wall left of a pale streak then traverse past the tufa.

⑲ Xorrollera Pinza Hut . . . [img][img][　] 6b
10m. Up the left-hand side of the big white tufa.

⑳ El forat negre . . . . . . [img][img][　] 6a+
10m. Up the right-hand side of the same white tufa.

㉑ Isma . . . . [img][　] 6b+
10m. The blunt rib to the right until the angle drops back. Head left to the lower-off

㉒ Pepe Blai . . . . [img][img][img][　] 6a+
10m. The open scoop is pleasantly pocketed. *Photo page 341.*

㉓ Juanot . . . . [img][img][　] 6c
10m. The rounded pillar is hard.

㉔ Patiras tendinitis . . . . . [img][img][　] 6c
10m. The 'other' scoop. There might be a warning in the name.

㉕ Patiras d'estrenyiment . [img][img][　] 6c
10m. The smoother wall to the right - trending right.

㉖ La petjada de tico . . . . . . [img][　] 6a+
10m. A more reasonable offering in between the two holes.

㉗ For ever? . . . . [img][　] 7c
10m. The near-impossible wall via the left edge of the streak.

㉘ Siniestra danza . . . . . . [img][img][　] 7c
10m. Similar climbing just to the right might be even harder.

㉙ Snake-men . . . . [img][　] 6c
12m. Further right is a short white scoop, climb it direct or via the left wall.

㉚ Erosión . . . . [img][　] 6a
12m. Pleasant balancy climbing up the rib to the right.

㉛ Centenario de vias . . . . [　] 6a+
12m. A right-hand line up the same piece of rock.

There are two lines up the rock to the right.

㉜ Ivana . . . . [　] 6b
12m. Trend right under the bushes then climb the wall.

㉝ Lour . . . . [　] 6a+
12m. The last route has a steep finish.

It is possible to descend the steep gully beyond the last route to pick up the approach from the car.

BELLÚS

Just to the north of the village of Bellús is an unspectacular looking hillside with scattered pig farms; not a promising location for a crag you might think. However tucked away here is a secluded dry valley called the Barranco Fondo with a south-facing wall consisting of good solid rock, about 500m long, and covered in some excellent and well-bolted routes. Although these are generally short they are action-packed with some fierce technical climbing on crozzly grey rock and steeper moves on the red sections. The location itself is remarkable when you consider that the approach takes in the aforementioned pig farms and an old quarry, but once you are at the crag you could not wish for a more pleasant and tranquil spot. It also rates as one of the best sun-traps on the Blanca.

Just to add to the attraction of the place there is a useful shady crag known as Cueva Pechina which is situated over the back of the hillside and can easily be visited on the same trip, especially if you need a bit of respite from the heat. This crag has the steepest and hardest climbing at Bellús and a few pleasant easier routes.

CONDITIONS

The crag is a well-sheltered sun-trap; it gets hot here even in the middle of winter. There are no big overhangs in the main gorge so there is little to do in the rain but there is little or no seepage and the crag will dry in minutes after any rain. Cueva Pechina offers shady climbing all day long and will give some dry climbing in light rain, albeit in the harder grades only.

APPROACH (area map page 305)

Bellús village is situated about 8km south of Xàtiva on the N340. It can be reached along the slow roads from Sella, via Alcoi and Albaida, however from Benidorm or Calpe it is best to approach from the Gandía ring road via the fast CV60 and follow this past Castello de Rugat to a junction with the N340. Turn right towards Xàtiva and Bellús. Drive through the town and turn right on a dirt road immediately north of the town and just before the road crosses a bridge. At the first cross-road turn left towards a landscaped quarry and park just before a barrier (about 1 hour from Calpe). Walk through the quarry, keeping left to its end where cairns mark the start of a path that picks a way up the hillside on the right. At the top of this is a track running left along a rocky terrace all the way up the right-hand side of the gorge to the cliff, 20 mins from the car.

For the Cueva Pechina continue straight on at the cross-roads, up a hill and between the farm buildings. Drive over a small hill before descending to riverside parking, two minutes from the cliff which is hidden just around the corner. Leave nothing in the car.

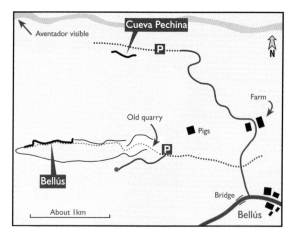

Alan James enjoying the slabby first sector at Bellus. The route is *Simpre igual* (6b) - page 355.
Inset: *Antesia* (6c) on the shady Cueva Pechina - page 356.

Routes 17 to 19
around corner

Approach from
Sector Bloques

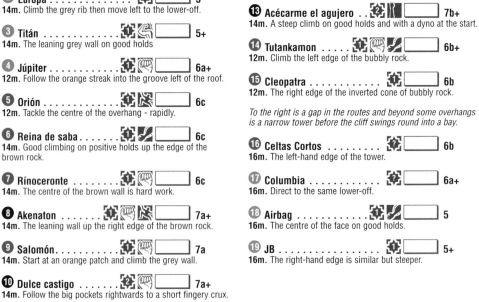

SECTOR BALCÓN

The far left-hand end of the crag has a good collection of short routes on steep, undercut, grey walls of good rock as well as some worthwhile pocket pulling. It is five minutes walk from the arrival point at the cliff.

1 Ganimedes 5
12m. The last/first route on the cliff traverses above the cave.

2 Europa 5
14m. Climb the grey rib then move left to the lower-off.

3 Titán .... 5+
14m. The leaning grey wall on good holds

4 Júpiter .... 6a+
12m. Follow the orange streak into the groove left of the roof.

5 Orión 6c
12m. Tackle the centre of the overhang - rapidly.

6 Reina de saba 6c
14m. Good climbing on positive holds up the edge of the brown rock.

7 Rínoceronte 6c
14m. The centre of the brown wall is hard work.

8 Akenaton .... 7a+
14m. The leaning wall up the right edge of the brown rock.

9 Salomón 7a
14m. Start at an orange patch and climb the grey wall.

10 Dulce castigo .... 7a+
14m. Follow the big pockets rightwards to a short fingery crux.

11 Campurriano ..... 7b+
14m. Steep and fingery moves up the wall left of the holes.

12 Capitán América .. 7b
14m. Climb to the edge of the big hole then step right, steep and fingery again.

13 Acécarme el agujero .. 7b+
14m. A steep climb on good holds and with a dyno at the start.

14 Tutankamon ..... 6b+
12m. Climb the left edge of the bubbly rock.

15 Cleopatra 6b
12m. The right edge of the inverted cone of bubbly rock.

To the right is a gap in the routes and beyond some overhangs is a narrow tower before the cliff swings round into a bay.

16 Celtas Cortos 6b
16m. The left-hand edge of the tower.

17 Columbia .... 6a+
16m. Direct to the same lower-off.

18 Airbag 5
16m. The centre of the face on good holds.

19 JB .... 5+
16m. The right-hand edge is similar but steeper.

SECTOR BLOQUE

Many of the routes on this well-named sector are very short, sometimes only 2 or 3 bolts long and occasionally the first bolt is missing! However they pack a lot in.

① Yertu primituvu .... ☐ 6a+
6m. The grey wall behind the bushes.

② Guapito bananas .... ☐ 6a+
6m. Direct to the same lower-off via the bulges.

③ Tócate los huesos .... ☐ 6b
8m. The left-edge of the grey rock beyond the caves

④ Peña el porru .... 🔧☐ 6b
8m. The leaning groove is awkward.

⑤ Carne Val .... 🔧💪☐ 6a+
8m. The steep orange rock leads to a tricky bulge.

⑥ Transilvania .... 🔧✋☐ 6c
8m. Climb out of the left-hand side of the cave.

⑦ Dràcula .... 🔧✋💪☐ 6c+
8m. The leaning right wall of the cave is butch.

⑧ Tarambanas .... 🔧✋☐ 6b
8m. The right edge of the cave and short bulging wall.

⑨ As de ases .... 🔧🤚☐ 7a
10m. The edge of the grey rock

⑩ Masacre .... ☐ 6a+
8m. Short-lived action up the face just to the right.

⑪ Halloween .... 🔧☐ 6a
8m. A right-hand line to the same lower-off.

⑫ Xíus .... 🔧☐ 6a+
8m. The left edge of the ear-shaped area of rock.

⑬ Comanche .... 🔧👊☐ 6b+
8m. Sharp pockets through the right edge of the overlap.

⑭ Pierdo verticalidad ... 🔧✋☐ 6a+
8m. The bulging line of holes and short wall above.

⑮ Colores de guerra ...... 🔧☐ 6a
8m. Good moves up the pockets and short grey wall.

⑯ Asmático .... 🔧🤚☐ 6b+
8m. Pass the left edge of the horizontal slot with difficulty.

⑰ Pedro Picapiedra ..... 🔧👊☐ 6b+
8m. The bulges and wall to the right.

⑱ Pablo Mármol .... 🔧☐ 5+
8m. The wall on good pockets

⑲ Hells Bells .... ☐ 6a
10m. Straight up the wall from the white scar.

⑳ Consejo de guerra ...... 🔧☐ 6a+
10m. Head up the rib to the end of the diagonal flake

㉑ Consejo de paz ...... 🔧👊☐ 6b
10m. Climb the grey wall on small edges, trending right.

㉒ Yeti .... 🔧☐ 6a+
8m. Straight through the centre of the overlap,

㉓ A escobazos con Guerola . 🔧☐ 6a+
8m. Good juggy climbing up the wall.

㉔ El atrofiat .... 🔧☐ 6a
8m. A hard start might leave you wasted.

㉕ El attolladero ...... 🔧💪☐ 6b+
8m. A direct line to the same lower-off.

㉖ Amordasat .... 🔧☐ 6a
12m. The tall tower on the right by its edge.

SECTOR VERANO

This Sector has some of the longest routes at the crag with some fine lines up steep shallow grooves, pocketed cracks and open walls - enjoy.

❶ Invertidos de la ostia . 🎯🪓 ☐ **6c+**
14m. Start left of a slot and climb the bulging wall.

❷ Les grapes . . . . 🎯📐 ☐ **6b+**
14m. Trend right up the wall and on through the bulges.

❸ Los mediocres . . . . . . 🎯📐 ☐ **6b**
14m. The tricky lower wall leads to juggier rock above.

❹ Micro . . . . 🎯📐🏚 ☐ **6c**
16m. Follow pockets past a big hole to a thin head wall.

❺ Pistacho . . . . 🎯🪓 ☐ **6b**
16m. The excellent bubbly wall and blunt rib above.

❻ El pastiset . . . . 🎯 ☐ **6a**
16m. Climb the red streak and then try to avoid getting too deep in the orifice!

❼ Momo . . . . 🎯🏚📐 ☐ **6b+**
16m. Start just left of the vertical floor-level slot and climb the wall, then trend left to finish.

❽ Parasit . . . . 🎯📐 ☐ **6a**
14m. A steep, blocky rib leads into a technical little groove.

❾ Bossím . . . . 🎯📐 ☐ **6a**
14m. The wall and bulge lead to the longer groove high up.

❿ Mister coki . . . . 🎯📐 ☐ **6b**
14m. Climb to a bay then up the steepening scoop above.

⓫ Amors . . . . 🎯📐 ☐ **5+**
12m. The leaning wall leades to a steep groove.

⓬ Pobre Olivera . . . . ☐ **6b**
12m. The steep wall to grotty ledges.

⓭ Karkamal . . . . ☐ **6a+**
12m. A red groove to the left of a blob.

⓮ El amagatall . . . . 🎯 ☐ **6a+**
12m. Gain and follow a black scoop.

⓯ Capello . . . . 🎯📐 ☐ **6c+**
12m. Start up a white pillar and head through the black bulge.

⓰ No me siento las piedras . 🎯 ☐ **6a+**
14m. The rib and bulge behind the bushes lead to a groove.

⓱ Yohan . . . . 🎯📐 ☐ **7a**
16m. The wall leads into a well cleaned groove. Exit rightwards.

⓲ Champion's League . . . . ☐ **7a**
18m. Climb the diagonal crack then head direct up grottier ground above.

19 Harley Davidson . . . . . 🔲🔀⬜ 6c+
18m. Gain a large diagonal hole then climb the short grey rib.

The impressive wall to the right should have a route up it!

20 Brea . . . . 🔲🔀🔀⬜ 7a+
16m. Just left of a chimney with a roof to finish. There are 2
bolts to the right which may be a poor right-hand start.

*There is supposed to be a route up the wall to the right, Ostia a
la cabeza 7c though there is little evidence of it apart from the
odd chip mark!*

21 La pancheta gueroleta . 🔲🔀⬜ 6b
14m. The steep wall. There is supposed to be another 6b to the
left of this but again there is no evidence of it.

22 Moco de pavo . . . . 🔲🔀⬜ 7a
14m. The chipped pillar.

*There is a big gap of climbable rock which has two routes
listed, Terminator, 7b+ and Guerotex, 6c+ but no bolts.*

23 Duracel . . . . 🔲🔀⬜ 7a
16m. Start up tufas to the awkward leaning groove - how's
your stamina?

24 Atlanta . . . . 🔲🔀⬜ 6b
16m. A diagonal line of pockets with broccoli-covered footholds
leads to the finish of the last route.

25 Popeye . . . . 🔲🔀⬜ 6c+
16m. The superb tufa is well-named. One of the best routes at
Bellús. Battle up the tufas to the roof then head out right!
Photo on page 304.

Murcia
Alicante
Benidorm
Calpe
Xaló Valley
Gandia
Gandia
Salem
Aventador
Montesa
Bellús
Barranc de l'Avern

Murcia
Alicante
Benidorm
Calpe
Xaló Valley
Gandía
Gandía
Salem
Aventador
Montesa
Bellús
Barranc de l'Avern

SECTOR ESCARCHA NEGRA

The first section reached on the approach from the car and some teams go no further. A good collection of steep wall climbs early on and then an excellent steep slab, ideal for honing technique. The grades might feel tough at 1st acquaintance - that's because they are!

ROUTE NUMBERS - The numbers scratched on the rock refer to the 2001 Rockfax guide (no we didn't do the scratching). Just deduct 29 for the new number.

1 Project . . . .
14m. The red streak into a shallow groove. Should be 6b/c ish.

2 Project . . . .
14m. Past a small niche. Should also be 6b/c ish.

3 Project . . . .
14m. A very steep line which will be in the high 7s.

4 Cacolat del Marroc . . . . **7a+**
14m. The leaning wall, then trend left to the lower-off.

Further right, past a blank section, is a big roof high up.

5 Alto Brons . . . . **7a+**
14m. Follow tufas to a rest below the roof, then pull the lip.

6 Código rojo **6c**
14m. Climb the white streak then negotiate the roofs.

7 Sed de dromedario **6b**
14m. The orange groove.

8 Mega . . . . **6a+**
14m. Start below a small tufa boss at 2m and climb direct.

9 Esquirol . . . . **6a+**
14m. The first route on the fine grey slab.

10 Psicosis . . . . **6b+**
14m. The next line is similar - but harder.

11 Alparrus . . . . **6a+**
14m. Another good slab climb - assuming you like the genre.

12 Sopletiste . . . . **6c+**
14m. Taxing moves up rock too steep to be slabby.

13 Trance **6c**
14m. Between the two grey streaks.

14 Moreno **6b**
14m. This one has got a decent hold - at three quarters height!

15 Rompe gafas . . . . . **6c+**
14m. Smoother rock leads with difficulty to the same lower-off.

16 Rompe cojones **7a**
16m. Desperately thin wall climbing.

17 Maldita sea mi suerte . . . **6b**
16m. Excellent, steep slab climbing that even has the odd hold.

18 Tiempo perdido **6c**
16m. Climb straight up the slab just left of a white scar.

19 Cuerdas gastadas . . . . . **6a+**
16m. Straight through the white scar.

The next 4 routes start behind a large bush. This bush provides the only shade at the crag and tends to be the gearing-up spot.

20 A todo tren **6b**
16m. The steep pocketed wall on the left.

21 La chicharra **6b**
14m. The easing wall behind the bush.

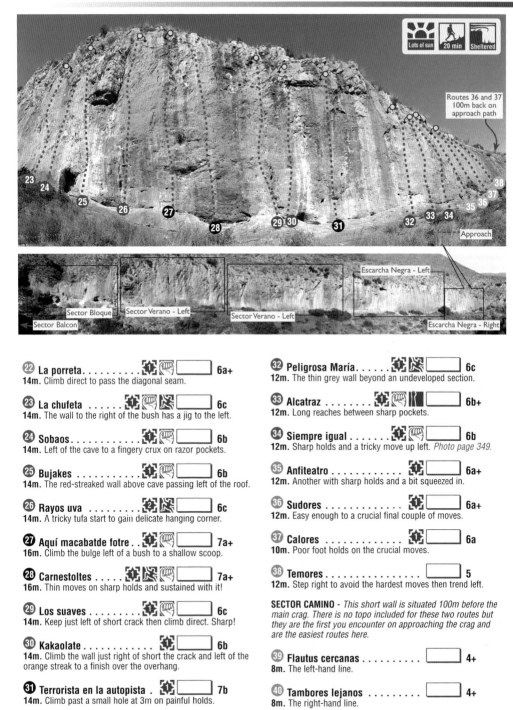

Routes 36 and 37
100m back on
approach path

Murcia · Alicante · Benidorm · Calpe · Xaló Valley · Gandia · Gandia · Salem · Aventador · Montesa · Bellús · Barranc de l'Avern

Sector Bloque · Sector Verano - Left · Sector Balcon · Sector Verano - Left · Escarcha Negra - Left · Escarcha Negra - Right · Approach

22 La porreta . . . . 6a+
14m. Climb direct to pass the diagonal seam.

23 La chufeta 6c
14m. The wall to the right of the bush has a jig to the left.

24 Sobaos 6b
14m. Left of the cave to a fingery crux on razor pockets.

25 Bujakes 6b
14m. The red-streaked wall above cave passing left of the roof.

26 Rayos uva 6c
14m. A tricky tufa start to gain delicate hanging corner.

27 Aquí macabatde fotre . . 7a+
16m. Climb the bulge left of a bush to a shallow scoop.

28 Carnestoltes . . . . . 7a+
16m. Thin moves on sharp holds and sustained with it!

29 Los suaves 6c
14m. Keep just left of short crack then climb direct. Sharp!

30 Kakaolate 6b
14m. Climb the wall just right of short the crack and left of the orange streak to a finish over the overhang.

31 Terrorista en la autopista . 7b
14m. Climb past a small hole at 3m on painful holds.

32 Peligrosa María 6c
12m. The thin grey wall beyond an undeveloped section.

33 Alcatraz . . . . 6b+
12m. Long reaches between sharp pockets.

34 Siempre igual 6b
12m. Sharp holds and a tricky move up left. *Photo page 349.*

35 Anfiteatro . . . . 6a+
12m. Another with sharp holds and a bit squeezed in.

36 Sudores . . . . 6a+
12m. Easy enough to a crucial final couple of moves.

37 Calores 6a
10m. Poor foot holds on the crucial moves.

38 Temores 5
12m. Step right to avoid the hardest moves then trend left.

SECTOR CAMINO - *This short wall is situated 100m before the main crag. There is no topo included for these two routes but they are the first you encounter on approaching the crag and are the easiest routes here.*

39 Flautus cercanas . . . . 4+
8m. The left-hand line.

40 Tambores lejanos . . . . 4+
8m. The right-hand line.

CUEVA PECHINA

A shady alternative to the main area with some steep routes and some very steep ones (plus a bit of slabby stuff).
GRADES - The grades are taken from the local topo, they appear to be on the stiff side!
APPROACH - Continue along the surfaced road past the turn off for the main area, between farm buildings, and down a steep hill to a parking spot at the end of the track. The crag is on the left.
CONDITIONS - This wall faces north and well-sheltered, the steeper routes will stay dry in light rain.

1 El rio **4**
16m. The left-hand line is a bit dusty and has a steep start.

2 El molino . . . . **4+**
16m. The left of the trio on the bigger slab.

3 Pera pares . . . . **4+**
16m. ....and the parallel line with a steeper start.

4 Pera nones . . . . . . **5+**
16m. A steep fingery start soon leads to easier ground.

5 El perro . . . . **5+**
16m. The left side of the wall to crucial moves up and right.

6 Casporillo. **5**
16m. Climb the flakes then the buttress surprising set of holds.

7 Es carlota **5**
20m. A classic, the steep flake and pocket line above.

8 Pure de pascueros . **7b**
20m. The smooth wall has some linkable pockets.

9 Coloquiadio . . **6c+**
20m. A continuous line of finger pockets gives great moves.

10 Warlock . . . . **7c+**
20m. Tough and tilted face climbing.

11 Anitesia **6c**
20m. Steep but bigger pockets leading to a deep groove, great!
Photo page 349.

12 Maldita Navidad . . **7c+**
18m. Powerful climbing up the wall left of the cave.

13 Mutante **8a**
18m. The left-hand line out of the cave - its all in the name.

14 Liante **8b**
18m. Bizarre and desperate climbing out of the cave.

15 Slayer **8a**
18m. The line out of the right-hand side of the back of the cave.

16 Anaslayer . . . . **7c+**
18m. The link-up for if you find the start of *Slayer* too much.

17 Anaconda . . . . **7b+**
18m. The right-hand line out of the cave.

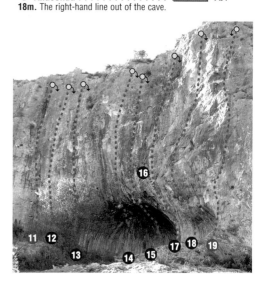

18 Gladiator . . . . 🔲🔲🔲 ⬜ 7a+
18m. A steep battle up the flakes to the right of the cave.

19 Colores . . . . 🔲🔲🔲 ⬜ 6c+
20m. The 'easy' looking line on the buttress front - it ain't.

20 Rompresas . . . . 🔲🔲 ⬜ 7a+
20m. Fierce fingery moves up the grey wall.

21 Extrema y Dura . . . . 🔲 ⬜ 6c+
20m. The slanting and technical groove.

22 El muro de las lamentationes . ⬜ 7b+
20m. The grey streak is desperate.

23 El trasgu . . . . ⬜ 7a+
20m. Through the middle of the bulges past a good pocket.

24 La pelota de manterol . . . . . . ⬜ 6b
20m. The right-hand edge of the wall.

After a gap is a new route then a fine wide wall.

25 El buitre pescador . 🔲🔲🔲 ⬜ 6a+
18m. A fingery move at half-height is a spoiler.

26 El albaran volador . . . . 🔲🔲 ⬜ 6a+
18m. Fine sustained climbing on good, though sharp, holds.

27 Odisea especial . . . . . . 🔲🔲 ⬜ 6b
20m. Steep and sustained linking pockets and good edges.

28 Mangurrian . . . . 🔲🔲 ⬜ 7a
20m. The grey streak directly below the capping tree.

29 Chocolate de patora . . . 🔲🔲 ⬜ 7b
20m. More hard and fingery climbing.

30 Cede al paso . . . . . 🔲🔲🔲 ⬜ 7b
20m. No queues likely on the smooth wall.

31 Centenario guay . . . . . 🔲🔲 ⬜ 6b+
16m. Start at a short black streak and climb direct.

32 Rock y ron . . . . 🔲🔲 ⬜ 6c+
16m. Tough moves through the overlap.

33 El clan de los cuerdos . . . 🔲 ⬜ 7a
18m. Trend right above the edge of the cave.

34 El clan de los locos . . . ⊖🔲 ⬜ 7c
16m. From behind bars make an escape up and right.

Murcia · Alicante · Benidorm · Calpe · Xaló Valley · Gandía · Gandía · Salem. · Aventador · Montesa · Bellús · Baranc de l'Avern

BARANC de l'AVERN

Murcia
Alicante
Benidorm
Calpe
Xaló Valley
Gandia
Gandia
Salem
Aventador
Montesa
Bellús
Baranc de l'Avern

The Barranc de l'Avern is a deep-cut twisting ravine with a lot of exposed rock and a busy road running through it. If it wasn't for the road it would be an extremely pleasant location but even with this drawback it is still a worthwhile venue for middle grades climbers. The rock is good and the climbs tend to follow vertical walls with some featuring small overlaps. The gear is a bit old on some routes however there is some replacement going on.

If the main gorge is a bit too noisy for you the Sectors Deposit and Visera should suite; they have an idyllic setting in a secluded valley, hemmed in by the hills and are a complete contrast to the other cliffs here.

The routes here were mostly equipped in the late 80s an early 90s by Guerola, Jordi, Nyanyes, Motosa, Héctor, Frequillo, Julian, Bosi, Rus and Pedro Pons.

Mitja vía (6c+) on Sector Gagallo de Gegant - *page 361.*

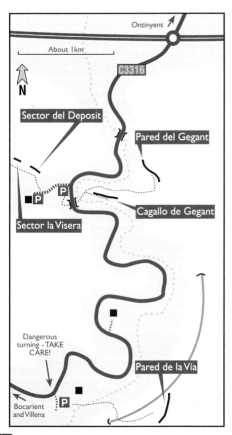

APPROACH (area map page 305)

The gorge runs south from the town of Ontinyent, and is reached by following the newly constructed ring road passing several impressive roundabouts. Take the C3316 (signed Bocarient and Villena) for just less than a kilometre from the last roundabout (the one with a Villena 35km sign) to a parking place on the right immediately before the second bridge in the gorge. This is the parking for the Pared del Gegant and Cagallo de Gegant, and is also the start of the road that runs up to the Sectors del Deposit and Visera. See the relevant pages for specific approaches to each sector.

CONDITIONS

Most of the sectors face south west and get plenty of afternoon sun. Although they are not exposed, it can be windy in the gorge however, this will have the benefit of drying the place out quickly if it has been raining. Sector la Visera may offer something to climb in light rain.

PARED DEL GEGANT

The spectacular grey sheet of rock offers some fine face routes in an impressive setting, high above the base of the gorge. Some of the climbs could do with being rebolted though on most of them the gear is at least adequate.

CONDITIONS - South-west facing, it gets plenty of afternoon sun but is not well-sheltered from the wind.

APPROACH - From the parking follow a track under a bridge, cross the dry river bed and scramble up to the rim of the water conduit. Follow this leftwards, crossing it at the first opportunity. Scramble up the bank passing to the left of a pinnacle (the top of the Cagallo de Gegant) to two prominent trees on the ridge. Behind, and to the right of these, a low rocky band is passed via an awkward chimney, to the second pylon on the ridge and just above this a ramp leads back down to the left to the foot of the face.

The first route starts up a rounded rib at a lower level which is most easily reached by a short traverse.

① Satiro . . . . **5+**
30m. Follow the rib passing old bolts and threads, and placing your own gear when required. Lower-off as for the next route.

② Milotxo . . . . **5+**
30m. The left edge of the main face has new bolts low down then older ones above. Reach it by a short traverse out from the end of the ledge. The lower-off is on the right at the top.

③ Bordi **6a**
28m. From the left end of the ledge trend slightly left to climb the rib and prominent thin crack. Above this follow flakes.

④ En un moment **6b**
28m. Start as for *Bordi* and follow the line of new bolts just to its right. Sustained and excellent.

⑤ Pinocho **6a**
28m. Trend rightwards up a line of older bolts that runs up a long black streak.

⑥ Tempranmillo **6a**
28m. Tackle the yellow streak marked by a line of old bolts.

⑦ Sangunsa . . . . . . **6c+**
28m. Climb the fine pillar of grey rock. Great climbing unfortunately protected by a mixture of old bolts and threads.

⑧ Botamonts **6c**
28m. Climb to a wriggling crack at 10m with a black drainage streak issuing from its base and continue in the same line.

⑨ Sandalio **7a**
28m. Take the tricky lower wall and pass the left edge of a veg-etated ledge. Climb the upper wall via scoops and bulges.

⑩ Sans Svesgota . . . . . . **7b+**
28m. Climb to the right side of the ledge to a hard finale with the lower-off just left of a bush on the crest of the wall.

⑪ Man kane . . . . **7a+**
28m. Fine, sustained climbing following new bolts, passing to the right of a large flowering shrub.

⑫ Hector **7a**
28m. The last route on the main section of the wall is protected by nice new blue bolts and has a tough upper rib.

The next routes are 20m further right on a steep orange wall.

⑬ Morir d'amor **7b**
20m. The left-hand line up the wall.

⑭ Tot ras . . . . **7a+**
20m. Good climbing passing to the left of the deep hole.

⑮ Sesion de noche **6c**
20m. Gain a deep hole from the right, then finish out right.

⑯ Te de tot . . . . **6b+**
20m. The less remarkable right-hand line.

A further 50m to the right are two more shorter climbs:

⑰ Anillo de cuero . . . . **6b+**
15m. On the left.

⑱ Punt mort **7a**
14m. ...and on the right.

CAGALLO DE GEGANT

Impolitely known as *The Giant's Turd*, the section of rock above the water channel is south-facing and has some good closely-packed climbs up to 20m in length. The climbs are generally better than they look.
CONDITIONS - This face gets plenty of sun and is better sheltered from the wind than some of the other faces.
APPROACH - From the parking place, follow the track under the bridge, cross the dry river bed and scramble up to the rim of the water conduit. Turn right and walk along the rim of the conduit until a plank can be crossed to the foot of the wall. The climbs are listed from left to right, starting to the left of the footbridge.

❶ S'has Golo . . . . 7a+
18m. Start 4m left of the bridge. The initial bulge is crossed by some harsh pocket pulling. Pass more bulges and a bush to a lower-off on the rim.

❷ Barrufets 6c
18m. Start 1m left of the plank bridge and pocket-pull around the right edge of the smooth bulges and then head up the easier rib above. The lower-off is rather antiquated.

❸ Pitufos 6a
18m. Start opposite the plank bridge at a bush. Climb the rib immediately right of the bulges - sustained and fingery - with particularly thin moves to enter the final crack.

❹ Pelawatios 6a
18m. Climb left of a yellow scar at 6m then through a bulge (old bolts) and up the steep wall to a new lower-off on the right.

❺ Espero Boxerini 6a
18m. The wall directly below the arete high on the cliff has one awkward move to gain the cleaned crack. The arete is pleasantly juggy and is climbed on layaways. Move left to the lower-off.

❻ Dolores 6a
18m. A line of new bolts up the wall. At the top step left and bridge the corner to a lower-off in the left wall.

❼ Caragol 5
16m. Start up a short rib above the narrowest part of the path and climb the wall, passing a couple of tricky moves at two thirds height, to a lower-off by a small tree.

❽ Tirali calceti . . . . 6a+
14m. Starting at a cave at the base of the cliff, climb direct up a narrowing slab, an orange groove and a short leaning wall.

To the right are four closely packed lines up the wall, all are pleasant but unremarkable.

❾ Cap de caixo 6a
14m. The first route right of the cave has a prominent bolt early on. Climb left of a yellow flake up two short leaning walls.

❿ Dolores con piano 6a
14m. Follow the line of new bolts over an overlap and straight on up the orange wall.

⓫ Flamingo 6a
14m. An older bolt above the 1st overhang marks the start. Climb grey bubbly rock and a left-trending shallow groove.

⓬ Tortugo 6a
12m. The face just left of an easy groove is reached over a couple of overhangs and climbed via a broken flake.

⓭ L'ortage 4
10m. The left-hand flake on the right side of the buttress is quite hard for the grade.

⓮ Obré Llaunes 4
10m. The odd wide yet shallow chimney feature is bridged or jammed to a selection of lower-offs.

To the right is an easy left-slanting ramp and then another buttress with the prominent flake crack of Va que's per hui towards its left-hand side.

⑮ Sopa de ganso . . . .  🪧 ☐ **6a+**
20m. The left-facing orange crack on the left side of the wall is followed to difficult moves out right to reach the lower-off.

⑯ Va que's per hui . . . . . 🪧🪧 ☐ **6a**
20m. Start immediately right of a large flake and reach the thin hanging crack via an overhang and some left-trending grooves. It gives excellent sustained climbing to a lower-off on the left.

⑰ Roca bola . . . . 🪧🪧🪧 ☐ **6a+**
20m. A steep start up a rusty red flake and grey wall, then the left side of the broad bulging rib. The route features plenty of unhelpful holds and a traverse out right to reach the lower-off.

⑱ Pancho verde . . . . 🪧🪧🪧 ☐ **7b**
20m. A line of green bolts up the blank rib is hideously hard.

⑲ Mitja vía . . . . 🪧🪧🪧 ☐ **6c+**
20m. A line through the smooth scoop. Start as for the last route but step out right to thin fingery climbing up the scoop. *Photo page 358.*

⑳ Man fotuto . . . . . . 🪧🪧🪧 ☐ **7a+**
18m. The right side of the scoop is a fierce sharp pitch.

㉑ Bon tacto . . . . 🪧 ☐ **7a+**
20m. A right-hand finish to *Man fotuto* up the rounded rib.

To the right the cliff bulges in its lower section and is capped by a long narrow roof. The routes offer good climbing on solid rock but the steep loose ledges at the foot of the cliff are a pain!

㉒ Si hay siroco . . . . ☐ **6c+**
18m. A line up tilted grey rock passing below the scar where a tree used to be, then trending left to the lower-off.

㉓ Ara no Bailo . . . . ☐ **6b+**
18m. The lower bulges are tackled via a hanging ramp/niche. Pull over the left end of the final overhang.

For the next routes, scramble up and right to where there are two low bolts close together at the base of the wall.

㉔ Marti Tirali . . . . 🪧 ☐ **6b**
18m. Pull over the right side of the lower bulge then trend left up the fine grey wall to the lower-off of the previous climb.

㉕ La penya dels Butifarras . . 🪧 ☐ **6a+**
18m. A direct line above the start of the last climb up the wall then across the small roof to finish.

㉖ Pablito clavo un clavito . . 🪧 ☐ **6b**
18m. Start from a flat ledge and climb past a big bolt into a scoop then follow a left-trending scoop to the lower-off.

㉗ De repente un parapent . . 🪧 ☐ **6c+**
18m. The same start leads to the rib just to the right and an exit rightwards through the roof.

㉘ Seccio homos . . . . 🪧 ☐ **6c**
18m. Follow the groove to the right of the rib to the roof and finish straight through these.

㉙ Desastre per a un sastre . . 🪧 ☐ **6b+**
18m. The last line here starts up the shattered bubbly rib on the right then powers leftwards through the roof.

On the far right is a small tower above a dam, with five short climbs and a longer offering just to the left.

㉚ Que contén qu'estic . . . . ☐ **6c**
18m. Climb scruffy rock passing two bolts and then better climbing up the smooth rib above.

㉛ Relajación . . . . ☐ **5+**
12m. The short left-hand line up a rib.

㉜ Opa ostil . . . . ☐ **7a**
12m. Very smooth rock just to the right.

㉝ Cap Finet . . . . ☐ **6b+**
10m. The central line passing a very useful hole.

㉞ Mano guarra . . . . ☐ **7a+**
10m. The centre of the orange wall directly above the dam.

㉟ La trampa . . . . ☐ **6a**
10m. Start up the brick work and then follow the rib above.

Murcia · Alicante · Benidorm · Calpe · Xaló Valley · Gandia · Gandia · Salem · Aventador · Montesa · Bailús · Baranc de l'Avern

Murcia
Alicante
Benidorm
Calpe
Xaló Valley
Gandia
Gandia
Salem
Aventador
Montesa
Bellús
Baranc de l'Avern

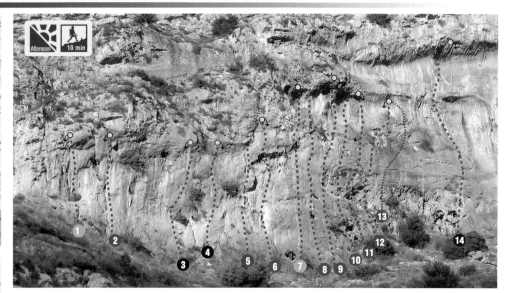

PARED DE LA VIA

This cliff is well up the valley (1.4km from the main parking area) and rises above an impressive railway embankment. It is the most extensive crag in the area and has a good selection of routes but there are also some wide sections of undeveloped rock.

CONDITIONS - South-west facing, it gets plenty of afternoon sun but is not well-sheltered from the wind.

APPROACH - The cliff is reached from a parking area amongst ruined buildings under the face. This is accessed via a short steep track that starts at a narrow entrance on the outside of the long right-hand bend directly opposite the cliff. This section of road is fast and GREAT CARE is needed when turning off here to avoid problems with traffic driving down the gorge. From the parking, cross the river (log) then take a steep track that diagonals up along the base of the impressive embankment to the railway line. Walk left 50m then scramble up to the foot of the face.

❶ Capoll . . . . ▢ **6a+**
12m. A short line up an awkward leaning white crack.

❷ Brimonster . . . . ▢ **6b+**
12m. The ragged overhanging crack starting from a bay.

❸ El principe . . . . ▢
18m. A project up a white rib and a thin wriggly crack line.

❹ Alex . . . . ▢
18m. Another project up a grey slab and yellow streak.

❺ Orelles curtes . . . . . . ▢▨ ▢ **7a**
26m. Climb the wall passing left of a prominent flake, through a bulge (crux) before trending right to reach the lower-off.

❻ Orelles Llargues . . . . . ▨▨ ▢ **6c**
26m. Start up a yellow wall, keeping right of the flake, passing through a large bulge, and finish up a leaning yellow wall.

Next is a steep grey slab up which the next three climbs start.

❼ Johnny Mendieta . . . . . ▨▨ ▢ **6a+**
28m. From a cave, climb the left side of the slab through a small overlap, up a yellow streak and over a juggy bulge.

❽ La ley del agarre . . ▨▨▨ ▢ **6b+**
28m. Good and hard for the grade. Climb left of a hole at 8m then up the slab (easier to the left) and through the bulges.

❾ Caxipolla . . . . ▨▨▨ ▢ **6c**
30m. Up the right edge of the grey slab then through a series of overlaps to a lower-off hanging from the overhangs above.

❿ No talles el teix . . . . . . ▨▨ ▢ **6b+**
30m. Climb steep rock then slabbier terrain until just below a bulging prow and make a finger-wrecking move out right.

⓫ El cerdo volador . . . . . ▨▨ ▢ **6c**
30m. Climb up the wall to below the final roof with the chains up and left. Reach them with difficulty.

⓬ Baixada 41 . . . . ▨ ▢ **6c**
30m. Climb an easy rib then the centre of the back wall of the shallow cave. Up the sharp grey wall then trend right.

⓭ Mocador blau . . . . ▨ ▢ **6b**
30m. Start as for *Baixada 41* but step right. Climb through the juggy bulges then move right and back left, to reach the same lower-off.

⓮ Unknown . . . . ▢
34m. The long line of bolts to the right looks excellent though nothing is known about it.

⓯ Calla . . . . ▨▨ ▢ **6b**
18m. Short but good. Climb the rib on sharp rock to below the prominent tufa. Make tough moves to reach it and go!

25m further right is the longest route on the cliff.

16 Les mil i una nir . . 🔲🔲🔲 7b
35m. The show piece of the cliff? Start up a grey slab then follow a direct line straight up the face pulling through bulges and finishing close to the top of the wall.

8m right the routes start coming thick and fast.

17 Orgullo blanca . . . . . . 🔲🔲 6b
30m. Climb the black slab (hard!) on crinkly holds then pull over an overlap and continue on much better holds.

18 La tacta rouga . . . . . . 🔲🔲 6c
30m. Climb to a bolt on the lower lip of a hole 10m up, then head through the centre of a patch of yellow rock riddled with holds. Cross the overhang and finishing up grey rock above.

19 Si te dicen que cai . . . 🔲🔲 7b
30m. Easy rock leads to the first bolt at 10m. Pass a hole then on up smooth powder-grey streak, and bulging wall to a hole and on through more bulges above; a majestic pitch.

20 Llum artificial . . . . 🔲🔲🔲 6c
28m. Climb easy slabs between bushes to reach a couple of old bolts. Above this new ones protect difficult moves up the steep wall to reach a diagonal break and the even steeper wall above.

21 Mollerunga . . . . . . 🔲🔲🔲 6b
28m. A tough pitch at the grade but well worthwhile. Move left and make hard moves to reach a large hole and harder moves to leave it. Continue on up the pumpy wall to easier climbing.

22 Que pallissa . . . . 🔲 6a
20m. Climb through some scoops then up a steep pocketed wall before finishing up a short rib on holds that keep appearing, and leading you to a conspicuous wire cable lower-off.

Up and right are two new routes that share a prominent lower-off at 12m. The right-hand one climbs the bulging rib and looks about 6c, the other passes just right of a tufa and looks easier. The last five routes are clustered around a bay at the far right side of the cliff.

23 Cinq-zero . . . . 🔲 6a+
20m. Climb the rib that forms the left edge of the right-facing flake passing a couple of ledges then continue up the scoop.

24 Si, que . . . . 🔲 6a
20m. Climb steeply into a right-facing corner and continue, passing some rock scars, and up the slab to the last bolt. Make a short traverse right to the lower-off.

25 Pipiolo . . . . 🔲🔲 6a
20m. Bridge up the back of the groove then swing left and mantleshelf onto a cleaned ledge. The slab gives sustained and delicate climbing, that slowly eases.

26 Cap amunt . . . . 🔲 5+
20m. Follow the easy rib and bulging wall then climb straight up the slab above until a couple of moves left lead to the belay.

27 Que facil . . . . 🔲 5
20m. Start as for the last climb up a bulging wall then follow a ramp up to the right. Take the right edge of the slab to a lower-off just short of the gully.

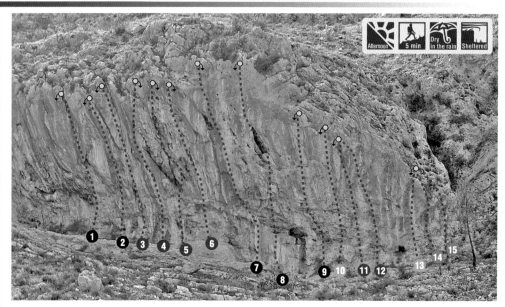

SECTOR LA VISERA

A steeply-tilted wall with some good strenuous climbs across the gully from the amenable Sector del Deposit.
CONDITIONS - The face is reasonably sheltered and it may give some dry climbing in light rain. The angle of the cliff coupled with its more easterly aspect means that it goes into the shade earlier than its immediate neighbour.
APPROACH - Turn up the track by the parking for the Pared del Gegant and drive up this for 200 metres to parking by the water pumping station. Do not block access or restrict the turning of other vehicles. The crag is five minutes walk up the valley to the right of the buildings and is reached by a scramble left along ledges.

❶ Misión Imposible. . . . .
14m. The first route on the face is (was?) a project.

❷ Callo largo 7b
16m. Get into the big hole at 4m then swing left on to the leaning rib which is followed to the lower-off.

❸ Eterna . . . . . 6c+
16m. Climb the grey and black tufa, then battle with the constricted and severely-overhanging groove above.

❹ Antropomorfo . . . . 6b+
16m. Tackle the smart left-slanting orange ramp that narrows as it rises to a tricky exit.

❺ Altair . . . . 6b+
16m. Steep jug pulling leads into a cave, then climb the steep pocketed rock to a lower-off on the rim of the wall.

❻ Prematuro 7a
15m. A leaning wall is climbed on finger pockets via an orange streak passing a hole with a bush in it. Finish up the rib.

❼ Polivalent 7b
20m. Tackle the right side of the hanging red rib - tufa climbing near the bottom then pocket pulling above.

❽ La cara al venta . . . . . 7a+
20m. The diagonal break that is main feature of the right side of the face is climbed by this route with a hard finish up a rib.

❾ Tot mon tesoro . . . 7a+
14m. Vicious moves up the steep wall.

❿ Fraude millonario . . . . 6a+
14m. The first line on the left side of the arete, with a bulging start, then easier above.

⓫ Tecnología puta 7a
14m. Green bolts protect this line on the right side of the arete.

⓬ Mata Castellanas . . . . 6b+
14m. Climb up a short sharp leaning wall, then more straightforward moves up the wall above.

On the right edge of the cliff is a rather scrubby slab. Three routes are on this and share a common lower-off.

⓭ Pelailla 5
12m. Climb steeply up a yellow streak for 4m then make easier above to reach the lower-off.

⓮ Teoría en la Practica 4
12m. A friendly wall climb.

⓯ Si una rosa es una rosa 4
10m. The rib and slab on the far right.

The main section of the narrow gorge of the Baranc de l'Avern is a rather noisy venue but the side valley is a tranquil and sunny spot to climb. Here Chris Craggs is climbing *Tatcham* (6a+) on Sector del Deposit - *page 366*. Photo: Sherri Davy

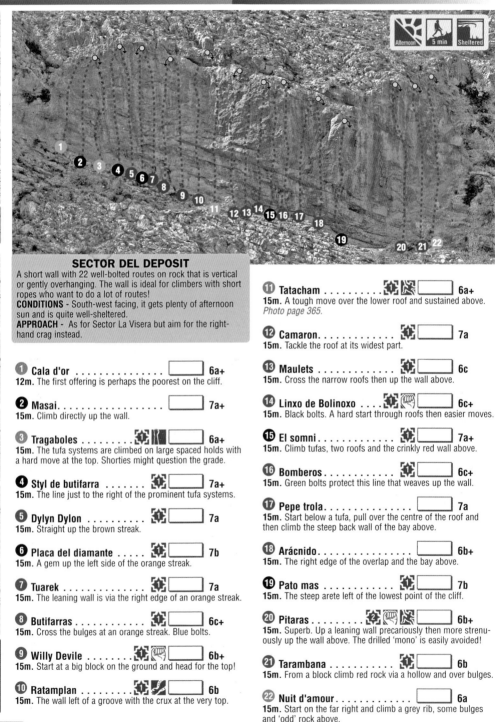

SECTOR DEL DEPOSIT

A short wall with 22 well-bolted routes on rock that is vertical or gently overhanging. The wall is ideal for climbers with short ropes who want to do a lot of routes!

CONDITIONS - South-west facing, it gets plenty of afternoon sun and is quite well-sheltered.

APPROACH - As for Sector La Visera but aim for the right-hand crag instead.

1 Cala d'or .... 6a+
12m. The first offering is perhaps the poorest on the cliff.

2 Masai .... 7a+
15m. Climb directly up the wall.

3 Tragaboles .... 6a+
15m. The tufa systems are climbed on large spaced holds with a hard move at the top. Shorties might question the grade.

4 Styl de butifarra .... 7a+
15m. The line just to the right of the prominent tufa systems.

5 Dylyn Dylon 7a
15m. Straight up the brown streak.

6 Placa del diamante 7b
15m. A gem up the left side of the orange streak.

7 Tuarek 7a
15m. The leaning wall is via the right edge of an orange streak.

8 Butifarras .... 6c+
15m. Cross the bulges at an orange streak. Blue bolts.

9 Willy Devile .... 6b+
15m. Start at a big block on the ground and head for the top!

10 Ratamplan 6b
15m. The wall left of a groove with the crux at the very top.

11 Tatacham .... 6a+
15m. A tough move over the lower roof and sustained above. *Photo page 365.*

12 Camaron 7a
15m. Tackle the roof at its widest part.

13 Maulets 6c
15m. Cross the narrow roofs then up the wall above.

14 Linxo de Bolinoxo .... 6c+
15m. Black bolts. A hard start through roofs then easier moves.

15 El somni .... 7a+
15m. Climb tufas, two roofs and the crinkly red wall above.

16 Bomberos .... 6c+
15m. Green bolts protect this line that weaves up the wall.

17 Pepe trola 7a
15m. Start below a tufa, pull over the centre of the roof and then climb the steep back wall of the bay above.

18 Arácnido .... 6b+
15m. The right edge of the overlap and the bay above.

19 Pato mas 7b
15m. The steep arete left of the lowest point of the cliff.

20 Pitaras .... 6b+
15m. Superb. Up a leaning wall precariously then more strenuously up the wall above. The drilled 'mono' is easily avoided!

21 Tarambana 6b
15m. From a block climb red rock via a hollow and over bulges.

22 Nuit d'amour 6a
15m. Start on the far right and climb a grey rib, some bulges and 'odd' rock above.

INDEX

COSTA BLANCA MAP

Check **www.rockfax.com** for a larger scale PDF version of this map

10km N